Animals

Animals-in-Law

Noël Sweeney LL.B Dip. Crim. I M.A.
of Gray's Inn, Barrister

This edition first published in Great Britain in 2013
by Alibi an imprint of Veritas Chambers,
186 High Street, Worle, North Somerset BS22 6JD

A catalogue record for this book is available from the British Library.

ISBN 978-1-872724-09-6

Printed and bound by CPI Group (UK) Ltd, Croydon, CR0 4YY

Preface

Animals are a natural part of the fabric of our society. Whether it is a Great Dane or an Irish wolfhound, be it domestic or wild, on a farm or on a plate, in a laboratory or in us, animals touch our daily lives in every sense. As that includes the economic and political and social sense, it is bound to be reflected in the legal one too. So as the lives of animals are inextricably connected with ours naturally we use our power to control them by law.

While there are numerous statutes and statutory instruments that govern our relationship with animals, it would be lubberly and unwieldy for the writer and the reader to attempt to cover them all. Therefore this book concentrates on the Animal Welfare Act 2006 (AWA) and the Dangerous Dogs Act 1991 (DDA). Those two statutes are the major ones that regulate and relate to our duty to animals generally and specifically dogs, whether we are affected as owners or victims. For often the owner will use his animal to create the victim. Equally the owner may actively make his animal another victim.

Though this book analyses both Acts in relation to all the authorities, it is an area that impinges on more than the strict legal position of the practitioner. So it is intended that laymen and lawyers alike will find the analysis useful. Indeed some may identify with the feeling of J. D. Salinger: 'I don't even like *old* cars. I mean they don't even interest me. I'd rather have a goddam horse. A horse is at least *human*, for God's sake.' To that end it is primarily aimed at all those persons who directly and indirectly are involved with animals as a result of their business or pastime or pleasure. Hence it is hoped that those who follow courses in jurisprudence, law and philosophy will find the book useful. Similarly it is intended to be of value to people who run welfare organisations and animal sanctuaries, plus the police and the legal profession as well as judges in the Crown Court and at Crufts.

How animals are unlawfully treated by others has repercussions for all of us. Illegal drugs are a serious problem in our society and have been for many years. Most drug addicts are compelled to resort or revert to crime to feed their addiction. In October 2012 it was confirmed by animal organisations in Scotland that such criminals are now feeding heroin to their dogs to make them more aggressive. That creates a legal and a social problem as in turn we share the cost of their welfare. Of course it is and has long been a proclivity of criminals to use a ferocious dog as a cat's-paw anyway.

The progress of the present English law can be traced by a gradual process starting in 1635 when the first legislation to protect farmers' property and their horses, being the same thing, was introduced in Ireland. Thereafter in 1641 the newly arrived Quakers settling in Massachusetts introduced anti-cruelty legislation in America. The changes in England can be seen when in the 17th Century it was considered by Charles Cock in *English-Law* in 1651 that butchers could not serve on a Jury in capital cases because they were inherently cruel by virtue of their occupation. That biased view of their brutality was shared by many at the time. Yet when in 1640 Thomas Hobbes, the Wiltshire philosopher, wrote in *The Elements of Law,* 'I pray, when a lion eats a man and a man eats an ox, why is the ox more made for the man than the man for the lion?', he was ridiculed as a fool and denounced as a knave for his heterodox views. In particular he was condemned by the Irish Bishop, John Bramhall, who countered his ideas in the *Castigations of Mr Hobbes,* that 'He acquitted the beasts from the dominion of man and denieth that they owe him any subjection... [he has become] an attorney-general for the brute beasts.' While that was meant then as the final religious curse now it would be interpreted by many as a spiritual compliment.

Historically animal law has been a piecemeal legislative process of amendments and repeals. This book covers all aspects of the two current main criminal statutes affecting animals. Both Acts account for almost all offences of animal abuse in every conceivable form relating to the duty of owners and their concurrent liability and responsibility. The DDA remains the first of its kind dealing with the inherent everyday danger to those who come into contact with dogs that are aggressive and out of control. The AWA is the first statute to incorporate the concept of welfare in relation to animals. Both Acts are analysed and criticised where, which is often, each is found wanting.

The aim of past legislators was to preserve our property and protect animals against the abuse by others. Now there is a substantive change in that the law is seeking to protect animals from the abuse by their owners too. The reason is where animals are concerned we have learned that in the seeds of their destruction we are in danger of sowing our own. Law is the universal language of natural justice. As a consequence these two Acts allow us to speak in a tongue that can protect those without one.

How close we are to those we control is now being considered by legal systems throughout the world. The mirror-image of the Great Apes has been relied upon by American and European lawyers in seeking to promote and recognise their legal status. A recent revelation proves their prescience. For in November 2012 researchers at the University of Warwick have identified that like so many men the Great Apes too suffer from a condition similar to a mid-life crisis. So the evolutionary circle remains unbroken. The problem now to be solved by the law is to square that circle.

Aristotle coined the phrase 'political animal' as he was one himself. However in relation to animals and law he had two unusual problems as he was blessed with power and privilege. As a result he considered all those who were not of a patrician class were automatically plebeians and hence inferior to him. His views extended to slaves and women and animals. Regardless of such questionable views which filtered through to our mores and in time our law, he was right on one part of his philosophy when he pronounced that 'Man when perfected, is the best of animals, but, when separated from law and justice is the worst of all.'

As to whether these two Acts as enacted are as imaginative as the ideas that ignited the ideals behind them remains in the balance for the future. Whether the aspiration is attained depends on the will of our representatives and us. Ultimately the answer will be provided by an interpretation of each Act by the courts and our independent conclusion. For though law and justice often collide, this is an area where the concepts should not merely meet but coincide.

Noël Sweeney

Dedication

To Joan, Maureen, Wendy, Nicole, Molly and all the other cats.

Acknowledgements

I am grateful for the information kindly given and inspiration provided by many organisations including in particular: Animal Aid, Animal Welfare Science Ethics and Law Veterinary Association, Animals Count, Association of Lawyers for Animal Welfare, Blue Cross, Compassion in World Farming, Department for Environment Farming and Rural Affairs, Dogs Trust, International Society for Animal Rights, League Against Cruel Sports, Oxford Centre for Animal Ethics, People for the Ethical Treatment of Animals, the Royal Society for the Prevention of Cruelty to Animals, the Suffrage Society and Viva!

Contents

Chapter 3: **Registration and Rescue**

Chapter 4: **Evidence and Prosecution**

Contents

Chapter 5: **Duty and Responsibility**

Chapter 6: **Sentencing**

Chapter 7: **Dangerous Dogs Act 1991**

Contents

Chapter 8: **Sentence**

Chapter 9: **The Legal Role and Status of Animals**

Contents

Table of Cases

Table of Statutes

Table of Statutory Instruments

Protection

1

Protection

A1 Property

It is and always has been their lot to be exploited. They have been abused, burnt at the stake, hanged at the gallows, tried and executed as criminals, vivisected and used as weapons of war. They have been subjected to every cruelty imaginable for reasons of economics, hedonism, politics, science, sport and war. They have been the perennial victims enchained by law. Their rights extend to the right to be killed at will. As to who and why the reason is the same: animals because they are animals.

As a result of that legal position animals were classified as property. The concept of animals being property led Richard 'Humanity Dick' Martin to introduce the first comprehensive animal cruelty legislation in the United Kingdom. He introduced what was known as Martin's Act or the Ill-Treatment of Cattle Act 1822 by cleverly concentrating on the benefits to the owner of protecting his property. That approach defeated the opposition as it gave a legal right to the owner to take action against anyone who damaged his property. The welfare of the animal was secondary.

Within two years Martin along with Arthur Broome and William Wilberforce set up the Society for the Prevention of Cruelty to Animals (SPCA). One of the primary goals of the SPCA was to ensure that Martin's Act was effective. The triumvirate set up the first national animal welfare body in the world. The sacrifices made by Reverend Broome, an Anglican priest, were quietly amazing in that in a short time he lost his livelihood, his home and his liberty. Broome was sent to prison in respect of debts he incurred during his constant task of trying to protect animals.

Wilberforce was involved for the most part of his life in trying to abolish slavery. It was finally abolished by the Abolition of Slavery Act 1833. By then he had turned to his next moral crusade, from humans in bondage to animals. His contribution to that crusade, though worthwhile was brought to an untimely end by his death in 1833.

A2 Man

Martin's Act was later amended and repealed, finally resulting in the Protection of Animals Act 1911. That Act was the anchor of all legislation dealing with offences of cruelty to animals throughout the 20th Century. The weakness of the Act was contained in section 15 which defined a domestic animal as any animal 'Which is tame or which has been or is being sufficiently tamed to serve some purpose for the use of man.'

That was one of the main problems with that Act. It was the legal ideal of protecting our property and being able to deal with it in any way we feel. To that end it signified that animals that were given a limited protection continued to be classified as property. Their value was based on how they served 'some purpose' for us. So a stuffed Steiff teddy was no different than a live spectacled bear yet to be exhibited by a taxidermist.

A3 Dominion

The root of the problem is that it is a concept that ran deep in Roman Law which percolated into and through English Law. It is a datum-line of our law that animals were and are purely our property. The concept was accurately outlined by M. I. Finley in *Ancient Slavery and Modern Ideology* [1980]: 'When Roman lawyers defined a slave as someone who was in the *dominium* of another, they used the quintessential property-term *dominium*. They were not dissuaded by the slave's human quality (not even when they used the word *homo* to refer to a slave, as they did frequently). Nor were the millions of slave-owners who bought and sold slaves, overworked them, beat and tortured them, and sometimes put them to death, precisely as millions of horse-owners have done throughout history.'

While Broome seems to have been forgotten his legacy lives on. Although he died in obscure poverty, as Fairholme and Pain confirmed in *A Century of Work for Animals* [1924] 'unwept, unhonoured and unsung', he ignited the spark that fired the repeal of the 1911 Act and ultimately resulted in the Animal Welfare Act 2006. Broome's mission statement in 1824 for the SPCA asked with rhetorical compassion: 'Is the moral circle perfect so long as any power of doing good remains? Or can the infliction of cruelty on any being which the Almighty has endued with feelings of pain and pleasure consist with genuine and true benevolence?'

Broome died in 1837. The SPCA gained Royal patronage from Queen Victoria in 1840. His ideas have now affected and influenced all sectors of society nationally and internationally. The opportunity to gauge whether his memory and legacy have been properly honoured is now embodied in the 2006 Act. How far his ideals and his principles chime with our law depends now on the coincidence of the minds and mores of society and the courts. If the views of Hawkins J in *Ford v. Wiley* 23 QBD 203 are shared by this generation of judges we have reason for optimism that the opportunity will be grasped and used: 'Constant familiarity with unnecessary torture to and abuse of dumb animals cannot fail by degrees to brutalize and harden all who are concerned in or witness the miseries of the sufferers, a consequence to be scrupulously avoided in the best interests of civilised society.'

Given that Hawkins J said that in 1889 it shows his judicial instinct was a barometer of the contemporary society's conscience. For over a century later his vision is no less relevant in relation to how we should treat animals. They are the lowest members of our society. How a society treats its weakest members reflects its own strength. The crucial question for us is whether the weak are to perish or will they be protected by the strong? It is a question to be resolved by compassion, compromise and conscience in our own interests as a civilised society.

" THE GREATNESS OF A NATION AND ITS MORAL PROGRESS CAN BE JUDGED BY THE WAY IT'S ANIMALS ARE TREATED " – MAHATMA GANDHI.

Animal Welfare Act 2006

2

Animal Welfare Act 2006

B1 Scope

The Animal Welfare Act 2006 (AWA) was a radical departure from the anachronistic Protection of Animals Act 1911 (POA) which it replaced after almost a century. In comparison to the POA which was primarily concerned with cruelty, the AWA is concerned with welfare. The words 'cruel' and 'cruelty' are not used in the AWA at all. Instead the word 'suffering' is used throughout. That is consistent with the twin legal limbs of duty and protection relative to people and animals. While the POA was riddled with legal inconsistencies, especially in the treatment of farm animals and wild animals in captivity, the AWA has a different slant altogether. The approach of the AWA is to place a legal burden on the person responsible to care for the welfare of the animal. To that extent it is a complete change of emphasis as the AWA seeks to protect animals from their natural predators, humans. Equally to that end the AWA restricts an owner's right to treat an animal in a way that harms its welfare.

It was a slow and thorough process that led to the passing of the AWA. Initially there was a public consultation between January and April 2002. That led to a draft Bill which was published in July 2004. The House of Commons Select Committee on Environment, Food and Rural Affairs then carried out a pre-legislative scrutiny of the draft Bill. The Select Committee published its report in December 2004. In March 2005 the Department for Environment, Food and Rural Affairs (Defra) published a response to the Select Committee's report. That

[handwritten margin notes:]
INSTEAD OF PROTECTING HUMANS' PROPERTY.
APPROPRIATE TO EARLIER PERIOD.
POA → CRUELTY
AWA → SUFFERING.
POSITIVE + NEGATIVE RIGHTS.
5 FREEDOMS
Qol MODEL.
REGULATORY PROCESS SEEKING PUBLIC INPUT
PASSING AWA 2006.

Committee published a further report a year later in December 2005.

Following that period of consultation and examination the AWA received the Royal Assent on 8 November 2006 and came into force on 6 April 2007. It was introduced earlier in Wales on 28 March 2007.

[handwritten:] REQUIRED TO MAKE BILL INTO ACT OF PARLIAMENT.

The AWA covers various aspects of animal welfare under 11 headings from the *Introductory* to the *General* category. The respective headings deal with the scope of the AWA through to the investigation of offences and the consequent sentences.

All the relevant headings are examined and analysed in the text except for the tenth one which covers sections 46 to 50 as they apply only to Scotland.

While those in the wild are still not largely legally protected, in given circumstances the AWA can extend to them too. The main protection is given to an animal that is owned by a person or there is someone who is responsible for it. Yet the offences relating to cruelty and fighting have a much wider application and catches those who are directly and indirectly involved in the crime. Although animal experiments and vivisection are outside the scope of this book, the AWA touches on that area as well. In general it extends the mantle of law to cover domestic and farm animals as both are often in equal measure used and abused by humans. The AWA seeks to identify and protect their interests.

To the extent that the AWA particularly covers areas that were previously overlooked or deliberately ignored, it is a rare example of Parliamentary prescience. Whether the Act is as revolutionary as it could be now depends upon the judiciary.

[handwritten:] FORE-KNOWLEDGE.

[handwritten:] COURTS.

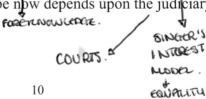

[handwritten:] SINGER'S INTEREST MODEL. & EQUALITY.

B2 Five Freedoms

It was an absurd situation that under the ancient legislation the authorities could only act after the animal had been abused. That was proved in sharp focus by a person representing Richard Martin who applied to the authorities to prevent the pending cruelty of a circus which advertised a spectacle 'A Tame Lion Bait with Dogs'. Wombell's Circus advertised it in 1825 just three years after 'Martin's Act' or An Act to prevent cruel and improper Treatment of Cattle 1822 was introduced. The mayor refused to stop the show. The magistrate refused to stop the show. They explained they could not act until the cruelty was committed. That purblind idea was enshrined in later legislation including the POA.

A crucial point about the AWA is that it allows the authorities to act before the offence is committed. That is a distinct difference between its power and effect as compared to the POA. The POA attempted to punish the owner of an animal after he had abused it. The AWA allows the authorities to bolt he stable door before he has harmed the horse. The essential reason for the difference is that the AWA is based on and incorporates the principles initially outlined by the Brambell Committee in their *Report of the Technical Committee to Enquire into the Welfare of Animals Kept Under Intensive Livestock Husbandry Systems*, in 1965. The effect of the Brambell Committee's Report was immediate and important. For as a direct result of their conclusions the term 'welfare' was adopted in the legislation to protect animals in Britain. By the Agriculture (Miscellaneous Provisions) Act 1968 the welfare of farm animals became a legal consideration which if breached could lead to a farmer being prosecuted.

The concept of welfare in the modern and legal sense that sprang from the Brambell Report was adopted and endorsed by the Farm Animal Welfare Council (FAWC – now Committee) which was

"WELFARE" INTRODUCED IN 2 LEGISLATION AFTER BRAMBELL REPORT.
↳ PROTECT ACTS BEFORE ACTS OF CRUELTY.

formed in 1979. In turn the result of the report by FAWC, *Report on Priorities on Animal Welfare Research and Development*, in 1993 led to the principles of the 'Five Freedoms'. These were established as the requirements that were necessary to ensure an animal's welfare was legally protected. FAWC concluded that all animals should have those basic Five Freedoms which are:

PROMOTION OF WELFARE, SECTIONS 9-12.

1. Freedom from <u>hunger and thirst</u> – by ready access to water and a diet to maintain health and vigour.
2. Freedom from <u>discomfort</u> – by providing an appropriate environment.
3. Freedom from <u>pain, injury</u> and <u>disease</u> – by prevention or rapid diagnosis and treatment. *→ MOTIVATIONS + FRUSTRATIONS*
4. Freedom to <u>express normal behaviour</u> – by providing sufficient space, proper facilities and appropriate company of the animal's own kind.
5. Freedom from <u>fear and distress</u> – by ensuring conditions and treatment, which avoid mental suffering.

Although those are far from perfect, it should be both emphasised and remember that they are the <u>minimum requirements</u> to ensure an animal is properly treated either by those who have a <u>duty</u> to <u>care</u> for it or are <u>responsible</u> for it or intend to kill it or all those matters. The requirements are now the central plank of the AWA and specifically detailed in sections 9 to 12. Indeed the heading of those sections, <u>Promotion of Welfare</u>, accentuates the aim and approach of the Act. For the regulations and the codes of practice and enforcement powers under the provisions of the AWA enable the authorities to be active in promoting animal welfare as well as reactive to abuse.

↓
ACTIVE + REACTIVE.

B3 Life

In the Scottish case, *Patchett v. Macdougall* [1984] SLT 152 (Note), the court held that when Patchett shot and killed a dog he had to be acquitted because there was no direct evidence or expert opinion that the dog had suffered prior to its death. Although the court condemned his act Lord Hunter said, 'the absence of a positive finding to the effect that the act of the appellant caused the animal suffering is fatal to the conviction.'

It was submitted to the court by the respondent that the fact the dog lost its life was tantamount to 'suffering' and hence an offence. Lord Wheatley laconically responded, 'Metaphysical considerations apart, I do not consider that the structure and purport of the Act opens the door to that view.'

That strict intellectual view was confirmed in essence in the High Court in *Isted v. DPP* [1998] Crim. L. R. 194 where a farmer, Isted, shot a dog, Lily, who was in his pig pen with teeth bared and barking, which resulted in her being wounded but not killed. Brookes LJ said, 'The present state of the law was unnecessarily confusing.' He went on to consider, 'the requisite mental element' under the Criminal Damage Act 1971 as compared to the POA and added, '…the relevant part of the 1911 Act was framed by the reference to the antique law underlying words like "wantonly or unreasonably" which was bound to continue to give trouble to those concerned with its administration.'

↳ SUBJECTIVE LANGUAGE VERACIOUS LEGISLATION.

That encapsulates all that was wrong with the POA. Brookes LJ added, 'It is time that policy [damage to animate property] was expressed in clear, intelligible and modern language, which would avoid the unnecessary legal expenditure devoted to cases like this.' The AWA has sought to obviate such abstruse language and provide a remedy to that inherent confusion.

Fortunately however that is now in the past. It is consistent with the aim of the AWA that the principle of the welfare of the animal is paramount. Moreover that is consistent with the approach of the Recorder of Aylesbury, His Honour Judge Tyrer DL, in *Gray v. RSPCA* [2010] A20090060 where he said accurately, 'In our judgment the old jurisprudence is no longer relevant.' [See **B8**; **B9**.]

Put in perspective, notwithstanding that animals are classed as property as a matter of law, there is no reason why it should be 'appropriate and humane' to deprive one of its life, except by a qualified vet or if it is in a condition of manifest distress. That would allow the caring person, be it the owner or a passing Samaritan, to act in the interests of the animal. The fact it is deprived of its life would be inappropriate and inhumane unless it was shown to be otherwise by the person carrying out the act or the omission. That approach would preserve the legal duty of care with the animals' welfare in remaining alive. Indeed given that such destruction is both final and irrevocable, it accords with the aim of the AWA too as stated specifically in sections 4(4) and 9(4) in the same terms: 'Nothing in this section applies to the destruction of an animal in an appropriate and humane manner'.

There is nothing metaphysical about concluding that if you hit an animal from behind so it is instantaneously killed, or there is no expert evidence, it does not suffer. For sections 4(4) and 9(4) do not stand on their own. They encompass the ethos of the AWA. As such the AWA protects the animal by confirming the manner of its destruction must be appropriate and humane in order to be legal. Whatever the method, depriving an animal of its life without cause or reason is neither appropriate nor humane.

B4 *Introductory*

The Introductory sections 1 to 3 specify which animals are within the protection of the Act.

14

[handwritten margin note: FAILURE TO FULFILL LEGAL / MORAL OBLIGATION.]

Animals to which the Act applies

Animal Welfare Act 2006, s.1

(1) In this Act, except subsections (4) and (5), "animal" means a vertebrate other than man. → INVERTEBRATES NOT COVERED

(2) Nothing in this Act applies to an animal while it is in its foetal or embryonic form. → FETUSES + EMBRYOS NOT COVERED.

(3) The appropriate national authority may by regulations for all or any of the purposes of this Act –

    (a) extend the definition of "animal" so as to include invertebrates of any description;

    (b) make provision in lieu of subsection (2) as respects any invertebrates included in the description of "animal";

    (c) amend subsection (2) to extend the application of this Act to an animal from such earlier stage of its development as may be specified in the regulations.

(4) The power under subsection (3)(a) or (c) may only be exercised if the appropriate national authority is satisfied, on the basis of scientific evidence, that animals of the kind concerned are capable of experiencing pain, or suffering.

(5) In this section, "vertebrate" means any animal of the Sub-phylum Vertebrata of the Phylum Chordata and "invertebrate" means any animal not of that Sub-phylum.

As a nod to the reality that we are all Darwin's cousins, the AWA defines animals to which the Act applies as 'a vertebrate other than man'.

Unlike the legal protection given to humans, the AWA does not apply to an animal while it is in its foetal or embryonic form. That seems a strange omission given that it would obviously be

↳ HARMING FOETUS/EMBRYO HARMS MOTHER.
↳ HARMING MOTHER CAN AFFECT WELFARE OF/KILL/TERMINATE FETUS.

[margin note, right side, rotated:] CAN REG (+ HAS BEEN) EXTENDED. [SPECF. OCTOPUSES PROTECTED IN ANIMALS (SCIENTIFIC PROCEDURES) ACT 1986]

an aggravating feature if suffering is caused to a pregnant animal. It is the precise reason why human foetuses have legal protection. After all if an animal is pregnant its needs and welfare are affected because of its condition. Moreover the unborn progeny can have its pending birth terminated and its welfare affected as well as a result of any abuse directed at its prospective parent.

Nevertheless the AWA specifically allows for changes in legal protection according to the advancement of knowledge and science. The 'appropriate national authority' which is defined by section 62(1), is the Secretary of State for England and the National Assembly for Wales. They have power to extend and make and amend the regulations. At present the AWA applies to vertebrate animals as those are currently believed to be the only perceived sentient animals. So those authorities can introduce other animals within the AWA according to scientific advancement. On 24 May 2012 the International Institute for Species Exploration confirmed the existence of 200 new animals and plants. They include such a variety as a sneezing monkey, a blue tarantula and a parasitic wasp. This provision would allow the authorities to include such creatures within the protection of the AWA.

The regulations referred to are the means of amending the AWA under section 12 by the national authority. It is typical of the Act that such regulations must relate to the promotion of animal welfare. That is why that power may only be exercised if it is satisfied 'on the basis of scientific evidence', that animals of the kind concerned are capable of experiencing pain or suffering.

It is noteworthy that 'pain' is not defined directly at all in the Act. While 'suffering' is defined under section 62(1) as 'physical or mental suffering and related expressions shall be construed accordingly'. That definition is particularly significant as we now know that animals can indeed feel mental suffering and in

[handwritten margin note, left side, vertical:] REGULATIONS EXTENDED IN ACCORDANCE WITH EVIDENCE OF SCIENCE.

[handwritten note, bottom:] SECTION 62 DEFINES SUFFERING AS PHYSICAL/MENTAL. → NOT PAIN.

16

— LASTING IMPACT OF MENTAL SUFFERING.
↳ FOUND IN POLICE/ARMY DOGS.

Animals to which the Act applies
↳ FINN'S LAW MAKES CAUSING UNNECESSARY
SUFFERING TO SERVICE ANIMALS ILLEGAL.

extreme cases even post-traumatic stress disorder. The resonance between the human reaction to conditions and animals are similarly related. Sometimes prisoners can become mentally disturbed, known colloquially as 'cabin fever' or 'stir crazy', which is a condition that can be reflected by animals in a zoo. Where animals are affected it is known as *'stereotypies'*: Pregnant sows whose feed is restricted bite at their stalls' bars and chew without anything in their mouths. In laboratory rats and mice, grooming is the most common activity other than sleep, and grooming stereotypies have been used to investigate several animal models of anxiety and depression…well known in stabled horses, usually developing as a result of being confined…'

Professor Victoria Braithwaite in *Do Fish Feel Pain?* [2010] states, 'In terrestrial zoo animals, like tigers, elephants, and polar bears, boredom, frustration, and enclosures too small and too plain sometimes lead to 'stereotypies' – repetitive actions or movements performed over and over again. Likewise, sharks and other fish species that typically have large home ranges, or make long distance migrations, also show stereotypies in public aquaria. These behaviours are not necessarily painful, but they do represent a welfare concern because they are expressions of frustration on the animal's part…' So the size of the cell and the bars on a cage can induce the same mental stress regardless of whether the one incarcerated is a human or an animal.

FAWC analysed the position of animals in the decades following the Brambell Report with regard to the implementation of the Five Freedoms. In their report, *Farm Animal Welfare in Great Britain: Past, Present and Future* [2009], they say, 'A common misconception is that the Fourth Freedom is to express natural rather than normal behaviour. Normal suggests behaviour that is not abnormal; stereotypic and other abnormal behaviours such as tail chewing are undesirable and a sign of poor welfare.'

NORMAL ≠ NATURAL.

17

Like the soldiers they serve beside the dogs of war are subject to the same psychological stress that affect the soldiers. Stanley Coren, a professor of psychology, said 'There was always that suspicion and we started to look at PTSD [post-traumatic stress disorder] when some of the dogs used at the Twin Towers after 9/11 started to show symptoms. In the past, the clinical world would have said you were crazy and anthropomorphising but the condition is now widely accepted.' Indeed in the same report in *The Times* of 10/12/11 Kevin Igo, a soldier, confirmed Gina, his 4-year-old German shepherd was traumatised after returning from service in Iraq. After a course of 'desensitisation and counter-conditioning', Gina changed and almost made a full recovery, though she was still affected by gunfire.

That definition in the AWA is and should be wide enough to include all aspects of psychological pain rather than relying on a vague definition that is open to a more limited interpretation. For that was precisely the problem with an austere analysis by judges under the POA. Given the present state of our knowledge, it can and should now be avoided. └→ PSYCHOLOGICAL PAIN DEFINED + RECOGNISED IN AWA. SOLUTION A PROBLEM OF POA.

"Protected animal"

B5   Animal Welfare Act 2006, s.2

An animal is a "protected animal" for the purposes of this Act if – ┌→ ETHICS OF THIS.

(a)   it is of a kind which is commonly domesticated in the British Islands; DEURO / UK - CENTRAL. └→ IGNORES CULTURAL DIFFERENCES.

(b)   it is under the control of man whether on a permanent or temporary basis, or └→ WHY SHOULD THIS MAKE A DIFFERENCE WHEN WILD ANIMALS

(c)   it is not living in a wild state. ARE JUST AS CAPABLE OF SUFFERING?

In order to be given a legal right in respect of its welfare, the animal has to be a 'protected' one. One problem among many

18

with the POA was that it was full of legal nuances borne of semantics that defied law and logic. The new definition is potentially much wider though it is still lacking in preventing suffering to all animals. A protected animal under the AWA is one that is domesticated or is under our control or is not living wild. That theme runs throughout the AWA in respect of the principal offences.

The meaning of a kind of animal that is 'commonly domesticated' would include stray dogs and feral cats. Essentially it covers animals who because of their collective conduct and life-cycle have been conditioned by being under human control. This would affect their physiology and breed too as normally they would have been subject to living conditions and behaviour dictated by us. There would be a degree of history about the relationship between the type of animal and the human control as it has to be one that we have commonly domesticated. So it would also include wild Dartmoor ponies and visiting Canada geese if people become involved in their feeding and living conditions.

As these are alternative states, if it is a wild animal that has been captured by a man whether on a 'permanent or temporary' basis, the mantle of the Act would provide protection. So the urban fox which occasionally becomes a pet could not be hunted on the High Street or killed at will if it suffered in the process. For it is plain from the Burns Committee Report, the *Report of the Committee of Inquiry into Hunting with Dogs in England and Wales*, in 2000 that a fox's welfare is affected when it is hunted to death: 'We are satisfied, nevertheless, that this experience seriously compromises the welfare of the fox'. In these days of the urban fox it is not so rare to extend care to them given that we have been instrumental in causing them to move towards us in order to survive. Therefore it would be no less than if it was an ordinary domestic cat. [See Foxes and Foxes in the City: Ch. 4: 1-8 May 2012; also **F3**]

Similarly in *R (Countryside Alliance) v. Attorney-General* [2008] AC 219, it was plainly confirmed that a fox's welfare is affected by people and dogs hunting it: 'There is, however, a body of reputable opinion which accepts that the pursuit and digging out of foxes, and their killing by hounds, imposes a degree of suffering. This accords with common sense. To suppose that the contrary is generally true strains one's credulity to breaking point' *per* Bingham LJ.

The term 'captive animal' which was used in the POA often seemed to confuse the courts and prosecutors. Conversely the term 'under the control' is a much wider clause. As a result that should enable the courts to avoid the many problems associated with the interpretation of the former term used in the POA. That limited expression, 'captive animal', has no relevance at all to the AWA. Now even if an animal was not handled by a human, given the new technology for tracking and tracing and trapping animals used by baiters and poachers, an animal could be under the control of them if it cannot escape.

That is underlined by the fact it can be on a 'permanent or temporary basis'. It would not even matter if it was still underground as a badger may equally suffer from a terrier attack as suffocate if its sett is blocked. For the baiter and hunter is intent on getting as well as keeping the animal under his control until it is killed by his dogs or him or both. So besides any other statute that covered the offence, a captive bird would also be caught within the AWA.

The purpose of the wider expression is also to include animals who are not presently under our control, but have been and are not yet living independently in the wild. It would apply to Nellie

20

the elephant who ran away from the circus. Or to the 'stir-crazy' tiger who escaped from the zoo. Their status is dependent on the fact that prior to their bid for freedom, both the elephant and tiger were controlled by us and are not 'living in a wild state'.

By extension any wild animal that is not normally within the AWA would become subject to it if it is captured and held or rescued by a person. It then remains protected unless and until its status changes upon being released whether by human choice or by an escape.

An animal that is adopted as a pet, whatever its origin is, becomes a 'protected animal'. Brian May, a lead guitarist with a pop combo, appropriately in this transgender age called Queen, is keen on most wildlife. He has nurtured some foxes with the intention of returning them to nature in due course. As he has adopted the animals he has accepted the legal duty that flows from and accompanies his voluntary action. While a rat may invoke strong feelings of the black plague and is generally wild, a pet rat would be within the AWA no less than any other pet.

Responsibility for animals

B6   Animal Welfare Act 2006, s.3

(1) In this Act, references to a person responsible for an animal are to a person responsible for an animal whether on a permanent or temporary basis.

(2) In this Act, references to being responsible for an animal include being in charge of it.

(3) For the purposes of this Act, a person who owns an animal shall always be regarded as being a person who is responsible for it.

(4) For the purposes of this Act, a person shall be treated as responsible for any animal for which a person under the

age of 16 years of whom he has actual care and control is responsible.

The thread that runs throughout the AWA is one of 'responsibility' for an animal. For in turn that responsibility affects all the main *Prevention of harm* and *Promotion of welfare* headings under sections 4 to 10. Similarly it affects the powers to make regulations and control registration under sections 12 and 13. Once the responsibility attaches to a person, the legal duty and consequences flow from that status.

The liability of the owner for an animal is joint and several. That avoids the useless legal nuances that we used to have to contend with regarding the definition of who is the 'keeper' of an animal. Now the responsibility for an animal does not shift with control or possession, but lasts as long as the ownership itself. When a person accepts or assumes responsibility for an animal the liability attaches to that status. The AWA confirms that such responsibility includes being in charge of an animal and for any person who is under 16 years of age for whom he has 'care and control'.

This section is deliberately wide so people do not escape liability by claiming, whether falsely or otherwise, that they do not 'own' the animal. The simple fact they have responsibility for it on a 'permanent or temporary basis' is enough for a legal duty to ensue. It is the same reason that it includes being in 'charge' of it. So if the actual owner is on holiday or in hospital or in prison, whoever has accepted the temporary care of the animal equally accepts and assumes the legal 'responsibility' for it. As a result all the consequent duties flow from and follow that joint role and status.

The interaction of sections 2 and 3 places the responsibility on anyone who has care of an animal by virtue of ownership or custody or for a specific purpose. As it applies to those who have daily care of it and those responsible for an animal on a temporary basis, it would extend to a vet caring for an animal overnight in his surgery, staff at a cattery as well as volunteers at an animal sanctuary.

It would also apply to a police officer who seizes a dog be it a pit bull terrier or otherwise, as their responsibility attaches to their decision. Even if it is illegal to own a dog, the responsibility for the welfare of it attaches to the person who assumes the control. That would include caring for an animal while the owner is in prison. [See **G17**; **G37**]

To appreciate how wide this section is can be immediately seen from section 3(4). The interaction of that provision with section 3(3) means the owner is not free from his responsibility merely because one of his children causes the animal to suffer. In that event they are both liable. DUTY TO PROTECT ANIMAL FROM CRUELTY.

In *Gray v. RSPCA* [2010] A20090060, The Recorder of Aylesbury, His Honour Judge Tyrer DL, dealt with the position head-on as counsel for the first appellant, James Gray Senior, sought to argue that the fifth appellant, James Gray Junior, his 14 year-old son, could not be 'responsible' in law for an omission. Julie Gray, the wife of James Gray Senior, was the second appellant. It was argued that the AWA would only cover the situation if he, the fifth appellant, had committed a positive act. The Judge specifically rejected the submission out of hand:

'She [counsel] submitted that if Parliament intended that the first appellant and the second appellant were to be responsible for animals for which the fifth appellant was responsible, then it would have said so.

In our judgment section 3(4) does mean that: it means that the first appellant and the second appellant can be responsible for

APPERSON WHO APPLIES TO A HIGHER COURT FOR A REVERSAL OF DECISION OF A LOWER COURT.

any animal for which the fifth appellant himself was responsible, if the fifth appellant was under the actual care and control of the first appellant and/or the second appellant at the time.

It does not mean that the fifth appellant cannot be responsible in law. What other purpose can section 3(4) have? If the fifth appellant cannot be responsible in law for an animal because of his age why did Parliament deal with the position of those who have actual care and control of him?

There is no ambiguity: the purpose of section 3(4) is to extend responsibility for any animal looked after by an under 16 years old to both the under 16 years old and to those who have care and control of him.

In short, an appellant must have had some responsibility for any animal during the period covered by the charge in question: some temporary or permanent custody or control, some ownership, some element of being in charge of the animal in question.'

The Recorder was not merely forthright, he was right. The submission was simply misconceived. For if it were otherwise the AWA would be a legal paper tiger without bite or teeth. Moreover the reliance on the POA was pointless as the AWA swept away all the old ideas and introduced completely new concepts that were hitherto unknown within animal law. [See **B8**; **B9**.]

B7   *Prevention of harm*

Unnecessary suffering

Animal Welfare Act 2006, s.4

(1)   A person commits an offence if –
    (a)   an act of his, or a failure of his to act, causes an animal to suffer,

24

(b) he knew, or ought reasonably to have known, that the act, or failure to act, would have that effect or be likely to do so,

(c) the animal is a protected animal, and

(d) the suffering is unnecessary.

(2) A person commits an offence if –

(a) he is responsible for an animal,

(b) an act, or failure to act, of another person causes the animal to suffer,

(c) he permitted that to happen or failed to take such steps (whether by way of supervising the other person or otherwise) as were reasonable in all the circumstances to prevent that happening, and

(d) the suffering is unnecessary.

(3) The considerations to which it is relevant to have regard when determining for the purposes of this section whether suffering is unnecessary include –

(a) whether the suffering could reasonably have been avoided or reduced;

(b) whether the conduct which caused the suffering was in compliance with any relevant enactment or any relevant provisions of a licence or code of practice issued under an enactment;

(c) whether the conduct which caused the suffering was for a legitimate purpose, such as –

(i) the purpose of benefiting the animal, or

(ii) the purpose of protecting a person, property or another animal;

(d) whether the suffering was proportionate to the purpose of the conduct concerned;

(e) whether the conduct concerned was in all the circumstances that of a reasonably competent and humane person.

Hell Farm

[handwritten margin notes:]
→ CALLOUS SLAUGHTER
→ ARGUE AN INSTANT + PAINLESS KILLING DOES NOT CAUSE SUFFERING.

(4) Nothing in this section applies to the destruction of an animal in an appropriate and humane manner:

This heading, prevention of harm, governs sections 4 to 8 and relates to suffering and animal fighting. The areas covered relate to harm that is potential as well as actual. To that end it extends culpability to both active and passive harm, be it by an act or omission. It seeks to avoid the narrow construction given to the text of the POA by the courts as the AWA simplifies what is both expected and forbidden.

The prevention of harm in section 4 deals with the core subject of 'unnecessary suffering'. That qualifying condition is significant as it is consistent with the duty imposed on the owner making him liable for harm that could and should have been prevented. Consequently it is a basic intent offence for which the *mens rea* is either an intentional or reckless one.

[handwritten:] i.e INTENTION / KNOWLEDGE OF WRONGDOING THAT CONSTITUTES PART OF A CRIME.

B8 *'Hell Farm'*

In *Gray v. RSPCA* [2010] A20090060 the importance of the new Act can be seen in operation. This was an appeal from Bicester Magistrates' Court by five members of the Gray family namely the husband and wife, two daughters and a son. All five had been convicted of various offences of animal abuse under the AWA, particularly under sections 4 and 9.

The case concerned a horse business run by the appellants at Spindles Farm in Speen between 2007 and 2008. The RSPCA Inspectors attended the Farm and seized and removed over 100 animals, mainly horses, ponies and donkeys and discovered the bodies of 32 equines. Given the extreme conditions present there it became known by those investigating the offences as *'Hell Farm'*: 'More than 30 animals were also found dead at what became known as "Hell Farm" in Chalk Lane, Hyde Heath...' [*Bucks Free Press*]

The various animals had numerous health problems, including strangles, salmonella infections, anaemia, parasite infections, impaired liver functions and internal organ damage.

It was one of the biggest investigations ever by the RSPCA and cost about £1 million. RSPCA Inspector Kirsty Hampton said, 'When we arrived at the farm we were confronted with an extremely distressing scene. The stench of decomposition and urine was overpowering. The sight of horses left in such a miserable state will stay with me forever and I hope I never have to see animals treated with such little care and compassion again.'

It was a formidable case. Initially it was a 12 week trial at the Bicester Magistrates' Court. There was an appeal against conviction, heard at Aylesbury Crown Court over about 2 months, by The Recorder of Aylesbury, HHJ Tyrer Dl, sitting with two Magistrates. A total of 16 veterinary surgeons were involved in examining and advising on the various animals' welfare. The Recorder in introducing his judgment said, 'The issues are wide ranging: factual and scientific.'

There was reference by the court to the POA. That anachronistic Act was the subject of numerous confusing cases and many inconsistent decisions. So the Recorder took the opportunity to fix the court's judgment on the principles of the AWA. He was firm in declaring the legal irrelevance of the POA to their decision:

'The only comment necessary is in relation to section 4(1)(b) and as to what is the necessary state of mind in an individual. Before the passing of this new Act, there was a great deal of case law on the meaning of the previous provisions of section 1(1)(a) of the Protection of Animals Act 1911. In our judgment the old jurisprudence is no longer relevant. The section is clear and it is in the alternative.

What has to be established is either subjective knowledge namely personal knowledge, or objective knowledge namely that the individual ought reasonably to have known that his or her act or failure to act would cause an animal to suffer unnecessarily.'

After dismissing most of the appeals, The Recorder added, 'None of you has shown any remorse. You continue to protest your innocence in the face of overwhelming evidence.' The main appellant, James Gray Senior, initially absconded before sentence, but in due course was imprisoned and banned for life from keeping equines. [See **B9**]

The Recorder's reference to the alternative offence is indicative of the fact the section has created two offences. One is the act of omission which causes the unnecessary suffering to an animal. The other is being responsible for an animal and permitting or failing to prevent another person causing unnecessary suffering to that animal.

This section places a duty of care on the owner to consider the welfare of the animal from each perspective namely the subjective and objective view. So there are distinct conditions and criteria which are relevant to take into account in order to determine whether suffering is unnecessary. The relevant 'considerations' under section 4(3)(a)-(e) include all aspects of the animal's welfare ranging from whether the suffering could 'reasonably have been avoided or reduced' to whether the conduct concerned was in all the circumstances that of 'a reasonably competent and humane person'.

The person is liable if his act or omission was intentional. That is a subjective test as his knowledge and act coincides with the cause. However it is much wider than that as otherwise the section would easily be defeated. So he would also be liable if he acted recklessly as he 'ought reasonably to have known' of the actual or potential effect. If it is 'likely to do so' it is an objective test.

The second offence is also wider than in previous legislation as it covers and extends to a vicarious and joint liability. Indeed it extends the liability to a person who is in a supervisory capacity as well as one who is not supervising the one who commits the offence.

In that respect it similarly includes a subjective and objective test so making both parties potentially liable. For each and every person commits an offence if he is responsible for an animal and acts or fails to act in a way that was reasonable in all the circumstances to protect the animal from the resultant unnecessary suffering. That is indeed the effect of section 4 of the new Act and the strength of it is exhibited by the judgment in *Gray v. RSPCA*.

B9 Spindles Farm revisited

In due course and by a circuitous route the defendants, James Gray and Julie Gray, having requested a case stated application which was rejected finally ended up in the High Court. James Gray relied on several points of law, while Julie Gray sought to challenge the costs order made against her. In the Administrative Court Toulson LJ explained that 'In order to make progress and curtail further debate as to the form of case stated... Ouseley J ordered' that the case should be resolved by judicial review.

The principal claimant, James Gray, initially faced and was duly convicted in 2009 at Central Buckinghamshire Magistrates' Court before District Judge Vickers of 11 offences under the AWA. All but two of the charges were under section 4. Charges 2 and 9 were under section 9. Four other members of Mr Gray's family, including his wife, were found jointly guilty with him on some of the charges. On each of the charges Gray was sentenced to 24 weeks' imprisonment concurrent and disqualified under section 34 for an unlimited time from dealing in, owning or keeping equines with a further stipulation that he should not be entitled to apply for a termination of his disqualification for a period of 10 years. Additional orders were made for deprivation and seizure of animals to which the various charges related. They had been suspended pending the appeal. Gray was successful on two charges, but his appeal was dismissed on the remaining nine. As a result he was ordered to pay £200,000 towards the prosecution's costs of the appeal in addition to the £400,000 costs ordered by the district judge.

Julie Gray was convicted on charges 2 and 9. She was sentenced to a community order and a disqualification order. She was ordered to pay £750 towards the cost of the prosecution. Then she was ordered to pay £200,000 in respect of the prosecution's costs of the appeal.

The draft case stated identified 6 points of law the main applicant was challenging in a root and branch attack on the findings of the Crown Court including the *mens rea*, interpretation of the Act, seizure of the animals, the jurisdiction of the court and duplicity of the charges. He and Julie Gray appealed against the costs.

Toulson LJ referred to the background and introduction of the AWA. He outlined all of the relevant sections for the appeal. During the hearing His Lordship made many salient decisions that marked the changes that resulted from the AWA: see *Gray v. Crown Court Aylesbury and RSPCA* [2013] EWHC 500 (Admin).

Toulson LJ set the scene by referring to the state of the respective animals:

'Numerous witnesses described in graphic terms the shocking conditions in which equines were held and the poor condition of many of them. Among the living equines there were dead and decomposing equine carcases. During those visits a total of 115 equines were seized by police officers purporting to act under section 18. According to the prosecution, the RSPCA had never previously been involved in the seizure of so many animals. The condition of three animals was such that they were destroyed. Many others were taken into custody for their protection. These actions were all taken on the advice of veterinary surgeons who considered such action to be necessary in the interests of the animals' welfare.

Charges 1 and 2 related to animals whose carcasses were found at the farm.

Charge 3 related to an animal...which was in such a condition that it was put down...the animal suffered unnecessarily by being neglected and starved. It could not get to food or water.

Charge 4 related to 13 horses...The court was satisfied that they had been neglected and left to starve.

Charge 5 related to a piebald pony...suffering from an infection of the penis which developed to such an extent that the pony needed to be put down. The court found that it suffered unnecessarily from a failure to provide veterinary treatment for its condition, and that if Mr Gray had taken proper steps to obtain treatment the pony would have survived.

Charge 7 concerned a horse which had to be put down. It was emaciated, suffered from an infected eye and exhibited chronic diarrhoea.

31

Charge 8 concerned a donkey foal...It was emaciated and starved to death, being finally overcome by salmonellosis.

Charge 9 was brought under section 9 and concerned ponies and other equines RS1-97. The veterinary surgeon who orally authorised their seizure conceded that most of the animals were in an acceptable condition but the court was satisfied that they had not been properly looked after and that the conditions at the farm were such that they were likely to suffer if their circumstances remained unchanged.

Charge 11 concerned 6 animals which were also the subject of charge 9...The animals were emaciated and close to death. The court found that they suffered unnecessarily as a result of Mr Gray's failure to provide them with a proper diet. [Gray's appeal succeeded on charges 6 and 10.]

The court considered the interpretation of "knew or ought reasonably to have known" in section 4(1)(b). Counsel claimed that the 'offence requires either actual knowledge or a form of constructive knowledge that the animal was showing signs of unnecessary suffering, and that negligence is not sufficient.' Somewhat strangely he relied on authorities relating to section 1(1)(a) of the Protection of Animals Act 1911.

Toulson LJ gave the submission less than short shrift: 'That Act [POA] was the corner piece of animal welfare legislation prior to its repeal and replacement by the 2006Act. The judge took the view that the language of section 1(1)(a) of the 1911 Act, and authorities as to its construction, were irrelevant to the construction of section 4 of the 2006 Act. The judge was right. The language of the provisions is significantly different. It would be wrong in principle to construe the provisions of the 2006 Act by reference to differently worded provisions of the repealed legislation.

Further, if there were ambiguity about section 4(1) of the 2006 Act (which is not the case), the explanatory notes, the departmental select committee's report and the government's response to that report make it clear that the offence was intended to capture unnecessary suffering caused by negligence... "...that the *mens rea* element of the clause 1(1) cruelty offence [which became section 4 in the 2006 Act] should be assessed by means of an objective test, so that the defendant's conduct will be assessed on the basis of what a reasonable person in the position of the defendant would have known about the consequences of his or her conduct."

The next point the court considered was the interpretation of "such steps as are reasonable in all the circumstances" in section 9(1)

Counsel for Gray relied on the same argument. The judge gave that a similar short shrift. He said, 'The offence created by section 9 was a new offence. Its purpose was to strengthen animal welfare protection in that previously no general offence was committed by neglect of an animal unless it could be proved to have caused the animal to suffer unnecessarily...the distinction between "the cruelty offence" and "the welfare offence" (which became respectively section 4 and section 9) should be whether the animal had suffered unnecessarily, not the mental state of the person concerned. The language of section 4 and section 9 is consistent with that approach. Mr Fullerton's argument as to the proper construction of section 9(1) mirrored his argument as to the proper construction of section 4(1)(b), which I have rejected. The judge was right to construe section 9(1) as setting a purely objective standard of care which a person responsible for an animal is required to provide.'

The court dealt with the issue of jurisdiction in a peremptory fashion: 'The operation of the deprivation orders was suspended pending the determination of the appeal, after which their operation was activated. There is no basis for holding that the Crown Court lacked jurisdiction to act as it did.'

The issue of duplicity was potentially a good point. For as Toulson LJ said, 'The question posed is whether a conviction under section 9 is bad for duplicity if it is based upon the same findings of fact as a conviction under section 4. There can be no objection to a person being prosecuted for both offences in relation to the same animal. There can equally be no objection to a person being convicted of both offences if the conduct proved in relation to the welfare offence is wider than the conduct which can be proved to have caused actual suffering to the animal.

The question posed for the opinion of the court is narrower. If a person is proved guilty of an offence under section 4, should there be a separate conviction under section 9 in circumstances where the neglect proved under section 9 was no wider than the conduct which caused the unnecessary suffering for which there was guilt under section 4? On those assumed facts the court should not in my view record a separate conviction for the less serious offence, because the conduct would be entirely subsumed within the conduct giving rise to guilt of the more serious offence. A separate conviction would therefore be otiose and a potentially misleading entry on the person's record. ... Otherwise every conviction under section 4 would be liable to bring with it a matching conviction under section 9.'

However the potential was not realised because, 'On the facts...there was no complete duplication. Charges 1 and 2 related to carcasses of animals found at the time of the RSPCA's intervention. Charge 1 was under section 4 and related to 15 animals. Charge 2 was under section 9 and related to 17 animals, 15 of which were the animals identified under charge 1...but there can be no objection to the fact of a separate conviction on charge

2 and no separate penalty was imposed. On charge 11 Mr Gray was found guilty of causing unnecessary suffering to 6 animals...they were emaciated and some were near to death. On charge 9 Mr Gray was convicted of a welfare offence in relation to 97 animals, including the 6 which were the subject of charge 11. Charge 9 not only included 91 animals which were not the subject of charge 11, but the lack of care of the animals was not confined to failure to provide them with a nutritionally balanced diet. They were not protected to the extent required by good practice...

The judge concluded, 'For those reasons I am not satisfied that a case has been made out for this court to interfere with Mr Gray's convictions on charges 2 and 9.'

His Lordship dealt with the lawfulness of the seizure of the various animals too. The point of law relied upon was a valid one, but the practical effect was nugatory as the evidence was nonetheless admissible. [See **C8**]

Finally Toulson LJ said, 'I would dismiss Mr Gray's claim for judicial review.'

Silber J, with whom Toulson LJ agreed, considered the issue of costs. Counsel for James Gray relied upon the maximum fines that could be imposed for the respective offences as the yardstick for what should have been the related costs. That would have limited the potential maximum sum to £140,000. He also claimed the costs should be paid out of income as opposed to capital. Silber J cut a swathe through the submission by saying, 'Indeed if Mr Fullerton was right and costs orders could only be made which would be payable out of income and not capital, it is difficult to see how costs orders could be made against serving prisoners as they would have no income but might have substantial capital in the form of a house.'

Silber J concluded, 'I should add that there is no merit in any of the other grounds put forward on behalf of the First Appellant and so his costs appeal has to be dismissed.'

The application on costs by Julie Gray was remitted to the Crown Court for a redetermination as the Trustee in Bankruptcy was involved with the First Appellant.

B10 Action

Taking those factors outlined in section 4(3) individually it shows a marked burden on the person doing or failing to do the act and causing the suffering to justify his action. While it does not shift the burden of proof, it does place an evidential burden on the person once it is shown that the suffering could have reasonably been 'avoided or reduced'. So if the prosecution introduce and adduce evidence from an expert such as a vet or an RSPCA Inspector that his action or omission could have been less or not done at all, then a *prima facie* case would be made. For once that evidence is adduced there would be a plain case for the defendant to answer as it is a basic intent offence.

If the 'conduct' that caused the suffering was in contravention of a code of practice or a licence or statutory instrument then that too is an evidential factor that would count against a defendant. It has the advantage for the prosecution of allowing them to rely on the breach of the code of practice or similar as evidence that the consequent suffering caused was 'unnecessary'. Conversely, if though it caused suffering, it was an inevitable consequence of complying with those practices then it would be unlikely to be an offence and, if a person is charged, it would provide a strong defence and powerful mitigation.

As the obverse side of that evidential coin, if the conduct was for the benefit of the animal, then the suffering could or would be necessary. So an operation performed by a vet could be properly performed yet it would cause the animal to suffer. Nevertheless that would be for a 'legitimate' purpose and so necessary, providing the vet was competent and acted professionally and humanely.

Similarly it would be for a legitimate purpose if the act was performed to protect a person or property or other animal. It would obviously be illegal to gratuitously kick or hit an animal. However if the act was against a dog that had attacked a child then it would be permissible self-defence to act in aid of the child. It would be the same if it was an out of control Rottweiler attacking your pet poodle. You would have to act reasonably in accordance with the principles of self-defence. That would equally apply if you were trying to protect your property. Although in that case the act of causing 'suffering' would be balanced against the type and value of the property. Of course given that an animal is only property too, it could be a farmer protecting his flock of sheep. The crucial factor is the purpose of the act itself.

It is not enough to simply rely on the conduct being for a legitimate purpose, it is also a consideration that the suffering was 'proportionate' to the purpose. So if an animal was killed or severely injured, that would not be justified unless the circumstances were extreme. If the suffering was prolonged, so that the animal was in constant pain over a period, that too would not be proportionate. That could be proved for example by a vet examining the animal if it limped or had a broken leg. Equally it could be shown by a post-mortem. For then it would show the progressive growth of an injury and how, if at all, it had affected the welfare of the animal prior to its death. To that end the medical evidence would tell the tale of the animal's suffering while it was alive.

The character of the person causing the suffering is another consideration for the court. The conduct that is the cause for concern must be carried out by a reasonably 'competent and humane person'. Allied to that the relevant 'circumstances' are also taken into account. If the person was genuinely doing his best, the fact it turns out wrong would not make him liable, providing he was acting competently and humanely. Conversely if it was a misguided bodger who interfered and caused greater suffering then it would not be a defence that he was doing what he honestly believed was in the best interests of the animal. So using some well-meaning, but wholly wrong treatment would be balanced against the urgency of the situation. For in an emergency a person may make a mistake yet had acted competently and humanely. That would apply if an animal was seriously injured in a road traffic accident and was in severe pain. The person treating it may exacerbate the condition even though he was acting with the best of motives. Then if the person causing the suffering had been incompetent or inhumane the liability would remain.

The advantage of those considerations for the animal is it allows the court to consider whether the suffering was unnecessary from the position of the victim. In that respect it must also be remembered that these considerations are inclusive not exclusive. That further allows a court to assess the action as it affected an animal by taking account of other relevant factors.

As a final provision section 4(4) states, 'Nothing in this section applies to the destruction of an animal in an appropriate and humane manner'. This allows for the killing of an animal. However to be lawful it has to be done in that qualified manner. That does not limit it to a vet or a professionally qualified person. It is the law that a person may do what they wish with their own property. Certainly under the POA a man could kill his pet dog providing he did not act so as to cause it unnecessary suffering. A single blow that instantly caused its death was legal whether carried out in a backyard by the owner or at an abattoir. It was the consequence of causing suffering that made the conduct unlawful. That is no longer the case.

All of those factors are discrete and so can be considered by the court when deciding whether the conduct caused unnecessary suffering. Yet they are related in that the prosecution could rely on any or all of those considerations to decide the issue. Conversely the person causing the suffering has the onus, once a case to answer has been raised and proved, of showing that he did not cause that result contrary to those considerations. In that respect there are considerable hurdles for a defendant. For even if he claimed he had acted in self-defence, it could still be contrary to a code of practice or a condition of his licence. If he could not rely on those considerations in his defence, the evidential burden on the prosecution would be discharged and move from an allegation to proof.

As the considerations are not exclusive the court is entitled to take into account in its deliberations and decision any other relevant considerations. That approach is consistent with the aim of the AWA. For the POA was introduced to directly protect the owner's property, the AWA was enacted to enhance the welfare of animals. So an animal now has the legal protection of not being the victim of suffering before or during its death.

There is a balance between those competing considerations that may arise. So a conflict between the concepts of necessity and humanity may have to be considered. Over all those factors the idea of proportionality is vital because prevention of harm is the focus of this section which aligns with the purpose of the AWA. For the protection of the respective animal is paramount. As that coincides with the 'promotion of welfare' under section 9 there is no reason why an animal should not be protected *per se* and so entitled as a matter of law not to be killed at will. Indeed there is every reason to consider that the aim and purpose of the AWA is to achieve that end. The significant change introduced by the AWA is that the owner's duty to care for the animal's welfare would include striving to keep it alive. It is the ethos that embodies and permeates the Act. [See **B3**]

Significantly under the general principles of criminal law a person has no duty to act to help another person who was in trouble be it in danger of drowning or being burned alive. The same principle applies to animals. However if the person is 'responsible' for the animal he would have a concomitant duty to assist the animal and try to abate its suffering. He has a legal duty to do so as otherwise by his act or omission he would be in breach of section 4. Similarly while a stranger would be exempt from liability for it as if he had no duty towards the animal or human, if he caused the initial injury the situation is different. For then his act or omission would be a breach of the duty imposed upon him by the same section.

Mutilation

B11   Animal Welfare Act 2006, s.5

(1) A person commits an offence if –
  (a) he carries out a prohibited procedure on a protected animal;
  (b) he causes such a procedure to be carried out on such an animal.
(2) A person commits an offence if –
  (a) he is responsible for an animal;
  (b) another person carries out a prohibited procedure on the animal, and
  (c) he permitted that to happen or failed to take such steps (whether by way of supervising the other person or otherwise) as were reasonable in all the circumstances to prevent that happening.

(3) References in this section to the carrying out of a prohibited procedure on an animal are to the carrying out of a procedure which involves interference with the sensitive tissues or bone structure of the animal, otherwise than for the purpose of its medical treatment.

(4) Subsections (1) and (2) do not apply in such circumstances as the appropriate national authority may specify by regulations.

(5) Before making regulations under subsection (4), the appropriate national authority shall consult such persons appearing to the authority to represent any interests concerned as the authority considers appropriate.

(6) Nothing in this section applies to the removal of the whole or any part of a dog's tail.

Using the word 'mutilation' is deliberate. It indicates that the animal is changed by the procedure and such change is or is likely to be inimical to the animal. That is why the 'prohibited procedure' is drafted so wide. As a corollary it is why under section 5(1) a person commits an offence if the mutilation, which is classed as a prohibited procedure, is performed on a protected animal.

Additionally a person commits an offence if he permits a prohibited procedure to be performed on a protected animal. The fact of 'permitting' it to happen has to relate to an animal for which he is responsible. To that extent he is liable if he acts or fails to act by allowing it to happen or failing to prevent it happening. Permitting is a wide term which includes knowledge and negligence via the Nelsonian blind eye. For if it is something that he could or should prevent he is liable. Hence the *mens rea* under section 5(2) means it can be committed by having an intention to do so or recklessly in not caring at all for the animal and so allowing it to happen.

This wide-ranging section creates three offences: (a) carrying out a prohibited procedure; (b) causing such a procedure to be carried out; and (c) permitting or failing to prevent another person doing so.

A prohibited procedure is a procedure which involves interference with 'the sensitive tissues or bone structure of the animal, otherwise than for the purpose of its medical treatment.' So it is one which alters the condition of the animal by some form of mutilation which is not for its benefit. It does not include the 'docking' of a dog's tail which is covered in section 6.

The sort of action the prohibited procedure is aimed at includes cutting a dog's ears to add fierceness for fighting or botched medical operations that border on butchery. Sometimes an owner will even treat an animal himself in order to save vet's fees. Those sort of actions may be performed by an amateur or a quack, though a qualified person would not be excused from liability if the procedure was prohibited. The crucial point is the need to protect an animal from those who should protect the animal but in fact cause it or permit it to be mutilated.

A complete exemption from the offences can be introduced by the national authority specifying by regulations that subsections (1) and (2) 'do not apply' in a given case. As that would effectively legalise what would otherwise be illegal, 'before' making any such regulations the national authority 'shall' consult such persons that appear to them to represent any interest as the authority considers 'appropriate'. That is a mandatory duty on the authorities. It has the inherent advantage that it gives an opportunity for any opposition to the intended exemption to be taken into account.

This new provision is controlled to a degree by the mandatory requirement that the authority 'shall' consult such persons that represent any interests that the authority considers appropriate. They must do so 'before' making regulations. To comply with that mandatory duty, the authorities would have to consult those persons. As those persons have to appear to be appropriate to the authority, there is a duty on the authority to seek out such interested persons. Moreover if they failed to take account of such interests and wrongly considered them to be inappropriate, any regulations they introduced could be challenged. For while it gives the authority a discretion as to whom they consult, if they fail to consult some relevant persons it could be subject to judicial review.

The importance of this provision in section 5(5) is plain from the fact it is repeated in a similar form throughout the AWA namely in sections 6(15), 13(9), 15(1), 16(1) and 17(3). They refer and are relevant to both regulations and codes of practice. Indeed the effect of the duty on the authorities and how it affects those who oppose their power can be seen in sharp focus in the landmark case *R (on the application of Petsafe Ltd and another) v. Welsh Ministers* [2010] EWHC 2908 where the introduction of a ban on dog collars by a regulation was challenged in the High Court. [See **B20**]

Docking of Dogs' Tails

B12   Animal Welfare Act 2006, s.6

   (1)   A person commits an offence if –
   - (a)   he removes the whole or any part of a dog's tail, otherwise than for the purpose of its medical treatment;
   - (b)   he causes the whole or any part of a dog's tail to be removed by another person, otherwise than for the purpose of its medical treatment.
   (2)   A person commits an offence if –
   - (a)   he is responsible for a dog,
   - (b)   another person removes the whole or any part of the dog's tail, otherwise than for the purpose of its medical treatment, and

(c) he permitted that to happen or failed to take such steps (whether by way of supervising the other person or otherwise) as were reasonable in all circumstances to prevent that happening.

(3) Subsections (1) and (2) do not apply if the dog is a certified working dog that is not more than 5 days old.

(4) For the purpose of subsection (3), a dog is a certified working dog if a veterinary surgeon has certified, in accordance with regulations made by the appropriate national authority, that the first and second conditions mentioned below are met.

(5) The first condition referred to in subsection (4) is that there has been produced to the veterinary surgeon such evidence as the appropriate national authority may by regulations require for the purpose of showing that the dog is likely to be used for work in connection with –

(a) law enforcement,

(b) activities of Her Majesty's armed forces,

(c) emergency rescue,

(d) lawful pest control, or

(e) the lawful shooting of animals.

(6) The second condition referred to in subsection (4) is that the dog is of a type specified for the purposes of this subsection by regulations made by the appropriate national authority.

(7) It is a defence for a person accused of an offence under subsection (1) or (2) to show that he reasonably believed that the dog was one in relation to which subsection (3) applies.

(8) A person commits an offence if –

(a) he owns a subsection (3) dog, and

(b) fails to take reasonable steps to secure that, before the dog is 3 months old, it is identified as a subsection (3) dog in accordance with regulations made by the appropriate national authority.

(9) A person commits an offence if –

(a) he shows a dog at an event to which members of the public are admitted on payment of a fee;

(b) the dog's tail has been wholly or partly removed (in England and Wales or elsewhere), and

(c) removal took place on or after the commencement day.

(10) Where a dog is shown only for the purpose of demonstrating its working ability, subsection (9) does not apply if the dog is a subsection (3) dog.

(11) It is a defence for a person accused of an offence under subsection (9) to showthat he reasonably believed –

(a) that the event was not one to which members of the public were admitted on payment of an entrance fee,

(b) that the removal took place before the commencement day, or

(c) that the dog was one in relation to which subsection (10) applies.

(12) A person commits an offence if he knowingly gives false information to a veterinary surgeon in connection with the giving of a certificate for the purposes of this section.

(13) The appropriate national authority may by regulations make provision about the function of inspectors in relation to –

(a) certificates for the purposes of this section, and

(b) the identification of dogs as subsection (3) dogs.

(16) In this section –

"subsection (3) dog" means a dog whose tail has, on or

after the commencement day, been wholly or partly removed without contravening subsection (1), because of the application of subsection (3).

A peculiar custom has grown up for many years whereby people dock the tails of their pets. It is often the result of misguided bar-room wisdom or old wives' tales. Sometimes it is no less than vanity of the owners or the fashion of myopic people who openly parade their egos at dog shows. The result is a dog will suffer for the simple reason he has been born with a particular tail because that is as nature intended. Be it long or short, straight or curly, the tail has a distinct purpose for a dog including showing emotion and assisting balance. It enables them to climb and run and act in defence when attacked by other animals.

Yet for some perverse reason some persons feel unable to resist the idea of docking a dog's tail. Whatever the reason, until recently it was prevalent. This section seeks to protect dogs from the perversity of their owners. So it prohibits tail docking unless it is done for medical treatment. It also prohibits showing docked dogs as often such mutilation appeals to those with power and vanity rather than judgement. A practising Scottish vet, Russell Lyon, who witnessed it first hand lamented in his autobiography, *Vet in the Country*, [2005], 'It is such a pity that docking dogs was not banned at the same time [as docking horses] … The Kennel Club could stop the horrible operation overnight if all dogs that were docked were prevented from entering the show ring. Dogs need their tails, and the public perception that spaniels, boxers or any other docked breed look better without tails has got to be changed.'

Now, in order to curb that 'horrible' practice which can be harmful and painful to the dog, it is strictly controlled by section 6. It creates five offences. If he is charged under subsection (1) or (2) it is a defence to show he reasonably believed that the dog was one to which subsection (3) applies.

When a dog has just been born his tail can be docked without it being as painful as at a later stage though it is still sensitive. As a result there is a special condition which in turn provides a defence to these offences. For neither 'subsections (1) and (2) apply if the dog a certified working dog that is not more than five days old.' This has become known as a 'subsection (3) dog' because the special meaning attached to it allows the docking which would otherwise be unlawful. Equally if it is certified to be a working dog within the subsection it has advantages for the owner. For under subsection (4) it must be certified by a vet that two conditions are met namely those contained in (5) and (6). Those conditions are that evidence was produced to a vet which complies with regulations made by the appropriate national authority. The second condition is that the dog is of a type specified by those regulations.

This section prohibits what is in effect the mutilation of a dog. By analogy with section 5 it is a prohibited procedure of any dog unless the person responsible for the dog has a defence.

By section 6(13) a regulation may be made allowing an inspector the power to check that there is no contravention of the AWA. That would entail them being able, for example, to read a microchip on a dog or inspect any vet's certificate in relation to the animal.

In 2010 a woman pleaded guilty to docking the tails of 5 of her Jack Russell puppies. A vet to whom she had taken them for a routine examination discovered the 'damage' to all of the dogs' tails. Her reason for doing so was her 'family had a history of docking dogs and she didn't know it was illegal.' She was given a conditional discharge.

It was confirmed in another case in the RSPCA Annual Report 2011 that docking the tails of 5 Jack Russell pups when they were 1-day old does cause 'pain and can be permanently sensitised to pain by trauma.' The defendant got another person to do the deeds. He was convicted and fined.

In summary section 6 creates five different offences. Those are if a person:

(a)   removes any part of a dog's tail other than for medical treatment;

(b)   permits it to be removed other than for medical treatment;

(c)   fails to identify the 'subsection (3) dog' as required by the regulations;

(d)   shows a docked dog to the public for a fee;

(e)   gives false information to a vet about a 'subsection (3) dog'.

Equally it creates four statutory defences that apply to the different forms which are:

(a)   a dog is certified by a vet that it complies with the regulations;

(b)   a reasonable belief that it was a 'subsection (3) dog';

(c)   the dog is shown solely to demonstrate its working ability;

(d)   a reasonable belief that the public did not pay to enter the event.

The Secretary of State has made a regulation namely the Docking of Working Dogs Tails (England) Regulations 2007 relating to England. A comparable one applies to Wales.

The status of a vet for the purpose of the AWA is defined by section 62(1). Only a vet may carry out the docking by the

Veterinary Surgeons Act 1966 and the Veterinary Surgeons Act 1966 (Schedule 3 Amendment) Order 1991. In that respect the Royal College of Veterinary Surgeons (RCVS) guidance, *Guide to Professional Conduct* (2000), states that it is 'unethical unless done for therapeutic or truly prophylactic reason.' In fact it even goes further in emphasising that 'Arguments for docking puppies on the grounds of tradition, or prevention of faecal soiling, or damage in "working" breeds unlikely ever to work, are considered scientifically and morally flawed by the majority of veterinary surgeons'.

Prior to the AWA it was still practised on a wide scale. Now it has to be remembered that a vet can only carry out the procedure if he complies with the AWA. So, unless he had a reasonable belief that the dog was only 4 days old, if he carried out docking on a 7 day-old dog he would commit an offence. That would require evidence from another vet or expert rather than relying on the shape of the dog's tail.

Over a century ago the practice of docking animals' tails was recognised and condemned in the classic animal welfare case *Ford v. Wiley* (1889) 23 QBD 203 where Hawkins J. said, 'Docking is another painful operation, which, no doubt, can occasionally be justified; but I hold a very strong opinion against allowing fashion, or the whim of an individual, or any number of individuals, to afford a justification for such painful mutilation and disfigurement.'

While it only took 100 odd years, the moral argument recognised by the RCVS is now encompassed by the AWA.

Administration of poisons etc.

B13 Animal Welfare Act 2006, s.7

(1) A person commits an offence if, without lawful authority or reasonable excuse, he –
  (a) administers any poisonous or injurious drug or substance to a protected animal, knowing it to be poisonous or injurious, or
  (b) causes any poisonous or injurious drug or substance to be taken by a protected animal, knowing it to be poisonous or injurious.

(2) A person commits an offence if –
  (a) he is responsible for an animal,
  (b) without lawful authority or reasonable excuse, another person administers a poisonous or injurious drug or substance to the animal or causes the animal to take such a drug or substance, and
  (c) he permitted that to happen or, knowing the drug or substance to be poisonous or injurious, he failed to take such steps, (whether by way of supervising the other person or otherwise) as were reasonable in all the circumstances to prevent that happening.

(3) In this section, references to a poisonous or injurious drug or substance include a drug or substance which, by virtue of the quantity or manner in which it is administered or taken, has the effect of a poisonous or injurious drug or substance.

Some people think it is hilarious to feed their pets anything from alcohol to drugs. All such substances and others, given their anatomy and digestive systems and size, can be harmful to an animal. For all animals can be affected adversely by a substance that is not a food naturally eaten by them. At best it can induce a deleterious effect on their organs while at worst it can be fatal. Therefore section 7 was introduced to cover a situation where a person feeds an animal a poisonous substance.

This is a wide section. Given the opportunity to abuse an animal and make money while doing so, both irresistible to some people, it covers any person who uses a poison to affect an animal. Primarily it is aimed at those taking advantage of an animal by making it take drugs to run faster, fight harder or grow fatter. While it is aimed at how the animal is affected by the substance, it would engulf anyone using such a substance in horse racing, dog fighting and bestiality.

There are few prosecutions in this area because the abused animal is rarely discovered at the time and so the drugs naturally disappear. An unusual case arose in 2011 when a defendant while being routinely interviewed by the police admitted abusing his greyhound, Jake, by giving him cannabis resin, sleeping tablets and sildenafil. His reason for doing so was 'to either suppress or enhance the dog's performance at the race track so he could bet on the outcome of the race.' The Hartlepool Magistrates held the offence was 'aggravated by the defendant's desire for commercial gain.' So they imposed a suspended sentence.

Obviously it also relates to cases of owners who find it amusing to abuse their pet by causing it to consume drugs. In *R. v. Wilson*: Bristol Evening Post [2009] Andrew Wilson beat his pet dog, Bronx, and fed him Stella lager. It was one of, if not the, first charge under section 7 of the AWA for the administration of poisons or injurious drugs to a protected animal. Wilson hit his dog, a bull mastiff, over the head and gave him the alcohol. Bronx was taken to the RSPCA Dogs and Cats Home and seen by the vet, Mandy Stone. Ms Stone said, 'Bronx had a nasty cut to his head and was staggering around, looking confused and generally depressed, it wasn't until Wilson was questioned and admitted that he gave Bronx alcohol that I realised why. He had a dangerous amount in his body and had Bronx been a smaller dog, may not have survived.'

The person committing the act would commit an offence unless he had 'lawful authority or reasonable excuse' for doing so. While 'administers' is a wide term, it also tends to indicate an intention to do the act as opposed to accidentally poisoning an animal. That is supported by the fact the person must know it is 'poisonous or injurious'. However if, as in *Wilson*, the defendant was drunk or drugged, it would not be a defence as it is knowledge of the drug as well as the dog that determines the mental element, not the act of administering that substance. The section creates two offences namely administering the drug or causing it to be taken by the animal. That position also covers 'causes' as the act would be dependent on his knowledge as if he was sober. If it were otherwise a drunk could use being drunk as a reasonable excuse.

The third offence is actually wider than previous legislation as it covers and extends it to a vicarious and joint liability. Indeed it extends the liability to a person who is in a supervisory capacity as well as one who is not supervising the one who commits the offence. As it includes an act or omission, the idea of 'permits' puts an onus on the person who is responsible to ensure his animal is not abused by another person. So there is no reason why in given circumstances, such as *Wilson*, recklessness would not suffice. To that extent it is a basic intent offence. For that would relate to the state of the owner and any other person, be they drunk or drugged or both. It would be consistent with a joint and vicarious liability.

Significantly it is not important or necessary whether the protected animal actually suffered as a result of a person administering a drug. For the prohibited act is the administering itself. The liability springs from the illegal deed. Further the width of the section can be seen by the fact the 'quantity or manner' of the substance being administered is the prohibited act. Therefore even a harmless substance could be harmful if it is given in a way that is injurious to the animal. Similarly a substance that is harmless in small amounts could be harmful if the dose is too high.

Plainly the offence is direct in respect of the knowledge of the person who administers the substance. However in appropriate circumstances there is no reason why, apart from a genuine accidental dose or accidental poisoning, a person could or would not be liable for a reckless state of mind. If it were otherwise a man who was like *Wilson* could claim he thought he was beating a carpet not his dog or he thought he was giving his dog a drink of water. So someone who had taken drugs would be able to escape from liability by claiming he did not understand what he was doing when he shared his spliff with his dog. Indeed in 2009 a man in France was liable for feeding his duck 'weed' or cannabis. [See *Criminal Law and Justice Weekly* 2009] Similarly in August 2009 a couple had an emaciated dog tied up outside their premises. A RSPCA Inspector said by virtue of the dog's condition it had not been fed for some months. The defendants admitted that was true. Instead of food they had fed it 'potentially lethal doses of tobacco.' They were each given a suspended sentence.

Fighting etc.

B14 Animal Welfare Act 2006, s.8

   (1)   A person commits an offence if he –
       (a)   causes an animal fight to take place, or attempts to do so;

    (b)   knowingly receives money for admission to an animal fight;

    (c)   knowingly publicises a proposed animal fight;

    (d)   provides information about an animal fight to another with the intention of enabling or encouraging attendance at the fight;

    (e)   makes or accepts a bet on the outcome of an animal fight or on the likelihood of anything occurring or not occurring in the course of an animal fight;

    (f)   takes part in an animal fight;

    (g)   has in his possession anything designed or adapted for use in connection with an animal fight with the intention of its being so used;

    (h)   keeps or trains an animal for use for in connection with an animal fight;

    (i)   keeps any premises for use for an animal fight.

(2)   A person commits an offence if, without lawful authority or reasonable excuse, he is present at an animal fight.

(3)   A person commits an offence if, without lawful authority or reasonable excuse, he –

    (a)   knowingly supplies a video recording of an animal fight,

    (b)   knowingly publishes a video recording of an animal fight,

    (c)   knowingly shows a video recording of an animal fight to another, or

    (d)   possesses a video recording of an animal fight, knowing it to be such a recording, with the intention of supplying it.

(4)   Subsection (3) does not apply if the video recording is of an animal fight that took place –

    (a)   outside Great Britain, or

    (b)   before the commencement date.

(5)   Subsection (3) does not apply –

    (a)   in the case of paragraph (a), to the supply of a video recording for inclusion in a programme service;

    (b)   in the case of paragraph (b) or (c), to the publication or showing of a video recording by means of its inclusion in a programme service;

    (c)   in the case of paragraph (d), by virtue of intention to supply for inclusion in a programme service.

(6)   Repealed

(7)   In this section –

"animal fight" means an occasion on which a protected animal is placed with an animal, or with a human, for the purpose of fighting, wrestling or baiting;

...

"programme service" has the same meaning as in the Communications Act 2003;

"video recording" means a recording, in any form, from which a moving image may by any means be reproduced and includes data stored on a computer disc or by other electronic means which is capable of conversion into a moving image.

(8)   In this section –

    (a)   references to supplying or publishing a video recording are to supplying or publishing a video recording in any manner, including, in relation to a video recording in the form of data stored electronically, by means of transmitting such data;

    (b)   references to showing a video recording are to showing a moving image reproduced from a video recording by any means.

It is often that bloodlust and blood-money has many followers. So those who are prone to gambling and particularly interested in profit engage in dog fighting in the animal world. While the forms of fighting are justified by them as a 'sport' no different than hunting or badger-baiting, it is closer to bear-baiting as it is a pastime that causes a lot of suffering and pain to the animals. They are dogs which, whether they win or lose in the fight, usually have numerous injuries. Regardless of their condition, they will be made to fight again. At worst they will die as a result of the injuries or because of their injuries be killed by the owner.

A fighting dog has a limited life as its value to the owner is its capacity to kill an opponent unless it is killed in the process. An injured dog would not be taken to a vet as if, as would be obvious to an expert, he realised the injuries were a result of dog fighting, he would report the owner to the RCVS and the police. A vet is under a professional duty to do so.

An indication of the new approach can be seen by the fact that 'fighting' which under the POA was just one of the factors which constituted cruelty. The provisions of the AWA simplified and widened that so the activity is illegal as it applies to animals and humans who are directly and indirectly involved in abusing animals by promoting fighting as a pleasure or sport.

While animal fighting mainly uses dogs, it also includes other animals such as badgers and spurred cocks. The Cruelty to Animals Act 1835 which applied to England and Wales was the first legislation in the world to make dog fighting illegal. The same Act banned badger-baiting, bear-baiting, bull-baiting and cock-fighting.

Yet using animals for fighting is on the increase in the United Kingdom, especially dog fighting which is common in places like Birmingham among immigrants who indulge in it in Pakistan where it is all but legal. The authorities there rarely if ever prosecute anyone for participating in their sport. It is also common amongst the gypsies where it is almost a custom according to a recent investigation shown on television. The producer of the programme followed the gypsies for two years. The content included bare-knuckle boxing, arranged fighting between children, cock-fighting and dogs attacking deer. The public were disturbed and lodged 300 complaints with the various authorities including the television company. Leo Maguire, the director, said, 'I was attracted by the violence of my two main characters...' The content so concerned the police and the RSPCA that both carried out investigations in relation to any potential offences. [See *Gypsy Blood*: Ch. 4: 19/1/12]

So this problem is now dealt with in a wide-ranging section that seeks to cover all areas of using animals to kill other animals. It extends to the unleashed atavistic violence by humans to that end as the definition in subsection (7) states it 'means an occasion on which a protected animal is placed with an animal, or with a human, for the purpose of fighting, wrestling or baiting'.

There are over 10 offences created by this section and many ways of committing them. A person commits an offence if he is involved in any form from causing a fight to take place up to training an animal for a fight. It extends to keeping any premises for that purpose. In this respect 'premises' are defined under section 62(1) as including 'any place and, in particular, includes –(a) any vehicle, vessel, aircraft or hovercraft; (b) any tent or moveable structure'.

It is extended to cover publications as similar to pornography films of animal fights are commonly sold to interested persons. Indeed there is a prevalence now of 'snuff' movies where animals are cruelly killed by women dressed provocatively so combining the perversion of pornography with cruelty. The videos are mass-produced and then sold on a connected secret network by the producers for profit.

Videos of animal fights are illegal in many ways too. In that context it includes that a person commits an offence if, without lawful authority or reasonable excuse, he knowingly supplies a video of an animal fight or possesses one intending to supply it. How close they are to our culture can be seen by the fact that the directors Lynch and Tarantino each used dog fighting as a backdrop in their films, *Blue Velvet* and *Pulp Fiction*. It has even recently featured in a radio play. [*Salvage of the Bones*: Radio 4 18/6/12]

What is potentially far reaching by subsection (3) does not apply if the video recording of an animal fight took place either outside Great Britain. Section 8(4)(a) is rather strange given that many animal fights actually take place outside Great Britain. Pure geography seems a rather odd reason to allow something to be legal which is otherwise illegal. If a person claims he believed it was made outside Great Britain, is that a reasonable excuse if it came from a place it is prevalent like Mexico or Pakistan? A film from Mexico could be used to influence other potential persons to become involved in promoting animal fights. Yet it would not be caught by the section as it is both a contingency and in the future. The section is mainly aimed at the present and arranged fight or possession of an item 'designed or adapted' to be so used. It appears to overlook the fact that animal abuse is growing internationally and has no borders.

Given the wide definition under section 8(7) of an 'animal fight' it is significant that it would cover any animal not just a 'protected' one within section 2. Therefore even if no one is responsible for the animal within section 3, an offence is still committed. Besides any other legislation it could cover the killing involved in badgers and cocks and foxes as well as stray dogs and abandoned kittens in the more conventional abuse of them in dog fighting.

As the definition of a 'video recording' under section 8(7) is similarly wide it would include images on a mobile phone or even a memory stick or a dongle. For from each a final image could be reproduced. It can capture the audience and participants in whatever capacity, even long after the initial event. So supplying or publishing a video recording by any means in any manner, including electronically, is caught within that definition. Evidence of that nature may take some time to be gained during an investigation. Therefore the extended time limit for a prosecution to be lodged under section 31 is now advantageous to the prosecutor. [See **D13**]

Similarly under section 8(8) 'showing' a video means showing a moving image reproduced from a video recording by any means. As that definition is so wide it could include a form which has not yet even been invented. It allows for advances in science to be matched by advances in law. Somewhat strangely as the definition is so wide, it only applies to a 'moving image' under both subsections. Therefore it would not apply to a still photograph.

A pest control officer acting within his employment which involved the use of one animal to catch another would not fall within the AWA. For in that case the licence would legalise the otherwise unlawful purpose. The primary legal purpose would be to control the activity of the animal designated a 'pest', not to cause it to be involved in baiting or fighting. Conversely if such a person nevertheless placed a bet on how many rats were killed or went outside the legitimate purpose of his employment which resulted in a 'fight', it would be an offence.

Badger-baiting, though outlawed since 1835 is still enjoyed by people who gain pleasure from inflicting pain on animals, even those they own and have as family pets. While a badger as a wild animal would not normally have the protection of the AWA, once it is 'under the control' of man it would become a 'protected animal'. Therefore it would be a double-breach of causing unnecessary suffering to each animal under that section.

The usual way an animal fight is arranged is for a series of friends and associates and strangers to get calls on a mobile phone at short notice. The definition of premises is deliberately wide as normally it is either a skittle alley in the back room of a pub that is temporarily rearranged with a ring for an animal fight or a barn on a farm. Betting usually takes place proportionate to how much blood and lust is spent by all those involved namely the animals and the participants and the spectators. It is often a family affair as many dogs will need to be trained for some considerable time to build up their strength. This can involve anything from pulling a car or being on a gym treadmill or attacking kittens swinging suspended from a tyre. It is often a mixture of those activities. For much like an athlete training for a marathon or the Olympics, the owners are intent on training their animals to be in the best shape in order to deliberately maim, wound and kill other animals.

In 2009 one of the biggest dog fighting gangs in the United Kingdom were convicted. Mike Butcher, a special investigator, said, 'A search warrant was executed in 8 counties across the UK and involved joint RSPCA and police teams. The operation unearthed 35 fighting dogs of which over half had sustained fighting injuries. Dog fighting paraphernalia was also found including treadmills and breaking sticks.' Following the investigation, which included an undercover reporter from BBC's Panorama programme, a total of 10 people were convicted.

Section 8(1) is primarily aimed at the main men, the organisers and participants. The persons whom the main man contacts who then attend or are informed on the grapevine and are present at the animal fight without 'lawful authority or reasonable excuse' commit an offence. Save for the informer or investigator or underground activist, it is difficult to know how a person would lawfully be there.

As the section is wide it applies to causing an animal fight to take place and attempting to do so. Further it catches those who directly and indirectly are involved as it also applies to all the attendant activities from start to finish of money and publicity and training that enables a fight to fructify.

Duty of person responsible for animal to ensure welfare

B15 *Promotion of Welfare*

Animal Welfare Act 2006, s.9

(1) A person commits an offence if he does not take such steps as are reasonable in all the circumstances to ensure that the needs of an animal for which he is responsible are met to the extent required by good practice.

(2) For the purposes of this Act, an animal's needs shall be taken to include –

(a) its need for a suitable environment,

(b) its need for a suitable diet,

(c) its need to be able to exhibit normal behaviour patterns,

(d) any need it has to be housed with, or apart from, other animals, and

(e) its need to be protected from pain, suffering, injury and disease.

(3) The circumstances to which it is relevant to have regard when applying subsection (1) include, in particular –
  (a) any lawful purpose for which the animal is kept, and
  (b) any lawful activity undertaken in relation to the animal.
(4) Nothing in this section applies to the destruction of an animal in an appropriate and humane manner.

The concept of welfare in the modern and legal sense sprang from the Brambell Report in 1965. After detailing the main areas for the prevention of harm under sections 4 to 8 that are unlawful, sections 9 to 12 are the core of the legal concept of welfare and in turn the anchor of the AWA. For those sections confirm the principles, the power of the inspectors, the responsibility of owners and others, plus the making of regulations to provide for the welfare of animals. Within this area of the AWA the most important one is section 9 because it places a defined duty on the person responsible for the animal.

That concept of welfare underpins the whole of the AWA. It is the cornerstone of the principles within it. While the idea of welfare was of concern as long ago as 18th century to John Lawrence, it has only had legal significance since the 1960's. Lawrence, a farmer, claimed in his book, *A Philosophical Treatise on Horses, and on the Moral Duties of Man towards the Brute Creation,* [1796] that our view of animals was that they had been created for our use so that their natural interests and welfare were secondary to man and 'sacrificed to his convenience, his cruelty or his caprice.'

The conclusions of the Brambell Report were endorsed by the FAWC in their 1993 report, *Report on Priorities for Animal Welfare Research and Development.* The result of those reports was that the Five Freedoms were established to ensure an animal's welfare was protected. Given the aim and intent of the Act, the promotion of animal welfare is at the heart of the reason it was introduced. Unlike the POA which tended to protect the proprietary and property rights of the owner of the animal, the AWA goes some limited way to provide welfare rights for animals. For it introduces the language of tort in terms of placing an active duty on the owner or person responsible for its welfare. Now a person charged with being responsible cannot escape liability by abandoning the animal or alternatively acting irresponsibly if he is the owner. [See **B2**]

Within the Agriculture (Miscellaneous Provisions) Act 1968, there is a power to make regulations to enhance the position of farm animals. As a result the Welfare of Farm Animals (England) Regulations 2000 was introduced to promote and protect the welfare of livestock on agricultural land. Similar provisions apply now to all animals for which someone is responsible by section 9 of the AWA. It is an active duty cast upon him. So he has to take steps to ensure the 'needs' of an animal are met consistent with the principle of 'good practice'.

Abandonment is a constant problem as people routinely abandon their pets. Often they will simply move away and leave the animals to fend for themselves. At worst they will leave a house full of cats and dogs starving to death, they then try to survive by eating their former companions. The POA was so inadequate it did not even cover the abandonment of an animal. So the Abandonment of Animals Act was introduced in 1960. The AWA repealed and replaced that Act. Now if a person who is responsible for an animal abandons it, he will commit an offence under section 9. If, as is often the case, an animal actually suffers as a result of the abandonment, usually through lack of food and water, he also commits an offence under section 4. In fact the suffering of the animal by distress and hunger is an aggravating factor which would make it a more serious offence.

The court can consider certain aspects of the alleged offence which may conflict with an activity that is a lawful practice. An animal, especially a dog, may be used by an army officer to help locate people after an explosion or to find a bomb before it has exploded. Similarly the police now often use horses to control protesting crowds or rioting thugs who then throw missiles of various forms from rocks to Molotov cocktails. If such a person was charged with an offence, the court would take into account how the lawful purpose or activity hindered his duty in meeting the animal's welfare needs, according to what is reasonable in the circumstances of the case. So if an animal is injured in such a situation it may not be an offence as the defence would be subject to the balance between the risk to the animal and the need to uphold the law. Crucially this does not provide a person with an absolute defence. It is simply a factor that the court will have to take into account. It does not mean that because the activity or purpose is lawful, no offence can be committed. The animal may have been injured because the owner was negligent or unprofessional in performing the activity. Everything depends on how it affects the animal in the circumstances including how the injurious result or effect could have been avoided. The 'considerations' would apply to the circumstances. That position applies to the police in an off-duty role too. The thugs throwing rocks would be guilty of an injury to the horse and if it was burnt, it would be arson too.

The needs of an animal are deliberately wide, though not limited to those outlined. For they include the Five Freedoms in aim and effect under subsection 2(a) to (e) which specifically considers the basic needs of an animal in relation to its behaviour and environment and protection from suffering. So it relates to the particular animal in question and thereby gives a greater protection than if it was merely a general provision. An animal might normally be content or better placed among other animals. However if it had a particular need to be housed separately then a failure to do so would be a breach of that duty. Conversely it may need to be with its mother or similar animals if it is to be healthy. Then separating it from its mother or the others would be a breach of that duty.

As an extension of those needs the animal has to be 'protected' from pain in its various forms. That may relate to prevention of any injury as well as protection in respect of an existing injury. So if where the particular animal is injured, whether accidentally or deliberately or even congenitally, its needs include being protected from further injury. While 'suffering' is defined under section 62(1) as 'physical or mental suffering and related expressions shall be construed accordingly', it is strange 'pain' is not defined at all. To that extent it would depend on expert evidence. If it were otherwise there is a danger its condition is assessed on an anthropomorphic basis with the result it could be overlooked as not being in pain or alternatively considered to be in real pain. Sometimes it would not be feasible or even possible to decide for certain until the death of an animal. In that event the fact of the suffering could be deduced from the state of its organs following a post-mortem.

Similarly 'disease' is not defined. That must be deliberate given the potential for widespread sudden diseases that affect a whole herd instantly such as BSE and Foot-and-mouth. Now animals should not be destroyed without strong evidence which is independent rather than just from a body such as Defra or some other government department or a self-interested body. That could only be achieved by independent evidence. For the person responsible would have to 'ensure' those infected do not affect the others. Equally those animals affected should not be subject to further avoidable pain as that would be contrary to their needs. If the condition continues so would the breach and the legal duty.

The 'circumstances' are wide-ranging too that the person has to consider when taking the necessary 'steps' to ensure the needs of the animal are met. Those are extended under section 9(3) so the circumstances include in particular any lawful purpose and lawful activity which pertain to the animal. Given that it states these are included in 'particular', it places a burden on the person to ensure it is not merely a profit-inducing machine, but is seen to be a sentient animal with appropriate needs. The purpose and activity is to take account of each animal's needs. It is not uncommon for owners to refrain from feeding an animal that is due to be slaughtered. That would unquestionably be a contravention of the AWA and consequently an offence.

B16 Whip

Where an animal is used for sport it is essential that though it is a lawful activity the animal is not abused. A controversial area recently arose with the use of a whip by jockeys who whipped horses until their bodies were visibly marked. Their only purpose in doing so was to gain a monetary prize. Although it appears the whip used was initially the result of interested parties, it was thereafter changed to a different type of a lighter whip and the number of strokes allowed decreased and during the race was limited to close to the finishing post. When some of the jockeys complained, a couple even going so far as refusing to race, it was changed again.

Of course notwithstanding that it is the result of the agreement between the various parties, it is pertinent that the use of the whip *per se* has never been tested in the courts. Given that it is very restricted in some countries particularly Norway it is plainly not an essential part of the race. After all it would not be legal to whip either a stallion or a stubborn mule outside of a racecourse. Therefore it appears profit and the policy and self-interest may be given priority over the needs of an animal. That, if true, would be a breach of their duty. In turn it would be a contravention of the AWA. As a corollary it is not an agreement between interested parties that decides the law. The only forum for a decision to protect any horse is the court. If the practice were tested in court, it would be unlikely to be upheld. By analogy with the DDA it was said in *Knightsbridge Crown Court v. The Commissioner of Police for Metropolitan Police v. Wells Street Magistrates Court ex parte Crabbe* [1996] EWHC 380 with accuracy by Mc Cowan LJ, 'After all it is for the court to decide whether the dog should be destroyed and not the Crown Prosecution Service.' Precisely the same principle applies to the whipping of horses. [See **G43**; horsesforlife.com]

Frankie Dettori, a jockey, whipped his horse so often in a race that there were numerous complaints about his conduct. As a result 'The Stewards held an enquiry into the use of the whip by Frankie Dettori , the rider of the winner, Rewilding, from two furlongs out. Having heard his evidence and viewed recordings of the race, they found him in breach of Schedule (B) 6 Part 2 in that he had used his whip with excessive frequency. They suspended him for 9 days as follows: from Wednesday 29 June to Thursday 7 July 2011 inclusive.' [See British Horseracing Authority: *Whip Policy*: 2008] Dettori explained his action by saying, 'When you are in the closing stages of a horse race – whether it is a Group 1 or a seller – the adrenalin pumps in both jockey and horse. Rewilding was responding to my pressure and we won the race – and that's what I'm paid by one of the top stables in the world to do.' It is equally pertinent that on 13/6/11 the BBC Sport reported that 'Winning jockey Jason Maguire was banned for five days for excessively using his whip in the closing stages on board Ballabriggs and the horse required oxygen after crossing the line.' If there was a prosecution it would be difficult to use excessive whipping as a defence. The elephant in the room in this area is why is it necessary to punish jockeys at all if the use of the whip does not affect the horse's welfare?

What if the oxygen Ballabriggs needed to survive never arrived? What if Rewilding collapsed and died? In that event are both deaths just a natural part of a lawful sport or would the manner of their death be the question to answer? Would whipping a horse be considered to be an appropriate and humane act by a court? For the last provision of the section, 9(4), states 'Nothing in this section applies to the destruction of an animal in an appropriate and humane manner'. That is a mirror-image of section 4(4) which covers unnecessary suffering. That is an important provision as obviously it would usually cause an animal some pain and suffering if it is killed. Yet it could be the only appropriate action. For if it is in acute pain the destruction may be the kindest act as death is the release from unavoidable misery. That would then be read in conjunction with section 18 which gives power to the police to destroy an animal in distress. However if it is killed instantly for some capricious or malicious reason it could still be an offence. For if not, contrary to the *raison d'etre* of the AWA, it would be appropriate and humane to kill an animal at will merely because he was tired of it being alive. [See **B3**]

There is an overlap between sections 4 and 9. That was the reason the prosecution in *Gray v. RSPCA* charged all the defendants with several offences against both sections. It was strengthened by the fact that the prosecution put the case on the basis of a joint liability. Hence the overall evidence of each allegation affected each defendant. [See **B6**]

Improvement notices

B17   Animal Welfare Act 2006, s.10

(1)   If an inspector is of the opinion that a person is failing to comply with section 9(1), he may serve on the person a notice which –

(a)   states that he is of that opinion,

(b)   specifies the respects in which he considers the person is failing to comply with that provision,

(c)   specifies the steps he considers need to be taken in order to comply with the provision,

(d)   specifies a period for the taking of those steps, and

(e)   explains the effects of subsections (2) and (3).

(2)   Where a notice under subsection (1) ("an improvement notice") is served, no proceedings for an offence under section 9(1) may be instituted before the end of the period specified for the purposes of subsection (1)(d) ("the compliance period") in respect of –

(a)   the non-compliance which gave rise to the notice, or

(b)   any continuation of that non-compliance.

(3)   If the steps specified in an improvement notice are taken at any time before the end of the compliance period, no proceedings for an offence under section 9(1) may be instituted in respect of –

(a)   the non-compliance which gave rise to the notice, or

(b)   any continuation of that non-compliance prior to the taking of the steps specified in the notice.

(4)   An inspector, may extend, or further extend, the compliance period specified in an improvement notice.

The inspectors ensure that the responsible person discharges his legal duty towards any animal he is responsible for in terms of its welfare. If the inspector is of the opinion he is failing in that duty he can issue that person with an improvement notice under section 10. That is an important step for two related reasons. If an improvement notice is issued the person responsible for the animal's welfare is notified he must act or action will be taken against him. If he fails to act, it will be. Then a prosecution will follow.

The improvement notice must be detailed and specific as it has clear legal implications. So it must state the reason for the inspector's 'opinion' and the person's failure to comply with the provision. It explains what he must do and when he must do it. The improvement notice is a clear warning that the person has to take action as otherwise he is in danger of being prosecuted. That is an interim stage where the duty has been breached and the remedy is in his hands. Therefore if it is served no proceedings can be taken under section 9(1) before the end of the specified period, the 'compliance period'.

While it puts the onus on the owner to carry out his duties, as if the specified 'steps' are taken within the compliance period no proceedings will be taken in respect of that potential breach of the AWA, it does not bind the inspector in respect of another or a different offence. As all the welfare aspects are concentrating on the animal's benefit, it places a legal burden on the person responsible for the duties towards the animal. So in that spirit the letter of the law favours compliance by the person so far failing in his duty. The inspector has a discretion under section 9(4) to 'extend, or further extend' the compliance period.

This gives an opportunity to the person with the duty to arrange for the work plus the finance to be carried out. Conversely if he is still failing to do so the fact that he ignored an Improvement

Notice and any extension of time to carry out his duties are matters of aggravation the court could take into account in any proceedings. In that event it would be relevant and admissible evidence during a trial. It would also be relevant if the person was convicted or, following a plea of guilty, for the sentence.

An inspector who makes the decisions under the AWA is defined by section 51 as 'in the context of any provision, means a person appointed to be an inspector for the purposes of that provision by the appropriate national authority, or a local authority'. An inspector is a vital part of the procedure in the functioning of the AWA. He is a person with legal power and responsibility combined with a defined legal immunity from liability under section 51(5). [See **E1**]

It has to be remembered that generally the type of person to whom an improvement notice is issued is often one who was irresponsible in his duties towards an animal within his care. He probably has potentially committed more than one kind of offence regarding his failure to properly discharge his responsibility for an animal. So although no proceedings can be taken in relation to the non-compliance specified in the notice, it does not prohibit such action in relation to any other offence. Therefore if the improvement notice specified particular animals, such as a failure to feed a group of pigs, he could still be prosecuted for failing to feed a group of sheep. Similarly in terms of his particular behaviour, if the improvement notice specified he did not provide adequate bedding for cattle he could still be prosecuted for failing to provide water for those same cattle.

Conversely if the person who is at risk of being prosecuted complied with the improvement notice within a specified time period, he will have a defence to the particulars specified of his failure.

Thus the inspector is giving the person a chance to change by issuing an improvement notice. He does not have to do so. If the circumstances are warranted, the inspector could take immediate action without issuing such a notice. Moreover he could also issue a subsequent improvement notice if the person lapses, having initially complied with the order. Either way it is his choice. The chance to change given to the person is wholly his choice. The chance to change given to the person is wholly dependent on the 'opinion' of the inspector.

As an inspector requires certain specific experience and knowledge, it is likely that the person appointed is a qualified vet. Given the extensive powers they possess, to at least put somebody out of business and at worst provide evidence that would put him behind bars, the role of the inspector is itself tightly regulated under section 51.

Transfer of animals by way of sale or prize to persons under 16

B18   Animal Welfare Act 2006, s.11

(1)   A person commits an offence if he sells an animal to a person whom he has reasonable cause to believe to be under the age of 16 years.

(2)   For the purposes of subsection (1), selling an animal includes transferring, or agreeing to transfer, ownership of the animal in consideration of entry by the transferee into another transaction.

(3)   Subject to subsections (4) to (6), a person commits an offence if –

(a)   he enters into an arrangement with a person whom he has reasonable cause to believe to be under the age of 16 years, and

(b) the arrangement is one under which that person has the chance to win an animal as a prize.

(4) A person does not commit an offence under subsection (3) if –

(a) he enters into the arrangement in the presence of the person with whom the arrangement is made, and

(b) he has reasonable cause to believe that the person with whom the arrangement is made is accompanied by a person who is not under the age of 16 years.

(5) A person does not commit an offence under subsection (3) if-:

(a) he enters into the arrangement otherwise than in the presence of the person with whom the arrangement is made, and

(b) he has reasonable cause to believe that a person who has actual care and control of the person with whom the arrangement is made has consented to the arrangement.

(6) A person does not commit an offence under subsection (3) if he enters into an arrangement in a family context.

Consistent with the aim of the AWA is that the person responsible for the welfare of the animal is a responsible person. So there are limits on when any person under the age of 16 years can be given an animal as a prize or a transfer by sale. Under section 3 of the Pet Animals Act 1951 it was an offence to sell a pet animal to children under 12 years old. So this extension to 16 years of age is a welcome aspect of the AWA. The age and conditions, which are controlled by section 11, enhance the welfare of animals.

The essence of the AWA is that it places a value on an animal as a living creature in its own right. Allied to that point it tries to curb the idea that animals are toys to be given away as prizes at a fair or in a competition. Similarly it takes a slight account of the oft-repeated phrase of the animal organisations that mop up the Boxing Day detritus of abandoned gifts: 'A dog is for life and not just for Christmas'.

The advantage of these provisions is that it puts the onus on the vendor of animals to ensure the buyer is a person over 16 years old. He must have a reasonable cause for such a belief. It applies to a direct and indirect sale in relation to what is an otherwise perfectly legal transaction.

It was commonplace everywhere from school fetes to passing fairs to offer animals as prizes as if they were cuddly toys. This section prohibits such an 'arrangement' unless the child is accompanied by someone over 16 years old.

To that limited extent section 11 makes it an offence to transfer animals by sale or a prize under various conditions. It is an offence if he sells an animal to a person whom he has a 'reasonable cause to believe' is under 16 years old. So that could be by physical appearance as a child being in a school uniform or in the company of other schoolchildren that would put him on notice. As the section uses the word 'transfer', it specifies that 'selling' an animal includes an actual or potential transfer of ownership of an animal as a result of another contract prior to the sale. So it includes a direct and indirect agreement. That is intended to avoid the transfer being a subsequent contract. If the result is a sale then the section takes effect.

As an extension of that idea of a sale and a contract, it is also an offence to enter into an arrangement with a person under 16 years who by the arrangement has the 'chance' to win an animal as a prize. As before the offence relates to the person having a reasonable cause to believe the potential winner is under 16 years. It is quite wide as the transfer does not have to be completed or even likely to be completed. For the mere chance of the prize is enough for culpability to arise.

While the mere chance is potentially very wide, there are provisions which attach to subsection 3 that provide a defence if the child is in the company of an adult. In that event a person does not commit an offence if he enters into an arrangement in the 'presence' of the person who is under 16 years and he is 'accompanied' by another person who is over 16 years. The seller has to have a reasonable cause to believe that the person is in the company of the other older person.

That provision also extends to the position where no one over 16 years is present when the arrangement is made, but he has reasonable cause to believe that a person who has 'actual care and control' of the child has 'consented' to the arrangement. That is a specific term as it relates to the person having care and control so it would have to be a parent or a guardian. Bearing in mind the arrangement would then be in the absence of the person having care and control, if he is challenged, the seller would have to have solid evidence to support his belief.

Indeed in relation to all of these potential defences it would not be sufficient to rely on some general or vague notion that, 'He looked over 16 to me', or 'His mate said it would be alright'. There would have to be real evidence that is reliable given the essence of the section is to protect animals at the point of sale and thereafter by ensuring the buyer is a responsible person. To that end the seller has to be too.

As this section is aimed at transferring animals to persons under 16 years, obviously this can and does often happen within families. So in those circumstances there is no offence. The subsection (6) specifies that it is legal 'if he enters into the arrangement in a family context'. The term family context is not defined but is wide enough to cover more than simply a parent to a child. It would also cover step-parents, older siblings and in given circumstances, relatives too. Nevertheless it must not be overlooked that the AWA makes both parties liable in the event of an offence under the AWA: *Gray v. RSPCA*. Ultimately that is the aim of the prohibition for while a child may demand the animal as a pet, it is usually not very keen on seeing to its daily needs. [See **B6**]

In *R (RSPCA) v. C* [2006] 170 JP 463 a 15 year old girl failed to ensure her cat was taken to a vet for treatment because her father told her it was unnecessary. It is significant that it was under the POA. The appeal was dismissed and the magistrates' decision to acquit her was upheld. Her father pleaded guilty. Newman LJ said, 'The issue which the justices had to decide was whether or not this…girl had acted reasonably or unreasonably in acceding to the opinion her father had expressed…That involved considering whether it was reasonable for her to go along with her father's view of the position, having regard to her age and position in the household, whether it was for her to take any other action, as she could have done, and whether it was reasonable or unreasonable for her to fail to take that other action.'

That case illustrates the essential change introduced by the AWA. For it is an objective test as to what is 'reasonable' in all the circumstances. Further it is axiomatic that a visit to a vet and necessary treatment for a sick cat would be consistent with 'good practice'. Therefore if those facts reoccurred the father's view of the position would not afford a defence. It would purely be a matter of mitigation. If it were otherwise it would defeat the very provision intended to both protect an animal and make the owner who is under 16 years jointly liable with the responsible parent. Indeed in *Gray v. RSPCA* the court confirmed that position.

Regulations to promote welfare

B19   Animal Welfare Act 2006, s.12

(1)   The appropriate national authority may by regulations make such provision as the authority thinks fit for the purpose of promoting the welfare of animals for which a person is responsible, or the progeny of such animals.

(2)   Without prejudice to the generality of the power under subsection (1), regulations under that subsection may, in particular –

(a)   make provision imposing specific requirements for the purpose of securing that the needs of animals are met;

(b)   make provision to facilitate or improve co-ordination in relation to the carrying out by different persons of functions relating to the welfare of animals;

(c)   make provision for the establishment of one or more bodies with functions relating to advice about the welfare of animals.

(3)   Power to make regulations under subsection (1) includes power –

(a)   to provide that breach of a provision of the regulations is an offence;

(b)   to apply a relevant post-conviction power in relation to conviction for an offence under the regulations;

(c)   to make provision for fees or other charges in relation to the carrying out of functions under the regulations;

(d)   to make different provision for different cases or areas;

    (e)   to provide for exemptions from a provision of the regulations, either subject to specified conditions or without conditions;

    (f)   to make incidental, supplementary, consequential transitional provision or savings.

(4)   Power to make regulations under subsection (1) does not include power to create an offence triable on indictment or punishable with –

    (a)   imprisonment for a term exceeding 51 weeks; or

    (b)   a fine exceeding level 5 on the standard scale.

(5)   Regulations under subsection (1) may provide that a specified offence under the regulations is to be treated as a relevant offence for the purpose of section 23.

(6)   Before making regulations under subsection (1), the appropriate national authority shall consult such persons appearing to the authority to represent any interests concerned as the authority considers appropriate.

(7)   In this section, "specified" means specified in regulations under subsection (1).

It is of no value to have such a wide-ranging statute as the AWA if it would soon become nugatory like the POA did shortly after it was introduced. So an important provision is contained within section 12 which allows the appropriate authority to make regulations to promote animal welfare. That is vital as it allows that authority to both react to changing circumstances as well as initiating regulations of their own volition. While it is a general power, the exercise of it is controlled by the conditions within section 12.

This new provision is controlled to a degree by the mandatory requirement that the authority shall consult such persons that represent any interests that the authority considers appropriate.

They must do so before making regulations. This power can only be exercised subject to that provision. It is an important balance and check upon an otherwise wide power that could be arbitrary or appear to be. [See **B9**]

As the AWA was introduced to reflect its name, this section allows for changes in circumstances and knowledge to be reflected in the promotion of their welfare. So if new scientific evidence became available to show some form of protection was necessary, this section would allow it to be introduced. Unusually, but a positive point, it also extends to the progeny of the animal. The section allows the appropriate national authority to make such provision as they 'think fit' for the purpose of promoting the welfare of animals for which a person is responsible, or the progeny of such animals. So the regulations can protect the progeny as well as the parent animal.

The section envisages contact and cooperation with various animal organisations plus bodies who could be introduced to cover areas of animal welfare in a wide context. While the section is general in application, the regulations may in 'particular' promote the welfare of animals.

The power to introduce new regulations goes hand in hand with a power to make breaches of the regulations illegal. Taking that point on a practical level, it includes a power to apply 'a relevant post-conviction power' to an offence under the regulations and to make different provisions for different cases or areas. It also allows for exemption to the provision which could be subject to conditions.

B20 Conviction

The reference to 'a relevant post-conviction power' is defined under section 62(6) as including one 'conferred by sections 33, 34,

37 or 42 of this Act'. It also relates to licences within seven other statutes such as the Pet Animals Act 1951 under which a person can be disqualified from holding a licence. The power is wide as the matters the authorities can take into account include making regulations to provide for people who are responsible for animals to meet their needs. That ties in with the definition under section 62(5) which states that 'references to the needs of an animal are to be read in accordance with section 9(2)'. That in turn includes the Five Freedoms. [See **B2**] So the duty of a person responsible for the welfare of animals can be specified in greater detail. The consequences for failure to attend to those needs can result in it being an offence by the regulations. Further it can apply to a 'relevant post-conviction power' which would allow the court to impose a greater sentence upon conviction. So the court could impose a disqualification from owning animals at all under section 34 following a breach of a regulation for specified conditions. The consequences take account of his culpability.

Given that the power to introduce such regulations is wide, there is a danger that the offences could be more severe than the existing offences. So it is made plain that that power does not include creating an offence triable on indictment or for imprisonment exceeding 51 weeks or a fine exceeding level 5 on the standard scale.

Nevertheless it does give a power under subsection (5) for the authority to make a regulation that a specified offence is to be treated as a 'relevant offence' for the purpose of section 23. That is an important provision as it gives extra 'entry and search' powers to an inspector or constable who is armed with a warrant. A 'relevant offence' is defined under section 23(3) as one 'under any of sections 4 to 9, 13(6) and 34(9). Those powers can assist an inspector to investigate offences that have been or are being committed. [See **D4**]

B21 Collars

Welfare regulations have been introduced for farm animals. The Welsh Assembly may adopt the same or introduce different types of their own. Indeed they have been more imaginative than the English authorities by banning dog collars which caused injuries to dogs. In a far-reaching decision, *R. (on the application of Petsafe Ltd and another) v. Welsh Ministers* [2010] EWHC 2908, they banned the collars despite powerful opposition. The issue in the case was whether the Welsh Ministers were entitled to prohibit the use on cats and dogs of any electronic collar which were designed to administer an electric shock. They introduced the Animal Welfare (Electronic Collars (Wales) Regulations 2010 under section 12 of the AWA. By the 2010 Regulations anyone using such a collar commits an offence punishable with up to 51 weeks imprisonment.

The First Claimant was a manufacturer and distributor of pet products. The products it distributes included electronic collars. The Second Claimant was an unincorporated association of four companies, including the First Claimant, which manufactured and distributed electronic training aids for animals. They sought permission to apply for judicial review of the 2010 Regulations and, if permission was granted, an order quashing the Regulations, which they claimed were invalid. A previous challenge was launched in September 2008. Permission in that case was refused on 31 March 2009 on the ground of prematurity.

In a detailed thought-provoking decision the High Court analysed all the issues in relation to English and European law. Setting the scene Beatson J said, 'The use of electronic collars and similar devices is controversial. A number of groups, including the Kennel Club, have been campaigning for some time to ban them because they have the potential to have adverse consequences for animals, and are cruel and unnecessary. Others maintain that the scientific evidence does not support a ban or regulation, and that the devices help to avoid injury to animals on roads or at the hands of farmers protecting their stock. During 2007 a number of government bodies in the United Kingdom considered the question. In England, the Department for Environment, Food and Rural Affairs, (Defra) commissioned research to assess the effect of pet training aids on the welfare of domestic dogs. In Scotland and Wales there were consultation exercises to consider whether electronic collars are harmful to dogs and cats and whether they should be banned.'

The court considered 'the Legislative Framework' of the AWA and specifically sections 2, 3, 12 and 62. The court went into a great deal of background information including making reference to a paper, *The Use of Shock-Collars and Their Impact on the Welfare of Dogs*, [2006] by researchers at the University of Bristol which reviewed the literature. It also considered the fact the Kennel Club campaigned for a ban on electronic collars and similar devices. The ban was supported by, among many other animal welfare associations, the RSPCA and the People's Dispensary for Sick Animals [PDSA]. The Welsh Association of Chief Police Officers [ACPO] had banned the use of electric-shock collars in 2000 and are not used by the police service.

The Explanatory Memorandum indicated that the Welsh Ministers had three areas of concern and that the purpose of the ban was the promotion of animal welfare. This was supported by Professor Christiane Glossop, the Chief Veterinary Officer for Wales and Head of Office of the Chief Veterinary Officer for Wales [OCVO] and Huw Jones, the Head of Animal Welfare at OCVO. The areas of concern included that the collars administered an electric-shock which causes discomfort and is of a sufficient intensity to affect an animal's behaviour whether or not the discomfort satisfies the International Association for the Study of Pain's definition of the term "pain". Also in untrained hands the device could cause pain and distress; that included "...significant psychological distress and harm when used improperly".

Beatson J said, 'In the *Countryside Alliance* case [*R (Countryside Alliance) v. Attorney-General* [2008] 1 AC 719] it was argued that the rationale of the Hunting Act 2004 could not be, as the courts below had found, the prevention or reduction of unnecessary suffering to wild mammals overlaid by a moral viewpoint causing suffering to animals for sport is unethical because if that was the purpose consistency would have required a more far-reaching measure. Lord Bingham rejected this argument. He described it as a traditional argument and stated he did not "think that doubt can be thrown on the rationale of the Act, as expressed by the courts below, by showing that the underlying principle, if carried to its logical extremes, would have justified a much more far-reaching measure". He also stated that the legislative practice had been "whatever seemed at any given time to the current Parliamentary majority to be the most pressing problem"...His observations are pertinent in the present context.

Baroness Hale, in the context of article 1 of the First Protocol, also rejected the "selectivity" argument, stating that protecting animals from avoidable compromise to their welfare fell well within the general interest and that the means chosen struck a fair balance. She stated "the fact the same principles might have justified a wider ban does not mean that a narrow ban cannot be justified". As to EC law, she agreed with Lord Bingham, and stated that the suggestion that the EC Claimants in that case might succeed while the Human Rights Claimants did not would be illogical and unjust.'

The court then referred to *Commission v. Italy* [2009] All ER (EC) 796 which stated "that the burden of proof cannot be so extensive as to require the Member State [here the Welsh Ministers], to prove, positively, that no other conceivable measure could enable that objective to be attained under the same conditions."

Beatson J continued after that complete analysis and concluded, 'In any event, in the *Countryside Alliance Case* Lord Hope stated it was not necessary for those promoting the legislation to engage in a close and careful examination of the factual basis for concluding that hunting for foxes with hounds was less humane than other methods of killing them. His Lordship stated that it was open to the legislators to focus on the nature of the activities without comparing them with others, bearing in mind that they were being engaged for sport and recreation. It was open to the legislators to form their own judgment as to whether they caused a sufficient degree of suffering in that context for legislative action to be taken.

Lord Hope also stated that, if it was open for the legislators to conclude that the activities that were to be prohibited were cruel if engaged in for sport, how could it be doubted that they were entitled to conclude that prohibition of those activities was necessary in order to prevent them from being carried on by those who wished to do so. That, he stated, was sufficient to meet what he referred to as the "condition of justification".

Given the fact that the prohibition in this case was a measure of social policy aimed at animal welfare and not aimed at intra-Community trade, the situation is broadly similar to that in the *Countryside Alliance* case. Any impediment on trade between Member States was a minor and unintended consequence which …bears more hardly on those in Wales than in other Member States. In these circumstances, I have concluded that the prohibition satisfies the requirement of proportionality under Community law and that the Regulations do not contravene that law.

While it is not conclusive that the notification process and the queries raised by the European Commission did not lead the Commission or another Member State to assert that the 2010 Regulations violate any provision of EU law, the fact that it has not done so is consistent with the reasoning that a ban on these collars pursues a legitimate aim and is necessary and proportionate. So too does the fact that such training collars are not permitted to be used in three other Member States, Finland, Denmark and Germany and that the Commission has not objected to the bans in those states or taken any enforcement action.

I also conclude that, assuming the ability to sell electronic collars is an economic interest in the nature of goodwill constituting a possession for the purposes of article 1 of the First Protocol, that the prohibition on their use, in order to promote animal welfare is a justifiable interference because of the views taken by the Welsh Ministers as to what is appropriate in the interests of animal welfare.'

He then ended with a view that chimed with the action of the Welsh Ministers: 'It makes it an offence for a person responsible for a cat or a dog to which an electronic collar is attached. "Responsibility" includes section 3 ownership, permanent or temporary responsibility, and "being in charge of" an animal. The argument that the provision is *Wednesbury* [*Associated Provincial Picture Houses Ltd v. Wednesbury Corporation* [1947] 2 All ER 680] unreasonable or irrational because of its perverse consequences depends on an assumption that a person, not previously responsible, who "takes charge of" or takes hold of the animal in order to remove the electronic collar is caught by the provision. Given the purpose of the enabling provision and the 2010 Regulations, that assumption involves an unreasonable and excessively literal construction. It is trite law that, in considering the unreasonableness of legislative acts such as regulations and by-laws made by public authorities, and in particular democratically accountable public authorities, a court should be slow to find that they are *Wednesbury* unreasonable or perverse.'

Having delivered that penetrating analysis Beatson J granted 'permission' to the Claimants. He then added, 'This application is dismissed.'

This was a positive interpretation of a positive measure boldly introduced by the Welsh Ministers notwithstanding the cost and considerable opposition and substantial legal arguments they had to meet and defeat. That it succeeded on all fronts is a credit to the vision of those Ministers. It also augurs well for the power of the AWA. [See **C5**]

The effect of the new legislation was tested in a landmark case in 2011 by the RSPCA. Inspector de Celis was alerted to a stray collie dog wearing an electric collar in Wales. He removed the collar and checked the dog, Doug, as he was microchipped. When the owner collected Doug from the kennels he was confronted by the staff with the fact of the illegal collar. Further, though he initially denied it, he accepted he had been 'warned' about it before. He was convicted at Bridgend Magistrates' Court and fined and the collar was forfeited.

This was the first case under the Regulation which was the first law of its kind in the UK. The negative aspect is it reflects the lack of vision by the English authority which has yet to grasp and address the issue.

3

Registration and Rescue

C1 Range

This chapter covers sections 13 to 21. These involve the various procedures which relate to persons who are either wishing to control animals or persons who rescue them if they are in distress. To control those who are in control of animals the former deals with licensing and registration of 'activities' concerning animals and their progeny. Allied to that there are Codes of Practice which are common in respect of farm animals. Now they are being used under sections 14 to 17 to promote the welfare of all protected animals. If any of those aspects of animal welfare within the AWA are breached it can and often does lead to consequent distress to animals. That extant distress is governed by sections 18 to 21 which covers the problem and solution including any relevant appeal. In that event the inspectors and police have extensive powers to deal with the animal including arranging for its death.

Licensing or registration of activities involving animals

C2   Animal Welfare Act 2006, s.13

Licensing and registration

(1)   No person shall carry on an activity to which this subsection applies except under the authority of a licence for the purposes of this section.

(2)   Subsection (1) applies to an activity which –
   (a)   involves animals for which a person is responsible, and

    (b)   is specified for the purposes of the subsection by regulations made by the appropriate national authority.

(3)   No person shall carry on an activity to which this subsection applies unless registered for the purposes of this section.

(4)   Subsection (3) applies to an activity which –

    (a)   involves animals for which a person is responsible, and

    (b)   is specified for the purposes of the subsection by regulations made by the appropriate national authority.

(5)   Regulations under subsection (2) or (4) may only be made for the purpose of promoting the welfare of animals for which a person is responsible, or the progeny of such animals.

(6)   A person commits an offence if he contravenes subsection (1) or (3).

(7)   The appropriate national authority may by regulations make provision about licences or registration for the purposes of this section.

(8)   The appropriate national authority may by regulations repeal any of the following enactments (which impose licence or registration requirements in relation to activities involving animals)-:

    (a)   section 1(1) of the Performing Animals (Regulation) Act 1925;

    (b)   section 1(1) of the Pet Animals Act 1951;

    (c)   section 1(1) of the Animals Boarding Establishments Act 1963;

    (d)   section 1(1) of the Riding Establishments Act 1964;

    (e)   section 1(1) of the Breeding of Dogs Act 1973.

(9) Before making regulations under subsection (1), the appropriate national authority shall consult such persons appearing to the authority to represent any interests concerned as the authority considers appropriate.

(10) Schedule 1 (which makes provision about regulations under this section) has effect.

This section provides an extensive power to regulate 'activities' that involve the use of animals. While what is an 'activity' is not defined the powers of the authority under section 13(7) are wide enough to cover any that exist or may be introduced that affects their welfare. The purpose of the section is to control those who control animals by only allowing them to do so by a licence. It applies to an activity which relates to an animal that the responsible person can only carry out if he has a licence.

Instead of a licence, it may be subject to registration. That has the advantage for the authority that it can control the bodies and the individuals who are concerned commercially or charitably with animals. Allied to that it enables them to be satisfied that any activity is properly carried out and monitored to ensure compliance with the welfare of the animal. That is the principal idea of the regulations as they can only apply when an animal and its progeny are those for which someone is responsible. The result is the activity that is subject to the licensing and registration by the regulations may only be made under subsection (5) for the purpose of promoting the welfare of such animals.

The consequence of the power is if a person carries out an activity without the necessary licence or registration, he thereby commits an offence.

The power is even wider as it can control activities which are legal at present and could in effect make it an offence. The power can be used to make provision about the licence or registration and even repeal them. There are specific statutes that are named such as the Performing Animals (Regulation) Act 1925. Given that this is a controversial area which governs animals used in circuses, many of those opposed to it could – and indeed should – be consulted under subsection (9) 'before making regulations'. A failure to do so could be challenged by judicial review. [See **B9**]

In 2011 the politicians initially claimed that they could not outlaw the use of animals in circuses because it would contravene the Human Rights Act 1998. That was shown to be untrue. As many offences were relating to the elephant, Annie, who was cruelly treated by numerous persons, that would strengthen the opposition and the potential for repeal. Though some politicians are attempting to change the law, so far the English authorities have failed to act.

Under these provisions the authority introduced the Welfare of Racing Greyhounds Regulations 2010. The power should be used to regulate the use of a whip in horse racing. Though the use of the whip has caused problems in England [as well as India], the authority now has the power to protect those that cannot protect themselves. There is no reason why jockeys should be allowed to whip their horse. All the reasons put forward do not justify their actions. They are excuses which should not be excused. The primary duty on the authority is not commercial interests or profit but to consider the effect of the 'activity' on the animals' welfare. If that were properly considered the use of the whip would be abolished. Its use is contrary to the AWA and consequently would be treated in the same way as electric-shock collars were by the High Court. [See **B15**; **B20**]

It is an important part of protecting protected animals that those involved with them are subject to licensing and registration and inspection. So the licence and the register for the activity to which it relates can be inspected by an inspector under section 51. The regulations under Schedule 1 allow for extensive entry and inspection as well as ensuring that the particular person or body has insurance in respect of the activity being monitored.

There are supplementary provisions relating to *Regulations under section 13* by Part 1 of Schedule 1. It specifies in paragraph 5 that a licence cannot run for more than 3 years. The other relevant aspects that affect the issue and monitoring of a licence include:

(a) a licensing authority must inspect premises before granting a licence;

(b) regulations may allow an authority to impose conditions on a licence or require it to do so;

(c) breach of a condition may be made an offence under the regulations;

(d) regulations may apply a 'relevant post-conviction power' to a conviction for an offence.

There are similar provisions relating to registration in Part 2. Given that the regulations could be repealed by section 13(8), an enabling provision allowing the preservation of the old licence conditions is contained in Part 3.

A licence for owners of dogs was a legal requirement from 1796 to 1987. The cost in 1878 was 37 p. It was the same in 1987 when it was abolished. Less than 50% of owners bothered to buy a licence. The cost of administering the dog licence scheme was disproportionate as it cost more to collect the small sum than was raised in revenue: the administration cost £3.5 million to collect £1 million. That was the fault of the government. So instead of increasing the fee they abolished it. Now it should be reintroduced with concessions and set high, at least £100, so that those responsible for the ownership of animals are equally responsible in law. For if they cannot afford a licence they cannot afford to properly care for a dog. As a further measure every dog should be micro-chipped. That would ensure the right person was prosecuted in the event of an offence being committed because of his irresponsibility. [See **B20**]

Codes of practice

C3   Animal Welfare Act 2006, s.14

Codes of practice

(1) The appropriate national authority may issue, and may from time to time revise, codes of practice for the purpose of providing practical guidance in respect of any provision made by or under this Act.

(2) The authority responsible for issuing a code of practice under subsection (1) shall publish the code, and any revision of it, in such manner as it considers appropriate.

(3) A person's failure to comply with a provision of a code of practice issued under this section shall not of itself render him liable to proceedings of any kind.

(4) In any proceedings against a person for an offence under this Act or an offence under regulations under section 12 or 13 –

    (a) failure to comply with a code of practice issued under this section may be relied upon as tending to establish liability, and

    (b) compliance with a relevant provision of such code of practice may be relied upon as tending to negative liability.

The Codes of practice can be made and amended and revoked. They are non-binding guidance, but were introduced after detailed consultation and agreed by Parliament. Evidentially they can be relied upon by a prosecutor if he is seeking to enforce the breach of any particular code. For any such breach can be taken into account by the court in considering the evidence relied upon to form the charge.

Sections 14 to 17 introduce the concept of *Codes of practice* being monitored by the appropriate national authority. That idea is consistent the ideas of the AWA as it allows for changing conditions within society that can be reflected in the best practice. It also allows for new scientific knowledge being gained which could be used for the benefit of animals. Farm animals have been protected by various codes of practice which promote their welfare for many years. They follow from the principles of the Five Freedoms and associated recommendations by the FAWC. In due course codes were introduced to cover areas such as cows, horse, pigs and sheep. Such codes are widely used at present to promote the welfare of farm animals. This provision extends the principle and purpose to non-farm animals. By the AWA the Code of practice extended the protection to non-farm animals. They now apply to all those animals within the mantle of the AWA.

The powers granted are extensive as the authority may issue such codes that offer 'practical guidance' in relation to the AWA. Equally it may even revise such codes as are introduced. It relates to any provision made 'by or under this Act'. So it could be pertinent to an existing section, or an amended one under the AWA, as well as a provision introduced by a regulation.

As the codes 'shall' be published in a manner the authority considers 'appropriate', it would have to be brought to the attention of those who could or would be affected, be they within the industry or the general public. Although any failure to comply with a code 'shall not of itself' render him liable to proceedings, nevertheless such failure has evidential weight. Therefore it is important in respect of both an offence and establishing a defence. For the tendency in either case is positive or negative depending on what was done or not done compared to the terms of the code. So there is a burden on the authority to inform those who are subject to the code as then the proof of non-compliance presents its own penalty.

Its significance goes beyond the normal criminal offences governed by the AWA in relation to the prevention of harm and promotion of welfare under sections 4 to 9. In relation to regulations under section 12 and licensing or registration under section 13, the same evidential provision applies. So it is wider in scope and application. The licensing and registration provisions affect the livelihoods of those involved in any such activities involving animals.

Essentially it provides practical guidance on how to care for animals to ensure their welfare is considered and to guard against avoidable bad practice. Though any breach of the code is not an offence the value of it is an inspector can use that to consider any relevant relative breach. Thereafter the court can also take that breach into account in relation to the welfare standards of the AWA. Conversely an allegation can be denied if the person has complied with the practice and base their defence upon that fact. The result for the prosecution is that evidentially non-compliance with a code goes some way to proving the case against an offender. It tends to 'establish liability' if the codes are breached. The defence may counter any allegation by showing compliance with the code as that can be relied upon to 'negative liability'.

The leading regulation to protect farm animals is The Welfare of Farmed Animals (England) Regulations 2007. As that was introduced by the AWA it is often used by the prosecution for a breach either in its own right or in conjunction with other offences within the Act, especially under sections 4 and 9. [See Appendix]

Making and approval of codes of practice: England

C4 Animal Welfare Act 2006, s.15

(1) Where the Secretary of State proposes to issue (or revise) a code of practice under section 14, he shall –
 (a) prepare a draft of the code (or revised code),
 (b) consult about the draft such persons appearing to him to represent any interests concerned as he considers appropriate, and
 (c) consider any representations made by them.

(2) If following consultation under subsection (1) the Secretary of State decides to proceed with a draft (either in its original form or with such modifications as he thinks fit), he shall lay a copy of it before Parliament.

(3) If, within the 40-day period, either House of Parliament resolves not to approve a draft laid under subsection (2), the Secretary of State shall take no further steps in relation to it.

(4) If, within the 40-day period, neither House resolves not to approve a draft laid under subsection (2), the Secretary of State shall issue (or revise) the code in the form of the draft.

 …

So that the codes have value and are respected by those affected, there are strict rules relating to them. A code can only be issued following a draft and consultation with interested persons and the approval of Parliament. Those persons who have such 'interests' would be able to challenge the draft if they had not been consulted. Even if they were and their views were disregarded, that negative decision could still be used to apply for judicial review. [See **B9**]

If the draft is disapproved by Parliament within a 40-day period then it cannot be introduced in that form. If the draft is approved by Parliament within that period then it can be introduced. However even where the draft has been 'approved' by Parliament, that is not the end of the matter. The Secretary of State can produce a 'new' draft of the proposed or revised code which is then laid before Parliament. For the strict rules ensure a code of practice is not introduced unless there is a consultation with interested parties as to the contents. Then it has to be laid before Parliament where can be disapproved within 40-day time limit.

When a code is revoked without being replaced, by section 61(3)-(5) a draft of the document detailing the revocation order must be laid before Parliament. By section 61(2) those regulations, if properly produced, also apply to section 1, 5, 6, 12 and 13. That detailed process tends to enhance the consequent evidential weight of the codes if and when a case comes before the court.

Making of codes of practice: Wales

C5   Animal Welfare Act 2006, s.16

(1)   Where the National Assembly for Wales proposes to issue (or revise) a code of practice under section 14, it shall –
(a)   prepare a draft of the code (or revised code),
(b)   consult about the draft such persons appearing to it to represent any interests concerned as it considers appropriate, and
(c)   consider any representations made by them.

A similar section with similar conditions covers the draft code for Wales. The National Assembly were in fact more proactive than the Secretary of State in that they introduced the far-reaching code that effectively outlawed the use of electronic dog collars that were deemed to be cruel and contrary to the welfare of dogs. That was a more imaginative and bold approach in using a new regulation to promote animal welfare which in turn led to one of the leading cases now under the AWA, *R (on the application of Petsafe Ltd and another) v. Welsh Ministers* [2010] EWHC 2908. It has been effective too as it has also led to the first successful prosecution for a breach. [See **B20**]

Revocation of codes of practice

C6   Animal Welfare Act 2006, s.17

(1)   The appropriate national authority may by order revoke a code of practice issued by it under section 14.

(2)   An order under subsection (1) may include transitional provision or savings.

(3)   Before making an order under subsection (1), the appropriate national authority shall consult such persons appearing to the authority to represent any interests concerned as the authority considers appropriate.

(4)   Subsection (3) does not apply to an order revoking a code of practice in connection with its replacement by a new one.

Given that the whole idea of a code of practice is to allow for changing circumstances and offer guidance to those concerned with the welfare of animals, it is important that a new code could replace the existing one rather than a mere revision. In that case the authority may revoke a code that has been issued under section 14. Before making any order to that effect the authority 'shall' consult such persons that appear to them to represent any 'interests' concerned as they appear appropriate. That only applies to a revocation. If it is a replacement by a new code then under subsection (4) it does not apply.

That provision shows how important it is for the regulatory body to both 'consult' with those interested persons and not to ignore their views. It follows, consistent with the similar provision throughout the AWA, that if they are not consulted at all they could challenge a code if they should have been. Equally if they had been consulted, but their concerns were ignored they could challenge the code. The burden would be on them to show they or their concerns were 'appropriate'. If they were in fact a relevant body with views that were relevant to the code, yet were ignored, it would give rise to an application for judicial review. For in that event the very purpose of the provision would itself be being ignored. [See **B9**]

Powers in relation to animals in distress

C7   Animal Welfare Act 2006, s.18

Animals in distress

(1)   If an inspector or a constable reasonably believes that a protected animal is suffering, he may take, or arrange for the taking of, such steps as appear to him to be immediately necessary to alleviate the animal's suffering.

(2)   Subsection (1) does not authorise destruction of an animal.

(3)   If a veterinary surgeon certifies that the condition of a protected animal is such that it should in its own interests be destroyed, an inspector or a constable may –

(a)   destroy the animal where it is or take it to another place and destroy it there, or

(b) arrange for the doing of any of the things mentioned in paragraph (a).

(4) An inspector or a constable may act under subsection (3) without the certificate of a veterinary surgeon if it appears to him –

(a) that the condition of the animal is such that there is no reasonable alternative to destroying it, and

(b) that the need for action is such that it is not reasonably practicable to wait for a veterinary surgeon.

(5) An inspector or a constable may take a protected animal into possession if a veterinary surgeon certifies:

(a) that it is suffering, or

(b) that it is likely to suffer if its circumstances do not change.

(6) An inspector or a constable may act under subsection (5) without the certificate of a veterinary surgeon if it appears to him –

(a) that the animal is suffering or that it is likely to do so if its circumstances do not change, and

(b) that the need for action is such that it is not reasonably practicable to wait for a veterinary surgeon.

(7) The power conferred by subsection (5) includes power to take into possession dependent offspring of an animal taken into possession under that subsection.

(8) Where an animal is taken into possession under subsection (5), an inspector or a constable may –

(a) remove it, or arrange for it to be removed, to a place of safety;

(b) care for it, or arrange for it to be cared for –

(i) on the premises where it was being kept when it was taken into possession, or

(ii) at such other place as he thinks fit;

(c) mark it, or arrange for it to be marked, for identification purposes.

(9) A person acting under subsection (8)(b)(i), or under an arrangement under that provision, may make use of any equipment on the premises.

(10) A veterinary surgeon may examine and take samples from an animal for the purpose of determining whether to issue a certificate under subsection (3) or (5) with respect to the animal.

(11) If a person exercises a power under this section otherwise than with the knowledge of a person who is responsible for the animal concerned, he must, as soon as reasonably practicable after exercising the power, take such steps as are reasonable in the circumstances to bring the exercise of the power to the notice of such a person.

(12) A person commits an offence if he intentionally obstructs a person in the exercise of power conferred by this section.

(13) A magistrate's court may, on application by a person who incurs expenses in acting under this section, order that he be reimbursed by such person as it thinks fit.

(14) A person affected by a decision under subsection (13) may appeal to the Crown Court.

Sections 18 to 21 cover a significant part of the AWA as it incorporates the underlying philosophy of the Act. For it allows those in power to monitor the welfare of an animal and then take immediate action to remedy an urgent situation that threatens their welfare, up to and including death. While unnecessary suffering is the backbone of the AWA and is defined, the element of 'distress' is not defined. This must be deliberate as it as it allows for an assessment of the condition of an animal by an inspector or a constable. For if either of them 'reasonably believes that a protected animal is suffering' he may take or arrange for the taking of such steps as appear to him to be 'immediately necessary' to alleviate the animal's suffering.

The protection for *Animals in distress* is a wide power which is added to by sections 19 and 20. Those additional powers allow entry to premises and orders made by a court. That is necessary in order to deal with the pressing problem of an animal in distress. As distress is never defined within the AWA the subjective opinion of the inspector or constable relates to a situation that presents a sense of urgency.

Section 18 is wider than previous related legislation in that the Protection of Animals (Amendment) Act 2000, which the AWA repealed, in three important ways namely: (a) action can be taken to protect an animal even if no proceedings have been issued; (b) it is not restricted to animals that are kept for a commercial purpose; (c) it allows an inspector or a constable to take into possession an animal that is already suffering and one that is likely to suffer if he does not take action. That is a prime example of the principles of the AWA in effect. For it is to protect those who are presently suffering as well as those who will be at risk in future unless they are rescued now.

For if either of those persons reasonably believes that a protected animal is suffering he may take or arrange for the taking of such steps as appear to him to be immediately necessary to alleviate the animal's suffering. While that section gives a wide discretion to the inspector or constable it does not authorise the 'destruction' of an animal. On any level it is an urgent situation. Indeed then, even without the certificate of a vet, under subsection (3) he may destroy the animal if it 'appears to him' there is no reasonable alternative to that final act.

The power to take the animal into 'possession' includes a power to take its dependent offspring into possession as well. To that end he may remove the animal and arrange for its care at a suitable place. When he does so he may 'mark' it or have it marked for identification purposes. That could be significant for the owner and the police if it becomes an exhibit in any subsequent proceedings or action taken by either party in due course. Any marking would have to be compatible with section 5 as if it was a mutilation it would be an offence. Once an animal is taken into possession the person exercising the power equally has a duty to look after its welfare. He remains responsible in terms of its welfare and ensuring any treatment that is necessary. That includes arranging for its care and the removal to the place of safety. If he decides to care for the animal on the premises, he can make use of any equipment on the premises. So the inspector or constable could use any of the apparatus on a farm without the farmer's permission or consent.

The usual way an animal is discovered to be in distress is following an investigation by the police or an inspector – often the result of a complaint by a member of public – they visit a farm and find a variety of animals in various states of distress, some even to a layman's eyes, in obvious need of immediate attention. In that event the usual procedure is to call an expert who will assess the situation professionally. Given the specialist knowledge that is required of an inspector the person appointed to the role will usually be a qualified vet. [See **E1**]

For that reason the AWA provides that if a vet certifies that the 'condition' of an animal is such that it is in its 'own interests' that it should be 'destroyed', an inspector or constable may destroy the animal or arrange for the destruction.

Similarly a degree of urgency may arise where an animal is involved in a road traffic accident and is plainly in severe pain on the highway. If there is an emergency the position of the animal is paramount. Either way the intervention by an inspector or a constable is allowed if he has acted with that 'belief'.

It may be the area or weather conditions or simply the time such that the emergency has arisen and no vet is available. While it then places a heavy responsibility for the animal's welfare on the inspector or constable, it equally applies a duty to release it by death if the suffering is such that it is in animal's 'own interests'.

If it is suffering and is so certified by a vet, but it does not need to be destroyed, then an inspector or constable may take possession of the animal. The vet must certify that the suffering will be likely to continue if its circumstances do not change. That would then allow them to seize the animal regardless of any opposition by the owner.

Even further than that position the inspector or constable can act without a certificate of a vet take an animal into possession for the same reasons namely the animal is suffering and will continue to do so if its circumstances do not change. The additional condition before they can act is that there is a need for action and it is not reasonably practicable to wait for a vet.

As these powers are really relating to an urgent situation or an emergency, is quite feasible that the owner or person 'responsible' in law for the animal is not at the scene. If the inspector or constable takes the action under this section without the knowledge of that responsible person, he must as soon as reasonably practicable after exercising the power take such reasonable steps to bring to the notice of that person the fact he has exercised that power.

It is one thing for a person to question or perhaps disagree with a person who is exercising the power under this section. That is acceptable as long as it is merely in a spirit of inquiry. However if he 'intentionally obstructs' the person exercising the power, he commits an offence.

When this kind of emergency arises there may well be attendant expenses in rescuing and transporting and treating the animals. In that respect the constable or vet acting under this section can apply to the magistrate's court for a reimbursement of their expenses. The court may then make such an order as it things fit. If it does make an order then the person affected has a right of appeal to the Crown Court. Although there is every reason he would wish to appeal if they refused to make an order. For then he would be more 'affected' by their decision.

As the affected animal will require care and comfort via veterinary treatment, any attendant expenses can be reimbursed on application to the magistrates' court. The person ordered to pay those expenses, he would normally be the owner or offender, has a right of appeal to the Crown Court.

The essential problem in relation to animals in distress is that so often those who might or would be most interested and expected to act on their behalf have little or no legal powers. That is the primary reason so many animal activists are involved as undercover operators who provide films and information in relation to the premises, particularly abattoirs. Similarly it sometimes leads to aggrieved employees becoming 'whistle-blowers' on behalf of the animals. Then they may still have to battle against the misguided view of the law by an official body like Defra. That was blatantly the case in *R. v. Wasiuta* [2012] where finally the CPS had to take over and take action. In the event both defendants, each of whom were responsible for multiple-abuse of animals in an abattoir, were prosecuted and sentenced to imprisonment. [See **F3**]

The position may move from an urgent one to an emergency. In that event the inspector or constable can take the animal into possession without waiting for a vet. That extends to the dependent offspring. So as they too can be taken into possession, the AWA provides for their protection too. Even if they are not presently suffering or likely to suffer, they are taken as well as their parent animal. If it were otherwise a forced separation on the contrary could make the progeny likely to suffer, mentally and physically. Both aspects are within AWA. Moreover the progeny would then become a protected animal in its own right.

A vet could examine and take samples from the animal, usually blood or urine, in order to satisfy himself as to whether the animal should be taken into possession or, depending on its condition, killed. A sample would also be relevant evidence to any charge against the responsible person.

C8 Words

The whole of this area is concerned with animals that are in need of varying degrees of urgent treatment. Therefore it is important to know, especially when a person has the right to kill the animal in question, what precisely the law requires to sanction that act. So does the certificate of the vet have to be in writing or is an oral opinion sufficient? The question was addressed in the High Court in *James v. RSPCA* [2011] EWHC 1642. Yvonne James pleaded guilty at Goole Magistrates' Court to three charges of causing unnecessary suffering to protected animals. The charges related to three horses which were found to have been 'living in atrocious conditions.' James appealed by case stated in relation to a 'costs' order for £38,644.56. She claimed it should have been reduced to reflect her 'ground' of appeal that the seizure and detention of the horses had been 'unlawful' as the vet's 'certificate' was not in writing.

The vet went to the stables where at the request of the RSPCA she examined the horses. The vet said, 'they were suffering and in need of veterinary attention. As a result, the police officer, who also had been requested to attend the stables by the RSPCA, assumed responsibility for the horses, and they were later cared for by the RSPCA.'

After outlining the facts Keith J said, 'The critical point is that the veterinary surgeon's certificate that the horses were suffering was not in writing. It was just what she said, and the first ground of appeal is that only a certification in writing amounts to a sufficient certification for the purposes of section 18(5).'

The question for the opinion of the High Court was:

"Is it lawful under section 18(5) of the Animal Welfare Act for an inspector or constable to take a protected animal into his possession if a veterinary surgeon present at the scene states orally that the animal is suffering?"

There were in fact three Crown Court decisions on the very issue. In *Rumachic* (Appeal No. A2008/0123) the Lewes Crown Court held it had to be in writing. But in *Shine* (Appeal No. A2009/0202), coincidentally at Lewes Crown Court, it was held it did not have to be in writing. The Recorder in *Gray v. RSPCA* ([2010] (A20090060) also held it did not have to be in writing.

Keith J said, 'The word "certifies" in section 18(3) is not defined in the Act...The word connotes a degree of formality, and the proposition that the degree of formality which is necessary is that certification be in writing is, in my view, supported by section 18(10)...If "a certificate" under section 18(5) is to be issued, that is more consistent with the certificate having to be in writing, because it is documents which tend to be issued rather than expressions of opinion.'

The RSPCA relied on two points. The first one was rightly rejected by the court as it related to section 6 which was concerned with the docking dog's tails. It was not of general application.

Keith J said, 'However the RSPCA's second point is a far more compelling one...The RSPCA contends that an animal might well be subjected to further suffering if a veterinary surgeon who is called to the scene is not in a position to produce a written certificate of the animal's condition immediately. That might happen, for example, if there are a large number of animals, some of whose seizure is necessary because they need urgent treatment, and some not, and there is not sufficient time to produce a written certificate covering only those animals whose seizure is necessary. It might also happen, for example, if the circumstances at the time made production of a written certificate impracticable, for example, if the weather was too bad for the appropriate documentation to be raised on site, or if the site was dangerous and the veterinary surgeon as well as the animal had to leave the site as soon as possible.'

Having analysed section 18(6) the court confirmed that applied *'before the veterinary surgeon has arrived.'* As a result Keith J concluded, 'It would, I think, be very surprising if section 18(5) were to be construed in a way which permits a police officer to act so as to put an animal out of its distress before the veterinary surgeon arrives, but does not permit the animal to be relieved of its suffering after the veterinary surgeon arrives, even though the veterinary surgeon thinks that the animal is suffering, but for one reason or another does not put that into writing.

For these reasons, I have concluded a section 18(5) does not require the certification to be in writing, and that the seizure and detention of Mrs James horses was not unlawful.'

However that was not the end of the matter. For the subject has been recently revisited.

In *Gray v. Crown Court Aylesbury and RSPCA* [2013] EWHC 500 the applicant, James Gray, raised an important issue as to the lawfulness of the seizure of numerous animals at his family farm in Hyde Heath on 4, 5, and 9 January 2008. In the High Court Toulson LJ outlined the issue for the court: 'The animals were seized in purported pursuance of section 18 by police officers acting on oral statements made by veterinary surgeons that they considered it necessary in order to protect the animals from likely suffering. After the animals were seized, they underwent examination and samples were taken for analysis. The results formed part of the evidence for the prosecution.' [See **B8**; **B9**]

There was a submission of no case to answer at the Crown Court on the basis the evidence was inadmissible because the seizures had been unlawful since there had been no written certificate by a veterinary surgeon. The court rejected that submission holding that section 18(5) did not require the certificate to be in writing. Further the court added that the unprecedented scale of the situation discovered on the visits resulted in pressure of circumstances such that "oral certifications were the only viable course to adopt". Moreover even if the seizures were unlawful, the court held that the illegality did not make the evidence inadmissible within the principle in *R v Sang* [1980] AC 402. Equally it was not unfair to admit it.

Defence Counsel submitted that the Crown Court erred in law in rejecting his submission about the lawfulness of the seizures and the admissibility of the resulting evidence.

Toulson LJ analysed the existing cases which caused the 'judicial disagreement about the proper interpretation of section 18(5).' His Lordship considered the authorities namely Judge Waddicor's view in *Rumachic* 23 October 2008 and *James v RSPCA* [2011] EWHC 1642 (Admin) where Keith J took a contrary view. Unlike Judge Waddicor, it was held by Keith J 'that section 18(5) does not require the certification to be in writing.'

Toulson LJ referred to the reasoning of Judge Waddicor and the Oxford English Dictionary definition of "certificate" as:

"A formal document attesting a fact, esp birth, marriage, or death, a medical condition, a level of achievement, a fulfilment of requirements, ownership of shares, etc"

He concluded, 'In my judgment, to be within section 18(5) the certifying must be in writing.' That was only part of the conclusion for he continued, 'However, it does not follow that the seizures in the present case were unlawful. As I have noted, the court found that the action taken in the present case was the only viable way to proceed. On that factual finding, it appears to me that the constable who seized the animals acted lawfully under section 18(6). Further, if that were wrong, I see no basis for holding that the court erred in law in its application of the principle in *R v Sang*. The court was entitled to conclude that the probative value of the relevant evidence justified its admission and that no significant prejudice was caused to Mr Gray by the fact that the veterinary surgeons' assessment of the animals' condition was not put in writing.'

Therefore the application for judicial review was dismissed.

That High Court decision was direct and right. While the evidence was relevant equally it was fair to admit it given that the defendant was the person who had in fact caused the abuse. If the court had decided otherwise it would have made the AWA unworkable. For it is as simple as the name itself. As it is for the' welfare' of animals, the role of a vet in alleviating an animal's suffering when it was unquestionably necessary would have been nugatory.

Power of entry for section 18 purposes

C9   Animal Welfare Act 2006, s.19

(1) An inspector or a constable may enter premises for the purpose of searching for a protected animal and of exercising any power under section 18 in relation to it if he reasonably believes –

(a) that there is a protected animal on the premises, and

(b) that the animal is suffering or, if the circumstances of the animal do not change, it is likely to suffer.

(2) Subsection (1) does not authorise entry to any part of premises which used as a private dwelling.

(3) An inspector or a constable may (if necessary) use reasonable force in exercising the power conferred by subsection (1), but only if it appears to him that entry is required before a warrant under subsection (4) can be obtained and executed.

(4) Subject to subsection (5), a justice of the peace may, on the application of an inspector or a constable, issue a warrant authorising an inspector or a constable to enter premises for the purpose mentioned in subsection (1), if necessary using reasonable force.

(5) The power to issue a warrant under subsection (4) is exercisable only if the justice of the peace is satisfied –

(a) that there are reasonable grounds for believing that there is a protected animal on the premises and that the animal is suffering or is likely to suffer if its circumstances do not change, and

(b) that section 52 is satisfied in relation to the premises.

So that there are no problems of entry to the premises where animals are in 'distress', the AWA gives the inspector or constable wide powers of entry for the purpose of doing their duty under section 18. In particular they may enter premises for the purpose of 'searching' for a protected animal. The person exercising any power under section 18 can do so if he 'reasonably believes' a protected animal is on the premises and is suffering.

He can action if the animal is 'likely to suffer' if he does not take action. That gives a wide subjective power to the person entering the premises as it is the potential for rather than actual suffering that is present in respect of the protected animal.

The power is strengthened by the fact that by paragraph 15 of Schedule 2, if he enters under that power or with a warrant under section 19(4), he may take the animal away and arrange for a post-mortem of any carcass. In relation to that and indeed generally, by paragraph 16, any obstruction of a person who is exercising such a power is itself an offence. Just how wide the power is can be seen by the fact that if he takes another person with him in exercise of that power of entry or a warrant, he too has these powers. Equally any obstruction of him would similarly be an offence.

While it is wide there is a potential flaw in the law as it does not authorise entry to any part of a 'premises' which used as a private dwelling. So if a person simply transfers the suffering animal from the farm to his lounge, how is it going to be discovered, let alone its condition alleviated? It has to be considered that in the growing animal abuse of dog fighting and badger-baiting, the usual course for the offenders is to take their dogs back home to recover.

'Part of premises' is defined under section 62(3) as a part 'which is used as a private dwelling include any yard, garden, garage or outhouse which is used for purposes in connection with it'. So while he could enter part of the premises used as an office, he could not go into the residential part unless he has obtained a warrant under subsection (4).

An inspector or a constable may find some resistance when they try to enter premises to search for an animal. It that event he can use reasonable force to gain entry. However he can only do so if it is necessary and he has to enter before a warrant for that purpose can be obtained and executed. That would be the case if an animal is suffering and it is imperative that he acts immediately as otherwise the suffering would be more severe. Schedule 2 would also apply in respect of any such resistance in the form of an obstruction which would be an offence. [See **E3**]

If force is necessary to gain entry and there is not that degree of urgency, a warrant has to be obtained. A justice of the peace may issue one which authorises an inspector to enter the premises and to use reasonable force. The warrant can only be issued if the justice of the peace is satisfied that the animal is suffering or is likely to if there is no change in its circumstances. An important additional requirement to that condition is that a justice of the peace must be satisfied in relation to section 52. That specifies strict conditions that must be met before a warrant can be issued. It includes one which allows for a warrant to be granted without notice to the occupier if the specified condition is satisfied. Without that condition any recalcitrant criminal would easily cock a snook at the aim of this legal protection. [See **D3**]

Orders in relation to animals taken under section 18(5)

C10   Animal Welfare Act 2006, s.20

(1)   A magistrates' court may order any of the following in relation to an animal taken into possession under section 18(5) –

(a)   that specified treatment be administered to the animal;

    (b)   that possession of the animal be given up to a specified person;

    (c)   that the animal be sold;

    (d)   that the animal be disposed of otherwise than by way of sale;

    (e)   that the animal be destroyed.

(2)   If an animal is taken into possession under section 18(5) when it is pregnant, the power conferred by subsection (1) shall also be exercisable in relation to any offspring that results from the pregnancy.

(3)   The power conferred by subsection (1) shall be exercisable on application by –

    (a)   the owner of the animal, or

    (b)   any other person appearing to the court to have a sufficient interest in the animal.

(4)   A court may not make an order under subsection (1) unless –

    (a)   it has given the owner of the animal an opportunity to be heard, or

    (b)   it is satisfied that it is not reasonably practicable to communicate with the owner.

(5)   Where a court makes an order under subsection (1), it may –

    (a)   appoint a person to carry out, or arrange for the carrying out, of the order;

    (b)   give directions with respect to the carrying out of the order;

    (c)   confer additional powers (including power to enter premises where the animal is being kept) for the purpose of, or in connection with, the carrying out of the order;

    (d)   order a person to reimburse the expenses of carrying out the order.

(6) In determining how to exercise its powers under this section, the court shall have regard, amongst other things, to the desirability of protecting the animal's value and avoiding increasing any expenses which a person may be ordered to reimburse.

(7) A person commits an offence if he intentionally obstructs a person in the exercise of any power conferred by virtue of this section.

(8) If the owner of the animal is subject to a liability by virtue of section 18(13) or subsection 5(d) above, any amount to which he is entitled as a result of sale of the animal may be reduced by an amount equal to that liability.

As animals are merely property in law they can be bought, sold, used, abused and damaged just like any other property be it a wooden rocking horse or a plastic duck. However if an inspector or constable has acted on a vet's certificate or of their own accord and taken an animal 'into possession' under section 18(5), it may be retained. There could also be dependent offspring of the parent animal. The person exercising the power can then apply to the magistrates' court for an order in relation to it. The magistrates can make an order for any matter relating to its future including treatment and sale. It could also order that it is disposed of or destroyed.

If the animal is pregnant when it is taken into possession, these powers extend to any offspring of the pregnancy. So if either or both the parent animal and any offspring required 'treatment' of a straightforward veterinary nature, that would be covered by caring for the animal under section 18(8)(b). If it was in need of more serious veterinary surgery, then the magistrates could make an order.

As the animal may have been taken against the wishes of the owner or, depending on the urgency of the circumstances, even without his knowledge, he still has a right to apply to the magistrates' court in respect of it. The owner could apply for the magistrates to order any of those powers including its return to him. Depending on the circumstances he may apply for its disposal or death.

The magistrates' court may also hear an application by 'any other person appearing to the court to have any sufficient interest in the animal'. So there could be a conflict between the owner and the other person as to what they would wish to have done with the animal. One may want to sell it, while the other may want to kill it. The paramount principle of the AWA is to protect the welfare of the animal. Therefore whether it is by a single application from the owner or a dual application by an interested party, the crucial decision is what is best for the animal. If there were conflicting applications the court could decide in favour of one or other or make a completely different decision. In order to make the right decision which would avoid a subsequent challenge on appeal, so protecting the court and the animal, the judicious course would be to seek the opinion of a vet.

As ownership is important as a legal concept, those powers of the court cannot be exercised unless it has given the owner an opportunity to be heard. However sometimes animals are abandoned in muddy fields, especially when travellers move on from a site. Or as happened in *Gray v RSPCA* [2010] where the owner, who is the main offender, absconds before or during the proceedings to avoid being sentenced. In the event of the magistrates' court being unable to contact the owner, it can carry out any of those powers if it is satisfied it is not reasonably practical to communicate with him. When the court makes any of those orders, it can enforce them by appointing a person to do so. Then the court gives directions for the procedure to be followed. [See **C7**]

There is a rather unusual provision in subsection (6) which indicates how the court should exercise its powers. It 'shall' have regard to, 'amongst other things', the desirability of protecting the animal's 'value' and avoiding increasing any expenses which a person may be ordered to reimburse. That appears to allow their determination in exercising those powers to place a mongrel or a stray at a lower premium than a pedigree poodle. While it states 'amongst other things', there is no reason to specify an animal's value in monetary terms when that could collide with its welfare now and in the future. If the decision is made to limit the expenses it could lead to the choice between a lower debt and immediate death. That is manifestly contrary to the purpose and principle of the AWA. For whoever caused the abuse should bear the burden of the cost.

There would be occasions when the owner or another interested person takes exception to any of those orders. He may indeed still have the animal on the premises as a place of safety under section 18. If he 'intentionally obstructs' the person carrying out the court order, under section 20(7) he thereby commits an offence.

Orders under section 20: appeals

C11   Animal Welfare Act 2006, s.21

(1)   Where a court makes an order under section 20(1), the owner of the animal to which the order relates may appeal against the order to the Crown Court.

(2)   Nothing may be done under an order under section 20(1) unless –

(a)   the period for giving notice of appeal against the order has expired, and

(b)   if the order is the subject of an appeal, the appeal has been determined or withdrawn.

(3) Where the effect of an order is suspended under subsection (2) –
   (a) no directions given in connection with the order shall have effect, but
   (b) the court may give directions about how any animal to which the order applies is to be dealt with during the suspension.

(4) Directions under subsection (3)(b) may, in particular –
   (a) appoint a person to carry out, or arrange for the carrying out, of the directions;
   (b) require any person who has possession of the animal to deliver it up for the purposes of the directions;
   (c) confer additional powers (including power to enter premises where the animal is being kept) for the purpose of, or in connection with, the carrying out of the directions;
   (d) provide for the recovery of any expenses which are reasonably incurred in carrying out the directions.

(5) Where a court decides on an application under section 20(3)(a) not to exercise the power conferred by subsection (1) of that section, the applicant may appeal against the decision to the Crown Court.

(6) Where a court makes an order under section 20(5)(d), the person against whom the order is made may appeal against the order to the Crown Court.

Given that under section 20 the powers are wide and the consequences are too, the 'owner' has a right of appeal against any of them to the Crown Court. That would have to be lodged within the normal time limit. While the appeal is pending, none of the orders made by the court can be enforced. They are suspended until the time for an appeal has expired or the appeal has been determined or withdrawn.

There may be a conflict between the application by the owner and the order of the court under section 20, especially where an animal requires 'treatment'. Then where on appeal the orders are suspended, given that we are dealing with a living creature, nevertheless the court may give 'directions' about how any animal subject to an order is dealt with during the suspension. Those directions are intended to protect the welfare of the animal pending the result of the appeal.

These provisions under subsection (4) are essential as the animal may be suffering meanwhile and in need veterinary treatment, notwithstanding any appeal. The owner's position is subject to the court's decision to minimise the animal's 'distress'. That is consistent with the purpose of their role and the AWA.

Besides any appeal the owner may make in his own right as against an order in favour of another person, he may also appeal where the court decides to make any other order. That would allow him to challenge an order that was made that was contrary to his application, particularly a refusal to return an animal to him. In relation to the expenses incurred in carrying out the directions and the reimbursement claimed, the person who is due to pay may appeal against the order to the Crown Court.

There could be a conflict of interest between the owner and any other interested person if an application is made by the former to sell the animal and the latter to have it returned to him. In that event the court has a discretionary power to grant either application or to reject them both. It has to make an order that is appropriate to the interests of the animal as compared to those of the human claiming it.

As a result there are two problems with this section. The court may have ordered that the person with a 'sufficient interest' in the animal under section 20(3)(b) has possession of it or decides against him. Either way his position is ignored under section 21 as it only applies to the owner. Allied to that, as it concentrates on the rights of the owner who is often the person who has abused the animal, it is plainly giving a balance that was not intended by the letter or spirit of the AWA. For a proper balance and the purpose of the AWA, an intermediary body should actually be appointed under section 20(3)(b) to automatically by law have a 'sufficient interest' in the animal's condition and life. To take account of their inherent vulnerability in their dealings with us there should be an Animals' Ombudsman. Then no less than a Public Trustee on behalf of children who are disadvantaged, he would look after the interests of those affected by the criminal acts of others yet cannot actively complain in their own right.

4

Evidence and Prosecution

D1 Enforcement

This chapter analyses all the actual mechanics of the AWA. While the foregoing sections 1 to 21 detail the background and prohibition of activities plus protection of animals, sections 22 to 45 are concerned with enforcement and prosecution and sentences upon conviction. Unlike most other statutes involving summary offences, the AWA takes account of the fact that the victims are animals. Hence as they cannot provide the evidence personally, the AWA grants power to the authorities for that purpose. That extends to the method and place and time to gain and obtain the evidence to effect a prosecution.

Seizure of animals involved in fighting offences

D2   Animal Welfare Act 2006, s.22

Enforcement Powers

(1)   A constable may seize an animal if it appears to him that it is one in relation to which an offence under section 8(1) or (2) has been committed.

(2)   A constable may enter and search premises for the purpose of exercising the power under subsection (1) if he reasonably believes –
(a)   that there is an animal on the premises, and
(b)   that the animal is one in relation to which the power under subsection (1) is exercisable.

(3)   Subsection (2) does not authorise entry to any part of premises which is used as a private dwelling.

(4) Subject to subsection (5), a justice of the peace may, on the application of a constable, issue a warrant authorising a constable to enter and search premises, if necessary using reasonable force, for the purpose of exercising the power under subsection (1).

(5) The power to issue a warrant under subsection (4) is exercisable only if the justice of the peace is satisfied –

(a) that there are reasonable grounds for believing that there is on the premises an animal in relation to which an offence under section 8(1) or (2) has been committed, and

(b) that section 52 is satisfied in relation to the premises.

(6) In this section, references to an animal in relation to which an offence under section 8(1) or (2) has been committed include an animal which took part in an animal fight in relation to which such an offence was committed.

Sections 22 to 29 govern the *Enforcement Powers* of the AWA. Those sections cover all the areas that arise where people who are involved with animals abuse them. The powers relate to and include entry and search of premises, seizure of animals and inspection of their condition and conditions.

The form and nature of animal fighting rings are that they are well arranged yet opportunistic and spontaneous. As the rings are always committing illegal bloody offences which are constantly being tracked by the authorities and informants, they operate by a series of secret meetings on a need-to-know basis by the cohorts. So often an area where the ordinary activity it is used for may be a game of skittles or a beer barrel storage yard becomes quickly transformed into a dog-fighting ring. The aim of the action is to feel the thrill of the kill and the prize money that is won and lost by betting on which dog does down the other dog to death. As it would be dangerous for the owners to take a heavily mauled dog to a vet who would recognise the origin of the wounds and have to inform the police, they remain licking their wounds. [See **B12**]

So the police need powers of entering premises to ensure they can act on suspicion alone where there is, prior to that visit, little or no proof. For mainly the 'information received' is the result of intelligence gained undercover or an underground animal rights activist who has infiltrated the secret network of the ring. That will filter through to the police officer and form the basis of his belief. [See **D5**]

To that end a constable may enter and search premises to seize an animal if he 'reasonably believes' an animal is on the premises in relation to which an offence under section 8(1) or (2) has been committed. Once the animal has been seized the police can ensure it is not used for further fighting offences. It can also lead to a deprivation order under section 33 against the owner or a disqualification order under section 34. As for the dog, there is a simple legal solution, as under sections 37 and 38 it could be killed.

However that is limited as the power does not authorise entry to any 'part of premises' which is used as a 'private dwelling'. That could be a serious lacuna in the AWA as the definition of a private dwelling in section 62(3) includes 'any yard, garden, garage or outhouse which is used for purposes in connection with it'. That provision would unquestionably hamper the investigation as entry to those areas are precisely where the dog fights are likely to be in full flight or alternatively areas disguised after the event. The hair and bones and blood will have been scrubbed from the scene.

The essence of the power of entry is to catch the perpetrators and participants and spectators while the fight is in motion. For you cannot have one without the other. Therefore that potential problem can be solved as the police can act with a warrant. A justice of the peace may issue a warrant to a constable to enter and search premises to seize an animal. As there can be no legal reason for the activity, there is often obstruction and resistance and assault by the perpetrators. Following a raid those present equally seek to or do escape. So the warrant gives a power to the officer to use 'reasonable force' if it is necessary.

It should be noted that only a constable can apply for a warrant under section 22(4). A warrant will only be granted however if a justice of the peace is satisfied in respect of two conditions. There must be 'reasonable grounds' for believing a section 8(1) or (2) has been committed. The second is section 52 must be satisfied in relation to the premises. The necessity could arise under section 52(3)(b) as a result of the occupier refusing entry to an inspector or a constable. The 'occupier' is defined under section 62(2) as 'the person who appears to be in charge' of the premises.

Section 52 is quite specific and strict in its terms and pays respect to the privacy that attaches to a person's home. So while it hampers the police in their investigation, it balances that with the right of a person to restrict those who enter his home. However if the heavy onus placed upon police is discharged, then the warrant can be issued even without advance notice to the occupier. [See **D3**]

Conditions for grant of warrant

D3   Animal Welfare Act 2006, s.52

    (1)   This section is satisfied in relation to premises if any of the following four conditions is met.

(2) The first condition is that the whole of the premises is used as a private dwelling and the occupier has been informed of the decision to apply for a warrant.

(3) The second condition is that any part of the premises is not used as a private dwelling and that each of the following applies to the occupier of the premises –

    (a) he has been informed of the decision to seek entry to the premises and of the reason for that decision;

    (b) he has failed to allow entry to the premises on being requested do so by an inspector or a constable;

    (c) he has been informed of the decision to apply for a warrant.

(4) The third condition is that –

    (a) the premises are unoccupied or the occupier is absent, and

    (b) notice of intention to apply for a warrant has been left in a conspicuous place on the premises.

(5) The fourth condition is that it is inappropriate to inform the occupier of the decision to apply for a warrant because –

    (a) it would defeat the object of entering the premises, or

    (b) entry is required as a matter of urgency.

There are four conditions relating to section 52. The first three conditions are a hindrance to any investigation as obviously once notice is given to the occupier of an intention to apply for a warrant, the evidence will be swiftly disposed of or destroyed, especially if it is a dog; it will be particularly if it is wounded as a bite could be powerful positive evidence of the illegal activity that produced it.

Hence the fourth condition counteracts that negative position by allowing the grant of a warrant if it is 'inappropriate' to inform the occupier of the decision to apply for a warrant. There are two alternative limbs either of which can be met. The first is because it would 'defeat the object' of the entry to the premises. The second is the entry is necessary as 'a matter of urgency'.

That condition within subsection (5) is essential as without it any investigation would often end before it began. For there is every incentive for a person involved in dog fighting to destroy the evidence if he is aware of a pending visit by the police.

It also relates to the fact that, depending on the condition of the animal, it is likely the occupier would have it at home to recuperate so it can be used to fight again in the future. So the point is clarified by section 22(6) which confirms that the section includes an animal which took part in an animal fight where an offence under section 8(1) or (2) was committed. That would include a dead dog as sometimes the most potent evidence is provided by a post-mortem. It can verify the nature of the wounds and the likely suffering as a result while the animal was still alive. Indeed it could prove the injuries led to its death.

If the owner seeks the return of a seized animal, given its legal status, he could apply to the court under the Police (Property) Act 1897. It would be similar to an application under section 20(1)(b) of the AWA, but stronger if the evidence is weak. For the former would place a burden on the police to justify their possession of his property.

Entry and search under warrant in connection with offences

D4   Animal Welfare Act 2006, s.23

(1)   Subject to subsection (2), a justice of the peace may, on the application of an inspector or a constable, issue a

warrant authorising an inspector or a constable to enter premises, if necessary using reasonable force, in order to search for evidence of the commission of a relevant offence.

(2) The power to issue a warrant under subsection (1) is exercisable only if the justice of the peace is satisfied –

    (a) that there are reasonable grounds for believing –

        (i) that a relevant offence has been committed on the premises, or

        (ii) that evidence of the commission of a relevant offence is to be found on the premises and

    (b) that section 52 is satisfied in relation to the premises.

(3) In this section, "relevant offence" means any offence under any of the sections 4 to 9, 13(6) and 34(9).

Once the warrant has been issued it is vital that it is executed with speed. Section 23 spells out in detail the power of an inspector or a constable where a justice of the peace has issued a warrant. Again it sets limits on the issue of a warrant in order to search for 'evidence' of the commission of a relevant offence. The warrant will authorise the use of reasonable force if it is necessary to give effect to the entry and search.

The issue of a warrant under subsection (2) is limited in that a justice of the peace must be satisfied on two separate but related grounds. First that there are reasonable grounds for believing that a relevant offence has been committed on the premises or evidence of it is to be found there. Secondly, similar to other sections of the AWA, section 52 has to be satisfied in relation to the premises. Therefore one of the four conditions therein must be met evidentially. [See **D3**]

A relevant offence means any offence within 'sections 4 to 9, 13(6) and 34(9)', which are the core sections of the AWA. Therefore it covers all the serious offences relating to prevention of harm from unnecessary suffering to a breach of the owner's duty of care. Within the promotion of welfare it also covers the responsible person breaching the licence or registration of activities involving animals. In meaning and extent it includes where a person breaches a disqualification. All those are essential as otherwise where there is a whiff of suspicion without proof it would go undiscovered as so often offences are committed behind closed doors where they remain hidden to most, except the perpetrators themselves. That is the precise reason this evidence provision is crucial to a proper investigation.

Significantly the conditions governing a warrant are set out in detail in paragraphs 1 to 3 of Schedule 2 under the heading, *Safeguards etc. in connection with powers of entry conferred by warrant*. It imposes strict conditions relating to an inspector and a constable in the application and execution of it. Allied to that power, so the warrant is effective, paragraph 10 of the Schedule confers additional powers on the person executing it including inspection of an animal, taking samples and seizing evidence. Paragraph 14 of the Schedule confirms the person is authorised to use reasonable force in exercising those additional powers.

Of course none of that would matter too much unless there was a sanction against those subject to the warrant. Therefore by paragraph 16 of Schedule 2 if a person intentionally obstructs a person exercising any of the powers 'conferred by this Schedule', he commits an offence. [See **E6**]

Entry for purposes of arrest

D5   Animal Welfare Act 2006, s.24

In section 17(1)(c) the Police and Criminal Evidence Act 1984 (power of constable to enter and search premises for purpose of arresting a person for offence under specified enactments), at end insert –

> "(v) any of sections 4, 5, 6(1) and (2), 7 and 8(1) and (2) of the Animal Welfare Act 2006 (offences relating to the prevention of harm to animals);"

The Police and Criminal Evidence Act 1984 gives extensive powers to a constable to enter and search premises for the purpose of arresting a person for an offence under various specified Acts and enactments. That is amended to allow a power of arrest to be extended for sections 4, 5, 6(1) and (2), 7, and 8(1) and (2) of the AWA. The officer has that power for all those sections that relate to the prevention of harm to animals namely suffering, mutilation, tail docking, poisons and fighting. Without that power the AWA would be considerably weakened. For that power of entry and arrest enables the police to find and hold the animal abuser and protect the animal as well as preserving the evidence.

Inspection of records required to be kept by holder of licence

D6   Animal Welfare Act 2006, s.25

(1)   An inspector may require the holder of a licence to produce for inspection any records which he is required to keep by a condition of the licence.

(2)   Where records which a person is so required to keep are stored in electronic form, the power under subsection (1) includes power to require the records to be made available for inspection –

    (a)   in a visible and legible form, or

    (b)   in a form from which they can readily be produced in a visible and legible form.

(3)   An inspector may inspect and take copies of any records produced for inspection in pursuance of a requirement under this section.

When a person owns animals for which he has a licence it is vital that he keeps records that are accurate. Those records have to be available to an inspector. If it was otherwise there would be no way to track and trace any case in which he breached his duty or failed to fulfil the conditions on which the licence was granted. So an inspector may require the holder of a licence to produce for inspection any records he is required to keep as a condition of his licence. Normally they would be in a paper form and signed by the owner. If they are in electronic form, the inspector has the power to require the records to be made available in a visible and legible form. That puts an onus on the licence holder. So if it is on a computer he can require the person to give him it on disc or a dongle rather than the inspector take away the computer. He could do that if the holder was uncooperative under paragraph 10 of Schedule 2.

The licence is granted under section 13. So if a person does an act which requires one without one, he commits an offence. Similarly if he breaches a condition of it he commits an offence. If he carries out an activity involving animals after the expiration of the licence period he commits an offence. In regard to his licence it is essential that he has reliable records that can be inspected. For if he has inadequate records it would be difficult if not impossible to know and check whether he has complied with the conditions. Moreover it would not be feasible to ensure any diseased animals do not enter – or have not already entered – the food chain intended for humans. Given the repercussions of 'mad cow disease' it could be serious if it spread through the mass consumption of beef burgers.

The grant of a licence can be for a limited period. In any event it cannot, under paragraph 5 of Schedule 1, be for more than 3 years. That allows for control of the holder during the period it is used and on application for renewal of the licence. How far the holder has complied with the conditions would be considered and become decisive. Accordingly his licence could then be revoked or amended or refused.

Inspection in connection with licences

D7   Animal Welfare Act 2006, s.26

(1) An inspector may carry out an inspection in order to check compliance with –

(a) the conditions subject to which a licence is granted;

(b) provision made by or under this Act which is relevant to the carrying on of an activity to which a licence relates.

(2) An inspector may, for the purpose of carrying out an inspection under subsection (1), enter –

(a) premises specified in a licence as premises on which the carrying on of an activity is authorised;

(b) premises on which he reasonably believes an activity to which a licence relates is being carried on.

(3) Subsection (2) does not authorise entry to any part of premises which is used as a private dwelling unless 24 hours' notice of the intended entry is given to the occupier.

A licence is defined under section 62(1) as one 'for the purposes of section 13'. An inspector may inspect the records and take copies of those produced for his inspection. If a person carries on an activity involving a protected animal without a licence or is not registered for the activity, under section 13(6) he commits an offence.

The purpose of keeping the records is to ensure that the owner is acting properly and the animals are cared for in terms of their welfare. There has to be cooperation between the inspector and the owner to ensure he complies with the licence conditions. An inspector checks he has complied with both the reason it was granted and the activity it covers. For if he breaches a condition of it, he commits an offence. Similarly if he carries out an activity involving animals after the expiration of the licence period, he commits an offence.

In order to carry out his duties the inspector may enter premises specified in the licence as where the activity is authorised. It is wider however in that he may also enter premises where he 'reasonably believes' such an activity is carried on. Without that extra power it would be difficult to control the licence holder as well as detect any breaches of the activity.

If the activity is being carried on in part of the premises which are being used as a private dwelling, then the inspector must give 24 hours' notice of his intention to enter to the occupier. The definition of the 'occupier' and the 'premises' and the 'private dwelling' is contained in section 62(1)-(3). [See **C8**; **D2**]

The 24 hours' notice is a balance between the privacy of the occupier and the power of an inspector. The notice has to be given as it is not within the serious offences of the AWA. Similarly there is no power to apply for a warrant under this section. The exclusion of notice under section 52 and the application of a warrant is reserved for the serious offences specified in the respective sections. [See **D3**]

Nevertheless it is wider than it at first appears as it includes the inspector checking any provision made 'by or under' the AWA which is relevant to the licence. Moreover it is an offence under section 13 to contravene the conditions of the licence. That is endorsed by conferring a power of entry under paragraph 10 of Schedule 2 which, if obstructed by the holder, by paragraph 16 is also an offence. Hence any refractory person could have his licence revoked if he prevents the inspector from fulfilling his statutory duty.

Although a warrant cannot be obtained under this section, an inspector could apply for entry with a warrant under sections 19(4) if there is an animal in distress and 23(1) if he reasonably believes an offence has been committed on the premises. In each case there would no need to give notice to the occupier.

Inspection in connection with registration

D8 Animal Welfare Act 2006, s.27

   (1) An inspector may carry out an inspection in order to check compliance with provision made by or under this Act which is relevant to the carrying on of an activity to which a registration for the purposes of section 13 relates.

   (2) An inspector may, for the purpose of carrying out an inspection under subsection (1), enter premises on which he reasonably believes a person registered for the purposes of section 13 is carrying on an activity to which the registration relates.

   (3) Subsection (2) does not authorise entry to any part of premises which is used as a private dwelling unless 24

hours' notice of the intended entry is given to the occupier.

The registration is closely connected with the licensing system as each relates to an activity that needs to be monitored by the authorities. So allowing an inspection of the licence only would be ineffectual. Consequently an inspector also has the power to check compliance with an activity that is registered within section 13. The inspector may enter premises where he reasonably believes a person is carrying on a regulated activity. So it would be a breach under section 13(3) if he had not been granted registration, but it was in fact required. That in turn would be an offence under section 13(6).

As with the proposed inspection in connection with a licence, so similarly 24 hours' notice of the intended entry has to be given to the occupier to any part of the premises which is used as a private dwelling. The same reason pertains with regard to that notice as with the licence namely the balance between the power of the inspector and the privacy of the occupier. Further the same position is applicable in relation to a warrant under sections 19(1) and 23(1). By corollary it extends to the additional powers under Schedule 2.

Inspection of farm premises

D9   Animal Welfare Act 2006, s.28

(1)   An inspector may carry out an inspection in order to –
   (a)   check compliance with regulations under section 12 which relate to animals bred or kept for farming purposes;
   (b)   ascertain whether any offence under or by virtue of this Act has been or is being committed in relation to such animals.

(2) An inspector may enter premises which he reasonably believes to be premises on which animals are bred or kept for farming purposes in order to carry out an inspection under subsection (1).

(3) Subsection (2) does not authorise entry to any part of premises which is used as a private dwelling.

(4) Subject to subsection (5), a justice of the peace may, on the application of an inspector, issue a warrant authorising an inspector to enter premises, if necessary using reasonable force, in order to carry out an inspection under subsection (1).

(5) The power to issue a warrant under subsection (4) is exercisable only if the justice of the peace satisfied –

  (a) that it is reasonable to carry out an inspection on the premises, and

  (b) that section 52 is satisfied in relation to the premises.

Before the introduction of the AWA the main statute relating to farms was the Agriculture (Miscellaneous Provisions) Act 1968. While that Act is still partly in existence, Part 2 was repealed by the AWA. The reason was it has given the authorities extra powers as it extends the monitoring of animals welfare to the inspection of farm premises.

The inspector may enter premises which he 'reasonably believes' to be premises on which animals are 'bred or kept' for farming purposes in order to carry out an inspection. However, as with other sections, this does not allow entry to part of the premises used as a 'private dwelling'. Nevertheless a justice of the peace may issue a warrant authorising him to enter any part of the premises to carry out an inspection. The power to issue a warrant, given it is an invasion of the privacy of the owner of the farm, is limited. It can only be issued if the justice of the peace is satisfied of two conditions namely that an inspection is reasonable and section 52 is satisfied in respect of the premises.

So that means the four conditions specified in section 52 apply. Hence any one of the four can be met. The first three conditions apply on the basis of giving notice to the occupier. Plainly that could often be self-defeating as the very animals the inspection is intended to protect could be immediately disposed of or destroyed. So the fourth condition can be met and a warrant issued if it would be 'inappropriate' to inform the occupier of an intention because it would defeat the object or there is an urgency regarding the inspection. Those two limbs are separate so either (a) the defeating the object or (b) the urgency would suffice. [See **D3**]

The benefit of using the provisions under the AWA is that the regulations made under it can also be specifically applied to it and amended, if necessary, to suit the conditions. To that end The Welfare of Farmed Animals (England) Regulations 2007 was introduced to cover the general position of animals on a farm as well as regulations relating to individual animals. The detail of the regulations covers all such animals while they are on the farm as well as travelling to and from it. [See Appendix]

An application for a warrant may be made by an inspector under this section, rather than by a constable. That is unlike section 22 which is the reverse. Though a constable has much wider powers under PACE which is now extended to the AWA under section 24. [See **D5**]

The additional powers conferred by paragraphs 10 and 14 of Schedule 2 apply to a person executing a warrant to enter the premises. Even then there are 'safeguards' on that position by paragraphs 2 and 3 of the Schedule. For if a warrant is granted under section 28(4) it is subject to conditions in relation to the application and its execution. That lays down strict conditions relating to the form and the method and the procedure. It also states it must be executed within 3 months of the date of its issue. Such conditions are present to protect the privacy of the occupier while ensuring entry is only gained to his premises on valid grounds. Indeed to put it in sharp focus, if the warrant does not strictly comply with the conditions in paragraphs 2 and 3 the entry to the premises 'is unlawful'. [See **E3**]

Inspection relating to community obligations

D10   Animal Welfare Act 2006, s.29

(1)   An inspector may carry an inspection in order to check compliance with regulations under section 12 which implement a Community obligation.

(2)   An inspector may enter any premises in order to carry out an inspection under subsection (1).

(3)   Subsection (2) does not authorise entry to any part of premises which is used as a private dwelling.

Numerous statutory instruments flow from the European Union which relate to animals in all aspects of their lives and death. An inspector may carry out an inspection to ensure compliance with section 12 which implements a Community obligation. It is wide in the respect that an inspector may enter 'any' premises in order to carry out an inspection. However that does not authorise entry to any part of premises which are used as a 'private dwelling'.

This provision is to check compliance with the European Community obligations. Essentially it is a similar provision to a power in the Animal Health Act 1981. It has the advantage of allowing for the changing circumstances in Europe to be taken into account by any regulations made under the AWA.

Power of local authority to prosecute offences

D11   Animal Welfare Act 2006, s.30

Prosecutions

A local authority in England or Wales may prosecute proceedings for any offence under this Act

The subject of prosecutions is significant in this area of law more than most because, while in appropriate cases there is nothing to stop an animal organisation or private individual taking a private prosecution, generally it is given to the local authorities in England and Wales. That includes a county council, district council and the county borough council respectively.

The right to lodge a private prosecution is a cherished right derived from the common law. For when, as sometimes happens for the best or worst of reasons, the police or other authority refuse to prosecute a person a private prosecution can always be mounted. Often that is the only way, even if it is later rather than sooner, to effect a positive change in the law. [See *Roberts v Ruggiero*: Unreported 3/4/85]

While there are bodies like Compassion in World Farming who took action in *Roberts,* most prosecutions are undertaken in England by the RSPCA. The position in Scotland is that the SPCA does not prosecute cases. It informs and provides evidence for the Procurator Fiscal who actually takes the proceedings to court. Moreover without the RSPCA there would be no or very few prosecutions.

The problem in this of area of prosecutions is that many cases of animal abuse are not discovered for some considerable time. Unlike say a burglary or robbery, an offence under the AWA may be a continuing one with regard to the animals' welfare. Even when a complaint is made or the allegation is discovered, the investigation may take some time. It may be dependent on expert evidence from a vet, including a post-mortem. Normally as they are summary offences the time limit for prosecutions once a summons is issued is six months. That would defeat the authorities in this case as there could be an Improvement Notice which is ignored, it may be necessary to try and trace the perpetrators who have since moved on and any progeny who are also affected, though born during the period the abuse or suffering continues. So who can prosecute is an important legal and social role.

D12 Prosecutor

The power of a body to prosecute on behalf of those who cannot do anything to alleviate their own suffering is a significant legal power. With it the plight of those who are otherwise helpless can be helped and the persons responsible for the abuse punished. That role and status was addressed head-on in *Lamont-Perkins v. RSPCA* [2012] EWHC 1002. This was an appeal by case stated against two rulings made by HHJ Ambrose sitting at Gloucester Crown Court. Each ruling was made in the context of an appeal to the Crown Court brought by Margaret Lamont-Perkins against her convictions by the Coleford Justices for offences of causing unnecessary suffering to a number of dogs contrary to section 4. The judge was sitting alone when he made his rulings. Both parties agreed that the judge alone should determine the legal issues which arose in the appeal.

The judge concluded that the information which been laid by the respondent against the Lamont-Perkins had been brought within the time limit specified in section 31(1). His second conclusion was that if the appellant wished to challenge a certificate the respondent had issued under section 31(2) she had to do so by an application that the issue of the certificate and/or the prosecution amounted to an abuse of process. Those rulings were the questions posed in the case stated.

Wyn Williams J in the High Court said, 'As I have said, Ms Howe, counsel for the Appellant, submitted that the Respondent is not and can never be "the prosecutor" within section 31(1) or 31(2)...the "prosecutor" in those subsections must be interpreted to mean a body which is authorised by some statute to in initiate prosecutions; the phrase is not apt to include a private person or organisation which initiates a private prosecution...HH Judge Ambrose rejected Miss Howe's submission upon the interpretation of section 31 of the 2006 Act. He concluded that the phrase "the prosecutor" within section 31 of the 2006 Act was apt to include any person or body initiating a prosecution; it mattered not whether the prosecutor was a body authorised to prosecute by statute or whether the prosecutor was an individual who or a body which had initiated what is known as a private prosecution. Was he correct to do so?'

The appellant relied, *inter alia*, upon the fact that section 30 expressly empowers a local authority to prosecute for any offence under the Act. So Parliament had 'in mind a restricted class of prosecutor.'

The respondent submitted that the judge's decision was correct. He relied upon the fact there was '...no proper basis to conclude that the phrase "the prosecutor" should be limited to a prosecutor who is exercising the functions to prosecute pursuant to some statutory provision.

Wyn Williams J concluded, 'I agree with the conclusion of the learned judge. First it is important to stress that section 31 of the 2006 Act must be interpreted in the context of the Act as a whole. In my judgment there is nothing in the Act, read as a whole, which leads to the conclusion that the phrase "the prosecutor" should be interpreted narrowly as Ms Howe contends.

I appreciate that the power to issue a certificate under section 31(2) is a considerable one. It is not a power lightly to be conferred upon any prosecuting authority. I am not persuaded, however, that the power to issue a certificate under section 31(2) is a conclusive indicator that the power is intended to be available only to a prosecutor which derives its authority to prosecute from statute.'

This was unquestionably the right decision. There are two specific reasons for that conclusion. There are many cases where an existing prosecuting body such as the CPS or Defra fail to be proactive in mounting a prosecution notwithstanding the state of the evidence. Without bodies like the RSPCA often there would be no prosecution at all in such cases. It is also in the interests of justice that animal abusers are punished. If not it would do more than merely ensure they escape their just deserts. It would also, because of the cruelty connection as practised by violent miscreants, put other animals as well as people at risk of being victims in the future.

So this right does not limit the right of who can prosecute under the AWA. It is merely an additional power that allows the authorities to do so too. The position of the RSPCA is however somewhat unusual as it is perhaps the best-known animal charity in the world. While conversely in *Line v. RSPCA* [1902] TLR 634 the court held it had no extra powers over the ordinary citizen. Yet like the police it is subject to PACE. In *RSPCA v. Chester Crown Court* [2006] EWHC 1273 it was said with accuracy by Sedley LJ, 'You are in a curious position. You are not a public authority in constitution; you are a charity. But, of course, you do have a statutory position as a prosecutor, which others do not have.'

Coincidentally with uncanny insight Beatson J added, 'You are like the NSPCC in relation to children.'

Animal abuse, which is rife in our society, would go unpunished without the RSPCA. It was started in 1824 by the Reverend Arthur Broome, Richard Martin and William Wilberforce, the slavery reformer. It was granted royal patronage in 1840 by Queen Victoria. In 2011 alone they prosecuted over 1000 people. Without them more animals would suffer more than they already do at our hands.

Time limits for prosecutions

D13 Animal Welfare Act 2006, s.31

(1) Notwithstanding anything in section 127(1) of the Magistrates' Court Act 1980, a magistrates' court may try an information relating to an offence under this Act if the information is laid –

 (a) before the end of the period of three years beginning with the date of the commission of the offence, and

 (b) before the end of the period of six months beginning with the date on which evidence which the prosecutor thinks is sufficient to justify the proceedings comes to his knowledge.

(2) For the purposes of subsection (1)(b) –

 (a) a certificate signed by or on behalf of the prosecutor and stating the date on which such evidence came to his knowledge shall be conclusive evidence of that fact, and

 (b) a certificate stating that matter and purporting to be so signed shall be treated as so signed unless the contrary is proved.

This is one of the most important and equally contentious sections in the AWA. The reason is that it gives a wide power to the prosecutor to take proceedings a long time after the alleged offence, subject to a certificate confirming the view of the evidence by him. While if the defence can raise the issue of the certificate being invalid, then the prosecution is likely to fail from the start or there may be no case to answer. So it has a practical value and effect for both parties.

The usual period of 6 months within which a magistrates' court may try an information does not apply if (a) within 3 years of the commission of the offence; and (b) within 6 months of which time the prosecutor 'thinks' the evidence is sufficient to justify the proceedings comes to his knowledge. The prosecutor must sign a certificate of his subjective belief as to the state of that 'evidence' and its effect. That is then 'conclusive' evidence of that fact. So if the certificate confirms that point and purports to be signed, it will be treated as so unless the contrary is proved.

While it is an unusual provision it is not unknown in different areas that depends upon a lengthy investigation before the evidence gained is strong enough to justify a prosecution. Nevertheless the prosecutor could be challenged and called upon to justify his decision. Therefore the court might raise the issue of the certificate of its own volition though it is more likely to be by the defence. In the latter case they would bear the initial burden of raising the reason why the signature was questionable. Indeed they could do so by expert evidence or on the facts by calling into question the delay during the statutory period.

There are three recent decisions that analyse the subject in considerable detail and are instructive in the court's approach to the validity of a certificate. The decisions resonate with guidance that applies now and in the future for all prosecutions under the AWA.

This provision is particularly pertinent in relation to animal fights as often it will only be possible to prosecute those responsible well after the normal 6 month statutory period as the evidence is only discovered when the investigation is complete. It may relate to telephone records or a video or items only on a computer. For like a paedophile ring or drug dealers, the dog-fighting perpetrators equally communicate covertly and in extreme secrecy. However in relation to those criminal activities, unlike dog fighting, each could be subject to proceedings in the Crown Court and so outside any statutory limits.

D14 Certificate

The function of the certificate is the pulse of a prosecution as animal abuse cases are different than most other criminal offences. They are similar to sexual offences against children in that they often come to light long after the event. Allied to that the discovery of evidence that is sufficient to mount a case is painstaking and delayed too. That was at the root of the issue raised in *RSPCA v. Johnson* [2009] EWHC 2702. This was an appeal by the RSPCA by case stated from the decision of the Consett Magistrates' Court on 30 October 2008. The District Judge refused to hear an information laid by the RSPCA on the basis that it was 'out of time'.

Paul Johnson was charged with an offence of causing unnecessary suffering to a thoroughbred stallion between 11 May and 11 June 2007 in County Durham contrary to section 4(1). The issue raised by Johnson was whether the information and summons dated 11 June 2008 were out of time. On that document the informant was stated to be "RSPCA Inspector Jackman 108 (on behalf of the RSPCA)". The RSPCA relied on the certificate. The Information was laid on 4 June 2008, that is before the end of the period of 6 months from the certified date of 21 December 2007 and thereby within the period provided in 31(1).

In the High Court Pill LJ said, 'I anticipate the respondent's submissions by stating that the relevant date for section 31 purposes was, in his submission, 10 December 2007, from which it would follow that the issue of the summons on 11 June 2008 was out of time...The judge found that Mr Jackman saw an injured horse, Hans Christian, at the farm on 11 June 2007. After examination by a vet the horse was put down 13 June 2007. A chip implanted in the horse's neck indicated, as inquiries with the British Horseracing Authority revealed, that the respondent was the owner of the horse. On interview, on 14 June 2007, Cecil Johnson said that the horse was owned by the respondent who was his son.'

Throughout June, July and August, and later as well at places other than the farm Johnson made concerted efforts to avoid and hide from Mr Jackman. He visited the farm in the course of his duties and contacted various bodies for information about the Johnson including the Department of Work and Pensions.

His visits to the farm continued after the December dates which are critical in his appeal; he visited on 23 January, 31 January, 13 February 2008. Finally on visits to a dental practice which was believed to be owned and operated by the respondent, he saw him on 27 May. Johnson said, "I am not interested in talking to you." Further visits by Jackman were subsequently made.

Pill LJ said, 'In discharging their duties, Inspectors of the Society clearly need to make inquiries. There is a public interest in prosecutions not being started otherwise than on good grounds and there is a public interest in fairness being shown to those whom it is proposed to prosecute...The judge found that there was, on that basis, sufficient evidence that the respondent owned the horse. The judge found that the Society is a body corporate. He concluded, first, that the Society had sufficient knowledge and evidence to issue a process within the usual six-month time limit, that is within six months of 17 June; secondly, he found that the certificate dated 4 June 2008 was a misguided attempt by the Society to extend the time for the issuing of an information. That appears to me to be a finding of bad faith against the Society...

The issues are whether the certificate is conclusive, if not then the judge was right to reach the conclusion he did. If on its face the certificate was conclusive, the judge was still able to investigate whether there had been fraud or an abuse of process. That will often involve, as it does in this case, going behind the certificate to look at the sequence of events. The judge's finding as to whether the certificate was valid on its face is, with respect, not altogether clear. What is clear is that he did go behind it and he found that there had been an abuse of process by the Society. He did so, it would appear, by reference to the delay between 17 June 2007, when the alleged ill-treatment was discovered, and the issue of the information/summons in June 2008.'

The court considered the position of Jason Fletcher, the Prosecution Case Manager for the RSPCA and that at that point on 21 December 2007 did "have sufficient evidence in my possession to justify proceedings in respect of Paul Johnson". So he claimed he complied with section 31.

Pill LJ continued, 'I have referred, in summary form, to the evidence of Mr Jackman and his very considerable efforts to trace and interview the respondent. It was when those were unsuccessful that he took further steps he described by way of letters to other bodies...including the British Horseracing Authority.'

Johnson's position was even if the certificate was on its face sound, there had been an abuse of process, as in effect found by the district judge. Sufficient evidence to justify proceedings had come to the knowledge of the Society as early the summer of 2007.

In the alternative they submitted sufficient knowledge came to prosecutor on 10 December 2007 there being evidence of the RSPCA Chief Inspector Charton knew of Mr Smith's letter dated 5 December on that date. Time began to run on that date, not on the date when the contents of statement were considered and assessed by Mr Fletcher. The documents took 11 days to reach him. Mr Jackman was away sick during at least part of that time.

The court considered several cases where statutory provisions materially identical to those in section 31 and some of the points now in dispute had been raised. In *Morgans v. DPP* [1999] 2 Cr. App. R. 99 Kennedy LJ stated in relation to section 11 of the Computer Misuse Act 1990 "The defendant contends that the words sufficient in the opinion of the prosecutor to warrant the proceedings as merely descriptive of the evidence and that the prosecutor would not have to form his opinion before time begins to run. I accept that submission, because otherwise the prosecutor, in full possession of all relevant information, can prevent time from running simply by not applying his mind to the case."

Kennedy LJ also stated that the provision is an exception to the ordinary rule in section 127(1) and as such "it should be construed strictly".

Similarly in *R. v. Haringey Magistrates' Court ex parte Amvrosiou* [1996] EWHC 14 in relation to section 6 of the Road Traffic Offenders Act 1988, Auld LJ said, "Conclusive evidence means that no contrary evidence will be effective to displace it, unless the so-called conclusive evidence is inaccurate on its face, or fraud can be shown".

In *Burwell v. DPP* [2009] EWHC 1089 Admin it was considered in relation to section 11 of the Computer Misuse Act 1990. Keene LJ stated: "I would emphasise, however, that that does not mean that a prosecutor can simply stall the start of the proceedings, or use a certificate to present a date which is patently misleading. The first exception referred to by Auld LJ would seem to encompass the situation where the certificate plainly (even if honestly) inaccurate, so that the decision of the prosecutor to certify would itself be amenable to challenge by way of judicial review on the usual grounds, or challengeable before the Magistrates' Court as an abuse of their process. But the certificate would have to be plainly wrong. The prosecutor is entitled to a degree of judgment as to when there is sufficient evidence available to warrant a prosecution. That, after all, is the purpose on the face of it of section 11(2)."

Pill LJ having reviewed the relevant authorities and considered the submissions for Johnson said, 'In my judgment there is no defect on the face of the certificate, which is conclusive, subject to arguments which arise in this case as they did in the cases cited, as to abuse of process. The judge found abuse in relation to the period between June 2007 and June 2008. I am unable to accept that any abuse of process is revealed by the conduct of the Society during the period up to the issue of the information. As in the case of *Amvrosiou* much of the delay was caused by the respondent himself. I have already referred to the public interest in careful enquiries being made and the more elusive someone is, the more likely an inspector will want to have the clearest evidence in case some point is taken – and unforeseen. point – by the elusive person when charged. Mr Jackman made very considerable efforts to get to the bottom of things. There was evidence available in the summer of 2007, but no evidence as to how reliable the chip is or the weight which could be attached to whatever information was on it. Mr Jackman acted reasonably, or at any rate not so that he was abusing the process of the court, by trying as he did to interview the respondent, and his considerable efforts having failed, seeking authoritative evidence from sources he consulted at the end of November...

There is no principle of law that knowledge in a prosecutor begins immediately any employee of that prosecutor has the relevant knowledge, and *Donnachie [R (Donnachie) v. Cardiff Magistrates' Court* [2007] EWHC 1846] does not establish one...There is, however, a degree of judgment involved in bringing a prosecution, and knowledge, in my judgment, involves an opportunity for those with appropriate skills to consider whether there is sufficient information to justify a prosecution.

It is in the public interest that prosecutions are brought only upon a consideration of the evidence by an expert mind.

Upon investigation of the circumstances, it appears to me there was no abuse of process in nominating 21 December, the first date on which Mr Fletcher had the information, as the date to be certified for purposes of section 31. Even if contrary to that conclusion, knowledge must relate to a somewhat earlier date, that is a date on 10 December or between 10 December and 21 December, I would hold that, mistaken though it was, the stating of the wrong date did not amount to an abuse of process, having regard to the considerable burden upon a defendant seeking to establish that a prosecutor has acted in that way.

This was a decision that was a small triumph for common sense. The reality of the situation was that Johnson was doing everything possible to avoid detection. As a result the RSPCA had to be sure they both had the right man and had strong enough evidence to convict him. Of that they had to be sure before they charged him. If they acted too soon he might have, as he almost did, escaped his deserts by an unwise decision. If the RSPCA had been at fault then they should have failed. Here the fault lay entirely with the defendant whose determined efforts to escape justice were foiled.

D15 Limitation

Less than 6 months later the same issue in a different form was raised again in the High Court in *RSPCA v. King* [2010] EWHC 637. This was an appeal by case stated from the Portsmouth Magistrates' Court who dismissed 6 summonses against Ian and Kathleen King alleging offences under the AWA. The judge upheld a submission at the close of the prosecution case that there was 'no case to answer' because the information had been laid more than 6 months after the date of the alleged offences and so outside the limitation period prescribed by section 127 of the Magistrates' Court Act 1980. The prosecution sought to rely on section 31 of the AWA 2006 which provides that a certificate is 'conclusive' evidence.

The certificate was similarly signed by Jason Fletcher, the Prosecution Case Manager, for the RSPCA. The copy attached to Fletcher's statement was unsigned. The RSPCA claimed there was 'evidence' (a) in Fletcher's statement of a certificate which complied with section 31 and that, in any event, (b) the statement was itself evidence the proceedings had been commenced in time because, when read with the exhibited document, that evidence was 'sufficient to justify the proceedings' came to the knowledge of the prosecutor on 27 December 2007.

King submitted that the prosecution were not entitled rely upon that statement because (a) Fletcher had not been called to give evidence and (b) the prosecution had not sought to introduce his statement before closing its case. Therefore the court did not have any signed certificate that complied with section 31(2). The respondent also made the point that this was no 'ambush' because they had made clear there was a live issue as to the prosecution's date of knowledge, an issue they had explored in cross-examination of Inspector Jan Edwards, who did give evidence and who was referred to in Fletcher's statement.

The District Judge concluded: "I was of opinion that, the prosecution having failed in presenting its case and before closing the same, and not having applied to reopen the same nor adduce further evidence, to produce a certificate as provided for by section 31(2) of the Act or other evidence to support the contention that the informations were laid before the end of the period of six months...it was not...open to me simply to infer that, when the informations had been laid and summonses issued under the rubber stamp signature of the Head of Legal Services, the requirements of section 31(1) were satisfied. And accordingly, I upheld a defence submission of there being no case to answer on the basis that the prosecution having failed to adduce any evidence in support of section 31(1) of the Act it was not open to me to continue to try the informations they being in essence time-barred."

The District Judge posed 6 questions for the opinion of the High Court. The critical question was: "In light of the signed facsimile copy statement of Mr Jason Fletcher, dated 13 August 2009, should I have accepted that evidence which he, as the 'prosecutor', thought sufficient to justify the proceedings came to his knowledge on 27 December 2007?"

The RSPCA had to accept the exhibit did not comply with section 31 because it was unsigned. However they submitted that section 31(2) does not require that it should be signed before proceedings were commenced, that the statement and the exhibit together constitute a signed certificate within the meaning of section 31(2). They argued that the court should look at the substantive matter and not the form. When the statement was read with the exhibit, it amounts to a certification that the date on which evidence the prosecution thought sufficient to justify proceedings came to his knowledge was 27 December 2007.

On appeal Toulson LJ said, 'I do not accept that argument. Given that a certificate in proper form is conclusive, subject to limited qualifications recognised in the case law, the court should not adopt a loose approach to the formal requirements of the subsection. Keene LJ gave a compelling reason for this approach in *Burwell v. DPP* [2009] EWHC 1069 which turned on a section in the Computer Misuse Act 1990, materially indistinguishable from section 31 of the Animal Welfare Act. He expressed the view that a prosecutor can only avail himself of the benefits of such a certificate if the certificate fully complies with the statutory requirements, and there is good reason for that. A statutory certificate when in proper form forecloses the issue, subject to some limited exceptions. Therefore, there is good reason to require that the certificate should be in proper form.

In this case, when Mr Fletcher signed his statement dated 13 August 2009 he was plainly not purporting to make a certificate under the Act. I regard that as a matter of substance and not merely of form. Good faith requires that somebody signing a certificate under section 31(2) should be applying his mind to what he is doing and should have at that time knowledge of matters which he certifying. In this case Mr Fletcher in his statement was recording a matter of historic fact, namely that several months earlier he had signed a certificate to the same effect summarised in his statement. The two are not the same. Moreover, there is ground to doubt the accuracy of his memory about the signing of that certificate. On the first day of the trial the respondent's counsel had been given by the prosecution, when this point was raised, a copy of a purported certificate in the same form as that exhibited to Mr Fletcher's statement, except that it was dated 8 February and not 29 January 2008. It is evident that when Mr Fletcher's statement was drafted by the solicitor appearing for the prosecution in the magistrates' court, the original draft referred to a certificate dated 8 February 2008 and not 29 January 2008. We know that because Mr Fletcher's statement had a fax which stated: 'Please note the date I signed the letter and the date on the letter are the same, being 29/10/08 and not 8/2/09 as in your draft statement. I am not sure where the date of 8/2 came from but you may wish to call me if there is confusion.'

There was indeed confusion because the letter of 9 February 2009 had been referred to in a schedule of unused material served by the prosecution but there was no reference to a certificate dated 29 January 2008, nor had that ever been shown to the defence. If a letter or certificate dated 29 January 2008 had been signed by Mr Fletcher, it is puzzling why a later certificate in identical form, dated 8 February 2008, should have been prepared under his reference for his signature. All that this goes to show is that there was at least some ground to doubt the accuracy of his memory of events surrounding the signature of a certificate by him early in 2009 at the time when he made his statement in August 2009. Moreover, he had not himself been involved in the investigation, as he stated in his letter. These matters illustrate the point that a person who is signing a certificate intended to have effect under section 30(1), (2) needs to have the relevant facts in mind at the time of making that certificate. They also illustrate the importance of requiring that a document should comply with the statutory requirements in form and in substance before being treated as a statutory certificate.' The appeal was dismissed.

That was the right decision as it put the RSPCA specifically and prosecutors generally on notice that it was essential that they should comply with the strict requirements of the AWA. Those conditions were strict with good reason. For if a certificate was valid even though the prosecution had been guilty of a loose use of language and procedure it would in time lead to a dilution of a provision that would be unfair to a potential defendant. That is why there is a difference under section 18(5) where a vet's certificate can be given orally as that provision is to protect animals in an emergency.

The provision in section 31 allows prosecutors more time but only if they can justify the delay and have not been dilatory in any way. So this decision should serve as a warning to all prosecutors that they fail those they are meant to protect if they in turn fail to see this case as a signpost to good practice. [See **C8**]

D16 Warning

The position of the prosecutor was spelled out in the clearest terms by the High Court in *Lamont-Perkins v. RSPCA* [2012] EWHC 1002. This was an appeal by case stated against two rulings made by HHJ Ambrose sitting at the Crown Court at Gloucester. [See **D12**]

Wyn Williams J said, 'The Appellant appealed against her convictions to the Crown Court. The Appellant did not appeal upon what might be termed the merits.' After dismissing the first ground of appeal as to the status of a 'prosecutor' he turned to the second ground which was a challenge to the RSPCA claiming they did not comply with the requirements of section 31: 'She wished to argue that the certificate issued in this case was wrong when it asserted that the date on which evidence came to prosecutor's knowledge such that the prosecutor thought it sufficient to justify criminal proceedings against the Appellant was 18 March 2008. Ms Howe submits (and submitted before the Crown Court) that the latest date upon which the prosecutor could have thought the evidence sufficient to justify criminal proceedings was 4 September 2007 after the Appellant had been interviewed under caution and informed that she would be reported to the Respondent's head office with a view to prosecution. Accordingly, Ms Howe submits that any certificate should have certified a date no later than 4 September 2007 and any prosecution should have been initiated before midnight on 3 March 2008.

Wyn Williams J analysed the factual and legal position and reviewed all the relevant authorities including *RSPCA v. Johnson* and *RSPCA v. King*.

Having done so His Lordship continued, 'I find it difficult to see how a certificate issued under section 31(2) is susceptible to challenge on the grounds that it is plainly wrong (albeit that the mistake can be innocent) with the suggestion that if it is challenged in the Magistrates' Court it must be challenged on the basis that an abuse of process has occurred in which some form of misconduct is involved. No real difficulty arises if it is challenged by way of judicial review. In such a challenge it would be possible to argue unreasonableness or irrationality, which, in context, would be likely to be very similar to if not identical with the notion that the certificate was plainly wrong. However, to repeat, if the approach in *Azam*, [*Azam v. Epping Forest District Council* [2009] EWHC 1069], is followed a challenge before the Magistrates' Court would appear to require proof of some kind of misconduct.

I acknowledge that this approach is not the one which was suggested as appropriate in *Burwell* and *Azam* and endorsed in *RSPCA v. Johnson*. However, the procedural issues raised in this case were not raised in any of those cases. Further, so far as I am aware, *Atkinson*, [*Atkinson v. DPP* [2004] EWHC 1457] , was not cited in any of those cases. For my part I consider the reasoning in the judgment of Auld LJ in *Atkinson* to be compelling.'

After that rather acute analysis there was a somewhat surprising turn of events. For when they were pressed the RSPCA were compelled to accept they had evidence sufficient to justify proceeding at an earlier date. Wyn Williams J said, 'As things stood at the hearing on the 22 November 2011 there was no obvious reason to conclude that H H Judge Ambrose and the magistrates had erred in law in concluding that a certificate had not been plainly wrong on its face. However, as I have said, there is now evidence available to this court which strongly suggests that the Respondent considered that it had sufficient evidence to justify a prosecution by no later than 8 January 2008. Certainly, there is credible evidence to that effect.

I am prepared to accept that there is at least a strong possibility that should this case be remitted to the Crown Court the court would conclude that the certificate issued by the Respondent was plainly wrong. However, that is not the end of the story. If the certificate is plainly wrong the court will disregard it. Nonetheless it will investigate whether or not the proceedings were brought within the time limit prescribed in section 31(1) of the Act.'

However, there was yet another surprising twist which had not been adumbrated. His Lordship concluded, 'I am not persuaded that the evidence of Mr Burrows would demonstrate that the proceedings brought by the Respondent against the Appellant were issued out of time. Further, I am satisfied that if the Crown Court was called upon to determine whether the proceedings were brought within the time limit specified in section 31(1) of the Act it would conclude that the proceedings were brought within time. H. H. Judge Ambrose must have concluded that the prosecutor was not fixed with the requisite knowledge on or about 4 September 2007. In my judgment, he was entitled to reach that conclusion. A prosecutor must be afforded a reasonable period of time after obtaining the relevant evidence in order to form an opinion about whether the evidence obtained justified a prosecution. There is no evidence available which begins to suggest that the Respondent considered it had sufficient evidence to justify a prosecution upon some dates between 4 September 2007 and 25 October 2007. These proceedings were commenced within six months of 25 October 2007. In my judgment, in these circumstances, no purpose would be served by remitting the case to the Crown Court for further consideration.

I acknowledge that the Appellant has persuaded this court that the procedure for determining the validity of a certificate under section 31(2) of the Animal Welfare Act 2006 is not that which was adopted in the Crown Court. However, there is no material available to this court which persuades me that there is a possibility that the proceedings brought by the Respondent against the Appellant were issued outside the time limit prescribed in section 31(1) of the Animal Welfare Act 2006. In those circumstances, it is appropriate that the convictions recorded against the Appellant should be upheld.'

Before leaving the case Wyn Williams J delivered a direct and stark message to prosecutors for the future. He said, 'This case has highlighted the need for *all* prosecutors to take great care when certifying a date under statutory provisions which have the effect of extending the time limit for bringing criminal proceedings. A prosecutor is exercising a crucial function when certifying such a date and it is incumbent upon the prosecutor to ensure the accuracy of the date.' [emphasis by judge]

For if the prosecutor is less than professional for him it is just another case that fails in embryo. However for society an animal abuser might have avoided a valid charge. That is more than a slight blight on society and the law. Consequently this is a vital provision within the AWA. Without it many cases of animal abuse would go undetected and the victims remain unprotected. Conversely it gives such a wide power to prosecutors it has to be controlled by the court. That fine balance is the reason the court is and remains vigilant. Now the responsibility for the right approach starts and ends with the prosecutors.

D17 *Post-Conviction Powers*

Sections 32 to 45 provide the core punishment and powers following a conviction. They cover all aspects of the AWA from sentence to expenses. In particular these powers govern the subject of disqualification of the defendant from owning or keeping animals. That is a crucial part of the sentence, especially if he has been convicted of any offence involving abuse of an animal or causing it unnecessary suffering. For the purpose of that part of any sentence is to protect the animal and other animals from him in the future. [See Sentencing and SC Guideline: **F1**; **F8**].

Imprisonment or fine

D18   Animal Welfare Act 2006, s.32

(1) A person guilty of an offence under any of sections 4, 5, 6(1) and (2), 7 and 8 shall be liable on summary conviction to –
(a) imprisonment for a term not exceeding 51 weeks, or
(b) a fine not exceeding £20,000, or to both.

(2) A person guilty of an offence under section 9, 13(6) or 34(9) shall be liable on summary conviction to –
(a) imprisonment for a term not exceeding 51 weeks, or

    (b)   a fine not exceeding level 5 on the standard scale, or to both.

(3)   A person guilty of an offence under regulations 12 or 13 shall be liable on summary conviction to such penalty by a way of imprisonment or fine as may be provided by regulations under that section.

(4)   A person guilty of any other offence under this Act shall be liable on summary conviction to –

    (a)   imprisonment for a term not exceeding 51 weeks, or

    (b)   a fine not exceeding level 4 on the standard scale, or to both.

    …

This section separates the seriousness of the offence and provides a sentence that is commensurate with the gravity of the act for which was convicted. For an offence under sections 4 to 8 there is a present maximum of 6 months' imprisonment or a £20,000 fine or both. [The 51 weeks provision has still not been enacted.] They all relate to offences within the prevention of harm category which includes various forms of causing suffering and fighting offences. All those carry the highest sentence as they are concerned with abuse of the animal. The fine is high to reflect that fact, but as a penalty it is rarely a deterrent as the abuse is often linked to profit, be it by gambling or killing or both. Further a fine is rarely paid.

A person guilty of an offence under section 9, 13(6) or 34(9) is subject to the same sentence except it is limited to a fine up to level 5. Those are concerned with failing in a duty of care for the welfare of animals, being involved in an activity without a licence or registration breaching an existing disqualification. It has the advantage of allowing the court to impose both imprisonment and a fine. The latter could be relevant, depending on its value, if the animal is sold or killed. [See **C9**]

A person guilty of an offence under regulation 12 relating to the promotion of welfare is by section 12(4) subject to the same sentence. The reason is that some breaches may be as serious as an offence under section 9 and so warrant the same sentence. Similarly an offence of a breach of a condition under regulation 13 may be subject to the same maximum sentence of imprisonment or a fine by paragraph 9 of Schedule 1. The reason is the same namely the potential seriousness of the abuse. Those sentences emphasise the importance of the offences against the welfare of an animal which is the reason for the existence of the AWA.

A person guilty of any other offence is subject to the same maximum sentence except it is limited to a fine up to level 4. The lower offences attract the lowest sentences and include an obstruction of an inspector and failing to keep records. Of course when that happens there are often more serious offences committed at the same time. Then a sentence for the more serious offence will be imposed to subsume the lesser one.

All the offences are summary only which is a problem within the AWA. That is largely historical as it echoes the POA. However that was introduced in a different climate, legally and socially, as well as a different century. The inherent problem is that the sentences are too low to prevent the prevalence of animal abuse. There is now no reason at all to keep that anachronistic tradition. The position is there are offences, not numerous it is true, but where numerous offences are committed which are so serious only a long custodial sentence is sufficient to mark the gravity of them and to act as a deterrent for others with a similar proclivity. Only the Crown Court could impose an adequate sentence but has no power to do so. That is a glaring inadequacy of the AWA.

Deprivation

D19 Animal Welfare Act 2006, s.33

(1) If the person convicted of an offence under any of sections 4, 5, 6(1) and (2), 7, 8 and 9 is the owner of an animal in relation to which the offence was committed, the court by or before which he is convicted may, instead of or in addition to dealing with him in any other way, make an order depriving him of ownership of the animal and for its disposal.

(2) Where the owner of an animal is convicted of an offence under section 34(9) because ownership of the animal is in breach of a disqualification under section 34(2), the court by or before which he is convicted may, instead of or in addition to dealing with him in any other way, make an order depriving him of ownership of the animal and for its disposal.

(3) Where the animal in respect of which an order under subsection (1) or (2) is made has any dependent offspring, the order may include provision depriving the person to whom it relates of ownership of the offspring and for its disposal.

(4) Where a court makes an order under subsection (1) or (2) it may –

(a) appoint a person to carry out, or arrange for the carrying out of, the order;

(b) require any person who has possession of an animal to which the order applies to deliver it up to enable the order to be carried out;

(c) give directions with respect to the carrying out of the order;

(d) confer additional powers (including power to enter premises where an animal to which the order applies is being kept) for the purpose of, or in connection with, the carrying out of the order;

(e) order the offender to reimburse the expenses of carrying out the order.

(5) Directions under subsection 4(c) may –

(a) specify the manner in which an animal is to be disposed of, or

(b) delegate the decision about the manner in which an animal is to be disposed of to a person appointed under subsection 4(a).

(6) Where a court decides not to make an order under subsection (1) or (2) in relation to an offender, it shall –

(a) give its reasons for the decision in open court, and

(b) if it is a magistrates' court, cause them to be entered in the register of its proceedings.

(7) Subsection (6) does not apply where the court makes an order under section 34(1) in relation to the offender.

(8) In subsection (1), the reference to an animal in relation to which an offence was committed includes, in the case of an offence under section 8, an animal which took part in an animal fight in relation to which the offence was committed.

(9) In this section, references to disposing of an animal include destroying it.

When a person is convicted of an offence under sections 4 to 9 the court can make an order depriving him of ownership of the animal and for its disposal. Deprivation can be an alternative or an additional sentence to imprisonment or a fine. Where the owner of an animal is convicted of an offence under section 34(9) because ownership of the animal is in breach of section 34(2), the court has the same power of deprivation and disposal.

These powers are particularly wide and were introduced to counteract the weakness of the POA. The AWA allows the court to make directions in relation to deprivation of the abused animal. The directions include a 'power of entry' which is essential in such a case. Where a court makes such an order under subsection (1) or (2) it may appoint a person to carry out the directions to give effect to its order. The court can make the offender pay the expenses of the confiscation and of carrying out the order plus any ancillary ones.

The aim of the order is to deprive an owner of the animal. It is limited to cases where there is an identifiable animal that has been abused. That is part of the value of allowing an inspector to 'mark' an animal under section 18(8)(c) and paragraph 10 of Schedule 2. The identification is crucial as otherwise the wrong animal could be subject to an order that affects its present and future. For where the animal has any dependent offspring, the power of deprivation and disposal extends to it too.

The power of disposal includes slaughter of the animal. That may be the only appropriate way of dealing with an animal that has been forced to engage in a fight. Its injuries may be so severe that to allow it to live would only prolong the existing resultant pain.

Deprivation of ownership may be the sentence in its own right. That would be unusual. The normal course for a court would be to subject the defendant to an additional sentence. This aspect goes to the root of the AWA as it is primarily to protect an animal and other animals in the future from the offender. So the existing victim is protected and so too are others who may otherwise be abused by him. So there is an onus on the court to consider an order in every such case under this section. For if it does not do so it has to justify its decision. In that event the court 'shall' give its reasons in open court. That applies to all courts dealing with such a sentence in a case involving an animal. If it is a magistrates' court it also has a duty to record its reasons in the register of its proceedings.

That does not apply where a person is disqualified from owning or keeping animals at all. No reasons are necessary as then the disqualification subsumes the deprivation. For that obviously is harsher and encapsulates deprivation and more as it effectively disqualifies him from dealing with animals at all.

When an animal is the victim of an animal fight under section 8, although that does not constitute direct abuse, it is plainly the case that it could only happen if a human mind is the instigator of the criminal action. The animal is included in the generic reference in subsection (1). It could include a badger or a fox or a stag as it is not limited to a 'protected' animal under section 8(7) which defines an 'animal fight'.

Disposal as a legal concept runs throughout this section and the AWA. Whilst 'disposal' of an animal can mean a simple transfer of ownership to a sanctuary or to another named person, it includes every measure that can be ordered up to and including death.

Disqualification

D20   Animal Welfare Act 2006, s.34

(1)   If a person is convicted of an offence to which this section applies, the court by or before which he is convicted may, instead of or in addition to dealing with him in any other way, make an order disqualifying him under any one or more of subsections (2) to (4) for such period as it thinks fit.

(2)   Disqualification under this subsection disqualifies a person –

    (a)   from owning animals,

(b) from keeping animals,

(c) from participating in the keeping of animals, and

(d) from being party to an arrangement under which he is entitled to control or influence the way in which animals are kept.

(3) Disqualification under this subsection disqualifies a person from dealing in animals.

(4) Disqualification under this subsection disqualifies a person-:

(a) from transporting animals, and

(b) from arranging for the transport of animals.

(5) Disqualification under subsection (2), (3) or (4) may be imposed in relation to animals generally, or in relation to animals of one or more kinds.

(6) The court by which an order under subsection (1) is made may specify a period during which the offender may not make an application under section 43(1) for termination of the order.

(7) The court by which an order under subsection (1) is made may –

(a) suspend the operation of the order pending an appeal, or

(b) where it appears to the court that the offender owns or keeps an animal to which the order applies, suspend the operation of the order, and of any order made under section 35 in connection with the disqualification, for such period as it thinks necessary for enabling alternative arrangements to be made in respect of the animal.

(8) Where a court decides not to make an order under subsection (1) in relation to an offender, it shall –

(a) give its reasons for the decision in open court, and

(b) if it is a magistrates' court, cause them to be entered in the register of its proceedings.

(9) A person who breaches a disqualification imposed by an order under subsection (1) commits an offence.

(10) This section applies to an offence under any of the sections 4, 5, 6(1) and (2), 7, 8, 9 and 13(6) and subsection (9).

Section 34 is intentionally wide especially when compared to the somewhat jejune provision in the POA. It allows a court to disqualify an offender from having any involvement with animals at all. As the period that can be specified is a discretionary power according to the gravity of the offence, it can be any time up to a life ban.

A person convicted of an offence under any of sections 4, 5, 6(1) and (2), 7, 8, 9 and 13(6) may be sentenced by the court to be disqualified for such period as it 'thinks fit'. Those are the main offences under the AWA as they are all within the prevention of harm heading which includes various forms of causing suffering and fighting offences. All those carry the highest sentence as they are concerned with abuse of the animal. It includes a breach of regulation 13. For that can be serious subject to the circumstances.

Disqualification can be an alternative or an additional sentence to imprisonment or a fine. It would be unusual for a sentence to be disqualification alone given the seriousness of the individual offences. An additional power relates to the case of where a person breaches a disqualification. Where the owner of an animal is convicted of an offence under section 34(9) because his ownership of the animal is in breach of section 34(2), the court has the same power of disqualification. Such a breach is not uncommon as where people have an emotional attachment to animals or animals provide their living, they tend to disregard the disqualification. In that event this allows the court to make a further disqualification more severe than the original sentence. Consequently the original sentence could be doubled or extended into a life ban. The court could extend the terms and time of the disqualification, besides imposing any other sentence.

The power of disqualification is so wide it can extend to a person being prevented from having any involvement with animals. That includes not merely owning and keeping animals, but participating in the control of and having any 'dealing' in animals at all. Lest there is any doubt about the width of such a ban it can even include transporting and 'arranging' for the transport of them.

The disqualification under subsections (2), (3) and (4) may be imposed in relation to animals generally, or in relation to animals of one or more kinds. In *Ward v. RSPCA* [2010] EWHC 347 Openshaw J made a salient point about the character of Anthony Ward when the High Court dismissed his appeal. He had been sentenced to a disqualification on two previous occasions. The court included 'cattle' in the order though the unnecessary suffering only related to two ponies. Openshaw J upheld the disqualification in respect of both kinds of animals as the suffering caused by Ward, 'is just as likely to be directed towards his cattle as towards his ponies.' That percipient conclusion confirms the guilt of the person in abusing an animal is the crucial factor not the kind of victim.

Yet it goes even further in that when a person is disqualified under section 34 he can normally apply for the ban to be lifted after one-year from the date of the order. Under 34(6) the court has power to specify a period for which the defendant may not make an application for a termination of the order under section 43(1). So the sentence could disqualify a person for say 10 years and not allow him to apply for a termination for 7 years.

Often there is an emotional aspect to such cases so the offender will lodge an appeal. In that event the court has power to suspend the order. It can also allow the offender time to make arrangements for any animal within the disqualification. While that power is discretionary, it is pertinent to note that otherwise a disqualification is not automatically suspended pending appeal. That is unlike all the other similar orders under the AWA within section 41. For by section 41 all the other relevant orders under sections 33, 35, 37, 38 or 40 are suspended once an appeal has been lodged. Conversely a disqualification can only be suspended pending an appeal by leave of the court. That allows the court to consider whether it would be a wise decision to allow the convicted person to still be in contact with animals and thereby have the opportunity for further abuse. The court would take account of his plea, the evidence and his antecedents.

If he has a violent character, be it towards animals or people, leave should not be granted.

Similar to an order of deprivation, there is an onus on the court to consider disqualification in every case. So where the court decides not to make in order it 'shall' give its reasons for the decision in open court. A magistrates' court must record the reasons and cause them to be entered in the register of its proceedings.

The POA was weak in that it did not allow the court to make orders to protect the welfare of other animals owned or kept by the disqualified person. Moreover it did not allow them to enter land to remove animals that were kept in breach of an order. In *Worcestershire County Council v. Tongue* [2004] EWCA 140 the Court of Appeal criticised this inherent weakness. This section and 35 were introduced to attempt to solve that problem.

That problem appears to be solved as the disqualification extends to all animals he has any dealings with at all. It would include every form of being involved with animals from 'custody' to 'care' in any capacity. That is proof of how wide the power of disqualification is and can be. Given that power the court can invoke the manifest principle of the AWA and protect all protected animals from all abusers.

Seizure of animals in connection with disqualification

D21 Animal Welfare Act 2006, s.35

(1) Where –
  (a) court makes an order under section 34(1), and
  (b) it appears to the court that the person to whom the order applies owns or keeps any animal contrary to the disqualification imposed by the order, it may order that all animals he owns or keeps contrary to the disqualification be taken order, into possession.

(2) Where a person is convicted of an offence under section 34(9) because of owning or keeping an animal in breach of disqualification under section 34(2), the court by or before which he is convicted may order that all animals he owns or keeps in breach of the disqualification be taken into possession.

(3) An order under subsection (1) or (2), so far as relating to any animal owned by the person subject to disqualification, shall have effect as an order for the disposal of the animal.

(4) Any animal taken into possession in pursuance of an order under subsection (1) or (2) that is not owned by the person subject to disqualification shall be dealt with in such manner as the appropriate court may order.

(5) A court may not make an order for disposal under subsection (4) unless –

    (a) it has given the owner of the animal an opportunity to be heard, or

    (b) it is satisfied that it is not reasonably practicable to communicate with the owner.

(6) Where a court makes an order under subsection (4) for disposal of an animal, the owner may –

    (a) in the case of an order made by a magistrates' court, appeal against the order to the Crown Court;

    (b) in the case of an order made by the Crown Court, appeal against the order to the Court of Appeal.

(7) In subsection (4), the reference to the appropriate court is to –

    (a) the court which made the order under subsection (1) or (2), or

    (b) in the case of an order made by a magistrates' court, to a magistrates' court for the same local justice area as that court.

(8) In this section, references to disposing of an animal include destroying it.

Where a court makes a disqualification order, often until that time the owner still has custody or control of the animal in question and sometimes other animals too. So the court has to take account of the position now and in the future. Thus 'all' those he owns or keeps can be taken into possession.

A court has a similar power where a person breaches an existing disqualification. Then when he is convicted again the court may order that all the animals he owns or keeps contrary to the disqualification may be taken into possession.

As with a deprivation order under the AWA, if a person is disqualified when his animals are taken into possession by a court order, then under section 35(3) it 'shall' have effect as an order for disposal of the animal. That includes, if necessary, killing them.

As all aspects of the welfare of the animal has to be considered by the court, it has to consider those which have been seized by a court order, but do not belong to the defendant or persons subject to the disqualification. Indeed the offence could have been committed without the owner's agreement or even knowledge. In that event the court has power to deal with it in 'such manner' as the appropriate court may order. That allows for the position where there may be an appeal. The 'appropriate' court is the one that made the order or if it was a magistrates' court, then it is one in the same local justice area.

As the court is dealing with the life and death of an animal who may be seen in emotional or financial terms, the court has to be aware of proprietary rights in it. To that extent a court cannot make a disposal under section 35(4) unless it has given the owner an opportunity to be heard. That is subject to discovering his whereabouts. In these days of technology that can track a person's movements this side of death, it would not seem to present a problem for the court to communicate with the owner. That places a burden on the court which would have to be discharged if they act without such consent or hearing his objection. However the animal's welfare is the primary consideration. So the court can act if it is satisfied it is not reasonably practicable to communicate with the owner.

Allied to that power, the person who is deprived of his animal by the disposal under section 35(4) has a right of appeal. If it was the magistrates' court it is to the Crown Court. If it was the Crown Court it is to the Court of Appeal. Consequently so there is a consistency between deprivation and disqualification the reference to 'disposal' of an animal includes killing it.

171

A court can combine a disqualification order with an order that any other animals he has may be seized too where continued ownership or possession would put him in breach of that order. Hence if he is convicted of an abuse under section 4 and disqualified for life or 10 years in respect of all or specified animals, others within that category or generally would be seized too as otherwise he would be in an immediate breach of the order.

In a similar situation if a person subject to a disqualification is found to be in possession of other animals they would be seized for the same reason. To that extent this provision is wider than a deprivation order under section 33 as that can only be made in relation to a convicted person. Under section 35 a seizure can be made against a person by virtue of the fact he is keeping animals in breach of that order.

A further distinction is that under section 33(2) the owner does not retain an economic interest in the animal. Under section 35(1) or (2) he is entitled to be given the 'disposal' proceeds less any expenses. It seems strange that the person who abused the animal may also profit from its death, especially given that he could have been the one that caused the suffering or been instrumental in the resultant abuse.

As a result, when an animal is seized because of the fact a person is disqualified it is automatically subject to disposal. A peculiar lacuna arises however in that under section 34 he has no immediate suspension pending appeal. He would need leave from the court. Notwithstanding that position, as the animal is seized under section 35, an appeal results in the order being suspended under section 41.

172

Section 35: supplementary

D22   Animal Welfare Act 2006, s.36

(1)   The court by which an order under section 35 is made may –

 (a)   appoint a person to carry out, or arrange for the carrying out of, the order;

 (b)   require any person who has possession of an animal to which the order applies to deliver it up to enable the order to be carried out;

 (c)   give directions with respect to the carrying out of the order;

 (d)   confer additional powers (including power to enter premises where an animal to which the order applies is being kept) for the purpose of, or in connection with, the carrying out of the order;

 (e)   order the person subject to disqualification, or another person, to reimburse the expenses of carrying out the order.

(2)   Directions under subsection 1(c) may –

 (a)   specify the manner in which an animal is to be disposed of, or

 (b)   delegate the decision about the manner in which an animal is to be disposed of to a person appointed under subsection (1)(a).

(3)   In determining how to exercise its powers under section 35 and this section, the court shall have regard, amongst other things, to –

 (a)   the desirability of protecting the value of any animal to which the order applies, and

 (b)   the desirability of avoiding increasing any expenses which a person may be ordered to reimburse.

(4) In determining how to exercise a power delegated under section (2)(b), a person shall have regard, amongst other things, to the things mentioned in subsection (3)(a) and (b).

(5) If the owner of an animal ordered to be disposed of under section 35 is subject to a liability by virtue of subsection (1)(e), any amount to which he is entitled as a result of sale of the animal may be reduced by an amount equal to that liability.

Plainly a court cannot merely make the order *per se*. To have effect it has to arrange for it to be executed. So the court has extensive powers to arrange for a person to carry out the order made under section 35. All those points are covered in section 36. The supplementary provisions are in fact and effect similar to those relating to the deprivation orders under section 33. To that end those provisions allow the court to appoint a person to carry out the order and give directions to enable it to be done. It also provides a power of entry which is essential for the person appointed to fulfil his duty.

As the court has to take into account the 'value' of an animal it may make an order disposing of it, the monetary aspect is important. The court has to exercise the power so 'any amount' the owner is entitled to as a result of the sale may be reduced by that sum if he is liable under section 36(5). That ensures whatever pain the animal has endured is balanced by the gain to the owner.

The offender or 'another person' can be ordered under section 36(1)(e) to reimburse the costs incurred. That other person, as he is not subject to a disqualification, must have some culpability or liability for or towards the animal. So while he may not have directly committed the offence he must have a responsibility that should reflect his contribution to the expenses. If it were otherwise, the court would be making a decision that could be open to challenge. Indeed in that event it would be a more expensive route to an appeal by that 'another' person.

Destruction in the interests of the animal

D23   Animal Welfare Act 2006, s.37

(1) The court by or before which a person is convicted of an offence under any of the sections 4, 5, 6(1) and (2), 7, 8(1) and (2) and 9 may order the destruction of an animal in relation to which the offence was committed if it is satisfied, on the basis of evidence given by a veterinary surgeon, that it is appropriate to do so in the interests of the animal.

(2) A court may not make an order under subsection (1) unless –

(a) it has given the owner of the animal an opportunity to be heard, or

(b) it is satisfied that it is not reasonably practicable to communicate with the owner.

(3) Where a court makes an order under subsection (1), it may –

(a) appoint a person to carry out, or arrange for the carrying out of, the order;

(b) require a person who has possession of the animal to deliver it up to enable theorder to be carried out;

(c) give directions with respect to the carrying out of the order (including directions about how the animal is to be dealt with until it is destroyed);

(d) confer additional powers (including power to enter premises where the animal is being kept) for the purpose of, or in connection with, the carrying out of the order;

(e)   order the offender or another person to reimburse the expenses of carrying out the order.

(4)   Where a court makes an order under subsection (1), each of the offender and, if different, the owner of the animal may –

(a)   in the case of an order made by a magistrates' court, appeal against the order to the Crown Court;

(b)   in the case of an order made by the Crown Court, appeal against the order to the Court of Appeal.

(5)   Subsection (4) does not apply if the court by which the order is made directs that it is appropriate in the interests of the animal that the carrying out of the order should not be delayed.

(6)   In subsection (1), the reference to an animal in relation to which an offence was committed includes, in the case of an offence under section 8(1) or (2), an animal which took part in an animal fight in relation to which the offence was committed.

Under section 37 the court has to consider the position where an animal is so abused it may be in its 'interests' to be killed. That could be the result of the direct abuse by the perpetrator or as a result of injuries sustained in fighting, usually arranged by the owner and his accomplices. However the crucial point is it has to be on the evidence of a vet. The meaning of who is a vet is defined under section 62(1). After all the animal is going to be killed, so plainly it is axiomatic it has to be as a result of a person with relevant professional knowledge and expertise.

So if a person is convicted of an offence under any of the sections of 4, 5, 6(1) and (2), 7, 8(1) and (2) and 9, the court may order the destruction of the animal to which the offence was committed if it is satisfied 'on the basis of evidence given by a vet', that it is appropriate to do so in the interests of the animal. As it is evidence given by the vet it should be in open court. Then that allows it to be challenged by the owner. Of course the court is also under a duty to be 'satisfied' so it should be exacting on behalf of the animal. For it may be there is no cross-examination, no opposition and no one to counter the claim for destruction on behalf of the animal.

As it is so final and an order, if it is executed, cannot be reversed, there are strict limits to the order especially as it is in the interests of the animal to die. So a court may not make such an order unless it gives the owner an opportunity to be heard. That can be overcome if it is not practicable to communicate with him. It would be hard for a court to justify that position as in these days of advanced technology it should be relatively easy to contact someone, whether they are deliberately evading contact or not.

Of course the simple fact is that often the abuser of the animal will have no interest in whether the animal lives or dies. Equally he may have conveniently become incommunicado in order to escape prosecution or further costs. He may not even be the person who was convicted of the offence in question. In that event the court would only hear the unchallenged evidence of the prosecution expert. That is contrary to the adversarial system as well as the ultimate interests of the animal. It is yet another reason that proves those interests could only fairly and properly be considered by the court if the victim was represented by an independent body such as an ombudsman for animals or at least an advocate as a 'friend' of the animal. That would aid the court too in coming to the right and reasoned decision.

Where the court makes an order for destruction it has the same powers as under sections 33 to appoint a person to carry out the directions of the court. That also ensures the owner or person responsible, if they are different persons, would be liable to pay the expenses incurred in carrying out he court order. Where the court makes an order for destruction the offender and the owner, if different, may appeal from the magistrates' court to the Crown Court and from the Crown Court to the Court of Appeal.

It includes sections 8(1) and (2) because like the power in relation to deprivation, it applies to an animal that was in a 'fight'. It is for the same reason namely that an animal may be so badly injured by being the victim in a fight that it is in its interests to put it 'out of its misery' by killing it. That applies to any animal, not merely a protected one, by virtue of the definition of an 'animal fight' under section 8(7). Indeed it includes a fight with a human.

There is a somewhat unusual section in 37(5) which states subsection (4) does not apply if the court directs that it is in the interests of the animal that the carrying out of the order 'should not be delayed'. That section that takes special account of the state of the animal as it may be suffering as a result of a failure of his duty to an animal or in a road traffic accident or a fight or abuse. The advantage for the animal is that the court is charged with only making such an order if it is appropriate in the interests of the animal. Moreover it can only do so if it is satisfied on the 'evidence' of a vet. That needs positive evidence to support a negative conclusion for the animal.

The problem that would arise is where the expert evidence is challenged. It would have to be fairly exact evidence for a court to rely upon it to exclude any possible appeal. The fact the section may exclude the ordinary avenue of appeal would not exclude the route of case stated or judicial review. For if it is a question of life and death, the High Court should intervene to assume and become a voice for the legally voiceless.

Destruction of animals involved in fighting offences

D24   Animal Welfare Act 2006, s.38

(1)   The court by or before which a person is convicted of an offence under section 8(1) or (2) may order the destruction of an animal in relation to which the offence was committed on grounds other than the interests of the animal.

(2)   A court may not make an order under subsection (1) unless –

(a)   it has given the owner of the animal an opportunity to be heard, or

(b)   it is satisfied that it is not reasonably practicable to communicate with the owner.

(3)   Where a court makes an order under subsection (1), it may –

(a)   appoint a person to carry out or arrange for the carrying out of, the order;

(b)   require a person who has possession of the animal to deliver it up to enable the order to be carried out;

(c)   give directions with respect to the carrying out of the order (including directions about how the animal is to be dealt with until it is destroyed);

(d)   confer additional powers (including power to enter premises where the animal is being kept) for the purpose of, or in connection with, the carrying out of the order;

(e)   order the offender or another person to reimburse the expenses of carrying out the order.

(4)   Where a court makes an order under subsection (1) in relation to an animal which is owned by a person other than the offender, that person may –

(a)   in the case of an order made by a magistrates'
        court, appeal against the order to the Crown
        Court;

(b)   in the case of an order made by the Crown Court,
        appeal against the order to the Court of Appeal.

(5)   In subsection (1), the reference to an animal in relation
        to which the offence was committed includes an
        animal which took part in an animal fight in relation to
        which the offence was committed.

This is a somewhat startling section in that it could effectively
exclude the main impetus and protection under section 37. For by
section 38(1) a court may, if a person is convicted of an offence
under section 8(1) or (2), order the destruction of the animal on
'grounds other than the interests of the animal'.

The immediate problem with that section is that it potentially
allows a court to completely override the 'interests' of the animal.
Given that the animal would have been involved in 'fighting' at
the instigation of humans it is hardly reasonable to kill it against
its own interests. Yet the court has the power to make such an
order. There is a restriction on the court in that it cannot do so
unless the owner is given the opportunity to be heard. That can
be overridden if the court is satisfied that it is not reasonably
practicable to communicate with the owner. But what if the
owner has deliberately absented himself in order to avoid
detection? Or absconds during the trial as the evidence unfolds
with the inevitable verdict looming, so as to avoid a sentence?
Who then attends to the interests of the animal?

How effective that restriction is can be seen by the very fact the
owner may be the perpetrator, but has escaped conviction. He
may have spent time and money training the animal to fight.
Hence he is unlikely to want to be found let alone seek an
opportunity to be heard.

Consistent with the same provision under sections 33 and 37 where a court makes an order it may appoint a person to carry out the order and give directions to that end. Similarly it may make the offender pay the expenses of those carrying out the order.

There is a further restriction on the order where the owner of the animal, if he is not the offender, has a right of appeal. In that event he can appeal from the Magistrates court to the Crown Court. If it is in the Crown Court then he can appeal to the Court of Appeal.

The inherent problem of this aspect of the Act is that the AWA was introduced to give vent to the welfare of the animals. That is the cornerstone and core of the AWA. It is reflected throughout in the powers of those investigating offences and those making orders against the offenders. However here the welfare of the animal could be overridden if it is considered to be for example very dangerous or particularly aggressive and so could harm other humans particularly children, if it is allowed to live. The problem of course is its 'character' may have been formed and manipulated by the owner and others whose interests are precisely against the interests of and welfare of the animal. [See **G36**]

The grounds that relate to 'other' than the interests of the animal can apply to one that is a danger to public safety. While there are other sections of the AWA that deal with 'fighting offences', they are mainly aimed at the criminals and only indirectly concerned with the animal in terms of its welfare. So if it is to be killed, the burden of death is for its own benefit. However this section gives a discretionary power to the court to destroy the animal even if it is against its interests.

By comparison with section 37 where in dealing with the same issue, the one who caused the suffering also causes the death, be that person the owner or offender, can appeal. Yet the animal has no legal representation to resist that human action. Perversely then it can only be taken on the evidence of a vet. What evidence does the court rely on in this case on behalf of the animal? Moreover, while there is a general right of appeal to the Crown Court and the Court of Appeal, who would know or care enough to even lodge an appeal? It is a flaw in the law that gainsays the ethos of the AWA.

Reimbursement of expenses relating to animals involved in fighting offences

D25   Animal Welfare Act 2006, s.39

(1) The court by or before which a person offence is convicted of an offence under section 8(1) or (2) may order the offender or another person to reimburse any expenses incurred by the police in connection with the keeping of an animal in relation to which the offence was committed.

(2) In subsection (1), the reference to an animal in relation to which the offence was committed includes an animal which took part in a fight in relation to which the offence was committed.

There are considerable expenses involved in the investigation of and prosecution of offences involving animals. The reasons are often a variety of authorities will be involved including the local council, the RSPCA, perhaps the Fire Service, the Health and Safety Officer, the police and expert evidence in the form of experts and vets. It also tends to be a continuing and prolonged investigation given the powers of those investigating it and the problem in obtaining evidence. One of the major obstacles in that respect is that the victim of any offence is both vulnerable and voiceless, so suffer in silence.

In *Gray v. RSPCA* [2010] the total cost to the RSPCA in investigating the *'Hell Farm'* run by the Gray family was approximately £1 million. [See **B7; B9**] As a result the costs are usually disproportionately high in relation to the conviction. So when offences are prosecuted and result in a conviction the offender can be subject to payment, as well as any other sentence, of the costs and expenses relating to the animal. That includes pre-trial, during it and after the sentence. A claim can be made where the offender or owner is convicted. While this is specifically relating to fighting there is a similar provision that could be used in sections 33, 36, 37, 38 and 41.

Similarly specifically in relation to animals involved in fighting, the court may order the offender or 'another' person to reimburse the expenses incurred by the police in connection with the keeping of an animal that is the subject of the offence under section 8(1) or (2). Who is the 'another' person is not defined, but as he is not he offender, any expenses would have to be both balanced and fair. [See **D22**]

The expenses borne by the police could be higher than usual for food and kennelling as it includes an animal which 'took part' in a fight in relation to which the offence was committed. It is not limited to that animal as, subject to the offences and circumstances, under section 18 any offspring and progeny may also be 'taken into possession'. Other animals he owned or kept may also have been seized under section 35 if he was disqualified for the fighting offence. In relation to those expenses it is also pertinent that the police then have a duty under section 9 to care for the welfare of any animals in their custody.

Forfeiture of equipment used in offences

D26   Animal Welfare Act 2006, s.40

(1)   Where a person is convicted of an offence under any of sections 4, 5, 6(1) and (2), 7 and 8, the court by or before which he is convicted may order any qualifying item which is shown to the satisfaction of the court to relate to the offence to be –
    (a)   forfeited, and
    (b)   destroyed or dealt with in such manner as may be specified in the order.

(2)   The reference in subsection (1) to any qualifying item is –
    (a)   in the case of a conviction for an offence under section 4, to anything designed or adapted for causing suffering to an animal;
    (b)   in the case of a conviction for an offence under section 5, to anything designed or adapted for carrying out a prohibited procedure on an animal;
    (c)   in the case of a conviction for an offence under section 6(1) or (2), to anything designed or adapted for removing the whole or any part of a dog's tail;
    (d)   in the case of a conviction for an offence under section 7, to anything designed or adapted for administering any drug or substance to an animal;
    (e)   in the case of a conviction for an offence under section 8(1) or (2), to anything designed or adapted for use in connection with an animal fight;
    (f)   in the case of a conviction for an offence under section 8(3), to a video recording of an animal fight, including anything on or in which the recording is kept.

(3) The court shall not order anything to be forfeited under a subsection (1) if a person claiming to be the owner of it or otherwise interested in it applies to be heard by the court, unless he has been given an opportunity to show cause why the order should not be made.

(4) An expression used in any of paragraphs (a) to (f) of subsection (2) has the same meaning as in the provision referred to in that paragraph.

There is no purpose in prosecuting a person under the AWA and allowing him to have the apparatus to continue to commit offences of a similar nature in the future. As often a perpetrator will use equipment to train the animal to become aggressive or vicious, or may use equipment to abuse the animal. So this is a section which is wide in that it allows the court, where a person is convicted under sections 4, 5, 6, 7 and 8, the court may order 'any qualifying' item which shown to the satisfaction of the court to relate to the offence to be forfeited and disposed of or destroyed.

What is a qualifying item is wide in its possible construction and includes anything and everything that is designed or adapted for committing the offence within the various forms covered in sections 4 to 8. That would include all the paraphernalia used by the amateur and professional animal abuser. So it could be any apparatus that is used for tail docking, mutilation, poisons, fighting and causing suffering to an animal. As the offences can be an attempt, the items do not have to have been used merely 'designed or adapted' for that illegal purpose.

Given that it could be an offence that is committed by a person who is not the owner of the animal, similarly he may be unaware his equipment was used. So the court 'shall not' order anything to be forfeited if a person claiming to be the owner or 'otherwise interested in it' applies to be heard by the court, where he has shown 'cause' why the order should not be made. The fact someone may have an interest in it could include a bank or an employer or a finance company. As the person claiming the interest has to show 'cause' there is an evidential burden on him to prove his claim and that it would be wrong to forfeit it. That evidential shift is consistent with established principles.

The person claiming the interest in the equipment would not tend to be the offender or liable in some way. For if he was culpable any qualifying items would be liable to be forfeited under the AWA and other Acts such as the Powers of Criminal Courts (Sentencing) Act 2000 section 143 as part of his criminal enterprise. In that case his culpability would destroy his ability to show cause.

Orders under section 33, 35, 37, 38 or 40: pending appeals

D27   Animal Welfare Act 2006, s.41

(1)   Nothing may be done under an order under sections 33, 35, 37 or 38 with respect to an animal or an order under section 40 unless –
   (a)   the period for giving notice of appeal against the order has expired,
   (b)   the period for giving notice against the conviction on which the order was made has expired, and
   (c)   if the order or conviction is the subject of an appeal, the appeal has been determined or withdrawn.

(2)   Subsection (1) does not apply to an order under section 37(1) if the order is the subject of a direction under subsection (5) of that section.

(3)   Where the effect of an order is suspended under subsection (1) –

(a) no requirement imposed or directions given in connection with the order shall have effect, but

(b) the court may give directions about how any animal to which the order applies is to be dealt with during the suspension.

(4) Directions under subsection 3(b) may, in particular –

(a) authorise the animal to be taken into possession;

(b) authorise the removal of the animal to a place of safety;

(c) authorise the animal to be cared for either on the premises where it was being kept when it was taken into possession or at some other place;

(d) appoint a person to carry out, or arrange for the carrying out, of the directions;

(e) require any person who has possession of the animal to deliver it up for the purposes of the directions;

(f) confer additional powers (including power to enter premises where the animal is being kept) for the purpose of, or in connection with, the carrying out of the directions;

(g) provide for the recovery of any expenses in relation to removal or care of the animal which are incurred in carrying out the directions.

(5) Any expenses a person is directed to pay under subsection (4)(g) shall be recoverable summarily as a civil debt.

(6) Where the effect of an order under section 33 is suspended under subsection (1) the person to whom the order relates may not sell or part with any animal to which the order applies.

(7) Failure to comply with subsection (6) is an offence.

As the powers under the AWA are wide and orders may be made which are against the interests of the animals or the offender or the owner, the orders have to be subject to any pending appeals. Therefore an order under sections 33, 35, 37 or 38 with respect to an animal or section 40 for equipment cannot be enforced if there is time for an appeal or one is pending. In that event it is temporarily suspended until either the period for an appeal has expired or the appeal has been determined or withdrawn.

There is an important exception in section 41(2) in that that limit does not apply if the order is subject to a direction under section 37(5). That relates to where the order directs that the animal is destroyed and it is in the interests of the animal that its death should not be 'delayed'. That would be extreme as, unlike section 38, that relates to a case where it is for the benefit of the injured animal that it is killed.

Sometimes the court will suspend the order, on application, until the result of a pending appeal. In that event the requirements and directions relating to it are also suspended. The court can however make directions in respect of the animal which is the subject of the suspension. That ensures the welfare of the animal is taken into account regardless of how long it takes to list the appeal. For meanwhile, though it may not be critical, the animal may nevertheless need veterinary treatment.

In respect of any directions under subsection 3(b) the court may make detailed directions in relation to the animal taken into possession including appointing a person to carry out the order. Given that the appeal may be delayed and the main exhibit is an animal the expenses continue to mount up for food and safety and shelter plus treatment. So the court can ensure that all the attendant expenses relating to the 'removal' and 'care' of the animal are recovered.

Given that the expenses relate to a criminal conviction, it might be considered that the provision would have a similar sanction. However that is not the case. For any expenses a person is directed to pay is recoverable as a civil debt. That has the advantage of being able to be recovered by bailiffs and by the sale of property and ultimately through the defendant's earnings.

When a person is subject to a deprivation order there is often an inclination to simply transfer or sell the animal in question. Many abusers simply part with the animal to another member of the family or a man they met in the pub or a friend of a friend whose name they cannot now recall. Or as sometimes happens the dog somehow mysteriously runs off and is never seen again as in *R. v. Richards* [2008] EWCA Crim 1427. The order cannot be defeated in that way for two reasons. If there is an order under section 33 and the effect is suspended, the person may not 'sell or part with' any animal to which the order applies. If he fails to do so and does breach that order, then under subsection (7) he commits another offence.

Unlike all the orders which are automatically suspended pending the appeal being determined, a disqualification order is not within that category. So an application has to be actually made by the appellant which the court, under section 34, can grant or refuse. That is a prudent course as it puts the onus on the offender to apply, given that he is the abuser. Sometimes the court will suspend the order, on application, until the result of a pending appeal. In that event the requirements and directions relating to it are also suspended. The court can however make directions in respect of the animal which is the subject of the suspension. That ensures the welfare of the animal is taken into account regardless of how long it takes to list the appeal. For meanwhile, at best though it may not be critical, the animal may nevertheless need veterinary treatment. At worst its condition may be critical so its death should not be delayed.

An unusual aspect of this area is that if a ban is not suspended and so remains, the appellant could breach the existing order by continuing to 'deal' with animals while disqualified. That is an offence under section 34(9) in relation to any other animals he owns or keeps contrary to the disqualification. Consequently they can be seized under section 35. So a disqualified person, who would usually be a convicted abuser, retains a right to the animals until his appeal is determined. As that is automatically suspended under this section it is contrary to the name and spirit of the AWA.

Orders with respect to licences

D28   Animal Welfare Act 2006, s.42

(1)   If a person is convicted of an offence under any of sections 4, 5, 6(1) and (2), 7 to 9, 11 and 13(6), the court by or before which he is convicted may, instead of or in addition to dealing with him in any other way –

    (a)   make an order cancelling any licence held by him;

    (b)   make an order disqualifying him, for such period as it thinks fit, from holding a licence.

(2)   Disqualification under subsection (1)(b) may be imposed in relation to licences generally or in relation to licences of one or more kinds.

(3)   The court by which an order under subsection (1)(b) is made may specify a period during which the offender may not make an application under section 43(1) fortermination of the order.

(4)   The court by which an order under subsection (1) is made may suspend the operation of the order pending an appeal.

There is little sense in convicting a person of an offence of causing an animal unnecessary suffering for example and yet still allowing him to continue to trade under any licence he possesses. If that were so he might just continue with any abuse. So where a person is convicted under sections of 4, 5, 6, 7 to 9, 11 and 13(6), the court may instead of or in addition to any sentence it imposes, it has extra powers. The court can cancel 'any licence' held by him and disqualify him for a period from even holding a licence.

The disqualification imposed under the section may be in relation to licences generally or to one or more kinds. For besides trading in animals, he may be a show judge of animals, may run a farm and may breed animals for sale. All of those activities could be curbed and controlled by the court.

As they apply to the main sections 4 to 8 which cover unnecessary suffering and abuse in various forms, it also relates to the welfare of the animal under section 9 and transferring an animal as a prize under section 11, it allows the court to control all such activities.

As with a disqualification under the other sections of the AWA, the court may specify a period during which the offender cannot apply for termination of the order under section 43(1). Nevertheless the court may 'suspend' the operation of the order pending appeal. That would be unlikely if there was a blatant breach of the animal's welfare or even less likely if he has antecedents for animal abuse. Moreover if an appeal is lodged it can be listed quickly so a suspension would be unnecessary. That approach would be consistent with the principle of the AWA and the paramount protection of protected animals.

Termination of disqualification under section 34 or 42

D29 Animal Welfare Act 2006, s.43

(1) A person who is disqualified by virtue of an order under section 34 or 42 may apply to the appropriate court for the termination of the order.

(2) No application under subsection (1) may be made –

    (a) before the end of the period of one year beginning with the date on which the order is made;

    (b) where a previous application under that subsection has been made in relation to the same order, before the end of the period of one year beginning with the date on which the previous application was determined, or

    (c) before the end of any period specified under section 34(6), 42(3) or subsection (5) below in relation to the order.

(3) On an application under subsection (1), the court may –

    (a) terminate the disqualification,

    (b) vary the disqualification so as to make it less onerous, or

    (c) refuse the application.

(4) When determining an application under subsection (1), the court shall have regard to the character of the applicant, his conduct since the imposition of the disqualification and any other circumstances of the case.

(5) Where the court refuses an application under subsection (1), it may specify a period during which the applicant may not make a further application under that subsection in relation to the order concerned.

(6) The court may order an applicant under subsection (1) to pay all or any part of the costs of the application.

(7) In subsection (1), the reference to the appropriate court is to –

   (a) the court which made the order under section 34 or 42, or

   (b) in the case of an order made by a magistrates' court, to a magistrates' court acting for the same local justice area as that court.

In many cases where a disqualification is imposed a person affected will lose his livelihood. The cases vary and are usually fact-specific. Generally the sentences often appear to be particularly lenient, depending on the circumstances of the offence. In *R. v. Wilson* Evening Post 7/1/09 the defendant who beat his pet dog and almost poisoned it to death by feeding it alcohol was disqualified for a year. In *R. v. Bale* the famous case of the woman who was caught on the internet when she caught the cat she had been stroking by the scruff of the neck and abandoned it in a dustbin for 15 hours, was disqualified for 5 years. Similarly in *Ward v. RSPCA* [2010] EWHC 347 a farmer who had two previous convictions, on his third conviction for abusing animals was only disqualified for 10 years from having ponies and cattle. Ward could not apply for a termination of the order for 3 years. [See **F1**]

While the power is wide a person who is disqualified can apply for a termination of the order. No application can be made until at least after a year from the date of the order. That would not apply if the court directed a period above that before he could apply under section 34(6). Then he would have to appeal initially in the usual way. If that succeeds he could apply within that time scale providing it is not more than a year. If so, he would have to wait until that period passes.

When an application is made the court may terminate the disqualification. Alternatively it may vary it by making it 'less onerous'. The court could refuse the application. In that event a person can re-apply after a further year has passed.

How a person acts and reacts to any disqualification can be decisive in such an application. For by section 43(4) when the court considers an application it shall have regard to the 'character' of the applicant, his conduct since the disqualification and any other circumstances of the case. That spells out the importance of character which is often significant in cases of animal abuse. For there is a clear connection between animal cruelty and child cruelty, plus those who are cruel to animals as children often become serious criminals who use violence on people. On 18 August 2012 a boy put a neighbour's cat in a microwave oven. As the boy was only 8-years-old he was below the age of criminal responsibility. However he is a potentially dangerous child who with time may become more violent. The subject is analysed with striking examples in *Cruelty to Animals and Interpersonal Violence* [1998] by R. Lockwood and F. Ascione. So this somewhat prescient provision would allow the court to take into account his 'character' in the criminal sense, particularly given the wide interpretation given to what constitutes a propensity for violence under the CJA 2003. It is an additional protection to animals which was foreshadowed in earlier legislation but never referred to specifically. The result is a rapist or a wife-batterer or a child abuser has a relevant bad character. He is the kind of character from whom people and animals need protection. [See *Animals and Children caught in a Cycle of Cruelty*: JP: 2004.]

That would be a reason to refuse the application, but there is no power to vary it by making it more onerous. The answer if a person breached the order would be to charge him with an offence and upon conviction the 'character' of the defendant and his antecedents would be taken into account. That would justify a longer ban and no application for a termination of it for given term. Indeed it should *per se* justify a longer sentence.

In fact the powers relating to disqualification are so wide if the court refuses an application for termination, it may specify a period during which a person may not make a 'further' application. That is an extension of the court's power to take into account the matters referred to section 43(4) too. For if his character is in issue or his 'conduct' or 'any other circumstances', the court could prevent him from reapplying again. Then he would serve the whole period of disqualification, which of course at worst could be for life. Indirectly it could be more onerous as if he was initially say banned for 10 years and could not apply for 2 years for a termination. If his application was rejected, the court could order that no subsequent application can be made for a further 5 years. So by subsection (5) it effectively becomes a minimum period of 7 years.

The court has power to make him pay all or any part of the costs of the application. That does not depend on the success or failure of the application. Although failure may result in the court considering it was a frivolous application, that is something that could be considered by the court. Nevertheless it could be ordered even if it was successful as after all, the ban was only imposed because he was convicted. Therefore the application springs from his criminal conduct towards an animal.

The 'appropriate' court at which the application should be made is to the court that made the order under section 34 or 42. If it was a magistrates' court it has to be one in the same local justice area. That has the advantage of local knowledge by the court.

Orders made on conviction for reimbursement of expenses

D30   Animal Welfare Act 2006, s.44

Where an order is made under section 33(4)(e), 36(1)(e), 37(3)(e), 38(3)(e) or 39(1), the expenses that are required by the order to be reimbursed shall not be regarded for the purposes of the Magistrates' Court Act 1980 as a sum adjudged to be paid by a summary conviction, but shall be recoverable summarily as a civil debt.

Throughout the AWA there are provisions for making people pay for the expenses incurred in looking after animals that are affected by the acts of owners or others. Although the expenses so incurred follow a summary criminal conviction, the sums specified 'shall' be recoverable as a civil debt. Therefore no criminal sanctions follow or flow from such an order.

That has the advantage of being able to be recovered by bailiffs or a court order against the goods and property of the convicted person, compared to a fine which can be simply discharged by a short prison term. The civil debt is a more effective method of enforcement.

Under the provisions specified in sections 33 and 36 to 39 a person can be ordered to pay the expenses of the orders in relation to the offences. That would include deprivation and caring for and looking after the abused animal. All those expenses can be recovered in the same way.

Orders for reimbursement of expenses: right of appeal for non-offenders

D31   Animal Welfare Act 2006, s.45

(1)   Where a court makes an order to which this section applies, the person against whom the order is made may –

(a) in the case of an order made by a magistrates' court, appeal against the order to the Crown Court;

(b) in the case of an order made by the Crown Court, appeal against the order to the Court of Appeal.

(2) This section applies to –

(a) an order under section 36(1)(e) against a person other than the person subject to disqualification, and

(b) an order under section 37(3)(e), 38(3)(e) and 39(1) against a person other than the offender.

Given the power to make such an order for expenses to be paid can also relate to a non-offender under sections 36(1)(e), 37(3)(e), 38(3)(e) and 39(1), he can appeal against any such order. He may have no knowledge of the acts of the offender or be responsible in any way for the abuse yet be liable for the expenses. In that event he may appeal as with other provisions of the AWA from the magistrates' court to the Crown Court and from the Crown Court to the Court of Appeal.

This is an important section not merely for the fairness which may flow from the fact it can relate to a non-offender, but equally because the attendant expenses in caring for the abused animal may be quite high as any care and treatment continues while it is recuperating. There would have to be some culpability or responsibility by the non-offender as otherwise he would be placed in jeopardy as a result of some other person's vicarious abuse. If so, besides the ordinary route of appeal, if it was an irrational or unreasonable decision by the court, it could be subject to judicial review.

5

Duty and Responsibility

E1 *General*

Sections 51 to 68 covers and completes the circle of the aim and end of the AWA in a general sense. It includes the duties and the responsibilities of inspectors, powers of entry and search as well as the general interpretation of the terms used throughout the AWA.

Inspectors

Animal Welfare Act 2006, s.51

(1) In this Act, "inspector", in the context of any provision, means a person appointed to be an inspector for the purposes of that provision by –
   (a) the appropriate national authority, or
   (b) a local authority.

(2) In appointing a person to be an inspector for the purposes of this Act, a local authority shall have regard to guidance issued by the appropriate national authority.

(3) The appropriate national authority may, in connection with guidance under subsection (2), draw up a list of persons whom the authority considers suitable for appointment by a local authority to be an inspector for the purposes of this Act.

(4) A person may be included in a list under subsection (3) as suitable for appointment as an inspector for all the purposes of this Act or only for such one or more of those purposes as may be specified in the list.

(5) An inspector shall not be liable in any civil or criminal proceedings for anything done in the purported performance of his functions under this Act if the court is satisfied that the act was done in good faith and that there were reasonable grounds for doing it.

(6) Relief from liability of an inspector under subsection (5) shall not affect any other person in respect of the inspector's act.

While the police and animal organisations have an interest in any offences to be investigated under the AWA, at the heart of the Act is the inspector. Their powers are wide even as investigative powers go. Throughout the sections that govern the search, seizure and at the forefront of the investigation, the power rests within the role and status of the inspector. The mechanism of the AWA depends on them. An Inspector is simply defined in subsection (1) as one who 'in the context of any provision, means a person appointed to be an inspector for the purposes of that provision by the appropriate national authority, or a local authority'.

In respect of that role the national authority may issue guidance which the local authority 'shall have regard' to in relation to the inspectors that they appoint. The national authority may give such guidance by compiling a list of persons whom they consider 'suitable' for appointment by the local authority. Those on that list may be considered 'suitable' for all purpose of the AWA or only such purpose as specified on the list.

Given the experience and knowledge and expertise that are required to be an inspector, in practical terms it is likely to be someone who is a qualified vet. That would be consistent with the guidance which specifies the criteria necessary for the role and status of an inspector. It is specific as a list of such suitable persons may be prepared. Even then those who appear on the list may only be suitable for some rather than all purposes. It would be limited by their skill and experience and qualifications.

All professionals occasionally make bad judgement calls, but usually they have a responsibility for their actions. An unusual aspect of the section, given the role and status and power, is that an inspector 'shall not' be liable in any civil or criminal proceedings for anything done in the 'purported' performance of his functions under the AWA if the court is satisfied that the act was done in 'good faith' and that there were 'reasonable grounds' for doing it. That gives an extremely wide power to an inspector as he could be acting in good faith but bad judgement. As for reasonable grounds, well any court would have to go some way to find the grounds were unreasonable if he acted in good faith.

It is rather peculiar that it exempts the liability in both civil and criminal proceedings. As the differing burdens of proof are relevant, the court in civil proceedings could find his act, even in good faith, to be unreasonable, but a criminal court could find it was reasonable.

The protection goes even further in that by section 51(6) that 'relief' from civil and criminal liability does not extend to 'any other person' in respect of the inspector's act. So as there could be a case involving joint or vicarious liability, the potential conflict is manifest. For if the inspector's act is considered to pass the test of reasonable grounds that would be persuasive in respect of any person who is charged with him or instead of him. It could be used to support a defence or, in an appropriate case, an abuse of process. On that point it must be remembered it is in the purported performance. The subjective element provides a further protection to the inspector on the touchstone of competency and honesty.

A problem would arise if an inspector recklessly or intentionally acted outside his powers while 'purporting' to be acting under those powers. Then his protection would not avail him as it is beyond his specified function. How far it would protect others would depend on whether they knew or were duped too.

Conditions for grant of warrant

E2   Animal Welfare Act 2006, s.52

One of 4 conditions must be met before a warrant can be granted. Significantly section 52(4) and (5) apply to dwellings and other premises. That is essential to deal with urgent situations and to take action in an emergency on behalf of a suffering animal.
It is usually a police officer or an inspector that investigates the initial complaint. To do so it often requires a warrant. The conditions that are attached to a warrant serves to protect an occupier in normal circumstances as he must be informed of their pending visit. In extreme cases where he is not informed, there must be a degree of urgency. That is consistent with the ethos of the AWA with seeking to protect animals from existing and continuing suffering. It has been analysed in an earlier chapter as it is relevant to several sections throughout the AWA from 19 to 28. [See D3]

Powers of entry, inspection and search: supplementary

E3   Animal Welfare Act 2006, s.53

Schedule 2 (which makes supplementary provision in relation to powers of entry, inspection and search) has effect.

This is a wide-ranging section which applies to all the provisions within the AWA and protects both those seeking evidence and those subject to the extensive searches, whether under a warrant or otherwise.

E4   Schedule 2 paragraph 7

Power to require assistance

(1)   This paragraph applies to a power of entry conferred by –

   (a)   section 19(1), 22(2), 26(2), 27(2), 28(2) or 29(2), or

   (b)   a warrant under section 19(4), 22(4), 23(1) or 28(4).

(2)   Where a person enters premises in the exercise of a power of entry to which this paragraph applies, he may require any qualifying person on the premises to give him such assistance as he may reasonably require for the purpose for which entry is made.

(3)   The reference in sub-paragraph (2) to a qualifying person is to –

   (a)   the occupier of the premises;

   (b)   any person who appears to be the person exercising the power to be responsible for animals on the premises;

   (c)   any person who appears to the person exercising the power to be under the direction or control of a person mentioned in paragraph (a) or (b).

(4)   In the case of a power under section 26(2), the reference in sub-paragraph (2) to a qualifying person also includes the holder of a licence –

   (a)   specifying the premises as premises on which the carrying on of an activity is authorised, or

   (b)   relating to an activity which is being carried on the premises.

This paragraph enforces *Schedule 2* which gives extensive extra power to the police and inspectors in terms of investigation. The powers are supplementary to those in the body of the AWA. They are the main powers in relation to entry, but the extra ones relate to the actions of an inspector under a warrant too. He will usually need the assistance of others, as indeed the police often do too. So to that end paragraphs 1 to 4 are entitled, *Safeguards etc in connection with powers of entry conferred by a warrant.*

This is wide as section 52 as a whole is concerned with the conditions which must be satisfied for the grant of a warrant. Section 53 relates to the power of entry, inspection and search as well as a warrant. The inspector has extended power as sections 15 and 16 of PACE apply to him when carrying out his duties under section 19(4) and 23(1) of the AWA.

The other paragraphs of Schedule 2 are mainly procedural and related to the conditions of granting and executing a warrant. It also specifies what an inspector and any other person he may take with him can do in respect of inspection and search plus the function of the entry itself.

This is an unusual aspect of the AWA as it places a burden on the defendant himself. The 'qualifying person' includes the occupier and any person who 'appears' responsible for animals there. It goes further by including those who appear to be under his control too. That is a welcome clause that gives claws to the inspector to grip the essence of his power.

Further if the power of entry is under section 26(2) then the qualifying person includes the holder of a licence which specifies that an authorised activity can be carried out on the premises. In effect that could result in a potential defendant helping the person with the power of entry to gather evidence which is then used to prosecute him. It is in fact even stronger than that position where a potential defendant becomes an actual one as to refuse such assistance is itself an offence. Hence it is in a sense one of self-incrimination. Depending on the circumstances that could arguably be contrary to Article 6 of the HRA. [See *Saunders v. UK* [1996] 23 E.H.R.R. 313; *Brown v. Stott* [2001] 2 All ER 97.]

E5   Schedule 2 paragraph 10

Functions in connection with inspection and search

(1)   This paragraph applies to –
    (a)   a power of inspection conferred by section 26(1), 27(1), 28(1) or 29(1), and
    (b)   a power of search conferred by a warrant under section 23(1).

(2)   A person exercising a power to which this paragraph applies may –
    (a)   inspect an animal found on the premises;
    (b)   inspect any other thing found on the premises, including a document or record (in whatever form it is held);
    (c)   carry out a measurement or test (including a measurement or test of an animal found on the premises);
    (d)   take a sample (including a sample from an animal found on the premises or from any substance on the premises which appears top be intended for use as food for such an animal);
    (e)   mark an animal found on the premises for identification purposes;
    (f)   remove a carcass found on the premises for the purpose of carrying out a post mortem examination on it;
    (g)   take copies of a document or record found on the premises (in whatever form it is found);
    (h)   require information stored in an electronic form and accessible from the premises to be produced in a form

in which it can be taken away and in which it is visible and legible or from which it can readily be produced in a visible and legible form;

(i) take a photograph of anything on the premises;

(j) seize and detain or remove anything which the person exercising the power reasonably believes to be evidence of any non-compliance, or of the commission of any offence, relevant to the purpose for which the inspection or search is made.

Similarly where the power of entry under paragraph 10 is used to gather evidence by inspection and searching of the premises, the persons on the premises must cooperate with the functions being performed. That could include supplying a 'document or record' in whatever form it is held. So again the potential defendant must 'cooperate' with the inspection and allow the person exercising the power of entry to assist by seizing 'anything' which he reasonably believes to be 'evidence' of either non-compliance or the commission of an offence. The evidence and hence his cooperation must be relevant to the purpose of the inspection or search. The duty to cooperate relates to 'anything' he can properly class as evidence.

It would be subject to any item which is itself subject to legal privilege. Such an item would be outside this power under paragraph 12 and section 10 of PACE.

Essentially this section allows a wide discretion to the investigator to obtain all the evidence there and then or for a later analysis. So anything that is taken can be retained as an exhibit for a pending trial or for forensic examination. In each case it must relate to a 'relevant offence' which is defined under section 23(3) as 'any offence under any of the sections 4 to 9, 13(6) and 34(9).'

E6   Schedule 2 paragraph 16

Offences

A person commits an offence if he:
- (a)   intentionally obstructs a person in the lawful exercise of a power to which paragraph 7 or 10 applies;
- (b)   intentionally obstructs a person in the lawful exercise of a power conferred by this Schedule;
- (c)   fails without reasonable excuse to give any assistance which he is required to give under paragraph 7.

While Schedule 2 is wide in scope its real power lies in the fact it is supported by a sanction. Its strength is that any failure to comply with either paragraph 7 or 10 is an offence. But it goes further. This is an overriding duty on a person to co-operate with such functions under Schedule 2. Although such cooperation may be against his own interests, it is not his choice to refuse. For once the request is made, he must comply or he will fail in his duty to cooperate. It is an all-embracing duty as an intentional obstruction of any power within Schedule 2 is an offence. The reason for these provisions is connected to the reality that if notice is given to the potential offender it is easy to destroy available evidence including the victim which might be the best evidence and main exhibit in any subsequent proceedings. Equally the victims cannot provide evidence except by the hand of a human in their inspection or by a post-mortem.

Power to stop and detain vehicles

E7   Animal Welfare Act 2006, s.54

- (1)   A constable in uniform or, if accompanied by such a constable, an inspector may stop and detain a vehicle for the purpose of entering and searching it in the exercise of a power conferred –

(a) by section 19(1), or

(b) by a warrant under section 19(4) or 23(1).

(2) A constable in uniform may stop and detain a vehicle for the purpose of entering and searching it in the exercise of a power conferred –

(a) by section 22(2), or

(b) by a warrant under section 22(4).

(3) If accompanied by a constable in uniform, an inspector may stop and detain a vehicle for the purpose of entering it and carrying out an inspection in the exercise of a power conferred –

(a) by section 26(2), 27(2), 28(2) or 29(2); or

(b) by a warrant under section 28(4).

(4) A vehicle may be detained for as long as is reasonably required to permit a search or inspection to be carried out (including the exercise of any related power under this Act) either at the place where the vehicle was first detained or nearby.

In the case of illegal activities involving animals especially dog fighting, badger-baiting and even transporting them without complying with a statutory obligation, the transgressors are usually using vehicles. So the AWA deals with that aspect by giving powers to both the police and inspectors to stop and detain vehicles.

A constable in uniform has extensive powers of search and inspection under this section. An inspector's power is more limited as he has to be accompanied by such a constable. An additional power allows them to detain the vehicle as long as reasonably required for a search or investigation to be carried out. As the search may be connected to any 'related' power under the Act, it would allow the police to undertake forensic tests which could relate to the vehicle and any blood, carcasses, weapons or other evidence found within it. That would allow the investigator to widen the initial reason for the detention of the vehicle and could lead to the detection of other offences, be they pending or after the event.

It also applies to activities committed illegally such as transporting horses and emaciated cattle to and from the abattoir. Given the wide definition of 'premises' which includes 'any vehicle ...or movable structure' under section 62(1), this section has a wider inherent power than at first appears. For section 17(1)(c) of PACE applies to the AWA by section 24. [See **D5**]

As a constable can stop and seize a vehicle for purposes of seizing an animal used in fighting, it is a practical power which can emanate from, depending on the section, a 'reasonable belief' or a reasonable suspicion or a warrant. So it can span everything from rescuing an animal in distress to inspecting farms.

Power to detain vessels, aircraft and hovercraft

E8   Animal Welfare Act 2006, s.55

   (1)   Where an inspector appointed by the appropriate national authority certifies in writing that he is satisfied that an offence under or by virtue of this Act is being or has been committed on board a vessel in port, the vessel may be detained.

   (2)   A certificate under subsection (1) shall –
      (a)   specify each offence to which it relates, and
      (b)   set out the inspector's reasons for being satisfied that each offence to which it relates is being or has been committed.

(3) Section 284 of the Merchant Shipping Act 1995 (which provides for enforcement of the detention of a ship under that Act by specified officers) shall apply as if the power of detention under subsection (1) were conferred by that Act.

(4) An officer who detains a vessel in reliance on a certificate under subsection (1) shall as soon as is reasonably practicable give a copy of it to the master or person in charge of the vessel.

(5) A vessel may be detained under subsection (1) until the appropriate national authority otherwise directs.

(6) The appropriate national authority may by regulations –

(a) apply this section to aircraft or hovercraft, with such modifications as the authority thinks fit, or

(b) make such other provision for the detention of aircraft or hovercraft in relation to offences under or by virtue of this Act as the authority thinks fit.

It is in keeping with the aim of the AWA that animals are protected even when in the air or on land or on the high seas. As the appetite for animals for food or pets or sometimes fashion ornaments grows internationally, the trade puts animals at risk of abuse. So here an inspector has wide powers in relation to those forms of travel. Where an inspector certifies in 'writing' that he is satisfied that an offence under or by virtue of the Act is being or has been committed on board a vessel in port, the vessel may be detained.

The certificate 'shall' specify each offence. That has to identify it in strict terms so the defendant knows what he has done or is doing wrong. It must also specify the inspector's reasons for his decision. That would have to set down the particular thing he is doing or has done which is unlawful. As the section is so wide and the results such a penalty as to detain the vessel, the inspector has to be on sure ground as his 'reasons' form the basis of the evidence which satisfies the test of the detention.

Section 284 of the Merchant Shipping Act 1995 allows specified officers to detain a ship. It is a wide-ranging section under which officers may detain a ship if it leaves a port without having permission to do so. That section of the 1995 Act shall apply as if the power of detention was conferred by the AWA. It extends the inspector's power to have that effect.

When an officer detains a vessel relying on such a certificate he 'shall' as soon as reasonably practicable give a copy to the master or person in charge of the vessel. That allows the master to both know the reason for the detention and to take any necessary legal action to protect the position of the vessel and probably the crew and himself. For once a vessel is detained it may be kept until the national authority 'otherwise directs'. The ship and crew may be foreign and so need interpreters too. The occupier of the premises is the one who appears to be in charge of it. This section would protect the cargo while monitoring the interests of the crew.

So that the power is not simply limited to animals being transported by sea, the authority may by regulations apply this section to aircraft or hovercraft. As a corollary it would include provision for the detention of any aircraft or hovercraft in relation to offences contrary to the AWA. Indeed the definition of premises under section 62(1) includes 'any aircraft or hovercraft' so all the other powers of entry and search would apply too.

While no regulations have been made yet under the AWA the power allows for changing conditions to cover new forms of transport. It is important to note in this regard that the definition of premises under section 62(1) 'includes any vehicle, vessel, aircraft or hovercraft; any tent or movable structure'. As a result the investigative powers extend well beyond a straightforward detention and search. A protected animal may be a cat that is a mascot on board a ship or a straggly dog companion with a travelling crusty. So it could and would include a yacht in the Isle of Wight as well as a tent at Glastonbury Festival.

Obtaining of documents in connection with carrying out orders etc.

E9   Animal Welfare Act 2006, s.56

(1)   Where –

    (a)   an order under section 20(1), 33(1) or (2), 35(1) or (2) or 37(1) has effect, and

    (b)   the owner of an animal to which the order relates has in his possession, or under his control, documents which are relevant to the carrying out of the order or any directions given in connection with it, the owner shall, if so required by a person authorised to carry out the order, deliver the documents to that person as soon as practicable and in any event before the end of the period of 10 days beginning with the date on which he is notified of the requirement.

(2)   Where –

    (a)   directions under section 41(3)(b) have affect, and

    (b)   the owner of an animal to which the directions relate has in his possession, or under his control, documents which are relevant to the carrying out of the directions, the owner shall, if so required by a person authorised to carry out the directions, deliver the documents to that person as soon as practicable and in any event before the end of the period of 10 days beginning with the date on which he is notified of the requirement.

(3)   A person who fails without reasonable excuse to comply with subsection (1) or (2) commits an offence.

There would be little or no point in having wide powers of investigation into animal abuse without a comparable power to obtain the evidence that underpins the abuse. That evidence, which is often in a documentary form, is essential for those persons charged with carrying out the directions of the court. To that end this power allows any person authorised to carry out an order under the various sections to request relevant documents of the owner. When there is such a request the owner has a duty to supply the documents within 10 days.

To have any positive effect and value, given that the power follows a conviction, the power must enable the authorised person to have the documents relating to the animal even if there is a pending appeal. So even if there is an appeal, where the court makes a direction under section 41(3)(b) which deals with how an animal is to be treated during any suspension of the order, it is still essential that the investigation continues pending the result. Therefore while the order may be suspended pending any appeal, when a request is made the owner remains under a duty to supply those documents within 10 days. After all, the abused animal may literally and legally be on the verge of death.

As with the provisions throughout the AWA, they would have no purpose if there was not a criminal sanction attending to such a request. So a person who fails 'without reasonable excuse' to comply with a request under the section commits an offence. It is significant that it places a burden on the owner for he is the one who would be likely to possess the documents. Even if he does not he would normally have the legal power to obtain them. So the excuse tendered would have to be legitimate and bear scrutiny. It would not suffice to offer something akin to the schoolboy chestnut that 'my dog ate my homework'.

Offences by bodies corporate

E10   Animal Welfare Act 2006, s.57

(1)   Where an offence under this Act is committed by a body corporate and is proved to have been committed with the consent or connivance of or to be attributable to any neglect on the part of –

(a)   any director, manager, secretary or other similar officer of the body corporate, or

(b)   any person who was purporting to act in such capacity he (as well as the body corporate) commits the offence and shall be liable to be proceeded against and punished accordingly.

(2)   Where the affairs of a body corporate are managed by its members, subsection (1) applies in relation to the acts and defaults of a member in connection with his functions of management as if he were a director of the body corporate.

The AWA has the aim of making all those liable for the welfare of animals if they deal in and with them. The advantage of that aspect is that it captures people who are in a position of authority and can make them vicariously liable for those whom they supervise or may have control of and over as employees or contractors. In that respect it would not be limited to those who are vicariously liable, but in an appropriate case relate to a joint and several liability too.

So the liability extends to intention and omission of those in charge of the activity leading to the abuse. The areas covered are almost any activity within a company that affects animals where the corporation is involved via its officers and extends to any person 'purporting' to be acting in such a capacity. So it is aimed at all those who are directly and indirectly in control of animals.

While that is extremely wide in aim and purpose, the powers are even wider. The legal status of a company can allow all the members to be in control of its affairs. In that event it would be pointless if that status stymied the legal effect in protecting animals. Hence where the affairs of a body corporate are managed by its members, the liability applies in relation to the 'acts and defaults' of a member in connection with his function as a manager as if he were a director of the corporation.

As by subsection (1) the offence is 'proved' to have been committed by any of the various officers of the company, there could be more than one or two proceedings in relation to the same subject of the charge. For it is difficult to have something 'proved' unless there is already firm evidence at least such as a signed confession or at the most a conviction against another person. The former could be used in the event of a joint charge or a conspiracy. In the latter case that conviction could be used to assist the police to prove the offence against those in charge.

The section catches any or all of those involved for some may have done so by actual 'consent' or even 'connivance', while for others it may be the result of 'neglect' by them. Equally it is a catch-all section that relates to a person who is in an official capacity as well as those 'purporting" to act in any such capacity. That would include ostensible authority. So the benefit of acting for the company has the balance of the legal burden of extended liability. This section shows the strength of the AWA as it captures all those who are responsible for the abuse of animals under their control and, be it direct or indirect, widens the net of their legal responsibility.

Scientific research

E11   Animal Welfare Act 2006, s.58

(1)   Nothing in this Act applies to anything lawfully done under the Animals (Scientific Procedures) Act 1986.

(2)   No power of entry, inspection or search conferred by or under this Act, except for any such power conferred by section 28, may be exercised at a place which is –

(a)   designated under section 6 of the Animals (Scientific Procedures) Act 1986 as a scientific procedure establishment, or

(b)   designated under section 7 of that Act as a breeding establishment or as a supplying establishment.

(3)   Section 9 does not apply in relation to an animal which –

(a)   is being kept, at a place designated under section 6 of the Animals (Scientific Procedures) Act 1986 as a scientific procedure establishment, for use in regulated procedures,

(b)   is being kept, at a place designated under section 7 of that Act as a breeding establishment, for use for breeding animals for use in regulated procedures,

(c)   is being kept at such a place, having been bred there for use in regulated procedures, or

(d)   is being kept, at a place designated under section 7 of that Act as a supplying establishment, for the purpose of being supplied for use elsewhere in regulated procedures,

(4)   In subsection (3), "regulated procedure" has the same meaning as in the Animals (Scientific Procedures) Act 1986.

The use of animals for experiments and vivisection is and always has been a controversial area of the law. While scientists have a vested interest in carrying out such procedures for reasons of their livelihood and research, equally many animal welfare bodies have criticised those acts as being immoral and wrong. Significantly the present Act that controls such procedures is called the Animals (Scientific Procedures) Act 1986 (ASPA) while the main and first Act to control those carrying out such experiments was entitled the Cruelty to Animals Act 1876.

There can be no question or doubt that the procedures that are allowed under ASPA are certainly contrary to the welfare of the animals. After all the basis of most are to test various products or research by experiments on animals and finally, when they have been so used, killing them. As a result there is a complete exemption for those engaged in such activities. Similarly those premises are not able to be entered or inspected or searched for the purpose of investigating or ensuring compliance with the conditions of the AWA.

The AWA does not apply to any act lawfully done if it is a scientific procedure within the ASPA. Even wider than that exclusion is the fact that section 9, which is the core duty of a person for an animal's welfare under the AWA, does not apply to an animal kept at a scientific procedure establishment for use in regulated procedures; or breeding or bred there or being supplied for use elsewhere in regulated procedures. Therefore it is allowing 'procedures', which are bound to affect the animal's welfare, by experiments and vivisection, to be performed which would otherwise be illegal.

Nevertheless the exemption under section 58(1) is in relation to 'anything lawfully' done under the ASPA. Therefore if the scientists carried out an experiment or activity that is not allowed under the licence granted under that Act by the Home Office, it would still be an offence. There would have to be reliable evidence from a 'whistle-blower' or an application under the Freedom of Information Act 2000. If that is applicable then a warrant could be issued under sections 28 and 52 which would allow the inspector to enter the premises without informing the experimenter. That has to be balanced by the fact it is an offence under section 24 of ASPA to disclose confidential information gained by an experimenter in discharging his functions. [See *Secretary of State for the Home Department v. British Union for the Abolition of Vivisection* [2008] EWHC 892]

The power of entry under the AWA does not apply to 'designated' places. The only exception is to the power of entry to inspect farming premises. Some ASPA places have a dual purpose of being a farm and an experimental place. So, subject to whether or not the 'farm' is designated to be 'a scientific procedure establishment', an inspector would have the right to inspect the premises to check whether any offence has been or is being committed under the AWA. However the power under section 28(2) of ASPA will only apply to animals that he reasonably believes are bred or kept for 'farming purposes'. Thus the power will not extend to animals bred or kept for an experimental or scientific purpose.

The ASPA provides a licensing system for people and projects and places where experiments on animals are carried out. As a result section 9 of the AWA, which protects the animals' welfare, does not apply if the experiments are within the ASPA. Nevertheless it will do so where an animal is at a designated place that is not covered by ASPA. That precise position could arise because the animal it is not of a type within the schedule or is not being used for a scientific procedure which is covered by the licence.

In terms the ASPA is legalising animal abuse. How wide the effect of the Act is in practice can be seen from section 2(1): A regulated procedure is any experimental or other scientific procedure applied to a protected animal which may have the effect of causing it pain, suffering, distress or lasting harm. For the avoidance of doubt it confirms that death of the animal is not an 'adverse effect' and so not classed as 'lasting harm'. [See *R (on the application of the British Union for the Abolition of Vivisection) v. Secretary of State for the Home Department* [2007] EWHC 1964]

Meanwhile a significant increase in animal experiments is contrary to the promise of the Coalition government in 2011 that they would, 'work to reduce the use of animals in scientific research.' In 2012 there were 3.7 million procedures which is 40% higher than in 2002.

Sir Roger Bannister, the legendary athlete and doctor, while in his medical practice some years ago wanted to test pyrogens. With the same spirit that made him the first 4-minute-miler he explained, 'To test my hypothesis I needed someone to experiment on, so I experimented on myself. It was dangerous, but it gave me the chance to verify my theory, and save lives.'

Fishing

E12   Animal Welfare Act 2006, s.59

Nothing in this Act applies in relation to anything which occurs in the normal course of fishing.

Given the long-term and continuing controversy over hunting which ultimately gave rise to the Burns Report in 2000 and the Hunting Act 2004, this section seeks to avoid any such doubt about the legality of fishing. This is a deliberately somewhat loose section in an otherwise detailed Act as what is or is not the 'normal course' of fishing is not clear. For it is often falsely claimed that fish are 'cold-blooded' and so do not feel pain. That is also used to distinguish fishing from the so-called 'blood-sports' of hunting which generally invokes 'hot-blooded' animals. So that leads to the conclusion that while the latter questionably feel pain, the former do not and so fishing is not cruel or concerned with animal welfare.

However the report of Lord Medway, *Report of the Panel of Inquiry into Shooting and Angling*, [1980] confirmed conclusively that the evidence for fish feeling pain is similar to and as strong as for other vertebrate animals. Hence it is legally limited to an activity that is 'normal' as an intrinsic part of the fishing process. So if a person uses some form of fishing before or during or after the actual catch which is not part of the 'normal' course of fishing, he could be caught by the net of the AWA.

The fishing activity would be limited to the ordinary activity of anglers. So if there was an unusual shaped hook that was a particularly barbaric method in that it caused severe pain or a fish was battered by a weapon while it was still breathing, that could be abnormal and therefore unlawful. The 'normal' activity is impliedly cruel. That is the reason it is exempt. So like experiments legalising what would otherwise be illegal. Thus it is a question of degree. For fishing is far from being totally exempt as it is subject to any abnormal activity being prohibited and so potentially illegal.

A fish may be a protected animal if it is under the control of a person, whether it is gained by a competition or by leisure. After all a fish at a fair is no different than one at a trout farm

The permitted course would include the use of live bait. However the common practice of 'catching and releasing' fish has not been tested in court. Professor Braithwaite assesses the position with the fish-eye of an expert: 'In Germany for example, laws forbidding the intentional release of fish over a certain size is have now been passed...a similar ruling was also recently introduced in Switzerland...Catch and release is an ethical difficult; knowing that fish feel pain and can suffer raises questions about whether it is appropriate to allow fish to be caught multiple times...' In truth the only difficult ethical issue is the same one that has been raised in other cruel pastimes from badger-baiting to hunting namely people enjoy it.

On her conclusion, answering the very question posed in the title of her book, Professor Braithwaite puts the position beyond doubt, ' "Do Fish Feel Pain?" Yes, they do. As demands for good animal welfare increase, this answer will change the way we think and act. Some will struggle with this change. Fish are still perceived as "different", but the deeper we delve, the more we recognise and appreciate many similarities with birds and mammals. The fish pain debate is gaining momentum.'

James Rose of the University of Wyoming has put forward a contrary view namely that fish do not feel pain, *The Neurobehavioral Nature of Fishes and the Question of Awareness and Pain*: [2002]. His theory has been grasped and is relied upon by anglers. However Professor Braithwaite counters that view as 'The review is now seven years old, and the field has changed rapidly during that time.' It is now a decade old. Meanwhile researchers at Edinburgh University have confirmed that fish do feel pain. Dr. L. Sneddon said, 'There were "profound behavioural and physiological changes" shown by the trout after exposure to noxious substances [that] are comparable to those seen in higher mammals.' Janicke Nordgreen of the Norwegian School of Veterinary Science came to the same conclusion. [See *Science Daily* 12/1/10]

The result is that many anglers' practices are suspect and unlikely to be consistent with the welfare of fish.

Katherine van Ekert, the president of the Australian organisation, Sentient, has criticised the killing of tuna in the old La Mattanza ceremony saying, 'The fish were shown to be lifted by hooks after attachment.

The suspension of the tuna's body weight is expected to cause pain and stress to the animals, as too would the tearing of their tissues as a result of gravity working against the hook.' The group are now lobbying politicians in Brussels and Rome seeking a total ban on bluefin tuna fishing.

Crown application

E13   Animal Welfare Act 2006, s.60

(1)   Subject to the provisions of this section, this Act and regulations and orders made under it shall bind the Crown.

(2)   No contravention by the Crown of any provision made by or under this Act shall make the Crown criminally liable; but the High Court may declare unlawful any act or omission of the Crown which constitutes such a contravention.

(3)   Notwithstanding subsection (2), the provisions of this Act and of regulations and orders made under it shall apply to persons in the service of the Crown as they apply to other persons.

(4)   If the Secretary of State certifies that it appears to him appropriate in the interests of national security that powers of entry conferred by or under this Act should not be exercisable in relation to Crown premises specified in the certificate, those powers shall not be exercisable in relation to those premises.

(5)   In subsection (4), "Crown Premises" means premises held, or used, by or on behalf of the Crown.

(6) No power of entry conferred by or under this Act may be exercised in relation to land belonging to Her Majesty in right of Her private estates.

(7) In subsection (6), the reference to Her Majesty's private estates shall be construed in accordance with section 1 of the Crown Private Estates Act 1862.

The AWA binds all government departments and other public bodies that are part of the Crown. It is the normal practice that the Crown is not subject to criminal liability. As the Crown is heavily involved in many areas of animal welfare, it is essential that it is bound by the AWA. To some limited extent it is as the High Court can 'declare' the questionable conduct is unlawful, be it an act or omission. That would cause the conduct to be controlled in the future.

While the exemption from criminal liability applies to the Crown as an entity, nevertheless the persons who would be liable do not share that exemption. For by section 60(3) it states it 'shall' apply to such persons. So the employees and staff are liable just as any other person would be. That is a crucial provision as otherwise the power of the Crown would be a shield from the sword of prosecution.

The exemption applying to the Queen may extend to her land. The Secretary of State may certify that entry to Crown premises should not be exercisable if it is not in the 'interests of national security'. An inspector or a constable does not have the power of entry granted under the AWA to enter the private estates of the Queen. Yet obviously offences may well be committed there. That is only a legal measure on the understandable grounds of national security. On that basis, if an offence is committed, they could enter but will require permission to enter her land. After all many members of the royal family and visitors use guns for shooting birds. Consequently it is essential that the Queen and her estate are not exempt from the provisions of the AWA as otherwise it could and would prevent the detection of potentially serious crime against people and animals.

6

Sentencing

F1 Powers

The powers under the AWA are:

(a) Imprisonment for 6 months and a fine or both: under section 32. [cf. ss. (5)]
(b) A deprivation order: under sections 4, 5, 6, 8, 9 and 36(9).
(c) A disqualification order: under sections 4, 5, 6, 7, 8, 9, 13(6) and 36(9).

The Sentencing Guidelines are set out in the section that follows at **F8**. The guideline sentences range from 26 weeks at the top for the worst category of animal abuse to a small fine at the lowest.

In order to consider the effect of the AWA the position before it was introduced has to be considered too. Then an accurate assessment of it can be made in relation to the changes in sentencing by the courts.

F2 Summary

When the POA was introduced in 1911 a person convicted of an offence of cruelty was liable to a fine of up to £25 and/or six months' imprisonment. The period of six-months had been increased from three months under previous legislation. According to A. W. Moss in the *Valiant Crusade* [1961] this caused a problem: 'It was found that this gave the right of the accused to trial by jury, but as so many prosecutions for cruelty were occurring at that time, the decrepit-horse traffic being still much in vogue, it often happened that on the juries were people who had faced such charges, with the result that many prosecutions were lost'. Consequently it was amended to three months, so making it a summary offence. Though by the Protection of Animals (Penalties) Act 1987 it was increased to six months' imprisonment it remained a summary offence.

Generally the courts were very lenient in sentencing persons convicted of cruelty to animals. The usual sentence was a low fine. Prison was rarely imposed even in flagrant cases. At a RSPCA meeting in 1929 reported in the *Justice of the Peace,* Sir Ernest Wild, the Recorder of London, suggested that the penalties for cruelty as compared to those for damage to property were unduly low. He recommended that there should be 'penal servitude of two to five years.' Captain Maclum, a RSPCA officer, agreed but added that the real problem was that 'many local benches do not administer existing law as strictly as they could.'

F3 POA

Many people who committed cruelty were merely cautioned. Prosecutions were undertaken as a last resort either where the perpetrator failed to respond to persuasion or the form of cruelty could not be overlooked.

Considering those points it is instructive to consider actual cases then and now. A comparison of the penalty of custody or non-custody [rather than disqualification] will show what, if anything, has changed:

1. In 1988 a ewe was seen at a market 'in great distress'. Its udder was 'a large foul-smelling mass, 13 inches long' and the animal's overall body condition was

'extremely poor'. The ewe had a prolapsed udder of which the last 7 inches was gangrenous. A vet examined it and had to destroy the ewe on site. The condition was the result of 'severe and untreated mastitis' such that the ewe had been suffering for at 'least six months'. The farmer pleaded not guilty to failing to provide the ewe with adequate care and attention. He was convicted. The farmer was fined.

2. In 1981 a neighbour found a pet dog in a coal shed. Its 'paws were tied with sticky tape and the bound legs were then tied together with nylon rope. Its mouth was bound with tape so tightly that the dog would have had difficulty in breathing'. The dog had 'three deep head wounds' where the owner had attacked it with an axe. Thomas Finley pleaded guilty to ill-treating the dog and causing it unnecessary suffering. Alwyn Eastland, the magistrate, told Finley, 'This is a case of cruelty... which no human being should be accused of carrying out.' It was in such a state the dog had to be destroyed. Finley was fined.

3. In 1988 a Badger Patrol found three men digging a well-known sett in a nature reserve. They claimed they were after foxes. Besides the spades, they had a sack with badger hairs inside, dog collars with radio tracking equipment and all the paraphernalia of the professional baiter. They had four terriers of which three had to be taken to a vet for 'urgent treatment'. One dog had 'part of its tongue ripped away and several teeth missing'. Another dog had been 'bitten through to the bone' of its face resulting in 'perforations of the palate'. The wounds could only have been caused by a badger or a large dog. All of the

dogs had numerous healed scars from previous fights. One dog had badger fleas which must have been 'a recent infestation'. They were charged with attempting to take a badger and cruelty to the dogs. They pleaded not guilty but were convicted. The three defendants were fined.

4. In 1987 a Shetland pony was in poor health. It owner, a farmer, knew of its condition but did nothing about it. The pony was riddled with arthritis which made it 'so grossly deformed' that its 'forelegs were permanently bent at right angles'. A vet who saw said it said there was no other course but 'immediate humane destruction'. The vet said the owner's neglect was 'the worst case of cruelty to an animal that he had ever seen during his 28 years in the profession.' The farmer was fined.

F4 AWA

Compared to the lamentable POA the AWA is progressive in promoting the welfare of animals, particularly with regard to the legal duty on the owner plus his taking of steps so as to avoid unnecessary suffering. How it compares in relation to sentencing is the acid test. For that does not rest with the statute, but an astute judiciary. This small representative selection exhibits the present and the likely future:

1. In 2010 Jamie Davies, Jason Jones and Daniel Silvestros admitted causing unnecessary suffering to a fox. The three men were out in Pontypridd in Wales when they called at the Tesco superstore to buy more alcohol. Some of Tesco's staff said that the fox 'was a friendly fox' and regularly approached the store. They 'fed it and had even given it a name.' The fox's

friendliness may 'account for the reason' the trio were able to catch it. At the time it was hiding in the car park just behind a parked car. Silvestros saw it and chased it and caught the fox. Silvestros then 'caught the fox by the tail' and swung it 'from side to side.' He dropped the animal after '10 seconds' because he said, 'The fox was "going nuts" as he swung it.' After he dropped it Jones then picked the fox up and in 'A very barbaric act, swung the fox from behind his back head-first into a wall, then swung it again, striking it on the floor.' Davies then joined in the attack. He began 'kicking and stamping on the fox's head.' After his attack Davies then picked it up and dropped the fox on the road. The staff at Tesco's were shocked and upset by what they saw, one woman was openly weeping. After the joint attack the fox was 'bleeding from the mouth and whimpering in pain.' As the fox was still alive all the defendants 'appeared to want to attack it again.' Someone told the defendants to 'clear off.' The fox died within 20 minutes from 'multiple injuries.' The three defendants were traced from CCTV which captured the attack. Each of the defendants received a suspended sentence.

2. In 2010 Melanie King was found guilty of causing unnecessary suffering to animals at Sittingbourne Magistrates' Court. King was a dog breeder. The RSPCA inspectors found 'more than 70 dogs living in squalor' at her business at Whents Farm in Feynham. Some of the dogs had 'untreated medical conditions.' The conditions many of the dogs were kept in were described as 'squalid and truly appalling.' Ray Bailey, a RSPCA Inspector, said 'King was totally irresponsible. She had been given previous warnings, but failed to take

action to safeguard the animals' welfare.' King received a suspended sentence.

3. In 2011 Dulcie Bickers and Amy Bickers each pleaded guilty to 7 offences of causing unnecessary suffering to animals. In relation to Dulcie it was horses and Amy it was cats. At Redhill and Reigate Magistrates' Court it was said that the police, vets, a RSPCA inspector and two field officers from World Horse Welfare had visited the women's family home in April 2010 following 'a tip-off'. At that location and nearby at Moorfield Stables in Chaldon they found 'a total of 37 horses in varying conditions, some without access to water and '17 cats were also removed'. One of the horses, an elderly stallion, was found to be blind and had to be killed. Five other horses, plus two unweaned foals, were moved into the care of World Horse Welfare. Those horses were found to be 'extremely emaciated, lice ridden or with long feet.' Both of the Bickers received a suspended sentence. For good measure the foals were weaned on their behalf and then returned to the defendants.

4. In 2010 William Osborne of Whitechurch near Blandford was sentenced at Weymouth Magistrates' court for causing unnecessary suffering to animals. He pleaded guilty to 20 offences. The offences included causing unnecessary suffering to 16 lambs by failing to treat fly strike (maggot infestation); failing to protect 8 animals from pain and suffering by not cleaning infected fleeces; failing to provide drinking water for a group of lambs; leaving broken wire fencing across a field; failing to properly dispose of carcasses and other animal parts; leaving carcasses exposed for

access by wild animals and birds; failing to comply with formal notices to dispose of carcasses; and providing false information to an animal health inspector from Dorset trading standards. The offences arose after a total of 23 visits by the various investigating officers who were often accompanied by Defra vets. Osborne received a suspended sentence.

5. In 2011 the defendant claimed his pet cat, Come-on-Then, scratched him. So he put her in the microwave oven and turned it on. The cat survived the ordeal and when a RSPCA Inspector saw her she was 'Panting heavily with her tongue hanging out and then collapsed on the kitchen counter...she was damp and hot to the touch.' The Inspector poured water over the cat to cool her down and rushed her to a vet. The vet found Come-on-Then had 'bloodshot eyes and abnormalities in her blood.' She was placed on a drip and monitored as 'microwaves can affect vital organs for some time afterwards.' The defendant pleaded not guilty to causing his cat unnecessary suffering under section 4. He was convicted. The magistrate at Portsmouth Magistrates' Court on sentencing said, 'This was a case of deliberate cruelty and so serious that only a custodial sentence would suffice.' The defendant received a suspended sentence.

F5 Prison

While immediate imprisonment is rare, when a prison sentence is imposed the term is usually unduly low.

1. In 2012 Piotr Wasiuta stubbed out cigarettes on the faces of pigs at an abattoir at Orchard Farm in Essex.

Kelly Smith, a fellow employee and co-defendant, also engaged in systematic abuse of the animals at the abattoir including beating them with excessive force and frequency. He hit one pig over 30 times in one minute. All their joint actions were captured on film by underground activists using covert cameras. Initially Defra decided that they would not prosecute because the evidence was not admissible as it was 'Evidence provided by a third party that it could not obtain under its own statutory powers.' That decision was inexplicable and incomprehensible and plainly wrong as a matter of law. After mass publicity in the media and protestations from Animal Aid whose undercover activists had obtained the evidence, Defra were forced to change their approach and eventually the CPS prosecuted both defendants. In the event Wasiuta pleaded guilty to 3 charges and Smith pleaded guilty to 2 charges. The court sentenced Wasiuta to 6 weeks' and Smith to 4 weeks' imprisonment. Given that they will only serve half the sentence that would be 3 weeks and a fortnight respectively.

Kate Fowler of Animal Aid said after the sentence, 'However, many other slaughterhouse workers, who also caused serious and deliberate suffering to animals, have escaped justice because this government refused to act.' Coincidentally they had secretly filmed the workers at other abattoirs which were randomly chosen. The result was that at 6 out of the 7 chosen abattoirs there were breaches of the animal welfare laws including 'animals being, kicked, slapped, stamped on, and thrown into stunning pens'. [See *The Independent* 19/11/10]

2. In *Gray v. RSPCA*, a case of sustained systematic animal abuse involving numerous animals over a long period, the main defendant absconded before his appeal was dismissed. He initially received 24 weeks' imprisonment which was increased by 2 weeks at the Crown Court. All of the other 4 defendants, who were members of his family and jointly liable, received non-custodial sentences. All of the defendants had pleaded not guilty and all had been convicted. Then they all appealed against their convictions. [See **B8; B9**]

3. In 2010 a man in Devon accompanied by two youths tortured a cat called Roxy. The man put her in a microwave and turned it on. He then took her out and put her in a washing machine and switched it on: 'Roxy could be seen rotating inside the machine.' The man took her out, 'grabbed Roxy by the scruff of her neck and put her into a freezer drawer…aided by one' of the youths. She was then let out, shivering, and one of the youths 'dumped her in the sink.' One of the youths filmed the whole of Roxy's ordeal. The footage on his mobile phone showed all 'The defendants laughing and making no effort to stop Roxy's torture.' Both of the youths pleaded not guilty but were convicted. The man pleaded guilty. The magistrate said, 'The offence was unpleasant, nasty and distressing.' The man received 126 days in prison so he would serve 61 at the most. Both youths received a Rehabilitation Order. All three defendants had previous convictions.

Further because of the severe overcrowding that is present in our prisons it is now unusual for most prisoners serving a sentence of four years or less to serve the full sentence. They are usually sent home after a much earlier time on licence or an electronic tag.

F6 Progress

All those cases at 1-4 under the POA occurred during the decade 1981-1988. There is no point to cite any more. Such cruelty happened every day in every county throughout this country. The sentences show how the courts and so the community they represented, viewed cruelty to animals. For throughout the whole of the 20th Century the courts consistently imposed lenient sentences for such offences, no matter how grave they were in intent and effect. It was rare, even in cases of extreme cruelty to many animals, for the court to impose a custodial sentence. Then even when a prison sentence was imposed it was for such a short term as to be futile as a punishment or deterrent. Those sentences sent out a clear message to the perpetrators and the public: cruelty to animals was undesirable but unimportant. [See **F3**]

These recent cases under the AWA are an indication the penalties are still too low and that is matched by the sentences. The POA placed little or no value on an animal's life. The AWA is a reflection of that imperfection. Little or nothing has changed under the AWA. It is one of the major flaws of the new law that it does not provide adequate punishment for extreme cases of animal abuse. The suggestion of Wild over 80 years ago was right then and remains so now. The sentences should be increased to at least 5 years so the offences can be tried in the Crown Court. So while avoiding meiosis, these examples suffice to show it is not the inadequacy of the AWA that is the problem, merely the inadequacy of the judges in taking appropriate action. [See **F2**]

F7 America

A horrific case of animal abuse in America changed both the law and how they deal with the subject itself. In 1994 in Mobile, Alabama, a teenage girl rejected a teenage boy. As a revenge he with two of his friends got her 3-month-old Chow-husky pup, Gucci, then hanged him from a tree by his neck, repeatedly smacked him in the face, kicked him 'and finally doused him with lighter fluid and set him on fire.' Gucci somehow managed to escape and ran and hid under a porch while still on fire. By sheer chance Dr. Doug James was visiting the area because he was selling a house he owned in the district. Gucci's owner could not afford to pay the vet to treat him. James took over and arranged for Gucci to see a vet. He rescued the dog and nursed it back to health. As a result he lobbied for years to change the law. After 6 years a new law, the Pet Protection Act ['Gucci's Law'] was introduced. Animal cruelty is now a Class C felony in Alabama which allows a maximum sentence of 10 years. [Other States have followed that legal suit.]

In 2007 Juan Daniels of Montgomery, Alabama was angry with his mother because she would not let him use her car. So he vented his spleen on his pet dog, now known as Louis Vuitton. He sprayed his dog with lighter fluid and then set him on fire. He also beat the dog with a shovel. Daniels was convicted of animal cruelty and was sentenced under Gucci's Law to 9 years and 6 months' imprisonment. He applied for parole in July 2010. Holladay Simmons, the vet who treated Louis immediately after the attack, told the Board of Pardons and Parole, 'The dog's wounds were as bad as she had ever seen.' Louis was brought before the Board. He still had scars from his head to his tail, white lines where the fire seared his skin. Ellen Brooks, the District Attorney, told the Board, 'The first reason to deny parole is to prevent him from hurting another animal or a person.' Daniels' appeal was rejected by The Board.

The case of Gucci and the change in the law should be a bell-wether for our legislators and judges.

F8 Animal cruelty: see Table

Animal cruelty	Animal Welfare Act 2006, s.4 (unnecessary suffering); s.8 (fighting etc.); s.9 (breach of duty of person responsible for animal to ensure welfare)

Triable only summarily:
Maximum: £20,000 fine and/or 6 months (ss.4 and 8)
Level 5 fine and/or 6 months (s.9)

Offence seriousness (culpability and harm)
A. Identify the appropriate starting point
Starting points based on first time offender pleading not guilty

Examples of nature of activity	Starting point	Range
One impulsive act causing little or no injury; short term neglect	Band C fine	Band B fine to medium level community order
Several incidents of deliberate ill-treatment/frightening animal(s); medium term neglect	High level community order	Medium level community order to 12 weeks custody
Attempt to kill/torture; animal baiting/conducting or permitting cock-fighting etc.; prolonged neglect	18 weeks custody	12 to 26 weeks custody

Offence seriousness (culpability and harm)
B. Consider the effect of aggravating and mitigating factors
(other than those within examples above)
Common aggravating and mitigating factors are identified in the pullout card – the following may be particularly relevant but **these lists are not exhaustive**

Factors indicating higher culpability	Factors indicating lower culpability
1. Offender in position of special responsibility	1. Offender induced by others
2. Adult involves children in offending	2. Ignorance of appropriate care
3. Animal(s) kept for livelihood	3. Offender with limited capacity
4. Use of weapon	
5. Offender ignored advice/warnings	
6. Offence committed for commercial gain	
Factors indicating greater degree of harm	
1.Serious injury or death	
2.Several animals affected	

Form a preliminary view of the appropriate sentence,
then consider offender mitigation
Common factors are identified in the pullout card

Consider a reduction for a guilty plea

Consider ancillary orders, including compensation
Refer to pages 168-174 for guidance on available ancillary orders
Consider disqualification from ownership of animal

Decide sentence
Give reasons

Dangerous Dogs Act 1991

7

The Dogs of Law

G1 Reason

The reason for the introduction of the Dangerous Dogs Act 1991 ('DDA') was positive and pragmatic. After a spate of vicious dogs running riot and biting members of the public who were both friends and strangers for no reason, the government had to act and act swiftly. They certainly did so. The DDA was badly drafted, ill-considered, a lousy piece of legislation that promoted confusion for judges and dog owners alike. It was completed in all its legislative stages in the House of Commons in a single day.

When it was first introduced it was Draconian in the literal and legal sense rather than merely metaphorical. For by the DDA there were two startling provisions that were contrary to the ordinary principles of law namely (a) if a dog was designated to be a particular type it was effectively deemed to be dangerous and equally doomed to die as (b) the burden of proof is on the defendant to prove it is not of that type.

How it hampered many a High Court Judge with a sense of ingrained justice can be deduced from the reaction of these distinguished judges, whose comments were unleashed as result of feeling frustrated in the face of an Act that was a jurisprudential dog's dinner:

(a) Rose LJ described it as 'Draconian' in *Bates v. DPP* [1993] 157 JP 1004.
(b) Popplewell J said in *Rafiq v. DPP* [1997] 161 JP 412 that, 'The Dangerous Dogs Act 1991 was, as is well

known, introduced in great haste by Parliament to deal with a number of unpleasant incidents in which a number of fierce dogs had seriously injured small children. It is a piece of Delphic legislation which is even worse than some of the directives coming out of Europe.'

(c) McCowan J asked himself in *R. v Secretary of State for the Home Department ex parte James* [1994] COD 167, 'What then is the position in law when an owner has made every reasonable attempt to get a certificate of exemption and has been foiled by reason of the conduct of others, and in particular the police? My reaction, I confess, is to ask myself: is there really no remedy?' After being compelled to ask that question he answered himself with a word, 'No'.

(d) Rougier J perfectly captured the Act's quintessential legal prejudice: 'Whilst acknowledging the obvious need to prevent the dogs which are, or have become, savage from injuring people, yet it seems to me that the Dangerous Dogs Act 1991 bears all the hallmarks of an ill-thought-out piece of legislation, no doubt in hasty response to yet another strident pressure group. Add to that the foolish nephew, an observant and zealous policeman and the result is that a perfectly inoffensive animal has to be sent to the gas chamber, or whatever method of execution is favoured, its only crime being to have a cough. It would take the pen of Voltaire to do justice to such a ludicrous situation' in *R. v. Ealing Magistrates' Court ex parte Fanneran* [1996] 160 JP 409.

(e) Underhill J simply said, 'It may be anomalous that one particular kind of private space – namely the common parts of a building shared by more than one dwelling

– should have been specially brought within the statutory definition when others are not; but this is a notoriously ill-conceived statute, and it is not for us to seek to re-draft it' in *Bogdal v. Regina* [2008] EWCA Crim 1.

The criticism was widespread and certainly not limited to the courts. For the DDA introduced a legal free-for-all attitude where any dog that resembled a pit bull terrier was seized off the street and then deemed to be dangerous. The biased view ensured its death. Given its introduction was a typically political act, its consequent lack of logic and fairness was reflected in the Act. It was criticised as 'this ill-considered, unjust law' in 1995 by the editor of the *Veterinary Record*. While in 2008 a solicitor in the *Law Gazette* analysed the decided cases and concluded the DDA was 'A dog's breakfast'.

The immediate result of the DDA was similarly not limited to legal confusion. One 'rescued' dog, Ebony, who had been badly abused by a former owner was alone and frightened in a car and unable to leave it despite the police trying to remove it. So they got a vet who arranged for her to be anaesthetised and then Ebony was killed. It was then discovered it was not in fact, contrary to their belief acting purely on appearance, a pit bull terrier but a friendly Staffordshire bull terrier too frightened of them to move: endangereddogs.com. Similarly the site cites the case of Mark Amston who was so worried when the DDA was introduced as he did not have insurance for his pit bull terrier, Sandy, that he had her put down. The following day he hanged himself from the attic door. He left a suicide note saying, 'Me and Sandy will never be parted again.' Dewi Pritchard Jones, the Coroner, said, 'In this case it was a family pet that had to be put down, not a fierce animal. There was no evidence that this dog was fierce. I think the lesson from this death is that legislation should be based on reason and not on panic...[his death] was a consequence of legislation rushed out and not properly thought out.'

With a certain perversity and irony a well-drafted Act is even more necessary now than before as in the summer of 2012 there was another spate of dogs biting people, particularly children. Allied to that there were also many unprovoked attacks by dogs on Guide Dogs for the Blind at a rate of eight a month. So on one level it is a problem that will not disappear. On the other level we have to equally consider the irresponsible owner that allows, or sometimes even encourages, their dog to behave aggressively. Ultimately it is usually the owner that causes the problem. That is the underlying reason the DDA puts an onus on the owner. Indeed it is where it belongs because the control is in his hands. The main purpose of the DDA is set out at length in section 1. While it has been amended over the past two decades, the strict import of its purpose remains as indicated in the Long Title: An Act to prohibit persons from having in their possession or custody dogs belonging to types bred for fighting; to impose restrictions in respect of such dogs pending the coming into force of the prohibition; to enable restrictions to be imposed in relation to other types of dog which present a serious danger to the public; to make further provision for securing that dogs are kept under control; and for connected purposes.

Dogs bred for fighting

G2   Dangerous Dogs Act 1991, s.1

   (1)   This section applies to –
      (a)   any dog of the type known as a pit bull terrier;
      (b)   any dog of the type known as the Japanese tosa; and
      (c)   any dog of the type designated for the purposes of this section by an order of the Secretary of State,

being a type appearing to him to be bred for fighting or to have the characteristics of a type bred for that purpose.

(2) No person shall –

    (a) breed, or breed from, a dog to which this section applies;

    (b) sell or exchange such a dog or offer, advertise or expose such a dog for sale or exchange;

    (c) make or offer to make a gift of such a dog or advertise or expose such a dog as a gift;

    (d) allow such a dog of which he is the owner or of which he is for the time being in charge to be in a public place without being muzzled and kept on lead; or

    (e) abandon such a dog of which he is the owner or, being the owner or for the time being in charge of such a dog, allow it to stray.

(3) After such day as the Secretary of State may by order appoint for the purposes of this subsection no person shall have any dog to which this section applies in his possession or custody except –

    (a) in pursuance of the power of seizure conferred by the subsequent provisions of this Act; or

    (b) in accordance with an order for its destruction made under the provisions; but the Secretary of State shall by order make a scheme for the payment to the owners of such dogs who arrange for them to be destroyed before that day of sums specified in or determined under the scheme in respect of those dogs and the cost of their destruction.

(4) Subsection (2)(b) and (c) above shall not make unlawful anything done with a view to the dog in

question being removed from the United Kingdom before the day appointed under subsection (3) above.

(5) The Secretary of State may by order provide that the prohibition in subsection (3) above shall not apply in such cases and subject to compliance with such conditions as are specified in the order and any such provision may take the form of a scheme of exemption containing such arrangements (including provision for the payment of charges or fees) as he thinks appropriate.

(6) A scheme under subsection (3) or (5) above may provide for specified functions under the scheme to be discharged by such persons or bodies as the Secretary of State thinks appropriate.

(7) Any person who contravenes this section is guilty of an offence and liable on summary conviction to imprisonment for a term not exceeding six months or a fine not exceeding level 5 on the standard scale or both except that a person who publishes an advertisement in contravention of subsection (2)(b) or (c) –

(a) shall not on being convicted be liable to imprisonment if he shows that he published the advertisement to the order of someone else and did not himself devise it; and

(b) shall not be convicted if, in addition, he shows that he did not know and had no reasonable cause to suspect that it related to a dog to which this section applies.

(8) An order under subsection (1)(c) above adding dog s of any type to those to which this section applies may provide that subsections (3) and (4) above shall apply in relation to those dogs with the substitution for the day appointed under subsection (3) of a later day specified in the order.

(9) The power to make orders under this section shall be exercisable by statutory instrument which, in the case of an order under subsection (1) or (5) or an order containing a scheme under subsection (3), shall be subject to annulment in pursuance of a resolution of either House of Parliament.

Initially the Act was limited to those two known types, the pit bull terrier and the Japanese tosa. Given the wide power under section 1(1)(c) the Secretary of State introduced the Dangerous Dogs (Designated Types) Order 1991 which came into force on 12 August 1991. That was the first one and by it the DDA was amended to include:

(a) any dog of the type known as the Dogo Argentino; and

(b) any dog of the type known as the Fila Braziliero.

It appears strange at first to have the 'type' of dog specified rather than a 'breed'. However on analysis the reason becomes obvious. By specifying breed it would limit it to a known kind of dog with a background and character within a certain or particular category. So by using the term 'of the type' it is more general and includes a much wider variety of the dogs that can be subject to that term.

Using type as the standard also allows for changing conditions so dogs would come within that term that were hitherto unknown. Criminals with an inclination towards pleasure and profit often resort to cruelty as a pastime. To that end they get involved in badger-baiting and dog fighting much as others might play cricket and bar skittles. At present there is a new 'type' of dog being bred by badger-baiters which is a cross between a bull terrier and a lurcher. [*Bristol Evening Post*: 1/2/12]. Regardless of whether the intention of those involved is contrary to the Protection of Badgers Act 1992, the benefit of the DDA is it allows the Secretary of State to amend that Act by including such a type if it was not already banned.

Collins J noted the flaw in the original law in *R (Sandhu) v. Isleworth Crown Court* [2012] EWHC 1658 (Admin): 'the Act was amended because it was recognised that there was a possibility that even pit bull type dogs might not be dangerous, particularly as the definition was not as tight as it might perhaps have been and so it might have comprehended dogs which actually were not inherently vicious and which could safely be kept.' [See **G37**]

G3 Type

Within a short time of the DDA being introduced a series of cases came before the courts that proved how oppressive the Act was in aim and effect. As a result two of those went to appeal and became the leading case of *R. v. Crown Court at Knightsbridge ex parte Dunne*; *Brock v. Director of Public Prosecutions* [1993] 4 All ER 491. *Dunne* was a judicial review application and *Brock* was an appeal by case stated. They were heard together because while the facts were not similar, the point at issue for the court in each was essentially the same, namely the interpretation of the phrase 'any dog of the type known as the pit bull terrier' in section 1(1)(a) of the DDA.

Gary Dunne was charged that on 26 November 1991 he had a pit bull terrier in a public place without it being muzzled. He was convicted at Wells Street Magistrates' Court and appealed to the Knightsbridge Crown Court. The court decided that (a) Dunne had failed to prove his dog was not of the type known as a pit bull terrier, but (b) the prosecution failed to prove that the dog was unmuzzled. Therefore the court allowed Dunne's appeal.

Dunne was advised he could not appeal against the Crown Court's conclusion that his dog was of the type known as the pit bull terrier. Therefore he applied for judicial review of that decision and was given leave. He sought: A declaration that the Crown Court erred in its interpretation of the phrase 'any dog of the type known as the pit bull terrier', and that on a proper construction of the statute the word 'type' should be defined in its technical sense – here equivalent to 'breed' – rather than given a broad, popular meaning.

Glidewell LJ outlined the findings of the Crown Court and particularly noted that Judge Mendl said: "if it were intended that it should refer to a particular breed, there would have been no difficulty in defining the breed by saying 'any American pit bull terrier', even though that breed is not accepted by the British Kennel Club. We therefore find that the meaning in the Concise Oxford English Dictionary is appropriate – a general meaning not a technical one. The words mean that a dog 'of the type known as a pit bull terrier' is an animal approximately amounting to, near to, having a substantial number of the characteristics of the pit bull terrier."

Judge Mendl summarised the evidence of Dr Mugford, an expert witness called by the defence and of witnesses called by the prosecution. 'He then said: "considering all the evidence we have heard and the burden of proof, we conclude the applicant has not discharged the burden of proving his dog was not of the type known as a pit bull terrier."

The court however then concluded that the prosecution had not satisfied the burden of proving that at the relevant time the dog was unmuzzled. Thus the appeal was allowed.'

Glidewell LJ then turned to the case of Karen *Brock* as it raised wider issues in respect of her dog, Buster, which she was convicted of having in her possession or custody which was a pit bull terrier. He said the case stated confirmed she 'admitted that

(a) she had the dog in her possession on 26 December 1991 (b) the dog had not been neutered, tattooed, implanted, insured nor registered. It was not therefore exempt on that ground from the prohibition against possession or custody of a dog to which section 1 of the Act applied.

Judge Zucker QC at Wood Green Crown Court traced the history of the dog: "Pit bull terriers were first bred in England as fighting dogs. Some time in the middle of the last century they were imported into the United States of America. When dog fighting was banned and died out in England about the middle of the last century, pit bull terriers were no longer bred here. The development of the breed however continued in the United States of America. In 1976 two female pit bull terriers were imported back into England, followed by a stud dog called 'Al Capone'. From that beginning pit bull terriers have been bred in England. (b) Dogs, generally, have breed standards which are laid down and recognised by different associations of dog breeders. The leading Association in England is the Kennel Club. Because of the long period when pit bull terriers were not bred in this country, The Kennel Club has no standard for pit bull terriers, nor has any other association in this country. (c) Because pit bull terriers have been bred over long period of time in the United States of America there are breed standards promulgated by associations of dog breeders in the United States of America. (d) One of those associations is that of the American Dog Breeders Association (ADBA). ADBA was founded in 1909, has always existed for pit bull terriers alone and has never registered any other breed. It is the most detailed standard. It deals with physical characteristics. It is widely used and accepted. The pit bull terriers originally imported into this country were registered with ADBA. (e) A second, less detailed standard is that of the United Kennel Club (UKC). ADBA does not recognise the standard of UKC and *vice versa*."

The Crown Court summarised the evidence of the defence expert, Dr Mugford. That related to pit bull terriers generally and the behavioural characteristics of Buster.

The Crown Court concluded that, "We accepted the evidence of the respondent's witnesses and did not accept the evidence of the witnesses called on behalf of the appellant. We found that the characteristics of the appellant's dog substantially conformed to the ADBA's standard and was of the type known as the pit bull terrier...The appellant therefore failed to adduce sufficient evidence to rebut the presumption that her dog was of the type known as the pit bull terrier. We therefore dismissed the appeal."

Glidewell LJ analysed that decision and said, 'Interpreting the phrase "of the type known as the pit bull terrier" in section 1(1) of the statute simply by the normal canon of construction, ie by giving the words their ordinary meaning, I entirely agree with the decision of the Crown Court in both cases that the word "type" is not synonymous with the word 'breed'. The definition of a breed is normally that of some recognised body such as the Kennel Club in the United Kingdom. I agree with the Crown Court in both cases that the word "type" in this context has a meaning different from and wider than the word "breed". I would so conclude by reading only section 1 of the 1991 Act. But that this is so is made even clearer by reference to a subsection to which I have not so far referred, namely section 2(4) of the 1991 Act. This provides: "In determining whether to make an order under this section in relation to dogs of any type the Secretary of State shall consult with such persons or bodies as appear to him to have relevant knowledge or experience, including...a body concerned with breeds of dogs."

In that subsection the two words are used in contradistinction to each other.'

The court was referred to two decisions of the High Court in Scotland. Glidewell LJ referred to one of them, *Parker v. Annan* [1993] SCCR 185, where the Lord Justice General said in dealing with the same issue:

"There is an absence of any precise criteria by which a pit bull terrier may be a identified positively as a breed and by this means distinguished from all other dogs. One must of course be careful not to extend the application of the section to dogs other than those which are described in it. A dog must be of the type known as a pit-bull terrier if section is to apply to it. But the phrase used by the statute enables a broad and practical approach to be taken, in a field in which it has been recognised that the pit bull terrier cannot, in this country at least, be precisely defined by breed or pedigree. For these reasons we do not think that the sheriff misdirected himself when he regarded as highly significant Mr Hayworth's evidence that Kim resembled a pit bull terrier more than any other type of dog and declined to rely on Dr Peachey's opinion that although she resembled a pit bull terrier she was not in fact one but was a mongrel. He was right to approach the case on the basis a dog could be the type known as the pit bull terrier although it was not purebred as such on both sides. We do not find anything in his use of words to suggest that he applied the wrong test in his approach to the evidence. The question whether the evidence as to Kim's characteristics was sufficient to show that she was not of this type was a question of fact for him to decide."

Glidewell LJ said, 'I would respectfully agree with and adopt that passage.'

His Lordship concluded, 'Having decided that the word "type" has a wider meaning than the word "breed", a court then has to adopt some guide for determining the limits of the phrase "any dog of the type known as the pit bull terrier". What that guide should be, and where those limits lie, are questions of fact for the decision of the magistrates or the Crown Court, on the evidence. In these matters, the courts in both cases heard evidence that the ADBA laid down a breed standard for pit bull terriers in the USA. The Crown Court in both cases were therefore entitled to use the ADBA standard as a guide. However, both courts were also entitled to find, on the evidence before them, that the fact that a dog does not meet that standard in every respect is not conclusive. Thus both courts could properly conclude that a dog was of the type known as pit bull terrier if, as the Crown Court at Wood Green found, its characteristics substantially conformed to the ADBA's standard or, to use the words of the Crown Court at Knightsbridge, if the dog approximately amounted to, was near to, or had a substantial number of the characteristics of the pit bull terrier as set out in the ADBA's standard.

That is sufficient to answer the question posed by Mr Dunne's application, and also to answer both questions (b) and (c) raised in the appeal of Miss Brock in the affirmative.'

Notwithstanding that conclusion the appeal of *Brock* raised an important point as to the relevance of the particular dog's behaviour. For the Crown Court position and several other cases showed that different judges had a different approach and answer to that vital question. In *Brock's Case* the Crown Court stated it was their "opinion that (a) In determining whether a dog was 'of the type known as a pit bull terrier' the behaviour of the dog, whether or not it had shown dangerous proclivities, was irrelevant."

Glidewell LJ referred to the point as 'A copy of the ADBA's standard is exhibited to the case stated in Miss Brock's appeal. In somewhat colourful language, the standard does refer both to bodily characteristics of a dog and to its behavioural characteristics. It is true it contains a long and detailed description of the bodily characteristics of an ideal pit bull terrier, but in another passage it is also said that the dog should have the following characteristics: (i) gameness, (ii) aggressiveness, (iii) stamina, (iv) wrestling ability, (v) biting ability.

No doubt the last three of these can be said to be functions of the dog's bodily characteristics, but the first two are obviously aspects of behaviour. Moreover, the standard concludes that, in judging the American Pit Bull Terrier, up to 10 points, out of a maximum of 100, can be awarded for the dog's attitude. To an extent, therefore, the ADBA criteria include behavioural characteristics.

So in my judgment it must follow, if the ADBA's standard is a proper starting point, that it is relevant to consider whether or not a dog exhibits the behavioural characteristics of a pit bull terrier, and evidence about the dog's behaviour cannot be irrelevant.

I emphasise that such evidence is not conclusive. It is clear from the long title to the 1991 Act that its purpose is "to prohibit persons from having in their possession ...dogs belonging to types bred for fighting". On appropriate evidence, a court would be entitled to express its conclusions in such words as: "We find that this dog has most of the physical characteristics of a pit bull terrier. The fact that it appears not to be game or aggressive is not sufficient to prove, on balance, that it is not a dog of the type of the pit bull terrier."

Nevertheless in my judgment for the reasons I have sought to explain evidence on this subject is relevant and must be given some weight.

For these reasons I would refuse to grant a declaration in terms sought by Mr Dunne. I would however answer the first question posed in the case stated on Miss Brock's appeal in the negative. Thus I would allow her appeal.'

The other Scottish case referred to was *Annan v. Troup* [1993] SCCR 192. There Lord Justice General Hope candidly identified the problem by suggesting the lack of certainty in the drafting of the DDA was, 'No doubt deliberate, in view of the many variables produced by cross-breeding...' He even openly acknowledged the manifest 'risk that different judges will form different views on the same facts.'

It follows that the prosecution have a distinct advantage over the defence in bringing proceedings as the 'presumption' under section 5(5) that the dog is of the alleged type is tantamount to proof 'unless the contrary is shown by the accused'. [See **G41**] Nothing much has changed since *Dunne* as while a pit bull terrier has a total of 54 characteristics, in truth a lot less than that number plus a dog's appearance are enough to ensure it is seized and killed: see *Dogs on Death Row*: BBC 1: 24/1/12.

Professor John Smith in his Commentary on the case at [1993] Crim. L. R. 854 makes a the point that though defence counsel accepted and Glidewell LJ confirmed that the burden of proof was on the defendant on the balance of probabilities, the section merely states 'show' rather than 'prove'. Professor Smith says, 'Sometimes draftsmen say "prove", sometimes "show", for no apparent reason. The presumption of innocence is constantly eroded by provisions of this kind.' It is a solid point as it is unusual to use different words in a statute with the same meaning. Indeed the same word 'shows' is repeated in section 1(7) presumably with the same effect. Yet conversely it states 'prove' in section 3(2).

In any event it is difficult to reconcile this decision with a legal burden of proof rather than an evidential one. Notwithstanding *Bates v. United Kingdom* [1996] E.H.R.L.R. 312 which was considered by the European Court, the better conclusion would be to follow the House of Lords in *R. v. Lambert* [2001] 2 Cr.

App. R. 28. Lord Slynn succinctly stated the point of principle in saying, 'Even if the most obvious way to read section 28(2) [of the Misuse of Drugs Act 1971] is that it imposes a legal burden of proof I have no doubt that it is "possible", without doing violence to the language or to the objective of that section, to read the words as imposing only the evidential burden of proof...even if this may create evidential difficulties for the prosecution as I accept, it ensures that the defendant does not have the legal onus of proving the matters referred to section 28(2) which whether they are regarded as part of the offence or as a riposte to the offence *prima facie* established are of crucial importance.' Thus the principle in *Dunne* should be revisited and challenged. [See **G7**]

Significantly in the civil case *Hunt v. Wallis* [1994] PIQR 128 the court was considering section 2 of the Animals Act 1971 in relation to harm done by a Border Collie. Pill J said, 'Where there is an identifiable breed of dog, a breed of long standing with acknowledged and identifiable characteristics, at least where it is a breed whose qualities are recognised as beneficial to man, the comparison should be with that breed or sub-species.' In another recent civil case under the same Act the court held that, 'A characteristic of an animal is something that is inherent in that animal and an unprecedented one-off action is not something inherent.' However that is precisely the reasoning relied upon by court-after-court to condemn a dog as being of a certain type with the consequence of ordering its destruction.

The uncertainty of the definition is confirmed rather than clarified by the present position as endangereddogs.com state, 'Unfortunately, since 1991 there have been three revisions of the ADBA standard, and the current version can be found on their website.'

G4 Gift

The restrictions as to the type of dog are strengthened by subsection (2) which curtails specified activities in relation to them. For it is forbidden to breed, or breed from, such a dog. Equally it is illegal to sell or exchange such a dog or offer, advertise or expose such a dog for sale or exchange.

The restrictions are wider in that a person cannot make or offer to make a gift of such a dog or advertise one as a gift. In that context any advertisement that is used to indicate an intention to give the dog away is defined by section 10(2) as: ' "advertisement" includes any means of bringing the matter to the public and "advertise" shall be construed accordingly'. So as it refers to any means it applies to temporary and permanent methods as long as the message is clear. Then the prohibited dog could not even be a gift-horse. [See **G37**]

G5 Intoxication

The most significant prohibition on such a dog is to allow it to be a plain danger to the public at large. So a person who is the owner or is for the time being in charge of it cannot allow it to be in a public place unless it is both muzzled and kept on lead.

It follows that the state of the owner, be it through alcohol or drugs, affects the fate of the dog. In *DPP v. Kellett* [1994] Crim LR 916 the prosecution appealed by case stated against a decision of the Crown Court to allow Kellett's appeal against conviction at the magistrates' court. Kellett was charged with being the owner of a pit bull terrier which she had allowed to be in a public place without being muzzled or kept on a lead contrary to section 1. The dog was registered as a pit bull terrier and otherwise complied with the Act. It had escaped from her flat as the front door had been left ajar and went into a public place. Kellett left the door ajar because she was drunk. The issue before the court was whether Kellett had 'allowed' the dog to be in a public place. The prosecutor argued that although the word 'allow' imported an element of *mens rea* into the offence, her voluntary intoxication could not provide a defence.

The court endorsed the dicta of Kennedy LJ in *R. v. Bezzina* [1994] 99 Cr App R 356 where it was accepted by the prosecution that the word 'allow' introduced some element of *mens rea*. In that case it was the absence of the word in section 3(3) of the DDA that rendered the offence under that section absolute. The court was referred to a number of Commonwealth authorities on the meaning of the word, which indicated it involved actual knowledge or connivance or consent or went beyond negligence or carelessness. In *Crabtree v. The Fern Spinning Company Ltd* [1901] 85 LT 549 Darling J said that 'a man cannot be said to allow that of which he was unaware or that which he cannot prevent.' The tentative view of the court was if Kellett had left the door ajar while sober and the dog, unknown to her, was able to get out, she could not be said to have allowed the dog to be in a public place even though she had been careless in not shutting the door.

However their tentative view was not conclusive as Kellett was only unaware of what she had done because she was drunk. As the offence under section 1 was a crime of basic intent her intoxication could not provide a defence. The appeal was allowed.

This is a policy decision which is questionable. For there is no *actus reus*. While voluntary intoxication negates the need to prove a basic intent it does not affect the prosecution's burden to prove the guilty act. The court was understandably concerned about the possible result if it allowed a drunken owner to escape the possible consequences of her behaviour. Nevertheless the reality is whether Kellett was drunk or not she did not 'allow' the dog to be there. Otherwise any workman who enters the kitchen to turn off her stopcock and lazily leaves the door open so her dog escapes into a public place would also make her liable. Though it is then the act of a third party the result is the same. His action would be transplanted onto her so as to make her liable for allowing the dog to escape. For 'the word "allow" refers to permitting or standing by as someone else causes that, effect or consequence': *Victor v. Chief of Naval Staff* [1992] 115 ALR 716. The result remains the same whether Kellett was as drunk as david's sow or as sober as a judge. [See **G32**]

G6 Necessity

How strict the DDA is interpreted can be seen by the fact necessity is not available as a defence. In *Cichon v. DPP* [1994] Crim LR 918 the appellant was convicted of allowing a pit bull terrier to be in a public place without being muzzled, contrary to section 1(2)(d). He appealed against the sentence to the Crown Court. Cichon argued that his mitigation revealed a defence, so his guilty plea at the magistrates' court had been equivocal. The Crown Court refused to remit the case to the magistrates for trial, but stated a case.

The mitigation was that Cichon had removed the muzzle because the dog had kennel cough, so it was cruel to keep the muzzle on whilst he was coughing. So Cichon claimed that was a defence of necessity. The questions for the Divisional Court were (a) whether the plea was equivocal and (b) whether it was right not to remit the case.

The Law Commission had drawn a distinction between a defence of duress and necessity. In duress the will of a defendant was overcome, whereas for necessity the defendant's freely adopted conduct was justified: see Law Commission No. 218. The question was whether a defence of necessity was available to a defendant who could show he did the deed to avoid serious harm to the dog.

The court rejected the claim because the aim of the Act was the security of the public. Schiemann J said, 'The Act does not in terms (and nor in my judgment does the common law) allow the person in control of the dog to make a value judgment as between what is good for the dog and what is good for the rest of mankind...We have here an absolute prohibition and a breach of that prohibition is to be followed by an order for the dog's destruction however blameless the dog and its owner.' So as the prohibition was absolute, Parliament cannot have intended a defence of necessity should apply.

In the Commentary Professor John Smith raises a significant point which casts doubt upon the decision. He refers to the fact the court 'thought that any defence of necessity there may be could not apply to the offence under section 1 of the Dangerous Dogs Act because it was an "absolute" offence. This does not follow. Statutes imposing an "absolute prohibition" exclude a requirement of *mens rea* but do not necessarily exclude general defences at common law. If the appellant had removed the dog's muzzle because an armed animal rights fanatic had threatened to shoot him if he did not, he would surely have had a defence of duress...Schiemann J states: "The Act does not in terms (and nor in my judgment does the common law) allow the person in control of the dog to make a value judgment as between what is good for the dog and what is good for the rest of mankind." That is right; but it is not inconsistent with a defence of necessity. Suppose that the dog was in great agony and the muzzle was removed by officers of the RSPCA, keeping the dog firmly under control until the muzzle could be replaced. A jury or magistrates, if they were allowed to decide the matter, might conclude that the evil prevented by breaking the letter of the law far outweighed any risk to the public arising from the breach.'

Kennel cough [acute tracheobronchitis] is a problem for a dog such that *Vetstream* in Fact sheet 265501 advises that 'It is very contagious and will spread rapidly around the dog population... it causes coughing that can go on for a month in some cases... If your dog normally wears a collar, take this off, to stop it irritating his throat, and exercise him outside with a harness or halter and lead.' If a person had an allergic-reaction to an electronic tag he had to wear as a condition of bail he would have a defence of necessity if he had to remove it. Similarly a prisoner if he was charged with an offence could rely on necessity if he had escaped from a burning cell. The comparison of the dog's kennel cough to a defendant's electronic tag which if a necessity arose because his ankle swole up or was aggravated by the metal in the tag or when breaching his bail he broke his ankle, would the tag not be removed and his condition and self-inflicted injury provide a lawful excuse? If so, what is the difference when compared to a kennel cough or a drink of water or an involuntary vomit? Why should or indeed would an excuse of justification and necessity be available for a man but a vicarious one be denied to the master of a dog?

There is a salient explanation on dogstrust.org which states: 'Kennel cough could be compared to human 'flu in that whilst it is very unpleasant, it is rarely fatal. Recovery from symptoms is usually complete in two to three weeks. However, severe cases in puppies, older dogs and giant breeds may lead to pneumonia if the condition is not treated, and could lead to death.'

Professor Glanville Williams notes with his usual acute insight in the *Textbook of Criminal Law* [1983] that 'necessity is not a general defence, but is recognised within the definitions of some particular offences. A few statutes painstakingly provide for the defence, at least in part, as when the Protection of Animals Act 1911 penalises the infliction of "unnecessary" suffering…'

Dickson J in the Supreme Court of Canada confirmed the point with clarity in *Perka v. The Queen* [1984] 13 D.L.R. (4th) 1. The cargo of cannabis due for Colombia was offloaded into Canada. The captain took that action to save the ship from sinking. Upholding the defence of necessity the Court endorsed the view of Macdonald J in another case: 'The objectivity of the criminal law is preserved; such acts are still wrongful, but in the circumstances they are excusable. Praise is indeed not bestowed but pardon is…' Cichon deserved a pardon rather than his dog being forced to pay the price.

Another matter which does not seem to have been properly raised by expert evidence is the effect of the defendant not taking action to alleviate the dog's suffering: if the kennel cough was such a condition that as a result of the muzzle not being removed the dog choked and died the defendant could have been convicted even under the POA. Now he would be failing in his duty under section 9 of the AWA. Moreover as he may have caused his dog unnecessary suffering, whatever was the result, he could be liable under section 4 of the AWA too. Both offences could only have been avoided if he took action which amounted in law to a necessity. The alternative for Cichon would be committing a crime. All in all the decision was wrong in law and logic; in principle too. [See **B7**; **B13**]

G7 Place

The greatest danger arises when a prohibited dog is in a public place. For then often there is a spontaneous attack upon a small child or another dog. Then when the parent or other owner comes to the rescue, he is in danger too. That can only happen obviously if the dog has no muzzle or is not on a lead or both, so it is out of human control.

In section 10(2) a ' "public place" means any street, road or other place (whether or not enclosed) to which the public have or are permitted to have access whether for payment or otherwise and includes the common parts of a building containing two or more separate dwellings'. [See **G49**]

Although that definition appears to be wide it nevertheless does not cover rather obvious areas and places which are not uncommon, but certainly are dangerous, namely private premises. So on its face it applies to privately owned land because the public often have access. Similarly communal blocks of flats even when they are secured-entry controlled. However the limit expressed in the section is not necessarily going to apply to ordinary residential property which is precisely where many attacks take place. For if the dog is 'permitted' to be on neighbouring land then the section does not bite as it is subject to section 3 and it is not a 'public place'. Moreover if a postman is bitten while he is there, there would be a statutory defence, in that the onus would be on the prosecution to prove the contrary. Similarly it would provide a defence by calling the neighbour, if there was a case to answer, to substantiate the defence. [See **G14**; **G22**]

What is or is not a 'public place' is central to the effect of the DDA. So the liability for the owner and the dog depends precisely on the place where the forbidden act happened.

While the definition under section 10(2) is potentially wide it has been interpreted not to include the garden path leading to the front door of a private dwelling. The path was accessible to all members of the public. Yet it was held in *Bates v. DPP* [1993] 157 JP 1004 to include the inside of a car that was parked in a public place. That was so even though the car was locked and his dog, Otis, could not escape. Moreover the public did not have access to it. Hence it was an interpretation based on policy plus the definition.

The tale of Otis began in the magistrates' court and ended up in the House of Lords. It started on 30 November 1991 when Henry Bates was driving his Ford Cortina in East London. He was stopped by PS Cherry in the Blackwall Tunnel who warned him of his potential criminal liability in relation to his dog who was loose in the car. The Officer said, which was admitted by Bates, that Otis was a pit bull terrier. There was a muzzle and a lead on the floor of the car by the front passenger seat. It was accepted that the dog was secure inside the car. Further 'there was no evidence from which it could be inferred that at some point in its journey the dog must have been at liberty on the highway.'

At his trial on 29 July 1992 it was submitted that there was no case to answer as his car was not a public place within the DDA. As he was not aware of the actual breed of his dog, no submission was made on his behalf challenging the prosecution's claim that Otis was of the type known as the pit bull terrier. The magistrate concluded that the interior of the car was a public place. Bates was convicted. So Otis was ordered to be destroyed.

Bates applied to the magistrates' court to state a case for the High Court on the question of whether the interior of his car constituted a 'public place' within the DDA. The defence claimed the car was not a public place. Moreover it is impractical to have a dog being held on a lead in a car. On 25 February 1993 the appeal was dismissed. Waller J said, 'This statute is a Draconian statute… This statute is ultimately aimed to exclude these types, those of a type known as a pit bull terrier, of dog from the country *in toto.*'

The Court followed the Australian cases of *McKenzie v. Stratton* [1971] VR 848 and *Mansfield v. Kelly* [1972] VR 744. In *Mckenzie* Nelson J said, 'Generally when an offence is defined in terms of a public place it is the public nature of the offences which is the evil which the legislature is designed to restrain.' Adopting that *dicta* Waller J said, 'One could even have the situation where the dog is left in a parked car with the window up and somebody, all be it wrongfully, lets the dog out.'

Rose LJ went even further and said, 'If the applicant is right, it would mean first that, no offence would be committed if an unmuzzled dog of this kind were in a car, the window, roof or tailgate of which was open, and secondly that, no offence or aggravated offence... would be committed if there was a dog of this kind in a motor car in a public place dangerously out of control.' His Lordship differed from Kenneth Jones J who somewhat strangely in *John v. Hillier* [Unreported 27/6/74] decided a car was a public place.

So it was in a public place. The High Court refused leave to appeal to the House of Lords. The House of Lords then refused leave to appeal to the House of Lords.

Finally *Bates v. United Kingdom* [1996] E.H.R.L.R. 312 arrived at the European Court on 16 January 1996. The court confirmed that on 4 December 1991 Bates was stopped again by the police while driving with Otis in the car unmuzzled and without a lead. He was charged under section 1(2)(d). Otis was seized and remained in custody in police kennels from then to date. Since 28 July 1994 Bates had to pay £8.81 per day for the kennelling. Otis was approximately five years old in December 1994.

Meanwhile Bates was busy gaining new evidence. Bates relied on the fact that he was informed in August 1993 by the police that they had not, prior to or during the hearing before the magistrates' court, caused the dog to be seen by an expert to give an opinion on whether Otis was 'of the type known as the pit bull terrier'. So on 8 September 1993 Bates had his dog examined by an expert. Thereafter he had it examined by a further three experts. All four experts 'concluded immediately that the dog was not "of the type known as the pit bull terrier" but rather a Great Dane cross-breed.'

The European Court considered the background to the appeal. Bates had applied for judicial review of his conviction and *certiorari* to quash it. The grounds were his new evidence as to the dog's breeding and the failure of the prosecution to have the dog examined by an expert prior to the hearing. On 29 June 1994 the High Court dismissed the application. That court noted Bates had failed to adduce any evidence as to the breed of the dog at the magistrates' court and had admitted that the dog was of a type known as a pit bull terrier. That court considered that 'the prosecution had not conducted such tests because it correctly relied on section 5(5) of the 1991 Act which placed the burden of proving this matter on the defendant and thus concluded that there was no failing in the conduct of the prosecution...' Further the High Court had considered the compliance of section 5(5) with Article 6(2) of the European Convention on Human Rights and ruled that it was not open to criticism in any way.

The European Court considered Bates' claims that he was 'Not aware of his dog's breeding at the time of the initial hearing and assumed that the police must have performed some sort of examination prior to the hearing. However...the breed of dog was evidently a basic proof in the case, that the terms of section 5(5) of the 1991 Act were clear and it is not therefore tenable for the applicant to submit that his mistaken assumption in such circumstances would render the presumption of fact unreasonable...the applicant claims that it is unfair that he would be obliged to definitively disprove the identity of his dog rather than simply cast some doubt on this, the Commission again recalls that the applicant did not even attempt any such evidential procedure and that...his various experts would have been in a position to present strong evidence that his dog was not a pit bull terrier. Therefore the Commission considers that section 5(5) of the 1991 Act falls within reasonable limits, even in light of what was at stake for the applicant, given the opportunity expressly provided to the defence to rebut the presumption of fact and that that section 5(5) was applied in a manner compatible with the presumption of innocence.'

Bates complained that he had no opportunity to put the facts of his case fully to any court. Having found against Bates on every point thus far they added another criticism saying, 'The Commission notes that it was the applicant's own choice to state a case to the High Court which led to his being unable to pursue a full rehearing before the Crown Court.'

Bates then argued that his keeping of a dog or his relationship with his dog fell within Article 8 of the Convention and that the measures taken against his dog were a disproportionate and unlawful interference with his right to respect for his private life. The Commission dismissed it as the keeping of a pet is not within the protection of an owner's private life for the purposes of Article 8: *X v. Iceland* [1976] D.R. 5.

The Commission then took each and every point raised by Bates and one-by-one dismissed them out-of-hand. Indeed even his claim that the term in section 1(1) to any dog of the type known as the pit bull terrier 'is vague in that identifying a dog of this nature is notoriously difficult' was rejected. The Commission placed the burden on Bates throughout the judgment. In this area alone they relied on the fact there was an 'exemption scheme provided by the 1991 Order, by which the applicant could have appropriately regulated his conduct, if he was in any doubt as to the dog's breeding.'

The best point raised by Bates was that the DDA did not strike a fair balance between the public interest involved and his right to the protection of his property. That placed an excessive legal burden on him. Moreover the mandatory destruction order was not proportionate as the immediate seizure of a suspected dog, 'the unavailability of "bail" for a dog pending trial together with extenuating circumstances in his case,' the dog being in his car, indicate the provisions of the DDA were disproportionate.

The Commission responded by saying it 'accepts that a conviction based on breed rather than past behaviour and the consequent mandatory destruction order, being provisions ultimately aimed at eradicating pit bull terriers as a breed from the United Kingdom, are draconian measures. However they noted that Bates was stopped on 30 November 1991 and warned of his potential criminal liability in light of the new legislative regime in relation to dangerous dogs. While Bates claimed that he paid heed to the advice and 'took steps to register his dog, he did not have his dog muzzled, on a lead or restrained in any way when he was again stopped four days later.'

The Commission emphasised the onus was on Bates as the owner. Although in terms of seeking an exemption, 'he claims he did so after 30 November 1991 which was after the time limit for adult dogs set down by the 1991 Order.' Finally the Commission concluded its judgment by confirming that the DDA provisions were a legitimate balance of public safety and proportionality between the means employed and the aim sought to be realised. Given 'the margin of appreciation enjoyed by the Contracting States, in this area,' it was not discriminatory within Article 14, so the Application was inadmissible.

There are several points of concern relating to this decision. The Commission criticised Bates for admitting his dog was a pit bull terrier, yet as a layman until he had the evidence of four experts he could not challenge the prosecution allegation. Indeed he had no reason to question the opinion of the police and every reason to believe they had conducted an examination of Otis. It would be a reasonable thing to do. They criticised him for not appealing to the Crown Court and yet that may have been a tactical decision on advice as his defence raised a point of law. They criticised him for failing to take action to register his dog after he was warned by the police as to the possible breach on 30 November 1991, which was the date it became an offence. As to the term in section 1 being 'vague', their view is irreconcilable with the view of Lord Chief General Hope in *Annan v. Troup* [1993] SCCR 192. Similarly the point on the burden of proof is irreconcilable with the principle defined in *R. v. Lambert* [2001] 2 Cr. App. R. 28. [See **G3**]

Further while *X v. Iceland* is a misguided decision, it is matched by *Bullock v. U.K.* [1996] E.H.R.R. CD85. *Bullock* endorsed the principle that keeping a pet does not come within a person's private or family life in Article 8 of the Convention. Each decision indicates a lack of understanding of the importance of an animal to the owner and within a family. It is a poor excuse of a court to deny a person a defence by being content to label an offence Draconian. For if the description is right there is more rather than less reason for there to be a defence.

G8 Stray

The final of the five forms that are prohibited is committed in two ways. It is an offence to abandon such a designated dog if he is the owner of it. If rather than being the owner, he is only in charge temporarily it is unlawful for him to allow the dog to 'stray'. Whether it is abandoned or simply allowed to stray the result is a dangerous dog is allowed to be an actual or potential ever-present danger to any unsuspecting member of the public, particularly any passing child or a blind person whose own dog as well as himself is then put at risk. When such a dog attacks it is usually sudden and often with severe consequences for the victim, be it a person or another dog. Of course the natural instinct in such a situation is for perhaps a passing stranger to intervene to protect the victim and in so doing may become one himself. Those perils are the precise reason the DDA is aimed at a public place. It is also the reason the definition of a public place is given a wide construction by the courts.

G9 Scheme

This section is so wide that before it was amended there was little either an owner or someone in charge of a prohibited dog could lawfully do with his dog this side of death. Initially there was a limited exclusion by subsection (4) which stated, subsection (2)(b) and (c) is not unlawful where anything is done with a view to the dog in question being 'removed' from the United Kingdom before 30 November 1991. That was the appointed day for the subsection to bite regarding 'possession or custody'. So for that short time it allowed a person to ensure the dog did not die by exporting the dog and the problem to another country. In a strange way that provision proved the perversity of an Act rushed through Parliament for political reasons.

The core question and position is covered in section 1(3) as by it no one can have possession or custody except on two grounds. It can be where he has seized it within the DDA. The second limb is he has it by an order of the court in order to destroy it.

As the appointed day was over twenty years ago it has limited practical effect now. However the later amendment by the

Dangerous Dogs (Amendment) Act 1997 [DD(A)A] does affect the position as it allows for exemption of otherwise prohibited dogs subject to certain strict conditions. There is a slight softening of the approach by section 1(5) which allows the Secretary of State to make an order that sections 1(3) 'shall not apply' to certain cases subject to compliance with specified conditions in a 'scheme of exemption' containing such arrangements as he thinks appropriate. Consistent with that limited exception the Dangerous Dogs Compensation and Exemption Schemes Order 1991 was introduced on 12 August 1991. The appointed day was 30 November 1991.

The result is no one can be lawfully in possession of or have custody of a designated dog except: (a) if it is seized under section 5; or (b) it is held under an order for destruction under section 4; or (c) it is exempt under a section 1(5) scheme.

Defra initially had an agent to carry it out. Since 2011 Defra have taken over the running of the Scheme. So it is only feasible to possess such a type now if the owner takes positive action including reporting the fact to the police, arranging for neutering, identification of the dog and third party insurance. If the owner complies with the strict conditions a Certificate of Exemption is granted. Even if the dog in question is within the Scheme of Exemption nevertheless it is subject to the restriction specified in section 1(2). For they are absolute and effectively the aim of the DDA is to control the number of such dogs. There is an Index of Exempted Dogs which can be checked to prove that any dog in question is or is not legally exempt. A breach of a condition results in the dog losing the legal exemption. Just as an irresponsible owner can cause its death, so a responsible owner can save his dog's life.

The number of convictions for having custody without control of such dogs is now increasing in direct proportion to the growing number of irresponsible owners. When a person is convicted of an offence under section 1 he is liable by subsection (7) to a term of up to 6 months' imprisonment or a fine up to Level 5 on the standard scale or both. [See **G37**]

G10 Advertisement

As an 'advertisement' means using any means of bringing a matter to the attention of the public under section 10(2), it would extend beyond the usual forms of a newspaper and television to a computer and texts and the ever-alluring twittering on various websites. In that regard a person who publishes an advertisement has a partial or complete defence to a charge under subsection 2(b) or (c). Then under section 1(7)(a) he will have a defence which, if proved, will limit the sentence. In that event he will avoid imprisonment if he 'shows' he published it for someone else and someone else 'devised' it. That puts an evidential and a legal burden on the defendant, but one which he must discharge to the civil standard.

He has a complete defence to such a charge and so would avoid any conviction if he shows a lack of knowledge and that he had 'no reasonable cause to suspect' that it related to the type of prohibited dog. That approach is consistent with the aim of the DDA. It also puts a legal burden on the person charged to prove his absence of both knowledge and suspicion. Each defence could apply to the same person or different persons.

G11 Adding

The Secretary of State may add any dogs of 'any type' to those already specified. In that event section 1(3) and (4) applies equally with the appropriate different appointed day. Without that provision, allowing a person a period to act lawfully, it would be an offence immediately the order under section 1(1)(c) was

270

introduced. The power was used to add the Dogo Argentino and the Fila Braziliero to the DDA. Moreover the provision under section 1(8) allows for the changing conditions of new types of dogs be it by discovery by the police or deliberate crossbreeding by criminals. [See **G2**]

The power to make orders which amend section 1(1) or (5), namely governing the type of prohibited dog and the scheme of exemption, can be made under subsection (9). In that case it is subject to being annulled by either House of Parliament. In comparison section 2 has to be approved by each House of Parliament.

G12 Abuse

As is plain from *R. v. Crown Court at Knightsbridge ex parte Dunne* [1993] 4 All ER 491 the defence have a defined disadvantage in proceedings under the DDA as the presumption that the dog is of the alleged type is unless he proves otherwise. [See **G3**] Therefore given both the general approach of the courts and the presumption against the defence under section 5(5), it is instructive to note that Pill LJ struck a blow for an alleged pit bull terrier on the basis both the owner and dog deserved a fair trial.

It arose in *R. v. Liverpool Magistrates' Court ex parte Slade* [1997] EWHC 529 (Admin). It was an application to quash the decision of the stipendiary magistrate who refused to stay an information against Noel Slade alleging an offence under section 1. Slade pleaded not guilty on 17 March 1995. The case was listed for a pre-trial review. At a hearing on 4 May 1995 it was made clear the sole issue was whether the dog was a pit bull terrier and the defence indicated they intended to call an expert witness. The trial was fixed for 16 June but the defence requested and were granted an adjournment because their expert was unable to attend court that day. The prosecution also intended to call an expert witness as was made clear at another pre-trial review on 29 June 1995. The trial was fixed for 7 September. On that date, due to an administrative error, the expert witness for the prosecution could not attend because of a commitment at Doncaster Crown Court. The magistrate refused to adjourn the case.

As a result the prosecution, in the absence of that witness, decided to call no evidence. The information was dismissed. The following day, the dog, which had been in police possession, was returned to Slade. In February 1996, another information was laid against Slade with respect to the dog alleging he was in charge of the dog in a public place on 8 September 1995. The case came before the magistrate on 10 June 1996. The defence sought a stay on the ground it was an abuse of process. The magistrate refused to do so.

In the High Court Defence Counsel submitted there was an abuse of process because (a) the prosecution had denied Slade the opportunity of a favourable finding on 7 September 1995 and (b) by returning the dog on the following day they played a crucial role in allowing him to commit the offence with which he is now charged and (c) because of the delay between September 1995 and February 1996.

The Defence relied upon *R. v. Haringey Magistrates ex parte Cragg* [1996] 161 JP 61. Pill LJ referred to that case and said, 'The prosecution offered no evidence upon a charge under section 1 of the 1991 Act and the charge was dismissed. The dog was returned to the owner who was not the defendant in the first proceedings. The dog was re-seized and proceedings were initiated for An Order for destruction of the dog under section 5(4) of the 1991 Act. Maurice Kay J, with whom Rose LJ agreed stated,

"At the end of the day the second proceedings, …involved the same dog which had remained in the same ownership throughout...it was wholly inappropriate and wrong for the Commissioner to take the second proceedings against this applicant...It matters not precisely what label is put on that analysis but in my judgment it is an abuse of process and ought to have been held to have been such."

Pill LJ then referred to the purpose of the DDA and concluded this appeal was different from *Cragg's Case* as although the dog had been in the same ownership throughout, the defendant was different. He also did not accept the delay as a valid ground of appeal.

Pill LJ having analysed that position said, 'Where the applicant is on stronger ground is in the circumstances upon which the information was actually laid. On 8 September the applicant was allowed to take the dog out of police custody and into a public place unmuzzled. He had expert evidence in his favour and he had been acquitted of the charge against him. On the evidence, there is no reason to doubt that, the prosecution not having proceeded against him on the previous day, and the charge having been dismissed, he reasonably believed he was entitled to act as he did. Unknown to him, the prosecution had already decided to base a further charge against him on observing him leave the police station in such circumstances.'

The court considered the principle that in "the conduct of the trial" it neither "initiates nor stifles a prosecution" (Lord Scarman in *R. v. Sang* [1980] AC 402). His Lordship added an important qualification that 'the defendant should be not be protected for all time from a trial of the issue as to the dog's breed. However, the power in a trial court, in deciding upon the sentence to be imposed, to have regard to the circumstances in which offence was committed is ordinarily a safeguard which mitigates the potential harshness of general principle.'

Pill LJ observed the fact that the statutory provisions in force at the time precluded any such safeguard. Section 4(1) made it mandatory upon conviction for a court to order the destruction of the dog. There was no discretion to mitigate the severity of the sentence by reason of the circumstances in which the offence was committed. He commented that if there had been a discretion, 'the circumstances in which the offence was committed may have high mitigatory value and, by analogy with *Sang*, this was undoubtedly a case for its exercise. The absence of the discretion is, in my view, a relevant consideration when deciding whether there was abuse of the process of the court.' He then considered how the prosecution and the police had acted and how that induced a belief in Slade that he would not be prosecuted. He ended with a firm view, 'The statutory provisions were such that the trial court, by way of mitigation of sentence upon conviction, was not in a position to protect him (or his dog) from the unfairness of the procedure followed. Given the consequences of a conviction, it was unfair to try the accused for the offence and offensive to the court's sense of justice and propriety, so as to be an abuse of process.'

Lest there was any doubt about the principle and it was interpreted as a one-off case, Pill LJ dispelled any such view saying, 'The Dangerous Dogs (Amendment) Act 1997, which provides some qualification to section 4(1) of the 1991Act, is soon to come into force but should not in my view bear upon the decision reached upon the facts in this case.'

Pill LJ is right in his view and conclusion. While the DD(A)A has now been available in practice for over a decade, the principle of *Slade* remains good law. For if the prosecution were able to take advantage of their own error or bad practice to condemn a dog to death it would destroy more than the dog: it would reflect badly on the law too. [See **G40**]

Other specially dangerous dogs

G13 Dangerous Dogs Act 1991, s.2

(1) If it appears to the Secretary of State that dogs of any type to which section 1 above does not apply present a serious danger to the public he may by order impose in relation to dogs of that type restrictions corresponding with such modifications, if any, as he thinks appropriate, to all or any of those in subsection (2)(d) and (e) of that section.

(2) An order under this section may provide for exceptions from any restrictions imposed by the order in such cases and subject to compliance with such conditions as are specified in the order.

(3) An order under this section may contain such supplementary or transitional provisions as the Secretary of State thinks necessary or expedient and may create offences punishable on summary conviction with imprisonment for a term not exceeding six months or a fine not exceeding level 5 on the standard scale or both.

(4) In determining whether to make an order under this section in relation to dogs of any type and, if so, what the provisions of the order should be, the Secretary of State shall consult with such persons or bodies as appear to him to have relevant knowledge or experience, including a body concerned with animal welfare, a body concerned with veterinary science and practice and a body concerned with breeds of dogs.

(5) The power to make an order under this section shall be exercised by statutory instrument and no such order shall be made unless a draft of it has been laid before and approved by each House of Parliament.

The introduction of the DDA was controversial. It remains so even now. Some are wholly against it as they claim it is so prejudicial the many good-natured dogs are sacrificed on the altar of a bad law. Others claim it is way too vague and should be strengthened to cover growing situations such as where children are attacked in public parks by irresponsible owners and tattooed drug dealers who also escape their legal deserts. They claim it should be extended to cover all dangerous dogs, just not fighting dogs. It is an emotional area and as ever subject to the caprice of opportunistic politicians.

So the powers given to the Secretary of State under section 2 allow him to impose an order in relation to dogs of any type that are not within section 1. He has to consider that those other types of dogs 'present a serious danger to the public'. In that event he can impose restrictions with such 'modifications', if any, as he thinks fit to all or any of those contained in sections 1(2)(d) and (e). That would apply to any dog which is not one of the four named ones in section 1 and any new designated dogs. So there would have to be something about them that makes them 'specially' dangerous over and above the natural disposition of any dog to defend its territory and itself.

So he can introduce restrictions relating to the dog if the owner or the person in charge in relation to it is irresponsible. That would apply to a muzzle and a lead. It would also apply to those persons who own or are in charge fail in their legal duty and abandon their dog or allow it to stray. Allied to that position and power the order may specify that 'exceptions' can be made from the restrictions. Equally it can order compliance with specified conditions. That would allow for changing conditions including a type of dog was suddenly stricken with some behavioural problem and had to be curbed while in public, though it was not a fighting dog *per se*. While any amendments he introduces may modify those conditions, he cannot introduce other restrictions.

Given that this is a wide power and would be likely to lead to corresponding new offences, there is a danger it could be more severe than the existing legislation. That is not possible presently as a matter of law. For subsection (3) only allows any new offence under the section to attract the same sentence as existing at present.

There is an important provision in subsection (4). As the powers are so extensive and the effect can be no less than death for those affected, that is a welcome and progressive provision in an otherwise harsh Act. Under it the Secretary of State 'shall' consult with persons having 'relevant knowledge and experience' before and in order to determine whether he should make any order at all. If it is necessary then the content is equally relevant to the submissions of the third party. The persons to be consulted include a body concerned with animal welfare, one concerned with veterinary science and practice and one concerned with breeds of dogs. That gives a balanced and fair approach covering most appropriate areas, though it is not limited to those bodies. It is essential that that approach is adopted when considering whether such restrictions are necessary at all when they are not dealing with designated dogs. It is too easy to introduce legislation in this area that continues in the tradition of Dracon. The third parties are a welcome and essential monitoring body to ensure there is a legal brake on a potential arbitrary power. There is an excellent example of the effect of the consultations in relation to the AWA in *R. (on the application of Petsafe Ltd and another) v. Welsh Ministers* [2010] EWHC 2908 (Admin). The number of groups who were consulted by the Welsh Ministers before new legislation was introduced included the Kennel Club, the Chief Veterinary Officer for Wales, the RSPCA and the People's Dispensary for Sick Animals. [See **B18**]

While the provision states he shall consult such bodies as 'appear to him' to have the relevant knowledge or experience, if he fails to do so it would give rise to a potential application of judicial review. The purpose of the consultation is that it is even-handed. Conversely if he consulted bodies that did not possess that knowledge or experience it would equally reflect upon his judgement and so be open to challenge. [See **B9**]

Significantly, while the amendments under section 1 come into force automatically unless they are annulled by either House of Parliament, this section requires both Houses of Parliament to endorse them. That gives greater control over any amendments which further apply to dogs not bred for fighting to become within a similar prohibited category.

Keeping dogs under proper control

G14   Dangerous Dogs Act 1991, s.3

(1)   If a dog is dangerously out of control in a public place –
   (a)   the owner; and
   (b)   if different, the person for the time being in charge of the dog, is guilty of an offence, or, if the dog whilst so out of control injures any person, an aggravated offence, under this subsection.

(2)   In proceedings for an offence under subsection (1) above against a person who is the owner of a dog but was not at the material time in charge of it, it shall be a defence for the accused to prove that the dog was at the material time in the charge of a person whom he reasonably believed to be a fit and proper person to be in charge of it.

(3)   If the owner or, if different, the person for the time being in charge of a dog allows it to enter a place which is not a public place but where it is not permitted to be and whilst it is there –

(a) it injures any person; or

(b) there are grounds for reasonable apprehension that it will do so, he is guilty of an offence, or, if the dog injures any person, an aggravated offence, under this subsection.

(4) A person guilty of an offence under subsection (1) or (3) above other than an aggravated offence is liable on summary conviction to imprisonment for a term not exceeding six months or a fine not exceeding level 5 on the standard scale or both; and a person guilty of an aggravated offence under either of those subsections is liable –

(a) on summary conviction, to imprisonment for a term not exceeding six months or a fine not exceeding the statutory maximum or both;

(b) on conviction on indictment, to imprisonment for a term not exceeding two years or a fine or both.

(5) It is hereby declared for the avoidance of doubt that an order under section 2 of the Dogs Act 1871 (order on complaint that dog is dangerous and not kept under proper control) –

(a) may be made whether or not the dog is shown to have injured any person; and

(b) may specify the measures to be taken for keeping the dog under proper control, whether by muzzling, keeping on a lead, excluding it from specified places or otherwise.

(6) If it appears to a court on a complaint under section 2 of the said Act of 1871 that the dig to which the complaint relates is a male and would be less dangerous if neutered the court may under that section make an order requiring it to be neutered.

(7)   The reference in section 1(3) of the Dangerous Dogs Act1989 (penalties) to failing to comply with an order under section 2 of the said Act of 1871 to keep a dog under proper control shall include a reference to failing to comply with any other order made under that section; but no order shall be made under that section by virtue of subsection (6) above where the matters complained of arose before the coming into force of that subsection.

Given that the DDA is aimed at protecting the public from dangerous dogs, section 3 is at the heart of the Act. For that deals with dogs that are dangerously out of control in a public place. Its purpose is to ensure that those who own or are in charge of a dog are truly in control. Otherwise by this power those persons will be controlled. Their dogs will be too. If they fail to do so the consequences are that at worst it could lead to a charge of manslaughter, though it is conceivable it could even lead to one of murder.

Many criminal gangs now adopt 'status' dogs as a weapon of choice to protect them and impress their friends while frightening their enemies. As a result the Metropolitan Status Dog Unit was set up in South London specifically to seize such dogs.

As the proclivity of criminals, especially drug dealers, is to possess dangerous dogs as an ersatz weapon who are sometimes encouraged or even trained to attack the police, there is no reason at all why in an appropriate case the owner could not be charged with murder. An interesting and not insignificant historical case is outlined in Evans prescient book, *The Criminal Prosecution and Capital Punishment of Animals*, [1906] where he documents one of the last animal trials in Switzerland in 1906. Scherrer and his son and their dog attacked Marger intending to rob him. During the attack the man was killed. All three were charged with murder. All three were convicted. The two men got a sentence of life imprisonment. The dog was duly executed.

Whether a dog is dangerously out of control includes by section 10(3) on any occasion when 'there are grounds for reasonable apprehension that it will injure any person, whether or not it actually does so...' It is applied to that behaviour in a public place which includes under section 10(2) 'any street, road or other place...to which the public have or are permitted to have access whether for payment or otherwise...' Depending on where and what happens it would at least lead to the simple offence and potentially the aggravated one. For the combination of the place and the lack of control covers the inherent twin risks of an irresponsible owner and a dog devoid of a master. [See **G48**]

G15 Expert

Throughout the authorities it is clear that the courts can often be guided by the absence or presence of expert evidence relating to the dog in question. It can result in either a severe or a lesser sentence for the defendant and the dog. Just how important an expert can be in this area of the law is exemplified by the Scottish case of *Swankie v. Procurator Fiscal* [1998] Scot HC 3. Swankie pleaded guilty as the owner of a collie type dog which was dangerously out of control in a public place. The offence was contrary to section 3(1).

When the case was listed on 13 August 1998 Terrence Swankie was not present but had submitted a letter of explanation. The procurator fiscal informed the sheriff that at about 11.45 am on a Friday, Alastair Gardiner had walked with his granddaughter past the gate of Swankie's home, when the dog ran towards them, jumped over the wall and approached them barking and growling. He successfully fended off the dog. About 15 minutes later a neighbour heard the sound of breaking glass and, on looking out, saw the dog running along the top of the wall. The dog jumped off the wall, ran towards a postman, barking and growling, and backed him up against a wall. The postman used his bicycle to ward the dog off. Gardiner came out of his house and with his assistance the dog was chased off and went back to its own garden. The police were called and when they interviewed Swankie the dog was on a lead and was excitable, but not aggressive.

The sheriff invited Swankie to attend court and give evidence to show that the dog was not dangerous as his letter was inconsistent with the prosecution case. Swankie could only explain the second incident when the dog broke the window and escaped. However as that did not explain the first occasion the sheriff concluded there were *two* incidents of aggressive behaviour by the dog. Lord Kirkwood in the High Court said, 'The sheriff then invited the appellant to provide him with evidence, perhaps from a veterinary surgeon, but the appellant declined to provide any evidence. So he concluded that the dog was a danger to the public…and he reluctantly made an order that the dog was to be destroyed.'

On appeal it was argued that as it was not an aggravated offence under section 3(1) the sheriff had a discretion whether or not to order the dog to be destroyed. Lord Kirkwood said, 'It was important to note that the appellant had not been legally represented at the hearing.' Swankie had misunderstood the situation and could not give further information to the sheriff as to how the dog escaped from the house for he had no further information. He did not realise he was being invited to lead evidence to show that the dog was not dangerous and did not appreciate his dog was to be destroyed. The court then made a crucial point in relation to the circumstances. For it was thought 'that there had been two separate incidents, the first of which was unexplained, had weighed heavily with the sheriff.' However on analysis that was wrong: it was one continuous incident in that the dog had somehow broken the glass, was frightened, escaped and then attacked two people. Lord Kirkwood said, 'On the basis of Mr Gardiner's statement, there had not been two separate acts but one continuous incident after the dog had fallen out of the window. In these circumstances it was understandable why the appellant could not give an explanation for two separate incidents 15 minutes apart, as the account the procurator fiscal had given the sheriff was factually inaccurate.'

Once Swankie realised the seriousness of the matter, Lord Kirkwood said, 'he had obtained evidence which clearly showed that the dog was not dangerous.' The court had a report from Dr Roger Mugford, Head of the Animal Behaviour Centre, Chertsey in Surrey...Dr Mugford stated that the dog was a good-natured and much loved family pet who had never previously been the subject of a complaint or caused danger to the public. She had escaped through the broken window and, unexpectedly finding herself outside the family home, had barked at passing strangers. Further, since the incident the appellant and his wife behaved in a neighbourly and responsible fashion and, as set out in the report, had instituted steps to prevent a recurrence of the incident. In his opinion the dog was not a danger to public safety and she had caused no physical injury. Counsel also produced a letter from Mr Gardiner stating since the incident in question he had noticed a marked improvement in the dog's behaviour. The dog is now much more amenable and he expressed the wish that she should not be destroyed. We were also told that numerous references had been obtained from neighbours and friends to the effect that the dog was a good-natured family dog.'

The court considered all the circumstances and concluded that, 'We have now been asked to take into account a considerable amount of information which was not before the sheriff...In these circumstances, and having regard to the interest of justice, we have decided to consider the information which has now been made available to us...' Lord Kirkwood said there was only one continuing incident which occurred because 'After the window had unexpectedly broken, the dog had fallen out and was understandably upset and agitated. Further, even in that condition she did not cause any injury.' As a result of the new information the Court allowed the appeal and quashed the destruction order.

The absence or presence of an expert is of such importance that without it the fate of the dog can be sealed in law. In *R. v. Harry* it made the difference between life and death. After the Crown Court judge refused an adjournment for an expert report, the Court of Appeal allowed it to be adduced and quashed the order for destruction. [See **G26**]

G16 Charge

Given the propensity of criminals to possess dangerous status dogs that are sometimes trained to attack people, they may be used as a weapon no less than a gun or a knife. Indeed the gravity of the offences that can be committed can be gauged by the fact that if the dog injures any person those liable are guilty of an aggravated offence. That liability under section 3(1) would extend to both parties namely (a) the owner and (b) if different, a person for the time being in charge of the dog.

How far that liability spreads is magnified by *L v. The Crown Prosecution Service* [2010] EWHC 341 (Admin). The High Court clarified the meaning of being in charge and confirmed that control is not relinquished by a short temporary transfer of the leash. This was a case stated appeal from the decision of Gott DJ at Newham Local Justice Area, who found the defendant guilty of being in charge of a dog, a Staffordshire Terrier, which was dangerously out of control in a public place and whilst out of control caused injury to Toby Rajit. He was charged with an offence contrary to section 3(1) and (4) of the DDA and an assault occasioning actual bodily harm contrary to section 47 of the Offences Against the Person Act 1861. The co-defendant, Louie Green, was also charged with the same offence. Green claimed duress saying he was 'scared' of the defendant. That defence was dismissed so Louie was convicted too.

In relation to the two charges that L contested Gott DJ made these findings of fact in the case stated:

(a) The appellant was not the owner of the dog;

(b) The appellant handed the lead to the co-defendant, Louie, while he tied his shoes;

(c) Louie then ran at Toby Rajit shouting, "get him, get him" and deliberately released the dog off the lead;

(d) The dog bit Toby on the upper thigh causing an injury that later became infected and required an operation;

(e) Louie was in physical control of the dog at the relevant time when the dog attacked Toby.

The issue was whether L was in charge of the dog despite having transferred physical control to Louie. The appellant submitted to Gott DJ that he was not in charge of the dog at the material time as there could not be two persons in control. At that moment Louie had the lead and was in control of the dog. As section 3(1)(b) refers to 'the person', there was no basis for treating two persons as being in charge of the dog at the same time. It was accepted that whether someone is in charge is a question of fact and degree as the Court of Appeal decided in *Rawlings* [1994] Crim. L. R. 433. It was equally accepted that L was in charge of the dog up until the point when he gave physical control to Louie.

Gott DJ rejected L's submission and found him guilty for these reasons:

(a) L was in charge of the dog when it was chasing Tekkai, an earlier victim who was not in fact physically injured, but was chased by the dog on an earlier occasion;

(b) L was in close proximity to the dog at all times;

(c) L knew the dog. It responded to his commands. L took control of the dog after it chased Tekkai;

(d) After the dog attacked Toby L regained physical control of and walked away with it;

(e) The dog was physically out of L's control for a very brief period of time at the point when it was handed over;

(f) Both Louie and L knew the dog was dangerous because they had both been present when it bit a person on a recent previous occasion;

(g) Case law indicated that being in charge is a matter of fact and degree;

(h) L was in effective control of the dog and in charge of it at all times;

(i) When Louie was in physical control L was still in charge of the dog.

After reciting all those facts and findings Elias LJ said, 'In short, the view of the judge was that both were in charge, Louie had physical control, but the appellant retained effective control. The judge posed the following question for the court: "Was I wrong in law to find that the appellant could remain in charge of the dog despite the transfer of physical control to Louie and to find that both defendants could be in charge of the dog at the relevant time?"

In my judgment there was no error of law by the judge in this case. It seems to me that the crucial finding is that at all times the dog responded to the commands of the appellant and he was in charge, both before and after Louie took physical control. The appellant would plainly remain in charge of the dog if it were let off its lead in the park, and I see no reason in principle why he does not remain in charge if albeit for a very short, temporary period he puts the dog in physical control of Louie. In my judgment the judge is entitled to conclude that a short and temporary transfer of actual physical control did not prevent the appellant from remaining in charge. He had the right and power to take the dog back at any time and was able to control the dog.'

Counsel for the appellant made an application using an analogy of somebody being in charge of a motor car as in *DPP v. Watkins* [1989] QB 821. Elias LJ gave that short shrift saying, 'I do not think that is an appropriate analogy.' Unlike where somebody handed the keys to a third party, here the appellant 'Was, as the judge found, at all times in a position where he was able to issue commands to the dog and the physical control did not preclude that...there was no reason why the singular precludes the plural as section 6(c) of the Interpretation Act 1978 makes the presumption it will do so.' Consequently the appeal was dismissed and on the assault conviction too.

That was the right conclusion for while the transfer was only temporary it was equally crucial that the dog responded to the 'commands' of L. Given the relationship between a dog and its owner, with a word he could have ended the attack before it began.

L and Louie were on alert by the earlier attack on Tekkai. What followed was well within their foresight too. So from start to finish it was a case of joint knowledge that led to a joint liability.

G17 Degree

Conversely the Court of Appeal in *R. v. Rawlings* [1994] Crim. L. R. 433 considered the case of a transfer which involved keeping a dog for a much longer period. Rawlings was charged with being a person for the time being in charge of a dog dangerously out of control in a public place and which, while so out of control, injured a person contrary to section 3(1). Rawlings was looking after an Alsatian dog for a man who was in prison. She fed and exercised it. One afternoon the dog left the house and injured a nine-year old boy. Rawlings had been out at work during the morning, returned home and then went out shopping; while she was shopping the dog got out although she had locked the house. Rawlings' defence was that the woman with whom she lived had returned and was in the house when the dog escaped. So she denied being the person in charge at that time within the meaning of the DDA. The judge directed the jury that she remained responsible even though she was out shopping. She appealed against conviction on the ground the judge had misdirected the jury and effectively withdrew her defence from them.

The court allowed the appeal as 'being in charge' was a question of fact and degree. There was an issue as to whether at the time the dog left the house Rawlings was still 'in charge' of it. Although there was 'powerful evidence that she was', the judge should have left the issue to the jury.

This was quite different from *L v. The Crown Prosecution Service* as there Louie and L were together in close proximity at all times throughout the incident. Significantly although Louie had the lead, L had the authority and the voice which the dog recognised. As L was present before and during and after the attack he could have stopped the dog in its tracks. His choice was to allow the attack to happen and continue. Conversely when Rawlings left the house the dog was in the company and control of the other woman. That woman could choose to keep the dog in or let it out or take it for a walk or indeed allow it to escape as happened. Rawlings was not able or capable of controlling the dog while she was absent from the house. So given those circumstances it was at least arguable that, as a matter of fact, Rawlings was not in charge at the relevant time. It is also why the defence in section 3(2) exists. [See **G21**]

G18 Absolute

Nevertheless if a dog injures a person while the owner is in charge of it the fact that the behaviour is unknown or unusual or both will not provide a defence. For if the dog bites the DDA does too. In *Regina v. Bezzina* [1994] 99 Cr. App. R. 356 the Court of Appeal held that although there was a presumption of law that *mens rea* was required before a person could be held guilty of a criminal offence, that presumption could be replaced where a statute was concerned with an issue of social concern and public safety. Hence where a dog in a public place was shown to be acting in a way which gave grounds for reasonable apprehension it would injure someone, section 3(1) imposed absolute liability upon the owner or the person for the time being in charge of the dog.

On 9 July 1993 Bezzina was convicted at Southwark Crown Court of an aggravated offence, contrary to section 3(1). He was fined £250 and had to pay £250 compensation to the victim. Further, an order was made that the dog be destroyed. The ground of appeal was that the judge had erred in ruling that the section 3(1) offence was one of strict liability. There were two other cases, *Codling* and *Elvin*, which raised the same issue and were heard at the same time. Both *Codling* and *Elvin* were convicted of the same aggravated offence. *Elvin* also raised an additional point.

After outlining section 3 Kennedy LJ said, 'On the face of it, therefore, when the words "dangerously out of control" are encountered in section 3(1) of the Act, one turns to section 10(3) to find out what they mean...Accordingly, it would seem that this Act by section 3(1), imposes strict liability on the owners of dogs of all sorts which are in public places and are dangerously out of control within the meaning of section 10(3) which, on the face of it, imposes or sets an objective standard of reasonable apprehension, not related to the state of mind of the dog owner.'

The court then considered the history of offences that do require a *mens rea* and indeed the presumption in favour of it as a matter of principle. As a result, while strict liability is rare it can be appropriate in dealing with issues of social concern and public safety. Kennedy LJ endorsed the principles outlined by Lord Scarman in *Gammon (HK) Ltd v. Attorney-General of Hong Hong* [1885] A.C. 1 and said, 'The fifth proposition: "Even where a statute is concerned with such an issue, [social concern and public safety] the presumption of *mens rea* stands unless it can also be shown that the creation of strict liability will be effective to promote the objects of the statute by encouraging greater vigilance to prevent the commission of the prohibited act."

Clearly, the terms of section 3(1), if read as imposing strict liability, are liable to have that effect.

Accordingly, we come to the conclusion that the terms of the statute in section 3(1) do not have to be read in the way we indicated at the start of this judgment. In other words, when one encounters the words in section 3(1) –"dangerously out of control" – one applies the meaning which is set out in section 10(3) and that means, in effect, that if a dog is in a public place, if the person who was accused is shown to be the owner of the dog, if the dog is dangerously out of control in the sense that the dog is shown to be acting in a way that gives grounds for reasonable apprehension that it would injure anyone, liability follows. Of course, if injury does result then, on the face of it, there must have been, immediately before being the injury resulted, grounds for reasonable apprehension that injury would occur.'

The court considered the objections to that interpretation but rejected them. As Kennedy LJ said, 'It is urged that an owner may have no realisation that his dog is liable to behave in a way which will cause injury to anyone until, for example, a child pokes the dog with a stick and the dog reacts. That, indeed, may be the case. But it seems to us that Parliament was entitled to do what in this piece of legislation we find that it has done, namely to put the onus on the owner to ensure, if that is likely to happen, he takes steps which are effective to ensure that it does not, either by keeping the dog on a lead or keeping the child away from the dog or whatever may be appropriate in the circumstances.'

The court then dismissed the three appeals.

Counsel for the respondent in *Bezzina* in the course of his submissions invited the Court to consider whether expert evidence should be called in relation to prosecutions under section 3(1) or admitted by judges hearing such cases. Kennedy LJ answered, 'In our judgment, having regard to the interpretation we place on the statute, there would seem in normal cases to be no room for expert evidence in relation to the primary issue. But, of course, it may be admissible in relation to other issues such as, for example, whether the dog did, in fact, bite anyone at all and it may be of considerable assistance to the court in relation to questions of sentence if there is, indeed, a finding of guilt.'

During the appeal counsel for *Elvin* raised the issue of a problem that may arise 'When a dog is which is properly secured inside premises, is let loose by a third party of whom the owner knows nothing, for example, a burglar.' He relied on a South African case *O'Sullivan v. Fisher* [1954] S.A.S.R. 333 and a New Zealand case *Kilbride v. Lake* [1962] N.Z.L.R. 590. While the Court acknowledged it is a problem that '...may have to be resolved. But it is a problem which does not arise...as the dog was not in a situation, as the learned judge found, where it was properly secured and not liable to escape until some third party intervened.'

The court referred to the remarks of HHJ Marder Q.C. at Isleworth Crown Court on sentencing: "On that occasion you left these two powerful and dangerous pit bull terriers at large that were inadequately secure for that purpose...they were quite inadequate to contain those dogs who were left free within the premises."

Kennedy LJ cited that finding and said, 'In those circumstances, it seems to us that the intervention, or the possible intervention, of third parties...simply does not arise on the factual basis in relation to which we have to consider this appeal.'

There are at least three potential troubling points that arise from this case. The finding that it is immaterial that a perfectly well-behaved dog might be killed as a matter of law because it reacts to being poked with a stick by a child is wrong. What if the child pokes it into the dog's eye? How could such provocative behaviour provoke a criminal liability? That is using the law as a big stick to beat both the owner and the dog. A 'reasonable apprehension' of injury cannot exist if up until the exact moment the dog reacts it had been pacific and when it did react it was purely an instinctive reaction because it was suddenly poked in the eye by a child waving a stick. Then it is not the dog that is not being controlled by its owner, but the child who was not being controlled by his parents.

If a dog unexpectedly bites a person and is immediately restrained thereafter, that cannot amount to a reasonable apprehension that it 'will' do so. As 'apprehension' is defined as 'anticipation especially with fear or dread' something that is unknown cannot induce that feeling. *Bezzina* is a bad decision that has been followed in subsequent cases where the reasoning is similarly flawed. The necessary apprehension is neither reasonable nor real. Whether objective or subjective, the various attempts by judges to try and justify the position in subsequent cases have only served to compound the legal *non sequitur*.

It is also wrong with respect to the idea there is no need for expert evidence in such cases. It is not simply necessary or relevant in terms of the *actus reus* or mitigation, as suggested. After a dog that suffers from post-traumatic stress disorder or is recovering from an operation may not be dangerous at all but if kicked may defend itself or its master. Indeed expert evidence would surely be admissible if it would tend to prove that the dog reacted as it did because its master or itself was attacked? For that would be relevant to and assist any decision of a magistrate or a jury. If it would be remiss of the defendant to obtain such evidence as the European Court considered in *Bates v. United Kingdom* [1996] E.H.R.L.R. 312, then surely the prosecution should do so too, especially where it affects the 'primary issue'.

As to the intervention of a third party, the problem stems from the fact the Court confined the effect of the section to one of strict liability. Why should an owner who has taken care to instruct a workman not to open the gate be liable if he disregards the request and behaves irresponsibly? Why should the dog die, as was potentially the position in *R. v. Harry* [2010] 2 Cr. App. R. (S) 395 prior to the appeal? It does not have to be so extreme or dramatic as to be a burglar. What if the workman was drunk or malicious or both? Every which way it is viewed *Bezzina* remains illogical. [See **G26**; **G55**]

G19 Notice

Even with such severe measures being applied, fortunately the concept of natural justice cannot be ignored. It was highlighted in *R. v. Trafford Magistrates' Court ex parte Riley* [1995] 160 JP 418, where Riley, the owner of a dog had an argument with her friend. Following the dispute and without Riley's knowledge, her friend took the dog to a nearby car park. Although the dog was on a leash, her friend was unable to restrain it with the result it bit a police officer. A summons was subsequently issued against her friend under section 3(1). She pleaded guilty and the magistrates ordered the destruction of the dog. Riley applied for judicial review of the magistrates' decision to destroy the dog, relying on the fact that she ought to have been given notice of the hearing.

The High Court held that although the magistrates had no discretion as to whether to order the destruction of the dog, had the owner been notified she could have attended the hearing and argued before the magistrates that, in all the circumstances, the prosecution was an abuse of the process of the court. Further, she may have argued that the car park was not a public place or that the friend had entered her guilty plea maliciously. Whether or not the magistrates' power was mandatory or discretionary, in any case concerning the destruction of property, the rules of natural justice required a known owner of property at least to be given the opportunity to be heard. As a result the order for destruction and the conviction was quashed. The matter was remitted to the magistrates' court. [See also *R. v. Ealing Magistrates' Court ex parte Fanneran* [1995] 160 JP 409: **G30**]

G20 Fit

In relation to section 3(1) the owner may have a defence under section 3(2) if he was not in charge of the dog at the material time and he proves the person who was, was someone whom he 'reasonably believed to be a fit and proper person to be in charge of it'. This has the advantage for the owner of providing a defence which is fair, especially as he would have been absent or not in charge of the dog at all at the 'material time'. So it could be actually temporary possession by the other person as while the owner even queued for or used a toilet, or longer if he went on holiday. Equally it applies of course if the owner allows the person to take his dog to the park where it then bites someone. The crucial point however is that it is for the defendant to 'prove' the person was a fit and proper person to be in charge. Hence the burden is on him to establish the defence. It could be a longer period such as when the owner is in hospital or prison. His choice would have to be a calculated decision as if he is charged with an offence the character of the one he chose could provide a defence.

The importance of that defence was considered by the Court of Appeal in *R. v. Harter* [1998] Crim. L. R. 336. Harter was convicted of being the owner of a dog dangerously out of control in a public place contrary to section 3(1). At a time when Harter was absent, a tethered dog bit a visitor to his scrap yard. His daughter, who also worked at the scrap yard, was present. When he was interviewed, Harter said, 'The Harter family own the dogs'. The co-defendant, his daughter, gave evidence that she was the owner of the dog in question. She produced evidence that it had been sold to her alone. Harter's defence was that he was not the owner of the dog. His counsel addressed the jury on the statutory defence in section 3(2). The judge did not direct the jury on that defence. Harter appealed on the ground that he should have done so. The Crown claimed there was no sufficient evidential basis to raise the statutory defence.

The court held that Harter's answer in interview provided evidence that, contrary to his primary defence, he was an owner of the dog. However after he had explained to the jury that the prosecution had to prove Harter was an owner of that dog, the judge should have directed them that if they found that he was an owner, they should then go on to consider the statutory defence, with appropriate directions. While the evidence was of 'a tenuous nature', the question was not whether the defence was likely to succeed, but whether the judge should have directed the jury about it. As it was raised in the evidence and was expressly raised in counsel's speech, the judge should have canvassed with counsel the necessity of directing the jury on the statutory defence. His failure to direct the jury was a material non-direction. As that went to a substantial defence, the conviction was quashed.

The judge at the Crown Court overlooked an important point namely as even if the defendant believed his daughter owned the dog because she bought it, the jury might have concluded that as it was the family pet he was a co-owner of it. So he should have been able to 'prove' that the dog was in the charge of a person whom he reasonably believed to be a fit and proper person. That is after all the precise purpose of section 3(2).

G21 Transfer

The Court of Appeal considered that defence again in *R. v. Huddart* [1999] Crim. L.R. 568 where Huddart was the owner of a Rottweiler dog. He was charged with not keeping a dog under proper control. It was alleged that a Rottweiler dog, roaming on its own, had bitten the victim when he was exercising his dog in a field. The issue for the jury was whether the Rottweiler dog that bit the victim was the same dog that was owned by Huddart. His defence was that, as his dog had not left his garden at the material time, it could not have been the dog in question. Although there was no formal transfer of charge to any third party, Huddart also relied upon section 3(2) claiming it applied to him, because it was his wife who allegedly opened the door of their house to let the dog into the garden. At the trial the judge directed the jury to disregard the statutory defence. Huddart appealed contending that the judge ought to have left that defence to the jury.

The court held that section 3(2) was not intended, in a situation where a dog was kept at home, to call for a minute analysis of which member of the family was in charge of it at any one moment. The fact that the door through which the dog got out was opened by a member of the family rather than by the owner was not evidence from which it could be inferred that the charge of the dog had been transferred to that other family member. The defence operated only if there was plain evidence that the dog had been placed in the charge of someone other than the owner. In order for there to be such a transfer, there had to be evidence which established, or permitted the inference to be drawn, that the owner had for the time being divested himself of responsibility in favour of an identifiable person. Here there was no evidence from which it could reasonably be inferred that the charge of the dog had been transferred from the owner to the owner's wife. To adopt such an approach would be artificial and contrary to the purpose of that subsection. So the judge was right. The appeal was dismissed.

The court was concerned that the statutory defence would be diluted and become ineffectual. While it is true who is in charge of a dog is one of fact and degree, here there was no evidence of at all that Huddart had actually transferred the charge to his wife. Indeed if so there is a danger for him as there is no reason why she should not be liable too. The court restricted the defence to cases where the owner has taken action to transfer the charge of the dog to another such as a vet or in a kennel or to a neighbour or a cohabitant as in *R. v. Rawlings* [1994] Crim. L. R. 433. [See **G16**]

The court acknowledged that even on this analysis a problem will still occur in cases where, for example, the person placed in control 'loses the dog'. Or of course acts with ill will against the owner by perhaps removing the muzzle or worse for some puerile prank.

Nevertheless section 3(2) is badly drafted. For both the owner and person in charge are potentially guilty, unless the owner can prove his defence. So it requires that the owner knew about the characteristics of the person actually in charge, but does not require that he has knowingly or intentionally transferred the charge of the dog. As the liability under this section is strict and the legal burden lies on the defendant, it is wrong except in a clear case to deny him the opportunity to rely upon it. It should be the jury who decides as their verdict may also decide whether the dog lives or dies.

While in this case there is no doubt that Huddart is the owner of the dog and he was present in the house at the time, it is feasible for him to claim that another was in charge. If his wife let the dog out of her own accord, she would then have been in charge of it, without any formal transfer of that duty by her husband. That would arguably be within the statutory defence. The court distinguished *R. v Harter* [1998] Crim. L. R. 336 because, unlike this case, the owner was absent from the premises. Although absence from the property by the owner would make it more likely that another has taken charge, there is no reason why an owner cannot be in the house and yet at that particular time his dog is in the charge of his spouse. It would be consistent with the section as the liability depends on who is in charge at the 'material time'.

In the Scottish Case of *Swinlay v. Crowe* [1995] SLT 34 the High Court confirmed that when an owner transfers the charge of his dog to another person his responsibility for it then ends. It is regained if and when he retakes charge of the dog. That is part of the reason the court is strict in its interpretation of the section for otherwise there would be a legal limbo where no one is liable.

G22 Allows

That position is accentuated by section 3(3) as if the owner or the person in charge allows it to enter a place that is not a public place but where it is not permitted to be he could commit the simple or aggravated offence. Which offence is committed depends on the result as if whilst it is there, there are grounds for reasonable apprehension that it will injure any person he is guilty of the simple offence. However if the dog actually injures any person an aggravated offence is committed. That is so even though there is no prior warning of how the dog will act. [See **G18**]

There are two offences created namely allowing the dog to be dangerously out of control in a public place and injuring any person. It is significant that both parties, the owner and any other person in charge of the dog, could be liable.

The offence under section 3(3) is committed if the person 'allows' a dog to enter the forbidden place. That can be by an act or omission. That requires a positive step or a failure to take one. Consistent with the social policy and public safety purpose behind the introduction of the DDA, the Divisional Court in *Greener v. DPP* [1996] 160 JP 265 decided that *mens rea* was not necessary under the section. Greener was the owner of a Staffordshire Bull Terrier. He had left the dog chained in an enclosure in his back garden. The dog had strained and bent the clip which released the chain. The dog then escaped from the enclosure and entered a nearby garden where it bit a 3 year-old child on the face. That was not a public place but was one where it was not 'permitted' to be. The magistrates convicted Greener and ordered the destruction of the dog. His appeal to the Crown Court was dismissed. This was a case stated appeal on the grounds (a) it had to be proved that he had allowed the dog to enter the garden by taking positive action and (b) there had to be a mental element in the form of intention or foresight of the consequences.

The court held that an offence under section 3(3) could be committed by omission. The word 'allows' included taking and omitting to take a positive step. Saville LJ said Greener 'had taken precautions to prevent the dog from escaping and genuinely intended that it should be kept secured by the chain in the enclosure...The precautions were, however, obviously inadequate since the fastening was not sufficiently strong to keep the dog chained, nor the enclosure so constructed as to prevent the dog from getting out.'

As for 'allows' Saville LJ said, 'As a consequence, the dog was able to get into the other garden. In my judgment, this, as a matter of ordinary language, meant that he allowed the dog to get into that garden.' He explained it was impossible to conclude that Parliament intended any mental element to be part of section 3(3) and added, 'In the present circumstances, however, to qualify "allows" in such a way [viz with *mens rea*] would be to reduce the section to little effect.' [See **G5**]

Blowfeld J said, 'I confess that I have been somewhat troubled by this case.' He referred to *Sweet v. Parsley* [1970] AC 132 and the fact, 'It is firmly established by a host of authorities that *mens rea* is an essential ingredient of every offence, unless some reason can be found for holding that it is not necessary.' After listening to the arguments and Saville LJ he added, 'I feel bound in logic to accept his reasoning and the decision.'

However Saville LJ did make an important point relating to causation and culpability namely, 'I entirely accept that there may well be cases where on the facts it simply could not be said that the defendant allowed the dog to get into a prohibited place. An example that immediately comes to mind, of course, would be the intervention of a third person coming into the appellant's garden and deliberately releasing the dog and enabling it to get out of the enclosure…' [See **G26**]

By corollary there is an aspect of this case that is important. As it requires no *mens rea* would the defendant be liable even if the weakness of the chain and clip was the fault of the manufacturer? While the Court confirmed that the prosecution must establish causation, that is simply on the basis that the owner allowed the dog to enter the place in question. If the dog is in a place where it is not permitted to be then the burden shifts to the defendant. It is the intruder-scenario revisited. Although it is right that the defendant should be liable for his own negligence it is hardly fair that he should be responsible for the recklessness or malice of another. For this is deceptively wide because while the same two parties, the owner and any person in charge of it, there is no defence provided to the owner similar to the provision in section 3(2). So if the simple or aggravated offence is committed the strict liability will aply with regard to both offences and both defendants.

The section will only be effective if the dog is in a non-public place it is not permitted to be. Therefore if it is a neighbouring property and the owner has permission for his dog to be there the offence, both simple and aggravated, is not committed. For in that event the neighbour's permission would be a licence for the owner. As a result, if while there it bit a postman, the permission would provide a defence as a matter of law.

G23 Penalty

Under section 3(4) the penalties on conviction reflect the nature of the offence. So if it is the simple offence of the dog being dangerously out of control, the person is liable on summary conviction to –

(a) imprisonment for a term of 6 months; or
(b) a fine up to level 5 on the standard scale; or
(c) both.

If the person is convicted of the aggravated offence then the sentence is –

(a) on summary conviction imprisonment for a term of 6 months or a fine up to the statutory maximum or both.
(b) on indictment imprisonment for two years or a fine or both.

Until 20 August 2012 there were no Sentencing Guidelines in relation to the DDA. As a result of various factors including an increase in the number of attacks by dogs, the seriousness of the injuries, the disparity of sentences around the country and the natural public concern, a consultation paper was produced. That took account of the views of those parties who contributed to the consultation and the conclusions which in turn led to the new Sentencing Council introducing the first Guideline on the DDA. [See **H1**]

The present position reflects the seriousness of the aggravated offence which could be committed to the Crown Court by the magistrates' of their own volition. It could also be sent there on the application of the prosecution or by the election of the defendant.

Up until that recent change the courts unusually impose imprisonment in such situations to reflect that seriousness.

Normally it is rare for them to impose a prison sentence. However in *R. v. Cox* [2004] 2 Cr. App. R. (S) 54 the Court of Appeal confirmed it was right in principle to do so. Jacqueline Cox pleaded guilty at Burnley Crown Court to an aggravated offence of keeping a dog which was dangerously out of control contrary to section 3(1). She lived with her husband and five children. The family had five dogs, a number of puppies and some cats. A man was exercising his dogs in a park saw 7 dogs run into the park. They came to a halt as a pack and attacked a seven-year-old boy. The boy's clothes were ripped from his body and he received a number of wounds. The boy was taken to hospital where he was found to have multiple wounds and lacerations. He required surgery for the wounds. The dogs were identified as those belonging to Cox. She pleaded guilty on the basis that she failed to ensure that the dogs were kept indoors. She claimed she was upstairs having a bath when the dogs escaped. She was sentenced to 9 months' imprisonment and banned from keeping dogs for 10 years.

The Court of Appeal considered that the negligence or the recklessness of Cox set the scene for the potential escape of dogs which, given the nature of dogs when roaming as a pack, created a risk of potentially extremely serious injury. While Cox did not intend any injury to anyone, the consequences of her behaviour had that result. Parliament required the court to consider that as a serious aggravating feature.

After reciting the facts Leveson J. said, 'No prior example of a sentence in a case such as this is apparent from a study of the authorities. We approach it from first principles. Keeping a dog dangerously out of control, contrary to section 3(1), is an offence which on summary conviction is liable to a maximum penalty of six months' imprisonment or a fine not exceeding level 5 on the standard scale. The aggravated form of offence is committed if the dog while out of control injures a person, is punishable on conviction on indictment to a term not exceeding two years' imprisonment or a fine or both. Thus Parliament demonstrated the clearest intention that the courts should in no small measure look at the consequences of the offence when determining the ultimate penalty. An analogy can be seen by comparing the offence of dangerous driving, which has a maximum of two years' imprisonment, and causing death by dangerous driving, which has a maximum of 10 years' imprisonment.

We have come to the conclusion that it was entirely appropriate for the recorder to pass a custodial sentence to mark the nature and extent of the obligation which owners of dogs owe to all who might be affected if they roam free. Nevertheless, we do not consider it necessary for the appellant to be deprived of her liberty for as long as nine months. She was, after all, a lady of good character whose plea was on the basis that she should have ensured that the dogs stayed at her home, not on the basis that she had frequently allowed the dogs to terrorise others... In the circumstances we reduce the term of nine months' imprisonment to one of three months' imprisonment. The 10 years' disqualification order in relation to dogs remains.'

The sentences thereafter have varied in degrees of leniency. In *R. v. Donnelly* [2007] EWCA Crim 2548 the Court of Appeal followed *Cox* and reduced his sentence of 12 months' suspended sentence to 35 weeks. Similarly in *R. v. Richards* [2009] 1 Cr. App. R. (S) 48 a sentence of 9 months was reduced to 4 months. However the courts in subsequent cases have been anxious to avoid any view that *Cox* served as any kind of guideline. The position was stated specifically by the Court of Appeal during the sentencing in *R. v. Lee* [2010] 1 Cr. App. R. (S) 94. Yet in *R. v. Baballa* [2011] 1 Cr. App. R. (S) 50 the court imposed a 6 months' suspended sentence for the aggravated offence under section 3. It is unlikely most of those will survive the new guidelines introduced on 29 August 2012. [See **H1**]

Destruction and disqualification orders

G24   Dangerous Dogs Act 1991, s.4

   (1)   Where a person is convicted of an offence under section 1 or 3(1) or (3) above or of an offence under an order made under section 2 above the court –

      (a)   may order the destruction of any dog in respect of which the offence was committed and, subject to subsection (1A) below, shall do so in the case of an offence under section 1 or an aggravated offence under section 3(1) or (3) above; and

      (b)   may order the offender to be disqualified, for such period as the court thinks fit, for having custody of a dog.

  (1A) Nothing in subsection 1(a) shall require the court to order the destruction of a dog if the court is satisfied –

      (a)   that the dog would not constitute a danger to public safety; and

      (b)   where the dog was born before 30 November 1991 and is subject to the prohibition in section 1(3) that there is good reason why the dog has not been exempted from that prohibition.

   (2)   Where a court makes an order under subsection 1(a) above for the destruction of a dog owned by a person other than the offender, the owner may appeal to the Crown Court against the order.

   (3)   A dog shall not be destroyed pursuant to an order under subsection (1)(a) above –

      (a)   until the end of the period for giving notice of appeal against the conviction or, against the order; and

(b)   if notice of appeal is given within that period, until the appeal is determined or withdrawn, unless the offender and, in a case to which subsection (2) above applies, the owner of the dog give notice to the court that made the order that there is to be no appeal.

(4)   Where a court makes an order under subsection (1)(a) above it may –

   (a)   appoint a person to undertake the destruction of the dog and require any person having custody of it to deliver it up for that purpose; and

   (b)   order the offender to pay such sum as the court may determine to be the reasonable expenses of destroying the dog of keeping it pending its destruction.

(5)   Any sum ordered to be paid under subsection (4)(b) above shall be treated for the purposes of enforcement as if it were a fine imposed on conviction. [

(6)   Any person who is disqualified for having custody of a dog by virtue of an order under subsection (1)(b) above may, at any time after the end of the period of one year beginning with the date of the order, apply to the court that made it (or a magistrates' court acting in the same local justice area as that court) for a direction terminating the disqualification.

(7)   On an application under subsection (6) above the court may –

   (a)   having regard to the applicant's character, his conduct since the disqualification was imposed and any other circumstances of the case, grant or refuse the application; and

   (b)   order the applicant to pay all or any part of the costs of the application; and where an application in respect of an order is refused no further application in respect of that order shall be entertained if made before the end of the period of one year beginning with the date of the refusal.

(8) Any person who –

(a) has custody of a dog in contravention of an order under subsection (1)(b) above;

or

(b) fails to comply with a requirement imposed on him under subsection (4) (a) above, is guilty of an offence and liable on summary conviction to a fine not exceeding level 5 on the standard scale.

When the DDA was introduced numerous dogs were rounded up and simply killed, often without cause or reason. Even when the cases came to court sometimes the judge would lament that his hands were tied so the dog died though it was without fault on his part other than being born. The comment in *Cichon v. DPP* [1994] Crim L. R. 918 by Schiemann J was typical of the court's concern when he said, 'We have here an absolute prohibition and a breach of that prohibition is to be followed by an order for the dog's destruction, however blameless the dog and its owner.' In the same vein Rougier J said in *R. v. Ealing Magistrates' Court ex parte Fanneran* [1996] 160 JP 409, 'It would take the pen of Voltaire to do justice to such a ludicrous situation.' [See **G1**]

As result of various serious misgivings of that nature plus the belated myopic realisation that the statute was rushed through for political reasons and consequently was badly drafted, it was amended by the DD(A)A. Previously it was a mandatory requirement that once a dog was deemed to be dangerous via its owner being guilty of an aggravated offence or was categorised as a fighting dog, the court 'shall' order it to be destroyed. By the DD(A)A the court has a limited discretion not to kill the dog.

Whatever happens to the dog, the court has power to disqualify the owner and the person in charge in relation to dogs. The provisions are inter-related in that an order against the dog may depend on the person's act or omission. For where a person is convicted of an offence under section 1 or 3(1) or (3) or contrary to an order under section 2 the court may order the destruction of any dog in respect of which the offence was committed. While that is now discretionary the position remains precarious for such dogs. For subject to section (1A), the court 'shall' order the dog's destruction in the case of an offence under section 1 or an aggravated offence under section 3(1) or (3). Allied to that power the court may order the offender to be disqualified for any period it thinks fit, from having custody of a dog.

That amendment under section (1A) governs the court's discretion. Now it does not have to order the destruction of a dog if it is satisfied (a) that the dog would not constitute a danger to public safety; and (b) where the dog was born before 30 November 1991 and is subject to the prohibition in section 1(3) that there is good reason why the dog has not been exempted from that prohibition. The 'good reason' is one that would have to be established by the defendant. So that puts an evidential burden on him to produce evidence to satisfy the court: [See **G9**; **G37**]

G25 Suspended

The DD(A)A was brought into force on 8 June 1997. Before it was introduced Pill LJ said in *R. v. Liverpool Magistrates' Court ex parte Slade* [1997] EWHC 529 (Admin) said it would not alter that case. [See **G12**]After its introduction the courts have tended to be balanced when interpreting the amended terms of the DDA as often the case involves an isolated incident that is unlikely to be repeated. That is particularly where the conditions imposed by the court for the safety of the public will be likely to be fulfilled by the owner.

In the leading authority of *R. v. Flack* [2008] 2 Cr. App. R. (S) 70 the Court of Appeal set out the principles in some detail. Flack pleaded guilty to being the owner of a dog, Star, which caused injury while dangerously out of control in a public place. He also pleaded guilty to being in charge of a dog, Snoop, while dangerously out of control in a public place. A couple walking through a public park, Ridgway Park in Lymm, with their three grandchildren noticed two dogs running towards them. One of the dogs attacked the female member of the couple, causing a severe wound to her leg. Flack pleaded guilty on a specified basis. The Crown Court made a contingent destruction order in respect of Snoop and a destruction order in respect of Star. The appeal was limited to Star.

Silber J said, 'The basis upon which the appellant pleaded guilty was that an unknown third party had opened the gate behind which the dogs were secured, thereby allowing them to escape.

Evidence was called before the recorder from Dr Candy d'Sa, an animal behaviour consultant, who explained that she carried out an assessment of the dogs Star and Snoop over a period of two hours. She concluded that they were both sociable to people, very friendly and very playful with each other. It was her view that there was no reason to fear them or to worry about their temperament in any way. Dr d'Sa said that the behaviour of the dogs at that time of the incident might have been consistent with heavy play which might seem aggressive. In her report Dr d'Sa said that Star was a neutered bitch Rottweiller crossed with a German Shepherd dog. She was used as a therapy dog to visit the elderly in care homes. This had required rigorous training so far as her temperament was concerned. Dr d'Sa considered that Star and Snoop were friendly and interactive and they responded to commands. The dogs displayed no signs of aggression. They were two of the most passive and friendly dogs which had been encountered by Dr d'Sa. She considered that the cause of the attack might possibly have been that the dogs had been anxious on escaping from their garden and that they had reacted with fear to unfamiliar stimuli. Her view was that their aggression would most likely show itself in a single reflexive bite rather than the attack described. She described the dogs as being calm in the presence of unfamiliar people and passing cars. They displayed no predatory or exploratory behaviour. Her conclusion was that there was no evidence that Star or Snoop were inherently aggressive or dangerous dogs and that Mrs Flack showed she was a capable and experienced dog owner.

There were eight references before the recorder in respect of Star.'

The expert evidence and the character of the appellant were relevant. Silber J considered the position of the recorder and the fact that he, 'concluded that the court would fail in its duty if it did not make a destruction order. In reaching that conclusion he had not overlooked the fact that the appellant and his wife were decent people with a history of caring for dogs.'

The grounds of appeal were that Star did not constitute a danger to the public and therefore should be exempted from destruction under section 4(1A)(a) of the DDA 1991. It was also contended that the statutory power should have been exercised to impose stringent conditions upon Flack in relation to the future behaviour of Star with the sanction of the dog being destroyed if he failed to comply.

Silber J then set out the 'relevant principles' in respect of a dog whose owner has been convicted under section 3(1). Those are:

1. The court is empowered under section 4(1) to order the destruction of the dog.

2. Nothing in that provision shall require the court to order the destruction if the court is satisfied that the dog would not constitute a danger to public safety: section 4(1)(a)...

3. The court should ordinarily consider, before ordering immediate destruction, whether to exercise the power under section 4(a)(4)...to order that, unless the owner keeps it under proper control, the dog shall be destroyed ("a suspended order of destruction").

4. A suspended order of destruction may specify the measures to be taken by the owner for keeping the dog under control whether by muzzling, keeping it on a lead, or excluding it from a specified place or otherwise: see section 4(a)(5)...

5. A court should not order destruction if satisfied that the imposition of such a condition would mean the dog would not constitute a danger to public safety.

6. In deciding what order to make, the court must consider all the relevant circumstances which include the dog's history of aggressive behaviour and the owner's history of controlling the dog in order to determine what order should be made.'

The recorder did not consider a suspended destruction order. It was relevant that Star had not previously been aggressive. There was evidence from an animal behaviour consultant. It was a relevant factor that Flack was a man of good character. Indeed the recorder regarded him as a conscientious dog owner. Silber J said the recorder made, 'No order disqualifying him from owning or being in control of dogs. We are not surprised by that conclusion. It is clear from the evidence before us that the appellant is a competent and conscientious dog owner.'

As a result the court quashed the order for destruction. Silber J said, 'Instead we make an order that, unless the appellant keeps Star under proper control, she will be destroyed. We also impose the same conditions that were imposed in relation to Snoop: (1) Star shall be muzzled in public places at all times; (2) she must wear a special collar to keep her under control; and (3) she must be kept on a lead at all times in public.'

The principles specified in *Flack* have become the benchmark for the courts in subsequent cases. For it has the advantage of being fair in aim and approach by taking into account all the relevant factors that affect the public, the owner and the dog. Moreover it pays particular account to the character of the owner. Those principles are consistent with the new Sentencing Guidelines. [See **H1**]

G26 Neuter

The principles framed in *Flack* were followed in *R. v. Harry* [2010] EWCA Crim 673. Jamie Harry appeared on 11 September, 2009 at Mold Crown Court and pleaded guilty to two counts of being in charge of a dog which caused injury while dangerously out of control in a public place contrary to section 3(1). Count 1 related to a male English Bull Terrier known as Snoop. Count 2 related to a Staffordshire female crossbred Bull Terrier called Millie. Harry was sentenced to a 12 months' conditional discharge on each count concurrent and a destruction order was made in respect of both dogs. Harry appealed against the destruction order.

The facts were noteworthy because of the absence of any direct fault by the defendant. On 13 August 2008 Harry arrived at his parents' home at Chestnut Avenue in Wrexham. His parents were absent. At that time the dogs were living inside as his parents were having building work done to the rear of the property. Harry released the two dogs into the garden. The builders had been told to ensure that the side gate, which gave access to the front of the house and the road, 'remained closed at all times'. So naturally one of the workmen left the side gate open. As a result both dogs escaped into the street.

At around that time the victim walked towards his car parked outside his girlfriend's house. The dogs ran towards him. At first they appeared friendly but when the first dog, Snoop, arrived it jumped up and bit the victim on his penis, the top of his legs, his stomach and his back. He ran to his girlfriend's house which was locked. He then ran to a neighbour's home. The dogs followed, both biting him on his back. He stumbled, threw his jacket at the dogs but they continued chasing him. He arrived at another house on Chestnut Avenue and a resident let him in. He trapped one of the dogs' heads in the door. The victim was taken to hospital. It seems he made a good recovery.

In the Court of Appeal Davies J outlined the facts and that Harry 'accepted that the gate had been left open. A letter was before the court from D & K Home Improvements Limited confirming that at some time during 13 August 2008 the gate was left open by mistake by one of the building team. In that letter Mr Small, a director of the company, stated that at all times when the work was being carried out the dogs had been in their cage and even when they were let loose in the back garden they caused no harm to any member of staff and were playful.'

Davies J referred to the fact that Harry was a man of good character and 'pleaded guilty on the basis that the workmen had left the side gate open and he had let the dogs out without first checking that the gate was secure. It was accepted by the recorder that Harry and his parents were conscientious dog owners, who cared for their animals and who had an excellent record of animal ownership. Neither dog had ever done anything of this nature before and neither dog had shown any propensity to act in the way that each did on this single occasion.' The court was shown photographs of the accommodation that had been built for the dogs at the rear of the property since completion of the building works. It was an enclosed and roofed kennel which would significantly reduce the chance of the dogs being able to escape.

The court referred to and analysed sections 4 and 5 of the DDA. Then the court cited and relied upon all the principles Silber J specified in *R. v. Flack*. Davies J referred to the grounds of appeal which were that recorder failed to have regard to those principles, in particular to the provisions regarding the potential for a suspended order. Further, the recorder failed to adequately consider both the owner's exceptional care for the animals and the fact that neither animal had ever done anything similar in the past.

Davies J added this important point: 'It is the appellant's case that if the Recorder was considering a destruction order, he should have allowed the application made on behalf of the appellant to adjourn that part of the hearing, to allow for the preparation of a report on the dogs by an animal behavioural consultant.'

Plainly he refused that request as there was now a report before the court from an expert. The court then relied on section 23(1) of the Criminal Appeal Act 1968 which allows the court to receive any evidence which was not adduced in proceedings relating to the appeal if it is in the interests of justice to do so.

That evidence was a report prepared by Madeleine Forsyth, a veterinary surgeon and a barrister. Miss Forsyth examined both dogs on 30 September 2009, in the absence of their owner but in the presence of a police officer and a representative from the kennels. She found Millie to be in good physical condition, extremely friendly and obedient. She described her as being obedient, placid in manner, displaying no signs of aggression, either to Miss Forsyth or her main handler from the kennels. She was in no doubt that Millie was anything other than friendly domestic pet.

Miss Forsyth described Snoop as a good example of his breed and in good bodily condition. She found him to be friendly and amenable to verbal command. He allowed examination without objection. He showed no signs of aggression but was boisterous and because of his size and musculature powerful. Neither dog displayed any aggressive attributes as a normal behavioural characteristic. The manner and demeanour of each dog was entirely consistent with the status of a friendly family pet. Davies J considered Miss Forsyth's conclusion that it was 'likely that Snoop was the instigator of the incident...it is unlikely that Snoop would behave aggressively in any other circumstances as he is fundamentally friendly, obedient although boisterous. However, in the excitement of his escape and with another dog for company, his dominance emerged with disadvantage to the victim...restraint and control of the dog, combined with castration would reduce his hormonal fuelled dominance.'

The Court concluded the evidence was relevant to the issue and allowed it to be adduced.

The Court then made a contingent destruction order for both dogs with a condition (a) they were kept under proper control and restraint and (b) Snoop was to be neutered within 56 days.

Given that the gate was opened by a third party who had disobeyed a direct instruction, there must also have been some culpability by Harry as otherwise he would arguably have had a defence which at least should be considered by a jury. His fault lay in not checking that the gate was secure before he let the dogs out. The onus was on him to do so.

G27 Which

How important *R. v. Flack* is on a practical level can be seen from the Court of Appeal decision in *R. v. Davies* [2010] EWCA Crim 1923. Davies was convicted at Harrow Crown Court on 17 December 2009 of an offence under section 3(1) of the DDA. The particulars of offence were significant. They alleged that he "on the 5th of September 2008 was in charge of a *dog* which was dangerously out of control in a public place namely Larkspur Close Kingsbury and whilst so out of control injured Caroline Foley". [emphasis added by Mackay J]

Mrs Recorder Bickford-Smith sentenced Davies to a Community Order and made a destruction order for his Alsatian dog. The appeal was limited to the destruction order.

Caroline Foley, a neighbour of Davies, was walking her dog on a lead towards a green space at the bottom of her road. At the same time Davies was walking his two dogs, an Alsatian and a Labrador. They were not on leads or otherwise controlled in any way. They ran towards Mrs Foley and attacked her dog. Mrs Foley tried to pull her dog away and in so doing placed her hand over its chest. One of Davies' dogs bit her finger inflicting a large open wound. She could not tell which of the two dogs had bitten her.

Mackay J said, 'So far as the appellant himself was concerned, and in so far as his circumstances were relevant to the destruction order, the pre-sentence report showed he left school at twelve, had received some home tutoring but had no formal qualifications or work experience. He lived at home with his mother and siblings on benefits and described himself as a loner. He was of previous good character but the probation officer said his lack of insight into his responsibility for what had happened shows that he failed to think of the consequences of his behaviour.'

The two limbs of the appeal were that (a) the recorder was wrong to find that the Alsatian bit Mrs Foley and (b), if the first limb does not succeed, the recorder was wrong to make a destruction order rather than, at most, a suspended destruction order.

The court considered sections 3(1), 4(1), 4A and 10(3) of the DDA. Mackay J said, 'There were two issues. The first was whether the Alsatian was "the dog in respect of which the offence was committed" within the meaning of section 4(1) and therefore the dog referred to in the Particulars of Offence in the Indictment?'

The court analysed the incident and the finding of the recorder that both dogs were involved 'in some form of joint attack...[the recorder] limited herself to identifying the dog which bit the victim. She found as a fact that that dog was the Alsatian...Thus the offence was committed whichever dog delivered the bite and caused her injury. The prosecution did not need to rely on any analogy with joint enterprise between human beings. Neither we nor the recorder were called upon to answer the question whether, if two dogs attack a *human* victim but only one causes injury, both dogs "injure" that person, or only one does. That is a question for another day.'

Mackay J relied on, as an appeal court often does, the fact denied to them that the recorder had seen the witnesses: 'The jury may have found themselves in some doubt about the involvement of the Labrador but still could still have convicted on the charge as drawn. The Recorder...was entitled when deciding sentence to make findings of fact provided they were not inconsistent with the jury's verdict. We consider her finding that it was the Alsatian which bit the victim unassailable in this court, albeit it may have been one which Mrs Foley and the appellant may have found controversial. But we do not consider it was not open to the Recorder on the evidence she heard.'

The Court then considered the second issue namely whether the recorder was right to make an order for immediate destruction?

In answering that vital question Mackay J said, 'Only the dog inflicting the injury is potentially liable to a mandatory destruction order under section 4(1)(a). Other dogs present and out of control but not causing injury may, depending on the charge or charges, qualify for discretionary disqualification under that same subsection. But in either event, whether the mandatory or discretionary version of the destruction order is engaged, before making any order the court still has to consider both sections 4(1A)(a) and 4A(4) and (5). As to the first of these the court does not have to make a mandatory order if it is satisfied that the dog will not constitute a danger to public safety. In our view applying normal principles the burden of so satisfying the court falls on the party making that assertion, ie the appellant, and to the civil standard. It is the appellant who is seeking to displace a mandatory consequence and it is the appellant who will normally be the owner of the dog or a person entrusted with its care and who will be best placed to know about and adduce evidence of its characteristics. Such evidence may be of an expert nature (as was led in *Flack* [2008] EWCA Crim 204) or it may be lay evidence relating to such matters as the dogs character, demeanour and general past behaviour. But the matter does not end there, because section 4A allows for a contingent destruction order even if a destruction order, mandatory or discretionary, is otherwise appropriate. That section was construed by this court in *Flack* by Silber J...in an analysis with which we agree.' The Court then set out and endorsed those principles.

Mackay J continued and concluded that, 'The problem in the present case is that the Recorder was not referred to any of these provisions. Initially she was under the impression that as she had identified the Alsatian as the biting dog a destruction order was mandatory...She was then reminded of section 4(1A) to which she replied – "I don't think it's necessary for me to say this, but I am quite sure it follows, and I say for the sake of clarity that it seems to me plain, that this dog is a danger to public safety." Defence counsel accepted that and said no more. He made no application to lead any evidence on this topic. He did not refer to the case of *Flack* or to the further obligation to consider a contingent destruction order under section 4A. In those circumstances...the immediate order for destruction cannot stand and must be quashed. It should be replaced by a contingent destruction order to this effect that the Alsatian dog be destroyed unless the owner keeps it under proper control and, in particular, the dog must, at all times when in public places, be muzzled, and kept on a lead.' So the appeal was allowed.

It is significant that the court not only followed *Flack* in aim and effect, but that Mackay J stated that defence counsel did not refer to it 'or to the further obligation to consider a contingent destruction order...' That placed a duty on the defence as well as the court.

G28 Identification

While in *R. v. Davies* Mackay J said that which dog caused the injury, 'Is a question for another day' he is right in the context of that case. However he is not right in evidential terms because of the connection between the identity of the culprit and the consequences of a human identification of the wrong dog. Indeed in *R. v. Huddart* [1999] Crim. L. R. 568 one of the grounds of appeal was identification. The Court of Appeal refused to apply the *Turnbull* rules to cases of identification of animals. The court relied on *R. v. Browning* [1992] 94 Cr. App. R. 109, where the Court of Appeal refused to apply the *Turnbull* rules to mass produced inanimate objects such as motor vehicles. However that is a false analogy. For as Glidewell LJ explained in *Browning*, 'As to the car, unlike a human being, the appearance of a car remains constant unless it is deliberately altered by having its colour changed or by having some pieces added to it.' [See **G21**]

The dangers of identifying animals are akin to those of identifying humans rather than cars, be it a poodle or an Irish Wolfhound. So there is no reason at all why the court should not apply *Turnbull* rules in such circumstances. After all if a human is wrongly identified it can be corrected on appeal as a miscarriage of justice. If a dog is wrongly identified no appeal could reverse the sentence where his legal destiny is death.

A sharp-eyed Taiwanese judge used the technology of a Google map to help him identify the owner a dog who injured his neighbour as it was seen in the defendant's garden: *The Independent* 7/7/12. That is evidence consistent with *Turnbull*, yet it is more as it provides corroboration of any identification by other witnesses. It also relates to an association with the dog which in turn could form part of the *res gestae*.

Professor Diane Birch makes a judicious point in this respect in the Commentary on *R. v. Walton Street Justices ex parte Crothers* [1992] Crim. L. R. 875: 'From the way in which the subsection [5(4)] is constructed it seems primarily aimed at the situation where there is nobody to argue Buster's corner, and in such cases a bull terrier who is the victim of mistaken identification may go to his death without so much as a reference to the *Turnbull* rules. But if his owner has a case to put, it should be heard.' [See G39]

Although that section has been repealed, the *Turnbull* point remains. For what if he has no owner or his owner chooses to be silent or being the abuser, chooses to abscond? It is a keen point for one reason above all: identification evidence is the weakest form of evidence that exists. It is neither fair nor just that a dog that is or may be wrongly identified is killed simply because it is an animal rather than a human.

In June 2009 Carol Cameron was walking with her schnauzer dog in Lily Hill Park in Bracknell when 'a rather large brown dog' approached her and attacked her dog. She got between them and 'launched my dog into a rhododendron bush to save him.' The dog then attacked her. Cameron decided she was not 'going down without a fight.' So 'I bit he dog…I bit the back of his neck.' After she was released from hospital she had to attend a 'dog parade': she had to identify the animal in the back of a police van. [See *Criminal Law and Justice Weekly* [2012]; BBC News 4/6/12.] While the principle is commendable the practice is akin to placing a single ginger-haired man on a parade to identify him.

It is not a fanciful or speculative suggestion for such a situation arose in *R. v. Baballa* [2011] 1 Cr. App. R. (S) 50. In August 2008 Moses Baballa was exercising his four dogs, in Melfort Park, Thornton Heath. Three of them were pit bull terriers and one, Crystal, was a mongrel. None of them had a lead or muzzle. Crystal approached Jalal Dawad and 'began to bark and jump up.' Dawad was scared and ran away. In the Court of Appeal Swift J said, 'The other three dogs then surrounded him. They were barking and jumping up and he was bitten. The effect of the prosecution's acceptance of the appellant's plea is that the bites must be assumed to have been inflicted by Crystal and Crystal alone.' In the event the judge at Croydon Crown Court made a destruction order in respect of the pit bull terriers. The Court of

Appeal quashed that order and substituted a contingent destruction order for the three dogs. There was no similar order sought for Crystal. Indeed there was even no application. As Crystal was 'assumed' to have acted 'alone' he was then duly killed. What if that assumption was wrong? Then again Crystal was only a mongrel.

Just over a decade ago in Bristol Crown Court counsel relied upon an 'alibi' for a dog. The defence was it was a case of mistaken identity. A dog was alleged to have knocked a woman off her bike and then bit her. She claimed it was Patch. The owner denied it was his dog claiming it was in a distant meadow at the crucial time. All the cross-examination and evidence as to the alibi was called as if Patch was on trial. So the real question for the jury was simply: Was it this dog? After a trial the defendant – and his dog – was acquitted. I know because like the soldier in the song I was that defence counsel.

G29 Natural

The principle of natural justice demands that a person is informed if he is to be deprived of his property. It does not even matter whether the order is right or wrong as a matter of law. The important principle remains that a person's property cannot be destroyed without his knowledge and the opportunity to raise an objection to that result. In *R. v. Ealing Magistrates' Court ex parte Fanneran* [1995] 160 JP 409 it was Fanneran's nephew who pleaded guilty to being in charge of a pit bull terrier in a public place without it being muzzled contrary to the DDA. He had removed the muzzle in order to allow it to be sick. When the defendant appeared before the Ealing Magistrates' court he was fined and the dog was ordered to be destroyed. Fanneran, who was the owner of the dog, obtained an injunction restraining the police from destroying the dog and applied for judicial review of the magistrates' decision. She submitted that as she was not notified of the hearing the magistrates order should be quashed. The High Court held that although in all probability the presence of the applicant at the hearing would not have made any difference the fact remained that she should have been told of the hearing. It was the duty of the magistrates to act in accordance with natural justice and that had not happened in the present case. Accordingly, her application for judicial review would be allowed. The destruction order was quashed and the case remitted to the magistrates' court.

Staughton LJ made a pertinent point relating to why the application was allowed: 'The notion that when the rules of natural justice have not been observed, one can still uphold the result because it would not have made any difference, is to be treated with great caution. Down that slippery slope lies the way to dictatorship.'

Rougier J made an even more penetrating point as 'No one can ever say for certain what must have happened in the circumstances which have not, in fact arisen. The robing rooms up and down this land are full of strange tales of seemingly impregnable cases foundering on some unforeseen forensic reef. It is not, in my opinion, for this court to employ its imagination to postulate facts which might or might not have succeeded had the rules of natural justice been followed.'

The High Court had endorsed the same principle six months earlier in *R. v. Trafford Magistrates' Court ex parte Riley* [1995] 160 JP 418. The court confirmed that no one should be deprived of their property without first being given the opportunity to object to its deprivation or destruction. That is consistent with the principle established by the House of Lords in *Wiseman v. Borneman* [1971] A.C. 297. There is one reason that is stronger than most which leans inexorably towards natural justice in this kind of case: For unlike the normal case of destroying a person's personal property which can easily be replaced even at a price, a dog that becomes a corpse cannot be revived. [See **G19**]

G30 Appeal

As the person convicted may not be the owner of the dog, there is a right of appeal under section 4(2) by the owner to the Crown Court. This allows the owner the opportunity to avoid the order for destruction. That was the position in *R. v. Ealing Magistrates' Court ex parte Fanneran* [1995] 160 JP 409. As a consequence the dog cannot be destroyed pending the appeal. So the court order cannot be effective:

    (a)   until the end of the period for giving notice of appeal against the conviction or the order; and

    (b)   if notice is given, until the appeal is determined or withdrawn.

There is a provision under section 4(3) that the owner or offender, if they are different, can give notice to the court that there is not going to be an appeal. In that event the order can be effective within the appeal period.

When a person is convicted of these kind of offences he is often reluctant to hand over the dog in question which is so often their pet. Similarly they sometimes transfer it to another person so it cannot be traced. Therefore the court has power when it makes such an order to appoint a person to arrange the destruction and require any person having custody of it to 'deliver it up' for that purpose.

To emphasise the liability of the offender under section 4(4), the court may order him to pay all the attendant expenses of destroying the dog. In that event it may also make him pay for the dog's keep prior to and pending the destruction. If the offender is ordered to pay those expenses it can be enforced as if it were a fine imposed on conviction. Therefore as with any actual fine it could lead to imprisonment if it is unpaid.

G31 Disqualified

A person may be disqualified for any period up to and including a life ban. Whatever the period, the person may apply for a direction terminating the disqualification once a year has elapsed after the date of the order.

The Court of Appeal considered the position in *R. v. Holland* [2003] 1 Cr. App. R. (S) 60 and gave useful guidance to any subsequent court which had to deal with an application by a disqualified person. Elizabeth Holland pleaded guilty at Liverpool Crown Court to allowing a dog she was in charge of to enter a property in Strawberry Road, where it was not permitted to be and injuring an 8 year old child, Kathryn, contrary to section 3(3)(a). Her son left his Staffordshire bull terrier, Rickson, with her. On Sunday afternoon her neighbours were entertaining their family including their grandchildren. Two of the grandchildren were in the garden playing with a ball when the dog forced its way through wire fencing and ran towards the children. Rickson attacked one of the children, Kathryn, gripping her ankle, then her leg and finally her clothing in the vicinity of her chest.

Pitchford J said, 'The ferocity of the dog's attack and its determination to remain locked on the child was such that it was able to resist punches and blows with a mop handle. It desisted only when the appellant called the dog away.' Kathryn was taken to hospital where it was found that she had an injury just above the right knee which would leave a permanent scar. Holland was fined and ordered to pay compensation and disqualified from having custody of a dog for 10 years. Rickson was ordered to be destroyed. She appealed against the length of the disqualification and the destruction order for her dog.

Pitchford J made a significant observation that 'There was before the recorder and before us no evidence that the dog was other than a danger in circumstances such as we have just described. The recorder expressly excluded the idea that the dog was being teased or tormented.' Hence it would have relevance if that were the position. [See **G18**]

From the start the court was unsympathetic to the appeal generally and dismissive of the evidence presented to it in support of the application. A petition signed by number of people who lived in the area of Liverpool before it moved to be with Holland at Strawberry Road, confirmed Rickson was not a dangerous dog. Somewhat wryly Pitchford J said, 'No doubt those persons who felt able to make that assertion would have made it on the day before this incident occurred. We are bound say that it provides no evidence of the type which the court would require to avoid an order for destruction.

Secondly, we are provided with a letter dated March 4 2002, the author of which is Mr Kenneth Fogg, who clearly has an association with bull terriers, as his letter heading is "Sublyme Bull Terriers" of Stockport in Cheshire. Mr Fogg makes it clear that he does not have a veterinary qualification and that the purpose of his visit to see the bull terrier named Rickson at the council kennels in Birkenhead was to assess the well-being of the dog. He specifically did not express any opinion about the circumstances in which the dog came to be housed in council kennels. Again, we find ourselves quite unable to attach to this letter any weight for the purpose of reaching a conclusion whether this was a dangerous dog in circumstances such as we have described.

We agree with the order made by the learned recorder. He had, in our view, no alternative but to make the order he did, and that order for destruction will remain.'

The court was equally unsympathetic to Holland. In considering the purpose of section 4 Pitchford J said, 'The purpose of the disqualification is both punitive and preventative. As to the punitive element as it concerns this particular case, we have been provided with a number of testimonials from persons who know both the appellant and the fact she has possessed dogs over many years…The recorder disqualified the appellant for 10 years on the express ground, not that he was punishing her, but that he wanted to ensure that Kathryn was protected from the worry that there might otherwise be a dog next door when she visited her grandparents.

It is asserted before us today, without evidence in support, that the grandparents have in fact moved. There is no confirmation of that bare assertion. In any event, it seems to us that fact alone would not meet the recorder's concerns as to the nature of the animal which the appellant might keep at this property in future.'

Conversely the court had 'sympathy with the recorder's purpose… A balance should, however, be struck between the sensitivities of the victim on the one hand and the restriction on the freedom of the custodian on the other. Disqualification prohibits the appellant from keeping not merely an aggressive or dangerous dog, but any dog at all.'

The court went even further than it might have by placing the case in context for the future lest Holland makes an application under section 4(6) and (7). Pitchford J said, 'We consider that the recorder was right to conclude that the risk of emotional, if not physical harm, to the child was a continuing one and that the onus of demonstrating that she was a fit and proper person to have custody of a dog should remain with the appellant...We would not intend to bind the court which hears such an application, but it is likely to be measured against the proposals of the appellant, first, as to the breed of dog she proposes to keep; second, as to the existence of secure fencing around her property; and, thirdly, who are her neighbours at the time when the application is made.'

The application on the destruction was refused. The appeal was dismissed.

While that was no surprise in the event, it was a surprise that the evidence was not provided to the court from an expert who could have examined the dog after the event. That is a usual course and one that often finds favour with the court: see *R. v. Haynes* [2004] 2 Cr. App. R. (S) 9. Indeed there appears to be a paucity of evidence available on Rickson for the court. Nevertheless the Court was wrong to be dismissive of the evidence provided by the petition and Fogg and the references on Holland. All of that is admissible and relevant to the decision of the court. Indeed it is specifically referred to in the leading authority of *R. v. Flack* [2008] 2 Cr. App. R. (S) 70. Such evidence may be of an expert nature or it may be lay evidence relating to such matters as the dogs character, demeanour and general past behaviour. Moreover the principles outlined in *R. v. Flack* were later followed by the Court of Appeal in *R. v. Davies* [2010] EWCA Crim 1923. It may account for this somewhat pale decision that *R. v. Holland* was decided 3 months before *R. v. Flack*. Lest it reoccurs the practical solution to the problem would be to seek the permission of the court to adduce further evidence and agree to an undertaking as to the owner's future conduct. [See **G32**]

The Court of Appeal have confirmed the position in *R. v. Baballa* [2011] 1 Cr. App. R. (S) 50 where Swift J put the duty of the judge beyond doubt: 'It seems that, although the possibility of a section 4A(1) order was considered, the case of *Flack* was not brought to the judge's attention. We consider that, if it had been, and if he had followed the approach set out in that case, he could and should have been satisfied that a contingent order of destruction would suffice.'

As a matter of practice the defence should unquestionably provide an expert report for the court as to the character and disposition of the dog. If it is favourable it should save the dog. If not, it would provide a ground of appeal. If a report is not available an adjournment should be sought to obtain one. If it is refused it could be a ground of appeal. [See **G15**; **G26**]

G32 Undertaking

The Court of Appeal solved a potentially problematic legal point in *R. v. Haynes* [2004] 2 Cr. App. R. (S) 9 by combining principle and pragmatism to find a fair resolution. Rodney Haynes was convicted at Woolwich Crown Court of three counts of being the owner of a dog which was dangerously out of control and whilst out of control, injured a person, contrary to section 3(1). The three counts related to the same incident. Haynes owned three dogs. He lived in a block of flats which adjoined two play areas, one for children and one for dogs. Haynes took his dogs to exercise in the dog play area. It was bounded by a hedge with a gate at each end. Haynes left the dogs there while he had a conversation with a neighbour on the balcony. The dogs escaped from their play area and attacked a seven-year-old girl who was riding a bicycle. They ran towards her and knocked her off her bike and surrounded her. The girl was taken to hospital which she was found have superficial grazes on her abdomen, superficial wounds to the front of her thigh and a graze below her eye. She was allowed to go home after about an hour.

Haynes pleaded not guilty. He did not dispute that the child had been attacked by his dogs, but suggested that the dogs had escaped from the dog area as a result of some other person opening one of the gates. He was convicted by the jury and sentenced to an order of forfeiture of the dogs under section 143 of the Powers of Criminal Courts (Sentencing) Act 2000 and disqualified from keeping a dog for three years under section 4 of the DDA.

HHJ Roberts in the Court of Appeal said, 'He suggested that someone, possibly the little girl herself, must have opened one of the gates of the dog area, in which he had left the dogs, and thus allowed them to escape. His case appears to have been that the incident was unforeseeable and there was no actual fault on his part. However, the offence under section 3 is an offence of strict liability and the jury had little alternative but to convict him.'

The court was sympathetic from the start to the position of Haynes as the appeal raised an unusual point of law and practice. For the specialist in animal behaviour found that the dogs were in excellent condition and that they did not show any signs of aggression. He recommended that Haynes should be permitted to retain one dog which should be surgically castrated, and the other two dogs should be allocated to other owners. However the statutory power available to the sentencing judge did not permit him to make such an order. As the judge was satisfied the dogs did not constitute a danger to public safety, a destruction order was inappropriate. There was no statutory power to disqualify a person from having custody of more than one dog and to specify conditions under which an offender might be permitted to retain one dog. So the judge made an order of disqualification on Haynes and as a consequence ordered forfeiture of the dogs.

HHJ Roberts said, 'Before the trial the appellant's solicitors had very sensibly instructed the well-known specialist in animal behaviour, Dr Roger Mugford, to examine all three dogs in police custody. Dr Mugford is the head of a referral practice which specialises in the treatment of aggressive dogs. He conducted his examination with a visiting Canadian animal behaviourist. He examined each dog on its own. He found that they were all in excellent condition...None of them showed any signs of aggression. They played happily and appropriately and related well to another dog to which Dr Mugford introduced them. He described them from all as friendly and attractive dogs, individually a delight, and he did not think any of them on its own presented a danger to the public. He attributed the incident to "pack behaviour" when left without human supervision and he thought their motives were more likely to have been playful than aggressive. However, as he rightly stated, whatever their motives were, the outcome for the little girl must have been extremely frightening and her physical injuries could well have been more serious.'

Dr Mugford recommended that none of the three dogs should be destroyed. He considered only one dog, Bow, should be returned to Haynes and that a condition of the return should be that it is surgically castrated. The remaining two dogs should, he believed, be transferred to the Metropolitan Police who would arrange to re-home them.

The court considered the position and resolved it by a judicial percipience that satisfied Haynes and saved the dogs too. HHJ Roberts said, 'We do not criticise the learned recorder for adopting the course which he did. However, we think there was another course open to him which, if he had been alerted to it, he would almost certainly have followed. In deciding whether to make a disqualification order and whether to order the forfeiture of any or all of the dogs, he was entitled to have regard to any voluntary undertaking offered by the appellant as to the appellant's future conduct. Such an undertaking would not form part of any court order, but it could be reduced into writing and a copy provided to the police...'

An undertaking without a sanction would be valueless. So the court spelled out the consequences to Haynes: 'It would follow that in the event of any further offence being committed by the appellant and it being found that he was in breach of his undertaking, that breach would be treated as a serious aggravating factor and would almost certainly lead to the loss of the dog or dogs in question.'

Haynes obviously impressed the court. For notwithstanding the recommendation of Dr. Mugford they concluded, 'We have not insisted that the appellant should include in the undertaking an agreement to have Bow castrated. That is a matter about which the appellant has very strong feelings, which we understand, and we do not feel that it is necessary to include that in the undertaking, so it is not included in it.'

As a result of the signed undertaking the court quashed the disqualification order and the forfeiture order in so far as it related to Bow. The approach of the defence in this case in this case was a prime example of good practice in gaining the expert evidence which plainly found favour with the court. [See **G31**]

G33 Character

It is significant and unusual that the court in considering any application for removal of a disqualification may have regard to the applicant's 'character', his conduct since the disqualification was imposed and any other circumstances of the case. It may then grant or refuse the application. Whatever is the result the court may order the applicant to pay all or any part of the costs of it. If the application is refused, then under section 4(7) no further application can be made until a year after the date of that refusal.

Two points are of interest in this respect. Given that the court can consider 'character' which is very wide now given the changes introduced by the Criminal Justice Act 2003, it could take into account any violent offences the applicant has been convicted of meanwhile if that could or would reflect on his disposition to own a dog. Allied to that there is a well-proven connection between violence to animals and people, in that if a person has a proclivity for violence that could reflect upon his conduct with dogs too. Indeed a violent owner may change the character of a dog to reflect his own. Collins J noted the precise point in *R (Sandhu) v. Isleworth Crown Court* [2012] EWHC 1658 (Admin): 'Frequently of course section 3 offences depend upon the dog having been treated by its owner so as to exhibit dangerous tendencies...' The cruelty connection is considered by the author in *Animals and Children caught in a Cycle of Cruelty* in *Justice of the Peace* [2004] [See **G36**]

Moreover, unlike the AWA, there is no provision for preventing a person from making an application after the one-year period. By the AWA the court can specify a period in which the defendant cannot apply or reapply. It is another deficiency of the DDA.

The orders are enforced by the power the court has in relation to any person who has custody of a dog in contravention of an order under section 4(1)(b) or fails to comply with a requirement imposed under section 4(4)(a). He is thereby guilty of an offence. He would be liable on summary conviction to a fine up to level 5 on a standard scale. Such a sentence seems rather lenient given that by then he has already been convicted of a serious offence. Yet again that reflects the inherent weakness of the DDA.

Contingent destruction orders

G34   Dangerous Dogs Act 1991, s.4A

   (1)   Where –
         (a)   a person is convicted of an offence under section 1 above or an aggravated offence under 3(1) or (3) above;
         (b)   the court does not order the destruction of the dog under section4(1)(a) above; and

(c) in the case of an offence under section 1 above, the dog is subject to the prohibition in section 1(3) above, the court shall order that, unless the dog is exempted from that prohibition within the requisite period, the dog shall be destroyed.

(2) Where an order is made under subsection (1) above in respect of a dog, and the dog is not exempted from the prohibition in section 1(3) above within the requisite period, the court may extend that period.

(3) Subject to subsection (2) above, the requisite period for the purposes of such an order is the period of two months beginning with the date of the order.

(4) Where a person is convicted of an offence under section 3(1) or (3), the court may order that, unless the owner of the dog keeps it under proper control the dog shall be destroyed.

(5) An order under subsection (4) above-,

(a) may specify the measures to be taken for keeping the dog under proper control, whether by muzzling, keeping on a lead, excluding it from specified places or otherwise; and

(b) if it appears to the court that the dog is a male and would be less dangerous if neutered, may require it to be neutered.

(6) Subsections (2) to (4) of section 4 above shall apply in relation to an order under subsection (1) to (4) above as they apply in relation to an order under subsection (1) (a) of that section.

As part of the amendment by the DD(A)A this contingent destruction order concept now forms a major part of the DDA. It gives a power to the court to impose conditions relating to the owner and the dog which 'suspends' any immediate destruction order. This power has been endorsed by the Court of Appeal in many recent cases as the initial step to be considered and taken in relation to a dog rather than resorting to immediate destruction. *R. v. Flack* [2008] 2 Cr. App. R. (S) 70 set the bar for all other courts as Silber J outlined the principles a court should follow in deciding an appropriate sentence prior to the death of the dog. In *R. v. Davies* [2010] EWCA Crim 1923 Mackay J made specific reference to the fact that the recorder had failed to consider that potential order and added, 'Defence counsel accepted that and said no more. He made no application to lead any evidence on this topic. He did not refer to the case of *Flack* or to the further obligation to consider a contingent destruction order under section 4A.' So the Court quashed the destruction order. [See **G25**; **G27**]

It is wide in scope as it extends to both apparatus for the dog as well as changing its physical and perhaps mental condition. The new section 4A applies where a person is convicted of an offence under section 1 or an aggravated offence under section 3. Then if the court does not order destruction of the dog under section 4(1)(a) and also where the dog is subject to the prohibition in section 1(3), its future depends on whether it has an exemption certificate. It is emphasised that the court shall order that, unless the dog is exempted from prohibition within the requisite period, the dog 'shall' be destroyed.

That allows a court to make the order that the owner contacts the authorities within two months from the date of the order, the 'requisite' period, to seek 'exemption'. He must contact the appointed Agency which controls the Index of Exempted Dogs. The court may extend the requisite period. While no details are given as to the criteria for doing so, as in the circumstances the dog's life is at stake, the owner would have to have a good reason for an extension to be granted, especially as it is following a conviction. If it was withheld for an irrational reason or on unreasonable grounds it could be subject to judicial review. Defra is the body now governing the granting of the exemption. [See **G36**]

The test for when a mandatory and discretionary destruction order applies has been clarified by the High Court in *Kelleher v. DPP* [2012] EWHC 2978 (Admin). Victoria Kelleher was the owner of two dogs, Amber and Shadow. Both dogs were subject to control orders following previous incidents in public places. Neither of those incidents resulted in any injury to a member of the public. The present incident arose in September 2009 when Shadow escaped from Kelleher and attacked another dog, Wooky. Shadow was muzzled at the time. While Kelleher tried to regain control of Shadow, she lost control of Amber who attacked Wooky too. Amber bit Wooky. Although Wooky's owner was 'exceedingly upset and distressed' he did not 'suffer any direct injury' from Amber or Shadow.

Kelleher pleaded guilty to two offences under section 3(1). The Magistrates' Court ordered destruction of the two dogs. The recorder at Bristol Crown Court upheld that order.

On appeal Collins J. said the recorder '...did get it wrong...section 4A(4) applies to both aggravated and non-aggravated offences. The power to make a destruction order applies in both cases. The distinction, which is made clear by section 4(1A), read with section 4A(4), is that in the case of an aggravated offence there must be a destruction order unless the dog would not constitute a danger to public safety, and in the case of a discretionary order the court has to decide whether it is appropriate in all the circumstances, having regard to the facts, to make a destruction order...the test, which, as it seems to me, should be applied in either case, essentially relates to whether the dog is a danger to the public.'

As over 2 years had elapsed and both dogs remained well-behaved in public, the Court quashed the orders and remitted the case to a differently constituted Crown Court.

G35 Otherwise

An important interpretation of the new power under section 4A was recently considered by the High Court in *Housego v. Canterbury Crown Court and the Crown Prosecution Service* [2012] EWHC 255 (Admin). Timothy Housego pleaded guilty to three charges of being the owner of a dangerous dog out of control in a public place. The magistrates made an order for the destruction of his dog, Kelly. Housego appealed against the destruction order to Canterbury Crown Court. Before the appeal was heard, the police seized Kelly and placed her into the care of Mrs., Margaret Todd at the Lord Whisky Animal Sanctuary. By the time of the appeal Housego had renounced ownership and was asking for Kelly to be permitted to stay at the Lord Whisky Sanctuary.

The Crown Court heard evidence about the owner of the home and from her , Mrs Todd, as well as a report from an expert, a Dr d'Sa, all to say that that would be a satisfactory arrangement. Mrs Todd was said to be very experienced and she and the sanctuary staff were well able to keep the dog safe. So Mr Recorder Byrne dismissed the appeal.

Irwin J then set out the progress of the appeal: 'On 19 February 2010 the claimant applied to the Crown Court to state a case. On 2 March 2010 the Recorder refused, on the ground that application was frivolous. On 8 April a pre-action letter was sent to the Recorder, making the point that the dog was not going to be returned to the owner, that a suspended destruction order could properly be made and asking for that to be considered. On 26 April the Recorder again replied in a response suggesting that the application was frivolous. On 7 June there was an application for judicial review to compel the Recorder to state a case…On 23 August 2010, on paper, permission was refused to compel the case be stated. That was renewed on 13 September 2010. On 2 October 2011 Collins J gave leave, on the basis that it was arguable that there had been a legal error by the Recorder.'

The Recorder and magistrates were not impressed by some of the written evidence from Dr d'Sa. Irwin J said, 'There had been no application to adjourn to get her oral evidence.'

Irwin J then noted a finding of the Crown Court:

"Whilst it is right to say that the Appellant suggested that Kelly could stay indefinitely at the animal sanctuary, the Court had no power under the Act to direct that the dog remain at a particular venue for the remainder of its life, or until such time as it no longer presented a danger to the public."

Irwin J, agreeing with the initial view of Collins J, confirmed, 'That was, in my judgment, an error of law. It is an error of law which is conceded by Mr Boyd, appearing for the Crown Prosecution Service.

The Dangerous Dogs Act 1991, amended by the 1997 Dangerous Dogs (Amendment) Act, gives the court power to suspend a destruction order based on specific conditions. Under section 4 A(5) an order for destruction may be contingent on measures for its control specified by the Court "whether by muzzling, keeping it on a lead, excluding it from specified places, or otherwise." There is an open-ended potential for making such conditions because the Act in effect says that any conditions can be imposed.

It follows that this Recorder misdirected himself. Even if Mr Housego had remained an owner, the Court had power to make such a contingent destruction order. In fact the sensible outcome of this case was so to do...The appropriate order sought is that the dog will remain for life in the Lord Whisky Sanctuary; that if the dog is ever taken from the grounds of the sanctuary that should only be when she is accompanied by Mrs Todd or a member of staff of the sanctuary; that Kelly should be kept on a lead at all times and should be muzzled at all times when she is removed outside the premises.

The Recorder failed to grasp that such an order was available to him. That was a material error.'

Irwin J concluded with a succinct comment observing what is so often overlooked by the court to the detriment of the owner as well as the dog: 'After this dog has been kept on death row, so to speak, for more than two-and-half years, it is time she was reprieved.'

Moses LJ added with finality: 'I agree. I only wish to express the gratitude of the court, both to solicitors acting in effect for the dog and to counsel and, of course, to Mrs Todd of the Lord Whisky Animal Sanctuary, all of whom are to be congratulated for their persistence in this appeal, faced with the erroneous approach of Mr Recorder Byrne.'

Given that this case was decided in 2012 it is a signpost of the guidance given by the High Court to the lower courts. It starts with the court having a duty to consider a practical solution where it is feasible as opposed to an immediate sentence of destruction. That is a sea change. Too often in the past what should be a last resort for the court has been the first one. This case holds up a mirror to that error.

G36 Treatment

In common with the purpose of avoiding killing a dog unless it is inevitable, now even where a person is convicted under section

3(1) or (3), the court may order that the dog is destroyed 'unless the owner keeps it under proper control'. So the onus is on the owner to follow the order which:

(a) may specify the measures to be taken whether by muzzling the dog or keeping it on a lead or excluding it from specified places or otherwise; and

(b) may, if it appears a male dog would be less dangerous if neutered, make a condition that it is neutered.

That power was used in *Housego v. Canterbury Crown Court.* The power is thus quite wide as excluding the dog from 'specified places' could include a hospital, a nursery, a school or any place that may place a child or adult at risk. So it could take account of vulnerable adults which is consistent with the new accent on sentencing which were introduced on 20 August 2012. As for 'otherwise', it could include an exclusion from public parks where the dog could become excited and attack other dogs. Strangely enough in that respect there is a growing problem with Guide Dogs being attacked by dangerous dogs. Moreover the Guide Dogs which are often Labradors, are of a gentle disposition and will not respond to their attackers: There were over 70 such attacks in 2011 without a single prosecution. It is a growing problem which in June 2012 was reported to be running at the rate of eight a month. However the inimical effect of these attacks extend beyond the trauma to the dog resulting in the psychological effect on the blind person who becomes a dual victim. For he can hear his dog being attacked and yet is helpless to act plus is immediately at risk himself.

Often a dog which is not innately dangerous becomes so by the deliberate acts of a violent owner. For such an owner can change the disposition of his dog to become vicious to match his own. Collins J pinpointed that precise position with arrow-like accuracy in *R (Sandhu) v. Isleworth Crown Court* [2012] EWHC 1658 (Admin):

(a) 'However, in 1997 the Act was amended because it was recognised that there was a possibility that even pit bull type dogs might not be dangerous, particularly as the definition was not as tight as it might perhaps have been and so it might have comprehended dogs which actually were not inherently vicious and which could safely be kept';

(b) Section 3 is the section which deals with dangerous dogs, or dogs which have behaved in such a way as is clearly dangerous, notwithstanding the dog itself is not regarded as one which is inherently likely to be dangerous. Frequently of course section 3 offences depend upon the dog having been treated by its owner so as to exhibit dangerous tendencies...

(c) 'The circumstances in which the dog has been treated is considered in the sentencing guidelines that have recently been issued in relation to dogs have been decided to be dangerous. We have had our attention drawn to guidelines that come into effect on 20 August of this year. In dealing with ancillary orders they provide as follows under the heading "Destruction order/contingent destruction order"...'

Defence Counsel 'has drawn attention to one of the matters set out as relevant circumstances, namely the owner's character: is the owner a fit and proper person to own this particular dog? It seems to me that that is material in relation to whether the dog should be regarded as a danger to the public. Clearly a dog, which has been badly treated by his owner may, as a result, not be able to shed the characteristics which apply to dogs, the subject of section 1, namely that they are likely to be inherently dangerous. So the treatment that the dog may have undergone is clearly relevant to that issue. Whether the owner is a fit and proper person to own a particular dog may be material in the future, but only to this extent: that it may result in a breach of the condition under article 10(2)(f), [of Certificate of Exemption] but that is not a matter which at the stage of deciding whether the dog is a danger to public can be, as it seems to me, a material consideration.'

That analysis has to be contrasted with *R. v. Donnelly* [2007] EWCA 2548. Ian Donnelly was convicted after a trial at Manchester Crown Court when his dog, Zak, a German Shepherd, had escaped from his front door on three separate occasions in 2004, 2005 and 2006. On each occasion Zak had bitten the respective person who went to Donnelly's front door. Donnelly was subject to an Anti-Social Behaviour Order ['ASBO'] in relation to the incident in 2004. HHJ Khokhar sentenced Donnelly to a suspended sentence of imprisonment and ordered the destruction of Zak.

The Court of Appeal upheld the destruction order. However the reason they did so are less than sound under scrutiny. Hedley J said, The learned judge heard evidence from an experienced person of veterinary qualifications, Miss Sarah Heath, to the effect that, although Zak was likely to bite, the reasons for his doing so were not inherent to him, but because of the way in which he was kept, and therefore it would be wrong in the circumstances to order the destruction of the dog on the basis that it related to the care the dog had received rather than its inherent nature…[the judge] took the view that he had to look at the position as it actually was. He had to consider whether Zak, in the condition in which he was and having regard to the circumstances in which he lived, constituted a danger to the public safety. He concluded that it had not been shown that the dog would not constitute a danger to the public safety. In our judgment that was a conclusion to which not only was he was entitled to come, but was clearly right to come in all the circumstances that we have set out.'

The inherent problem with that legal solution is that Zak was killed because of the care he had been given as compared to his inherent nature. It would have been a better solution to transfer the dog to another owner such as in *Housego*. It would also have the advantage of allowing the dog an opportunity to be retrained by an expert to regain its natural character. That would be a progressive approach consistent with the principle in *Housego*. It would provide the control and opportunity to remove the conditioned change that had been caused by Donnelly. It was and is not right that the crimes of the owner should be visited on his dog. For in upholding that sentence in the face of expert evidence the court made Zak a victim too. *Flack* was decided 3 months later and is the leading authority.

A trainer may indeed teach an old dog new tricks and even aid his ambition. Uggie, the Jack Russell terrier in the black-and-white silent film, *The Artist*, in 2012 was a rescued dog. He had according to *The Times* in January 2012 been 'rejected by at least two owners for being "too wild" and was sent to a pound.' Omar von Muller, his trainer, then adopted him. Uggie was 70 years old in dog years when a short time later he won an Oscar for that film. Zak like Uggie deserved a chance to change too. By corollary there is an aspect of *Donnelly* that undermines the decision and underlines why it is wrong. Donnelly was reckless regarding his control of his dog. Yet Donnelly had his sentence reduced from 12 months' imprisonment to less than 9 months'. That relates to the normal principles of sentencing including punishment and rehabilitation. As a feck there is no reason why Zak should be denied the opportunity of rehabilitation, especially as it was not his nature that made him dangerous but his nurture by the defendant.

G37 Exemption

The exemption under the Dangerous Dogs Compensation and Exemption Schemes Order 1991 is subject to several conditions all of which must be complied with before the dog can be placed on the Index. Those conditions include that:

(a) Article 6 has been complied with which involves reporting to the police with all the details of the dog;

(b) Article 7 has been complied with which involves neutering the dog by castration or spaying by a vet and having a permanent identification;

(c) Article 8 provides Third Party Insurance is in place in respect of the dog;

(d) Article 9 specifies the Fee is paid to the Agency;

(e) Article 10 confirms a Certificate of Exemption is issued and in force; and

(f) The requirements specified in the Certificate are complied with by the owner.

Those conditions are strict and cover everything about the animal from notifying the Agency to the change of address of the dog in excess of 30 days, from the insurance to having a tattoo. It is a complete file that details everything about the dog from the moment of its birth up to and including its death.

Besides all those stringent conditions, lest they are not sufficient, the Agency has power to include 'additional requirements', including the imposition of time limits, as they may 'reasonably require' to ensure compliance with article 10. In *R (Sandhu) v. Isleworth Crown Court* [2012] EWHC 1658 (Admin) Collins J said, 'No doubt any additional requirement could relate to ensuring that the dog was kept in sufficiently secure conditions. As it seems to me, it could also require that the dog was kept at a particular address, if that was something which was material in the circumstances of any given case.'

Once a person is granted a Certificate he has to produce it if requested within 5 days. Certainly that condition concentrates the mind of every responsible owner as if he fails to produce the certificate he cannot show that his dog has the right to live.

The High Court in *R (Sandhu) v. Isleworth Crown Court* considered the use of Exemption Certificates in some depth. It was an application for judicial review of a decision of the Isleworth Crown Court whereby the court made a contingent destruction order in relation to two dogs of a pit bull type, Bullet and Cuddles. Sandhu argued that the judge was wrong when making that order not to deal with and consider specifically the circumstances in which the dog was to be kept following the court's decision.

Collins J outlined the system which 'required, in order to enable a contingent destruction order not to be put into effect, that the dog was granted what is called "a certificate of exemption", the position is that Defra now, …since, I think, August of last year, have been responsible for dealing with what is called the Index of Exempted Dogs, applying the court order and deciding whether, in this circumstances, it is indeed possible for the individual dog or dogs, the subject of the order, to be provided with the necessary exemption.' He analysed the reason for the introduction of the DDA and considered sections 1, 3 and 4 in relation to the application. He said, 'The court is empowered in the case of a section 3 offence to impose such conditions as it considers needed because, as subsection 5(a) specifies, the measures go on having identified various specific matters, to use the words, "or otherwise". That extended power does not apply in cases where there is a conviction under section 1 of the Act.'

Collins J dealt with the circumstances of the case coming before the Crown Court and the appeal. He said, '…There was evidence from a veterinary surgeon that these two dogs were not dangerous. That evidence was not disputed by the prosecution and so the court had before it the evidence, which was accepted, and so made a finding of fact, which on the evidence was an inevitable finding of fact, that the dogs would not constitute a danger to public safety. Defra has been joined as a Defendant to this claim because it has a real interest in knowing what the extent of the court's powers are in making orders under section 4A in the Act, and further what its obligations as being responsible for the carrying out of the requirements of the order are.

In fact the claim, as amended, seeks various forms of relief against Defra: a mandatory order that Defra exempt both the dogs and an order of prohibition to prevent the destruction of both dogs pending the court process. In fact we understand that the dogs have been kept in kennels since the decision of the Crown Court and the institution of these proceedings. We have also been informed that keeping dogs in kennels is not cheap and no doubt that is partly the reason for the relatively short period of two months, which is imposed as the time limit generally within which decisions must be made whether a certificate of exemption should be issued if a contingent destruction order is made. Thus the first question we have to decide is essentially whether in deciding under section 4(1)(a) of the Act whether the dog would constitute a danger to public safety, the court is concerned only with the characteristics of the dog or should go further and consider the circumstances in which the dog is to be kept so as to keep it under control in the future.'

In a significant development the Court then considered and relied upon the pending Sentencing Guidelines which were not due to come into force until 20 August 2012. That is a vital development because the court has to consider, 'The circumstances in which the dog has been treated...' That goes to the root of whether it is fair and just to kill the dog or make a contingent destruction order.

For the court now has to consider the character of the dog in relation to the character of the owner. Collins J said, 'Is the owner a fit and proper person to own this particular dog? ...So the treatment that the dog may have undergone is clearly relevant to that issue.' [See **G35; H1**]

Having considered that position generally Collins J said, 'What section 4(1)(a) is looking at is the nature and characteristics of the dog. If it is a pit bull type dog the approach of the Act is that it is *ipso facto* to be regarded as dangerous, but there may be evidence in relation to a particular dog, as there was evidence in relation to these two dogs, that it is not to be regarded as inherently dangerous and therefore is not to be regarded as a danger to the public... We are told that Defra has been concerned because courts have imposed as conditions that a dog should reside at a particular place, or with a particular keeper. That has been put forward as something which should dictate whether in the circumstances a certificate of exemption should be granted...In my view the court has no power under the legislation to apply any such condition in relation to a section 1 dog. The position is of course different in relation to a section 3 dog...All that the court can do, and should do, if satisfied that the dog in question would not constitute a danger to public safety, because it does not have the inherently dangerous characteristics that pit bull type dogs are believed to have, is make a contingent destruction order if asked to do so, so that attempts can be made to obtain a certificate of exemption. After all, that would not be altogether surprising because a dog is not to be regarded as a danger to the public, then it is *prima facie* wrong that the dog's life should be brought to an end.'

After considering the general principles the court concluded that the certificate of exemption should be granted. Then the court considered the particular position of the application for that certificate as it was made by the Sandhu's cousin given that he was unavailable. For Sandhu was 'Sentenced to substantial periods of imprisonment for offences other than those relating to the dogs. He will be in prison apparently for at least two years and possibly somewhat longer. Accordingly it is necessary, if these dogs are not to be destroyed, that they are looked after by someone else in the meantime. There is no question of transferring ownership. It is simply making the cousin the keeper of the dogs, or transferring possession of the dogs to the cousin for the period during which the Claimant remains unable to look after them because, in this case, he is in prison.'

The court was aware of the potential problem when Sandhu was released from prison. Dealing with the matter in a practical way Collins J said, '...since the certificate contains the undertakings, which very properly are exacted, it is obviously important that the person who applies for the exemption should indeed be the person who is to have control of the dog for a relevant period. It is not for us to consider on this application what should occur when Mr Sandhu is released from prison and if he then wants to recover possession of the dogs in question. That is a matter for the future...'

The other interesting thing that emerges is that the lower courts have been imposing conditions which are void as a matter of law and they cannot be imposed except in respect of a 'section 3' dog, not a 'section 1' one as Collins J named it. That is now clarified. To that end it is significant that Defra was joined as a party to the appeal as the exemption scheme is now run by Defra itself. So the judgment will have more impact now that the new sentencing provisions have been brought into effect.

Sandhu was an excellent example of a judicial interpretation of the DDA to give a positive effect to what could have been an obvious defect and injustice. Another decision that was a welcome analysis of this area of the DDA is *R. v. Metropolitan Police and the Index of Exempted Dogs ex parte Wheeler* [1993] Crim. L. R. 942. It was a case that the High Court called with an understated accuracy, 'a legal and bureaucratic nightmare'. The Index of Exempted Dogs was the trading name of the company which at the time was the designated agent for the Home Office in discharging its functions under the DDA. Wheeler had a pit bull terrier, Joker. He had obtained a Certificate of Exemption in October 1991 from the agency following the neutering of and implantation of a transponder in Joker by a vet. On at 11 August 1992 he was stopped by the police for a road traffic offence. Joker was in the car and he was charged with unlawful possession of the dog and with having an unmuzzled dog. On 25 September the CPS discontinued the case. However the dog was detained by the police as they considered he was in breach of the statutory requirements by not having had Joker tattooed. The police advised the agency and asked it to confirm the suspension of Wheeler's exemption certificate. The agency duly advised him that, due to the lack of a tattoo on Joker, his certificate had lapsed and he had no legal right to possess his dog. Wheeler issued a summons under the Police (Property) Act 1897. As a result the magistrates ordered the police to return the dog to him. The police acknowledged their liability to return it but advised Wheeler's solicitor that this would be a formality as the dog would be reseized. Subsequent attempts by Wheeler to visit the dog with a tattooist, so that the reference number could be put on Joker, were frustrated. It was contended by the police and the agency that the tattoo should have been done by 1 March 1992 at the latest. Now it was too late so Joker must be killed. The central issue was whether (a) the certificate was valid on 25 September 1992 when the CPS decided not to proceed and (b) the threat of reseizure was justified.

The High Court considered the requirement of a tattoo was purely for administrative convenience and was not connected with the neutering or implanting of the transponder. A tattoo enabled the police and the agency to identify a dog more readily. The exemption had been granted under the Dangerous Dogs Compensation and Exemption Scheme Order 1991, part of which required third party insurance be in place in respect of a dog to which the Act applied. There was no reference there to the tattoos or other identifying marks on the dog; nor was there any specific indication as to the termination of the certificate if any of the requirements ceased to be met. Before any amendment order came into effect, there was no express statutory reference to tattooing. It was clear from a 25 November statutory instrument and a letter circulated by the agency that tattooing was an additional requirement to the permanent identification required by article 7(1). The tattoo requirement was introduced for administrative convenience and became statutory on 25 November 1991. Before that date it followed that a certificate, which was otherwise lawfully issued, did not become invalid nor was it invalid merely because the dog was not tattooed. The agency had signed a certificate that the relevant conditions had been complied with and the applicant had ample grounds for a reasonable and legitimate expectation that the certificate was valid, which continued to be soundly based in the absence of notification of the additional requirement of tattooing after 25 November.

Wheeler was willing to have Joker tattooed and it would have been done by now if the police had permitted access. It was therefore unnecessary to decide whether there was a lawful requirement upon him to do so. The insurance certificate expired on 7 October 1992 and he could not obtain insurance whilst the dog was in custody. Wheeler was in a "catch 22" situation if it was said that he had allowed the insurance to lapse. He should be able to obtain insurance to take effect when the dog was released and any technical breach of the insurance requirements in the intervening period was not a ground for prosecution. The court granted a declaration that the certificate remained valid, subject only to Wheeler now complying with the conditions of the insurance.

A significant point of administrative law arose when it was argued by those opposing the application that there was no relevant 'decision' which could be the subject of a judicial review. The court dismissed that fanciful notion: for the decision of the Agency gave the court jurisdiction to make a declaration that their letter to Wheeler was void.

Destruction orders otherwise than on a conviction:

G38   Dangerous Dogs Act 1991, s.4B

   (1)   Where a dog is seized under section 5(1) or (2) below and it appears to a justice of the peace –

   (a)   that no person has been or is to be prosecuted for an offence under this Act or an order under section 2 in respect of that dog (whether because the owner cannot be found or for any other reason); or

   (b)   that the dog cannot be released into the custody or possession of its owner without the owner contravening the prohibition in section 1(3) above, he may order the destruction of the dog and, subject to subsection 2 below, shall do so if it is one to which section 1 applies.

   (2)   Nothing in subsection (1)(b) above shall require the justice of the peace or sheriff to order the destruction of a dog if he is satisfied –

(a) that the dog would not constitute a danger to public safety; and

(b) where the dog was born before 30 November 1991 and is subject to the prohibition in section 1(3) above, that there is good reason why the dog has not been exempted from that prohibition.

(3) Where in a case falling within subsection 1(b) above the justice or sheriff does not order the destruction of the dog, he shall order that, unless the dog is exempted from the prohibition in section 1(3) above within the requisite period, the dog shall be destroyed.

(4) Subsections (2) to (4) of section 4 above shall apply in relation to an order under subsection (1)(b) or (3) above as they apply in relation to an order under subsection (1)(a) of that section.

(5) Subsections (2) and (3) of section 4A above shall apply in relation to an order under subsection (3) above as they apply in relation to an order under subsection (1) of that section, except that the reference to subsection (2) in of that section shall be construed as a reference to the justice or sheriff.

The second amendment to the DDA was also quite far reaching because it gives wide powers to the court even though there has not been a conviction. It extends the discretion to the magistrates' court. So the destruction is now discretionary compared to the position prior to this amendment via the DD(A)A, when it was mandatory.

It arises where a dog has been seized by a constable or an officer under section 5(1) or (2). In that case there are two situations that affect the dog's position and future. If it appears to a justice of the peace that (a) no person has been or is to be prosecuted for an offence under the DDA or an order under section 2 in respect of that dog or (b) that the dog cannot be released into the custody or possession of its owner without the owner contravening section 1(3), he may order the destruction of the dog. [See **G40**]

That discretion towards destruction is clarified by confirming that if the dog is one within section 1, he 'shall' order its death. However that is subject to subsection (2) which governs their discretion. As a result the justice of the peace is not bound to order the destruction of a dog if he is satisfied it would not constitute a danger to public safety.

There must be some evidence from someone to show that the dog is not a danger to public safety. Normally that would be a vet which could be supported by lay persons and referees consistent with the principles set out in *R. v. Flack* [2008] 2 Cr. App. R. (S) 70 and followed in later cases in the High Court and the Court of Appeal. [See **G25**] The prosecution may not accept that position and instead obtain their own vet's report and/or expert evidence. Indeed in many cases the prosecution report is often the only expert evidence available. That position will increase as legal aid for defendants disappears. Yet that could be more problematic as in the circumstances the owner may not be found. Indeed he may have made himself scarce in order to avoid a potential prosecution. In that event it is manifestly a disadvantage to the dog to have no one to represent its interests including staying alive. That is inconsistent with its welfare and more under the AWA.

So who then speaks for the speechless? If that is the case the court ought to, whether of its own volition or under a statutory duty, appoint an *amicus* or 'friend' as the dog's legal voice. Moreover even if the owner can be found he may well disown the dog. In that case it is hardly fair that his lack of interest would determine the dog's fate and destiny.

If the justice of the peace, in a case within section (1)(b), does not order the destruction of the dog, he shall order that unless the dog is 'exempted' from the prohibition in section 1(3) within the 'requisite' period, the dog shall be destroyed. So it is plain the onus is on someone, who may not be the absent or missing owner, who should ensure then that an application for exemption is made. It is unclear as to who is responsible for making such an application if the owner is unavailable be it because of incarceration or otherwise.

The justice of the peace may order the destruction of the dog and if he does so he may order a person to be appointed to carry it out. If the owner is not found it seems reasonable to assume that the person appointed would need to be paid. The DDA does not make it clear who pays to keep the dog alive, let alone kill it.

The requisite period is 2 months. As that applies to section 4A and 4B, the period could be extended by the court. That is discretionary as it is a condition precedent to avoid destruction. So the court would have to be satisfied that the owner had a good reason for not taking the necessary action. As the regulations are strict it could be necessary to take action against the controlling body, Defra. [See **G37**]

While there is no conviction in this case, if nevertheless there is a destruction order, that can be subject to an appeal to the Crown Court. Given the vagueness of the DDA, it is unclear in the circumstances where the owner cannot be found who will appeal on behalf of the ownerless dog? Why would anyone wish to do so? If the unchallenged evidence of the prosecution is accepted because no one knows or cares, how is that reconcilable with the adversarial system? What if that unchallenged evidence is unreliable or wrong? There is no legal voice for the dog and his own would soon be stilled.

G39 Same

The same dog in a different case raised issues that are fundamental to the power of the police and the criminal justice process itself. The first case was *R. v. Walton Street Justices ex parte Crothers* [1992] Crim. L. R. 875 where Crothers sought judicial review of the respondent's decision to order the destruction of his dog under 5(4) of the DDA. The dog was seized by the police on 25 October 1991. The applicant was charged with being the owner of a pit bull terrier which he had allowed to be in a public place without a lead and unmuzzled and to be dangerously out of control. An application was made under section 2 of the Dogs Act 1871 that the dog be kept under proper control or destroyed. Crothers claimed that his dog, Buster, was not a pit bull terrier, but a Staffordshire bull terrier. On February 20 1992 the prosecutor served notice of discontinuance of the proceedings and that no order would be sought under the 1871 Act. The dog remained in police custody. On March 6, without notice to Crothers, the police applied for a destruction order under section 5(4) of the DDA. Crothers challenged the order on the grounds (1) that a condition precedent to the jurisdiction was not satisfied because he had been prosecuted and (2) that he should have been given an opportunity to be heard.

The High Court held that a person who has been summonsed but against whom the proceedings had been discontinued has nonetheless been 'prosecuted'. Consequently as section 5(4) confers upon the court a power which Parliament must have intended to be exercised within the principles of natural justice, the owner should have been informed. The court relied upon the House of Lords case of *Wiseman v. Borneman* [1971] A.C. 297 which held that property must be protected. Therefore the application was allowed as in any case involving the destruction of property the rules of natural justice required at least that a known owner of that property should be given an opportunity to be heard.

Professor Diane Birch makes a strong point in commenting that section 5(4) would have sealed his fate except for the fact, 'It seems his owner had amassed a volume of evidence to show he was in fact a Staffordshire bull terrier ...[so] his destruction should not been ordered without resolving that issue and to resolve it without hearing from the person who, as Buster's owner, had the greatest interest in arguing against destruction would have been a quite unnecessary departure from the rules of natural justice...But if his owner has a case to put, it should be heard.'

Two years later the same dog with a different defendant came before the same magistrates' court. In *R. v. Walton Street Justices ex parte Crothers* [1996] 160 JP 427 it was a different High Court with a different point of view. After the judicial review in his favour Crothers gave the dog to his son, the applicant. The police released Buster to the applicant and immediately reseized claiming he was the owner of an unregistered pit bull terrier. No prosecution was lodged but the applicant was notified that an application was being made under section 5(4) to the magistrates' court for destruction of Buster. Crothers attended court with a witness and applied for an adjournment so he could be legally represented. The magistrates refused that application. They refused to hear the witness. They then ordered Buster's destruction. Like his father the son applied for judicial review. The grounds were (1) if a person had been prosecuted under the DDA section 5(4) could not apply; (2) an adjournment should have been granted; (3) the witness should have been allowed to give evidence.

All and any of those grounds seemed reasonable or at least arguable. The court did not think so. Buxton J said, 'The police acted entirely properly, having given the dog momentarily back to Mr Crothers junior in reseizing it again, and were within their powers so to do. It is from that point of siezure onwards that the powers under section 5(4) have to be looked at. The fact that in respect of some previous event in connection with some previous seizure, another person – on Mr Crothers junior's own case, someone entirely different, unconnected now with the dog – had been prosecuted, does not in my view in any way affect the ability of the magistrates to proceed under section 5(4). What they were doing was to accept that the dog had been seized on 27 July 1992 [that related to the second seizure] and then decide what to do about it. The fact that previously there had been some other prosecution in respect of another seizure of that same dog seems to me nothing to the point at all.' The court equally held that they were right to refuse the adjournment as that was within their discretion. In relation to the final ground the court held that the magistrates had erred in law as they wrongly believed that as it was a civil case they could not hear from any witness. However the court overlooked that fact and was consistent in rejecting the appeal. Buxton J said, 'Although the magistrates were wrong, it could not be said that any injustice had been done.'

Initially this seemed to be just another bad decision and irreconcilable with the elementary principles of fairness and natural justice, when at a moment's notice a proper hearing might have saved the dog's life. The court dealt with the case as if Crothers was an irresponsible owner who deserved to be deprived of his property. They seemed to ignore the fact the magistrates erred in law and that a fair trial includes hearing from the accused and about another potential victim, his dog. On balance the court merely made a bad decision by applying a bad law.

The court should have followed the principle adopted by Collins J in *Knightsbridge Crown Court v. The Commissioner of Police for Metropolitan Police v. Wells Street Magistrates Court ex parte*

Crabbe [1996] EWHC Admin 380 where he said, 'However, because of the lack of the right of appeal and the lack of safeguards in the bare words of section 5(4), it seems to me that it is all the more important that the Magistrate, before whom the matter comes, ensures that there is a fair trial; in particular, that the owner of the dog, who is disputing the application that the dog be destroyed, be able to produce all the evidence that he wishes, providing of course that evidence is relevant.' [See **G44**]

It is of little value for the court to seek a solace by resting on the belief that no injustice was done. The reality is that unless and until it is tested no one knows what the result will be. The reasoning of Rougier J in *R. v. Ealing Magistrates' Court ex parte Fanneran* [1995] 160 JP 409 applies here with equal force. Crothers, like Fanneran, should have been granted the opportunity of a hearing. [See **G29**]

G40 Fair

That second *Crothers* case was considered by the High Court in *R. v. Haringey Magistrates' ex parte Cragg* [1996] EWHC Admin 162. *Cragg* was also decided under the DDA before it was amended by the DDA(A)A. However it is instructive for the bold analysis of the issue and the fair decision on the facts. Jeanette Cragg, was the owner of a dog, Kizzie. Alan Bailey, her friend, was seen in a public place in North London with Kizzie on 12 July 1992. Bailey was charged under section 1 with an allegation that Kizzie was a pit bull terrier. The trial started on 25 May 1993 and was adjourned part-heard. Maurice Kay J. said, 'The sole issue in the case was whether Kizzie is of the type of dog known as a pit bull terrier, and that was a matter for expert evidence.'

The adjourned hearing was listed in October 1993. However one of the experts for Bailey was known to one of the magistrates so the trial was halted and adjourned to a different day with a different bench. The new trial was scheduled for January 1994. However, in December 1993, the Crown Prosecution Service decided not to proceed. They wrote to Bailey indicating they had sent a notice to the magistrates' clerk 'discontinuing' the case under section 23 of the Prosecution of Offences Act 1985 because 'It is not in the public interest to proceed'.

Bailey was a man of some mettle. When he received that letter he was not willing to simply accept it. Bailey insisted on the matter being brought back to court under section 23(7) of the 1985 Act. When it came before the court on 24 January 1994 the CPS offered 'no evidence' and the charge was dismissed. Maurice Kay J said, 'It is akin to a verdict of "not guilty" by direction in the Crown Court.'

Kizzie was not then 'unreservedly returned' to either Bailey or Cragg. Instead on 10 February 1994 Kizzie was handed over but immediately reseized. Maurice Kay J said, 'That in my judgment, was most probably because the police officers were unhappy with the decision that had been taken by the Crown Prosecution Service to discontinue the prosecution of Mr Bailey...an application was made to Haringey Justices by a police officer, pursuant to section 5(4)...it is an application of a civil nature.'

At the hearing expert evidence was called on both sides. Indeed four experts were called on behalf of Cragg. The burden of proof was on the police to the civil standard. The stipendiary magistrate found the complaint proved. Once he found the complaint proved he was bound to make a destruction order for Kizzie. So he did.

On 13 April 1995 the stipendiary magistrate was asked to state a case. He refused to do so, taking the view that the matters raised were purely factual. So an application was made for judicial review. Leave was granted in January 1996. Meanwhile it was over 4 years after the initial seizure when the application came before the High Court.

The main ground of Cragg's appeal in the High Court was that the proceedings under section 5(4) was an abuse of process, either because they were *ultra vires* or they amounted to an attack on the acquittal of Bailey.

The Court referred to the later case of *R. v. Walton Street Justices ex parte Crothers* [1996] 160 JP 427 where one of the points was whether the proceeding under section 5(4) related said Maurice Kay J 'to double proceedings in relation to the same dog or double proceedings in relation to the same seizure of that dog.' He referred to that case, particularly the reasoning for the decision and said, 'That case brought to an end a somewhat sorry saga of litigation about the dog in question. The facts of that case were somewhat different to those in the present case and there had been rather less argument and submission about the law. I am bound to say that, with the greatest respect, I have some doubt about the construction there placed upon the section by Buxton J (with whom Beldon LJ agreed) on the point. However, it is not necessary in the present circumstances for me to resolve that doubt for a number of reasons.'

Dealing with Cragg's appeal Maurice Kay J specified the reasons namely, 'The first is that in the present case there was, in effect, an acquittal in the first proceedings and not just a discontinuance. Secondly, if the present applicant had been the defendant in the first proceedings, there is no doubt – and Mr McGuinness on behalf of the Commissioner frankly concedes this – that it would be wrong and in appropriate to proceed against her under section 5(4). Thirdly, the change in parties – that is to say, the Commissioner rather than the Crown Prosecution Service and the applicant rather than Mr Bailey – whilst it might be fatal to a technical argument based on estoppel or *res judicata*, is not, in my judgment, so fatal when one takes a broader look at the facts as this court is entitled and is asked to do. At the end of the day the second proceedings, that is to say the ones against the applicant, involved the same dog which had remained in the same ownership throughout. In my judgment, in these circumstances, it was wholly inappropriate and wrong for the Commissioner to take the second proceedings against this applicant, and the application which was made to the stipendiary magistrate to stop those proceedings as an abuse ought to have succeeded. It matters not precisely what label is put on that analysis, but in my judgment it is an abuse of process and ought to have been held to have been such. As these are civil proceedings I doubt whether the authorities on abuse of process in criminal proceedings are strictly relevant but my finding of abuse would be the same in any event.'

That analysis by the judge was an imaginative interpretation of an Act that was unfair in form and biased in substance. However his critical reasoning led to the right decision.

Seizure, entry of premises and evidence

G41   Dangerous Dogs Act 1991, s.5

(1)   A constable or an officer of a local authority authorised by it to exercise the powers conferred by this section may seize –

(a)   any dog which appears to him to be a dog to which section 1 above applies and which is in a public place –

(i)   after the time when possession or custody of it has become unlawful by virtue of that section; or

(ii)   before that time, without being muzzled and kept on lead;

(b)   any dog in a public place which appears to him to be a dog to which an order under section 2 above applies and in respect of which an offence against the order has been or is being committed; and

(c)   any dog in a public place (whether or not one to which that section applies) which appears to him to be dangerously out of control.

(2)   If a justice of the peace is satisfied by information on oath, ... that there are reasonable grounds for believing —

(a)   that an offence under any provision of this Act or of an order under section 2 above is being or has been committed; or

(b)   that evidence of the commission of any such offence is to be found, on any premises he may issue a warrant authorising a constable to enter the premises (using such force as is reasonably necessary) and to search them and seize any dog or other thing found there which is evidence of such an offence.

(3)   A warrant issued under this section in Scotland shall be authority for opening lockfast places and may authorise persons named in the warrant to accompany a constable who is executing it.

(4)   Repealed.

(5)   If in any proceedings it is alleged by the prosecution that a dog is one to which section 1 or an order under section 2 above applies it shall be presumed that it is such a dog unless the contrary is shown by the accused by such evidence as the court considers sufficient; and the accused shall not be permitted to adduce such evidence unless he has given the prosecution notice of his intention to do so not later than the fourteenth day before that on which the evidence is to be adduced.

This is the widest and perhaps most controversial area of the DDA because it raises the 'presumption' that the dog is of a 'type' that it is illegal to possess unless the owner proves otherwise. It also gives wide powers of seizure of dogs who are then subject to the rigours of the law because of their appearance and conduct. While there are according to the officers responsible for enforcing this law a total of 54 characteristics of a pit bull terrier, in truth many dogs are seized purely on their apparent resemblance to a known type. Then the burden shifts to the owner to prove otherwise or face the penalty.

Some police forces have a Dog Legislation Officer [DLO] who has in-depth training on dog-related legislation. As a result they may have a good knowledge of the prohibited types. Indeed some forces even run courses on the role of the DLO. In time such officers, especially if they are dog-handlers too, may acquire the knowledge of and so gain the status of experts. However this is an area that is rife with errors and disputes as to the identification of the family pet as a pit bull terrier. For once the pet is deemed to be one, that label may lead inexorably to its death.

Under this section a constable or an officer of a local authority may seize any dog which 'appears to him' to be a prohibited dog which is in a public place. There are additionally two alternative conditions relating to that power before it can be exercised. Those are either (a) after the time when possession or custody of the dog has become unlawful by that section or (b) before that time, it is not muzzled and kept on lead.

This applies to the four types who are designated dogs under section 1 of the DDA. The officer has to be authorised by the local authority to exercise those powers. So it is strange given the powers and consequences of exercising them that neither an 'officer' nor a 'local authority' is defined anywhere within the DDA.

Additionally the constable or officer may seize (a) any dog in a public place which appears to him subject to a section 2 order and an offence against the order has been or is being committed; and (b) any dog in a public place which appears to him to be dangerously out of control. So apart from the prohibited dogs that are designated under section 1, this allows seizure of it if it is a 'specially dangerous dog' under section 2. While initially there was a mandatory condition of death for the designated dogs who were seen as a danger by virtue of their fighting tendencies, these were not in that category yet did present a serious danger to the public. Consequently there could be 'restrictions' placed upon the dog plus the ultimate restriction namely its destruction.

By an extension of those powers a constable or officer could also seize any dog, regardless of any breach of any section or order, which appears to be 'dangerously out of control'. That enables the seizure if it is in a public place and for whatever reason the dog is an actual or potential threat to people. Like the previous two provisions under this section 5(1)(a)-(c) the power applies to 'any' dog.

As with all of these provisions, it gives a lot of power to the person seizing the dog as it is purely a personal decision. So providing it is reasonable the subjective view namely, 'which appears to him', is all that matters. The power lies in the eye of the beholder. Thereafter the consequences for the owner and the dog can be detrimental to both.

While Crothers did not want to give evidence in *R. v. Walton Street Justices ex parte Crothers* [1996] 160 JP 427, he did want his witness, Mr Smith, a 'breed expert' to do so. However the magistrates refused his request as they were advised that legally they could not do so as there was no power because the defendant had not given the required 14 days notice. The High Court decided they were wrong in law as that related to criminal proceedings whilst this was a civil application. That error of law did not affect the Court's decision. Axiomatically in such an application the presumption as to type still applies though the burden of proof on the defendant was on the balance of probability.

G42 Entry

Allied to those powers an application for a warrant can be obtained by a constable to enter premises and gain further evidence. By section 5(2) if the justice of the peace is satisfied, by information on oath, that there are reasonable grounds for believing (a) an offence under any provision or section 2 is being or has been committed or (b) evidence of the commission of any such offence is to be found on any premises he may issue a warrant.

This is an additional power which could be a further investigation of an existing offence or one that has been brought to his notice. It would be particularly relevant if he saw a dog which 'appeared' to him to be or acting contrary to the DDA and he wanted to enter the premises of the owner or the offender. If he is granted a warrant he could enter and use reasonable force to gain entry if it is locked. While there he could carry out a search and seize any dog or 'other thing' found there which is evidence of the commission of such an offence.

The power is wide, but the dog or thing seized must relate to the past or present in that it has happened or is happening. So it would not be the 'commission' of any offence, depending on circumstances, if it is to be arranged to happen in the future. Given that dangerous dogs and drug dealers are wedded together like thieves and handlers, it is a power that could be enhanced for the police by section 17(1) and 19 of PACE, especially as that applies to the AWA. While it could be the commission of an offence by omission, the evidence could also relate to the commission of one in the future. In that event it could be charged as an attempt or a conspiracy.

As the power is so wide it is unsatisfactory that the term 'premises' is not defined at all. So does it pertain to all areas or only those specified in the warrant or would it be vague so it is the subjective view of the constable as it specifies 'any premises'? It is a potentially problematic area as premises can exclude the private living area which is perversely the very area the evidence is likely to be found. The reality is it is another example of what was a flawed piece of legislation which was initially badly-drafted and continues to be in that condition.

G43 Adduce

Once it is alleged by the prosecution that a dog is one to which section 1 or an order under section 2 applies, it shall be presumed that it is such a dog. The burden of proof then immediately shifts to the defendant who has to prove the contrary by 'such evidence as the court considers sufficient'. There is a further onus on the defendant in relation to any evidence he intends to adduce to meet that burden. He will not be permitted to do so unless he gives the prosecution notice of his intention 14 days before the evidence is to be adduced. That allows the prosecution time to either accept or obtain their own evidence which is likely to be from an expert .The 14 day period of notice envisages a criminal proceeding. It does not apply if a person is contesting the civil application for destruction under section 4B(1). [See **G39**; **G 44**]

It would not be sufficient for the defence to simply say via the defendant and his friends and neighbours, "He's a lovely dog. He's great with children. He's a pussycat", and the like. What the defendant would need to show is solid evidence that effectively at best proves his defence and shifts the legal presumption back onto the prosecution. At the least he must adduce evidence which, if it does not destroy the presumption itself, raises a real doubt as to whether the presumption is accurate and reliable and true. Hence the court would decide in his favour on the civil burden of proof. Therefore to be effective in meeting the burden of proof and presumption, the defence would need evidence from an expert or an animal organisation or a vet or ideally a combination of them all.

The truth is this harsh provision is aimed primarily at pit bull terriers. While it is necessary to control such dogs that are plainly dangerous largely as a result of irresponsible owners this is problematic *per se*. For how can you positively identify a pit bull terrier when the appointed experts do not agree? That is the precise reason it indicates type rather than breed. Many dogs were seized and due to die which were shown to be merely of similar appearance, but turned out to be a Staffordshire bull terrier or other cross-breed which are not pit bull terriers. The experts and Defra do not agree on the origin and genetics of the pit bull terrier. To that extent the position remains the same. In *R (Sandhu) v. Isleworth Crown Court* [2012] EWHC 1658 (Admin) Collins J said, 'However, in 1997 the Act was amended because it was recognised that there was a possibility that even pit bull type dogs might not be dangerous, particularly as the definition was not as tight as it might perhaps have been and so it might have comprehended dogs which actually were not inherently vicious and which could safely be kept'. The one certain point about this area of law is its inherent uncertainty.

G44 Money

When there is limited legal aid available and the defendant is poor, there is a premium on him having a fair trial. The position was brought into sharp focus in *Knightsbridge Crown Court v.*

The Commissioner of Police for Metropolitan Police v. Wells Street Magistrates Court ex parte Crabbe [1996] EWHC Admin 380. This was an application for judicial review involving a dog called Elsa who was alleged to be a pit bull terrier. The Commissioner of the Metropolitan Police applied under section 5(4) and the Stipendiary Magistrate decided that Elsa was a pit bull terrier and so should be destroyed. [That action was a civil claim which prior to its repeal was an easier procedure for the police to initiate and prove.]

What is remarkable about this unusual and welcome decision on the DDA is the fact McCowan LJ was concerned about the fate of and there being a fair trial for the dog. Leslie Crabbe sought an Order quashing the decisions of the Commissioner and the Stipendiary Magistrate. Crabbe had the dog 'dumped on him by his girlfriend'. She had not bothered to get the dog registered. Although the CPS decided not to prosecute Crabbe under section 1, the court did not know the reason for their decision.

Meanwhile Elsa remained in the possession of the Commissioner who sought the destruction order. His problem was he had expert evidence Elsa was a pit bull terrier. The Commissioner sought a decision as McCowan LJ said, 'After all it is for the court to decide whether the dog should be destroyed and not the Crown Prosecution Service.'

Crabbe wanted Elsa to be examined by an expert, Dr Roger Mugford. He is an animal behaviourist. McCowan LJ said, 'He is an expert on how dogs behave, and apparently it has become clear that how a dog behaves is a very important part of the test of whether it falls within the prohibited description in section 1.'

However when Crabbe tried to have the dog examined by Dr Mugford the police said he could only do so at Teddington Police

Station. In that event McCowan LJ said he, 'would have to pay £300 towards the administrative costs...The Applicant did not have the means to pay this, as was made plain to the first Respondent. However he stuck by his decision. In consequence of that when the matter came before the Stipendiary Magistrate, the applicant had no such evidence and, in particular the evidence of Dr Mugford which he wanted.' So the Stipendiary Magistrate ordered the destruction of Elsa.

Then Crabbe appealed to the Crown Court. Meanwhile facilities were in fact granted so Dr Mugford and a vet, Dr Larkin, on behalf of Crabbe could examine Elsa. They both concluded that it was not a pit bull terrier. So Crabbe approached the appeal with some optimism. However McCowan LJ said, 'at Knightsbridge Crown Court before Judge Privite he ruled that there can be no appeal to the Crown Court for an order under section 5(4) of the Act. That is now accepted on behalf of the Applicant to be correct. The Stipendiary Magistrate accepts that too, although he did not know it at the time of the hearing before him. The result is that the Order for destruction stands, although the Applicant has expert evidence which it is accepted could save her life.'

Mc Cowan LJ then outlined a classic brief exposition that emphasised the trial process must ensure fairness for both the owner and his dog: 'I would not criticise the Commissioner for making the application, it is important, in my judgment, that if the application were to be made, no steps should be taken which would prevent the dog having a fair trial. The relevant facts were that the applicant had no legal aid, no right of appeal to the Crown Court and no means to pay the £300. As I say, £300 is an inordinately high sum. A much fairer sum could surely have been achieved by having the dog examined at another police station or, perhaps better still, at the police dog kennel. As it was, by insisting on a figure of £300 contribution to be made by the

Applicant, the Commissioner made it well near impossible for the Applicant to get a fair trial for his dog. I think that the learned Stipendiary Magistrate may well have taken a different view about granting an adjournment had he not mistakenly believed that an appeal did lie to the Crown Court and that the Applicant could call his expert evidence then.'

McCowan LJ concluded, 'In view of the combination of factors to which I have referred, I think there was not, in the result, a fair trial.' The destruction order of Elsa was quashed. A rehearing was ordered before a different Stipendiary Magistrate.

Collins J endorsed those points and added, 'Accordingly, like my Lord, I see no reason why the Commissioner should not have decided, as he did, to pursue the matter under section 5(4). However, because of the lack of the right of appeal and the lack of safeguards in the bare words of section 5(4), it seems to me that it is all the more important that the Magistrate, before whom the matter comes, ensures that there is a fair trial; in particular, that the owner of the dog, who is disputing the application that it will be destroyed, be able to produce all the evidence that he wishes, providing of course that evidence is relevant.'

Dogs owned by young persons

G45   Dangerous Dogs Act 1991, s.6

Where a dog is owned by a person who is less than sixteen years old any reference to its owner in section 1(2)(d) or (e) or 3 above shall include a reference to the head of the household, if any, of which that person is a member or, in Scotland, to the person who has his actual care and control.

It used to be a common excuse for a young person to say the dog in question did not belong to him. It was often claimed as a defence by a child that the dog belonged to his father or mother or older brother. This section was introduced to meet either excuse or truth as now both persons could be liable.

Now when a dog is 'owned' by a person under 16 years old any reference to its owner in section 1(2)(d) or (e) or 3 'shall' include a reference to the head of the household, if any, of which that person is a member. Of course there are many more children in care now than in the past so the head of the care home would be equally liable for the behaviour of the dog. The better phrase to describe the relationship and cover different social situations is the one used in Scotland, 'actual care and control.'

There also used to be problems as to who is a 'keeper' of animals. This section is aimed at an ideal family and only has a limited purpose for the Kellogg sunshine happy family of mother and father and two children. Nowadays with the rise of feminism, one parent families and multiple-marriages, the head of the household cannot be assumed to be the husband or father of the child. Indeed whether by choice or compulsion there may not even be a man on the premises. So the head of the household remains legally liable if the owner is under 16 years old.

Muzzling and leads

G46   Dangerous Dogs Act 1991, s.7

(1)   In this Act –
   (a)   references to a dog being muzzled are to its being securely fitted with a muzzle sufficient to prevent it biting any person; and
   (b)   references to its being kept on a lead are to its being securely held on a lead by a person who is not less than sixteen years old.

(2)   If the Secretary of State thinks it is desirable to do so he may by order prescribe the kind of muzzle or lead

to be used for the purpose of complying, in the case of a dog of any type, with section 1 or under section 2 above; and if a muzzle or lead of a particular kind is for the time being prescribed in relation to any type of dog the references in subsection (1) above to a muzzle or lead shall, in relation to any dog of that type, be construed as references to a muzzle or lead of that kind.

(3)   The power to make an order under subsection (2) shall be exercised by statutory instrument subject to annulment in pursuance of a resolution of either House of Parliament.

The fact that a dog is deemed to be dangerous and so has to be muzzled runs as a theme throughout the DDA. Similarly the use of a lead for such a dog is a recurrent theme. Both are plainly to prevent the dog from biting people and to protect the public. It is pertinent that the courts have also consistently ordered that a dog is muzzled when a contingent destruction order is imposed either initially in the magistrates' court or usually on appeal. In fact when a court orders a dog to be muzzled there is a usual condition precedent that it must be done within a given period normally 56 days. That concentrates the mind of the owner as if he fails to do so within that time the dog will be killed. [See **G26**]

In that regard it is spelled out that 'references' to a dog being muzzled are to it being securely fitted with a muzzle sufficient to prevent it biting any person. As it is never enough merely to have it muzzled, it is emphasised that references to it being kept on a lead are to it being securely held on a lead. That is endorsed by the fact the person holding the lead must be at least 16 years old. Moreover if the person in charge of it cannot hold the dog on the lead because it is too strong or he is too weak, then in the event of it biting someone the liability would follow. [See **G19**]

It is clear beyond doubt, given the strict liability on owners and the presumption as to the type of dog – as well as a matter of public policy – the courts narrowly interpret the DDA. So a muzzle has to be worn at all times to comply with the provisions of the DDA or a court order. The strength and weakness of that policy can be seen in a sharp and blunt focus by *R. v. Ealing Magistrates' Court ex parte Fanneran* [1995] 160 JP 409. Fanneran's nephew pleaded guilty to being in charge of a pit bull terrier in a public place without it being muzzled as he had removed it order to allow the dog to be sick. At that moment he was guilty. Just how narrow that interpretation is can be seen by the fact necessity is not available as a defence. One of the worst examples is *Cichon v. DPP* [1994] Crim LR 918 where Cichon had removed the muzzle because the dog had kennel cough, so he felt it was cruel to keep it on whilst the dog was coughing. Cichon was instantly guilty. [See **G6**; **G29**]

That places an onus on the owner to ensure any person who is in charge of the dog is over 16 years' and the muzzle and lead are secure. In respect of the condition the only safe course for an owner to avoid the metaphorical lash of the law on him and his dog is to follow the convict Magwitch to avoid becoming one: '…count upon me always having a genteel muzzle. Muzzled I have been since that half a minute when I was betrayed into lowness, muzzled I am at the present time, muzzled I ever will be.'

Additionally the Secretary of State may prescribe what kind of muzzle or lead to be used to comply in the case of a dog of 'any' type within section 1 or section 2. If it is specified that would be part of the condition in section 7(a). The potential regulation relating to a prescribed muzzle and lead relates to a dog of any type. So far there have not been any regulations to prescribe either kind of muzzle or lead.

The owner would have to ensure that the lead and muzzle is fit for its purpose. Therefore if it is cheap and breaks under strain or is badly fitting and allows the dog to escape, the owner would be liable. The poor quality would be the equivalent of an insecure gate.

Like the power under section 1, as compared to section 2 which requires a resolution of both, it can be annulled by either House of Parliament.

Short title, interpretation, commencement and extent

G47 Dangerous Dogs Act 1991, s.10

...

(2) In this Act –

"advertisement" includes any means of bringing a matter to the attention of the public and "advertise" shall be construed accordingly;

"public place" means any street, road or other place (whether or not enclosed) to which the public have or are permitted to have access whether for payment or otherwise and includes the common parts of a building containing two or more separate dwellings.

(3) For the purposes of this Act a dog shall be regarded as dangerously out of control on any occasion on which there are grounds for reasonable apprehension that it will injure any person, whether or not it actually does so, but references to a dog injuring a person or there being grounds for reasonable apprehension that it will do so do not include references to any case in which the dog is being used for a lawful purpose by a constable or a person in the service of the Crown.

...

This is an important section of the DDA as it defines what a 'public place' is in law. Much of the DDA is related to that fact as the reason for its introduction is to protect the public from attacks by dogs that are dangerous and vicariously, owners who are irresponsible.

Given the aim of the DDA the definition is wide enough to include fee-paying places like the cinema, dancehall, theatre and the zoo. Equally it extends to all public buildings, the communal areas of multiple-occupied residential buildings as well as temporary places like a school fete or a visiting fair or a music festival. The 'common parts' of a building would include the passages, stairways and lifts in a block of flats and other shared residential premises. It would not include the interior of such premises. So it would exclude the interior of blocks of flats where there is a security-controlled entry telecom as people would enter generally under a licence such as postmen and delivery drivers plus visitors and their friends. Obviously it would exclude a burglar, but what if a burglar in attempting to escape from his victim's home lets the dog out so it is free to roam and then it injures a member of the public? What about a neighbour whom you are on bad terms with who is either not welcome to visit or after an argument about the hedge storms out and slams the gate rather than closing it so the dog escapes and injures his child? [See **G18**]

It is a blurred area of law because it can stray into areas of civil liberties for members of the public and private householders as well as liberal-spirited local councillors. In February 2012 the Bath and North East Council proposed to force dog owners to keep their pets on leads and banned them from some open spaces altogether. The Council spokesman said, 'The plan drew very strong views' from the public and canine welfare organisations.

A Dogs Trust spokesman said it was 'Draconian'. As a result of the public reaction the Council withdrew the plan.

Although the area may be a private shopping precinct, that is not crucial to the definition. The legal test is whether the public is permitted to be there. It could cover areas which the public have access to even as ramblers under a covenant or as amateur cricketers on common ground or gypsies on the village green. How many members of the public use the area is not the acid test, only that they can and do so.

However it has been held to include a car which initially seems strange but on analysis is right. While the car itself was not a public place, the car was in a public place. Consequently the defendant was guilty as a person in charge of a designated dog in a public place. To hold otherwise would not merely dilute but defeat the DDA. [See **G7**]

So while the definition is wide nevertheless it is limited when it refers to private premises as it then encroaches into the cherished area of long-held civil liberties and every Englishman's right to indulge in crapulence on his own lawn.

G48 Infer

In *Cummings v. Director of Public Prosecutions* [1999] *The Times* 26 March 1999 the High Court considered the point on a case stated application. Christopher Cummings was convicted at Highbury Magistrates Court of being the owner of a dog which was dangerously out of control in a public place under section 3(1). Cummings kept his two dogs in a grassy area enclosed inside a wall, which was adjacent to a block of flats owned by the local council.

Blofeld J. said, 'A young boy entered the area via an unlocked gate and was bitten by the dogs. There were signs indicating that the flats were council owned property, but no signs indicating the grassy area was private property, that it was anything other than council owned or that entry to it was not permitted.'

Cummings claimed he had obtained permission from residents of the flats to leave his dogs in the grassy area and padlocked the entrance gate. His appeal centred on the point that the magistrates were wrong to find that the fact the area was owned by the local council was 'sufficient to show' that it was a public place, without any specific evidence that it was actually 'used' by the public.

Blofeld J turned that proposition on its head and said, 'There was no evidence that the council had given the appellant permission to use the area privately. The area was publicly owned, it was open for any member of the public to use and accordingly it could be inferred that it was a public place. There was no need to show evidence of public user.'

He was direct and right. If it were otherwise every prosecution would fail if any public area had to be so proved by use. The social arrangement allowing Cummings to use that area was not valid in law as if it were they could also by a private arrangement exclude others from using publicly owned land. It was purely an agreement written in water that could not change the place from public to private.

G49 Path

While at first glance the definition seems to be very wide, in its application it is actually narrower than it appears to be. That is particularly with regard to visitors to property. In *DPP v. Fellowes* [1993] Crim. L. R. 523 the High Court analysed what was a public place in respect of a paperboy visiting a house to deliver papers. Fellowes walked down the path from the door of his maisonette to accept a newspaper from a delivery boy, who had made previous deliveries there. As the boy handed the paper over Fellowes' Rottweiler bit him on the thigh. Fellowes was charged with being the owner of a dog which was dangerously out of control in a public place contrary to section 3(1). The magistrates concluded that as the boy had an implied and unrevoked licence to enter, having regard to the general purpose of the DDA, the garden was a public place as the public were permitted access to it. So Fellowes was convicted.

The appeal ground was that the garden path was not a public place because those who entered it did so, not as a member of the public, but as a visitor to the appellant's home. The Crown argued that while the path was private property, it was also a public place within the special meaning of the statute.

The court considered that there was considerable force in the Crown's argument if you simply read the statutory wording of the DDA. However in *R. v. Edwards* [1978] 67 Cr. App. R. 228 concerning the Public Order Act 1936 and *Williams v. DPP* [1992] Crim. L. R. 503 concerning the Criminal Justice Act 1967, the definition was specific and wide. While *Williams* contained no definition of private premises, the definition of public place in that statute and the one under consideration was 'almost identical', save that "public place" in the CJA 1967 was said to include the various places referred to, whereas in the DDA "public place" was said to mean any of the places it referred to. The difference in meaning was not material, although, if anything, the DDA definition was narrower. The other difference was section 10(2) of the DDA included the common parts of a building containing two or more separate dwellings. The Court considered that was presumably as result of the decision in *Knox v. Anderton* [1983] 76 Cr. App. R. 156 which confirmed the upper landing of a block of flats where the public could freely enter was a public place.

Given the meaning of public place in the POA 1936 and particularly in the CJA 1967, the path leading to Fellowes' front door was not a public place within the meaning of the DDA. The paper boy had visited it *qua* visitor and not *qua* member of the public. It was not possible to reach any different conclusion by consideration of the 'purposes of the DDA' alone. The only circumstance in which the DDA provided for an offence in a private place was in section 3(3), which is 'a very narrow provision'. As Parliament had expressed this offence in narrow terms, it was not wide enough to include events which occurred in places to which people were invited to attend as visitors, whether by express or implied licence. The court allowed the appeal.

While the court was in the circumstances reluctant to come to that conclusion, it was the right decision. For if the postman, the paper boy and the gas meter reader was protected, then it would have extended the law to protect visitors whether invited or tolerated from the unwelcome nosy neighbour from hell and every passing hawker to the tarmac cataian and concerned mother-in-law.

If the term were given a wider interpretation it would affect the civil liberties of every house owner and occupier of premises. That would distort the purpose of the DDA and be contrary to the reason it was introduced. Nevertheless it continues to exercise the politicians and the public as even as recent as March 2013 a 14-year-old schoolgirl, Jade Lomas-Anderson, was savaged to death by five dogs in a neighbour's house, where she was a guest of her friend. The government is considering introducing a 'public spaces protection order'. There are over 200,000 dog attacks each year. [See *The Independent on Sunday* 31/3/13.]

G50 Driveway

The Court of Appeal considered the subject in some depth and detail in *Bogdal v. Regina* [2008] EWCA Crim 1. Michael Bogdal appealed against his conviction and sentence in Hull Crown Court for three offences under section 3(1). The primary issue the court had to decide was whether the location at which the offences occurred was a public place within the meaning of the DDA.

Bogdal was the owner of a property called Wawne House in Hull. The only person living there at the material time was his mother, Mrs Janina Bogdal, who was aged 87. Underhill J described the property as, 'Wawne House lies a little way back from the main road with an extensive area of lawn as its front garden. In what used to be its back garden is a property called Sycamore House, which is a private care home for the elderly. It was built by Mr Bogdal some years ago but subsequently sold by him. A broad tarmac driveway runs in a horseshoe shape to and from the road round the edge of the front garden of Wawne House and around the back to Sycamore House; one limb of the horseshoe is bordered by shrubs but the other is unscreened from the lawn. The driveway constitutes the main means of access to both buildings and may be used by any person with legitimate occasion to visit either Wawne House or Sycamore House. It is not a public right of way. There are no gates where the driveway meets the road, but there is a large sign for Sycamore House at the principal opening.'

On three occasions in the summer of 2005 visitors walking on the shared driveway were attacked and bitten by an Alsatian dog. On the first occasion the victim, Ms Bowering, was going to visit her mother, a resident in Sycamore House. She was on a bicycle. The dog was tethered to a rope which is attached to a stake driven into the lawn in front of Wawne House; but the rope was not short enough to prevent it from attacking her on the driveway. The second occasion was the following day. A police officer, WPC Atkinson, had been there to investigate the incident involving Ms Bowering. The dog was again tethered to a stake in the front garden. While WPC Atkinson was talking to Mrs Bogdal at the door of Wawne House she saw that the dog was becoming excited by the presence of some children who were shouting at it. She went over to intervene. She remained on the driveway but the dog ran over to her and bit her on the buttock. The third occasion was when Ms Alexander, a district nurse, went to Sycamore House to ask directions for another care home she was seeking. As she walked back up the driveway to her car the dog jumped on her and bit her leg.

Bogdal was charged with the three offences on the basis he was the owner of the dog. When the matter came before the magistrates' court Bogdal applied for a stay on the ground the driveway where the incidents occurred was not a 'public place' within the DDA. His application was refused and the case was committed to the Hull Crown Court. He renewed the application for a stay. Miss Recorder Otton-Goulder QC dismissed the application and ruled that the driveway was a public place. Given those rulings and a *Goodyear* indication, Bogdal pleaded guilty on the express basis he reserved the right to appeal on the grounds the rulings were wrong. He received a suspended sentence.

The Court considered *Knox v. Anderton* [1983] 76 Cr. App. R. 156, *DPP v. Fellowes* [1993] Crim. L. R. 523 and *R. v. C* [2007] EWCA Crim 1757. Underhill J referred to the recorder's reasoning where she said:

"If the *ratio* of the garden path case – that is, the *Fellowes* case – is that it is a matter of invitation, whether explicit or implied, that cannot arise when one is dealing with a shared drive, because while a person may be implicitly or explicitly invited by let us say the owners of Wawne House, so far as Sycamore House is concerned there is no invitation whatsoever, whether explicit or implicit, and the same of course applies *vice versa.*" She further said that the terms of the common parts provision showed, "by analogy" that common access routes of this kind fell within the terms of section 10(2).'

Underhill J concluded, 'With respect to the recorder we cannot accept that reasoning.'

His Lordship explained that was so in relation to the driveway as, 'Members of the public were only entitled to use it as visitors to Wawne House or Sycamore House. We cannot see it can make any difference in principle that there are two properties served by the driveway: the right of members of the public to use it remains *qua* visitor, whichever property they happened to be visiting.'

Underhill J then considered the 'common part' provision and followed *R. v. C.* The Court confirmed it could not be distinguished from *Fellowes* either and so they followed it. Finally Underhill J gave a rather telling example to show the court's reasoning in the distinction between *qua* member of the public and *qua* visitor which resonated with the intoxication of common sense: 'And on closer consideration such a distinction can be seen to be essential if the concept of a "public place" is not to lose touch with ordinary usage and with important liberties. If every householder's front garden was a "public place" by reason only of the fact that the postman or the Jehovah's witness has an implied invitation to make their way to the front door, the result would be that not only could he not keep his dangerous dog outside but that he could neither carry a knife within his own curtilage nor enjoy the pleasure of being drunk and disorderly on his own front lawn.'

Referring to the submission of counsel for the respondent Underhill J said, 'of course many kinds of commercial or institutional premises to which members of the public have access as such – examples from the decided cases include football grounds, public car parks, shops, and places of entertainment – but not every institution is of that character. The borderline between public and private places may not always be easy to define, and there will be some doubtful cases. But we cannot see that it is arguable that the public as such has access to a private care home – or, still less, to a driveway leading to such a home through a private garden.'

Underhill J shot a warning towards Bogdal for the present and indeed the future lest the decision gave him an undue optimism: 'The fact that that driveway is not a public place does not mean that they may not incur civil liabilities arising out its behaviour or get into trouble with the law in other ways than under the 1991 Act.' That was directed at Bogdal as he represented himself throughout the proceedings. The Court quashed the conviction.

The case which the Court relied upon, *R. v. C,* is important as it covers an everyday situation. The complainant had been attacked by two dogs 'in a fenced area, used for depositing rubbish, which lay off a pathway leading from a block of flats to the car park serving the flats. The area formed part of the common parts of the block of flats, in the sense that it was part of communal area, but it did not form part of any building. Only occupiers of the flats or their licensees would be entitled to enter it.'

Given that last vital point the Crown Court Judge ruled against the prosecution and held that area was not a public place. The prosecution sought leave to appeal under section 58 of the Criminal Justice Act 2003. Royce J dismissed the application and approved the judge's reasoning. In particular he endorsed the principle that as it was a penal statute it had to be strictly construed and it was consistent with *Fellowes*. Significantly *R. v. C* was decided after the conviction in *Bogdal*.

G51 *Cul-de-sac*

The High Court added to the definition of 'public place' in *DPP v. Zhao*: [2003] 167 JP 521 where the evidence of the prosecution relied upon a police officer's local knowledge. It was an appeal by the DPP by way of case stated. Pauline Zhao appeared at Liverpool Magistrates' Court on 9 April 2002 charged with having a dangerous dog in a public place contrary to section 3(1). Zhao ran an electrical supply business from a warehouse off a *cul-de-sac* street, in an industrial area of Liverpool. On 30 November 2001, an HGV driver, who was collecting goods from Zhao was bitten by a dog under her control. The incident took place on the street just outside the entrance to her warehouse. During the trial a police officer who patrolled the area where it happened gave evidence she had seen children playing on the road where it occurred and had seen cars parked there by the general public. She was unable to give specific dates as to when she had seen members of the general public on the road. The DPP also adduced photographs as evidence to prove the road where it occurred was a public place. At the end of the prosecution case, the defence submitted that (a) the DPP had failed to show the area where the offence occurred was a 'public place' within the DDA and (b) there was no case to answer. District Judge Lomax agreed and dismissed the case.

On appeal the High Court held that the officer's evidence was *prima facie* evidence that the area where the incident happened was a public place. That evidence was consistent with the physical appearance of the road contained in the photographs relied upon by the DPP. The District Judge had erred as a matter of law in holding that the road was not a public place. So the appeal was allowed. The case was remitted to the magistrates' court.

Although the definition is potentially wide, the interpretation by the court in *DPP v. Fellowes* [1993] Crim. L. R. 523 highlights the importance of section 3(3). Often a dog will be taken by neighbouring children for a walk or be welcome onto its garden and property. That would be relevant in respect of a defence. For if the dog is 'permitted' to be on the neighbouring land then the section does not bite as it is not a 'public place'. Moreover if a postman is bitten there, there would be a statutory defence, in that the onus would be on the prosecution to prove the contrary. Similarly it would provide a defence by calling the neighbour, if there was a case to answer, to substantiate the defence.

G52 Control

The other important matter that runs throughout the DDA is the fact of a dog being 'dangerously out of control'. That term is referred to in section 3. It is defined under section 10(3) as 'a dog shall be regarded as being out of control on any occasion on which there are grounds for reasonable apprehension that it will injure any person, whether or not it actually does so'.

Therefore it is not the actual but simply the potential effect of the dog's behaviour. It does not have to 'injure', but merely act and behave so that persons in the vicinity have that fear. The 'reasonable apprehension' can be either for their personal well-being or even another's safety. That would apply to a parent fearing for their child or a nurse for her charge. Indeed it could be where a dog attacks a Guide Dog and the blind person then has a 'reasonable apprehension' he would be attacked too.

When the police have to control crowds they often have to resort to using specially trained dogs, particularly Alsatians; dog-handlers of the Crown do too. Both are exempt from this section and the consequences of their dogs being out of control if it is being used at the time for a 'lawful purpose'. Similarly it applies to prison officers for the same reason as they have to search visitors for drugs and smuggled goods by using their dogs.

G53 Apprehension

While there are many bad decisions under the DDA, *Regina v. Bezzina* [1994] 99 Cr. App. R. 356 is amongst the worst. It interpreted the DDA narrowly and strictly and as a consequence allowed the authorities to seize and kill numerous dogs whose real crime was being born. The case has been considered in relation to the section 3 and the absence of *mens rea*. [See **G18**] During the judgment the Court of Appeal also analysed the aim and effect of section 10(3). It was decided that it sets an objective standard of reasonable apprehension which is unrelated to the state of mind of the owner of the dog. While that may or may not be right the reasoning was blatantly wrong. For Kennedy LJ initially considered the purpose of the section and said, 'Accordingly, it would seem that this Act by section 3(1), imposes strict liability on the owners of dogs of all sorts which are in public places and are dangerously out of control within the meaning of section 10(3) which, on the face of it, imposes or sets an objective standard of reasonable apprehension, not related to the state of mind of the dog owner.'

After a detailed examination of the reason for legislation which covers social concern and public safety, Kennedy LJ justified his conclusion on the basis that Parliament was entitled to enact such an Act with such a provision. While that is fine as far as it goes he then sought to support his reasoning with a specious example saying, 'One applies the meaning which is set out in section 10(3) and that means, in effect, that if a dog is in a public place, if the person who is the accused is shown to be the owner of the dog, if the dog is dangerously out of control in the sense that the dog is shown to be acting in a way that gives grounds for reasonable apprehension that it would injure anyone, liability follows. Of course, if injury does result then, on the face of it, there must have been, immediately before the injury resulted, grounds for reasonable apprehension that injury would occur…It is urged that an owner may have no realisation that his dog is liable to behave in a way which will cause injury to anyone until, for example, a child pokes the dog with a stick and the dog reacts. That, indeed, may be the case. But it seems to us that Parliament was entitled to do what in this piece of legislation we find that it has done, namely to put the onus on the owner to ensure, if that is likely to happen, to take steps which are effective to ensure that it does not, either by keeping the dog on a lead or keeping the child away from the dog or whatever may be appropriate in the circumstances.'

That is an absurd example that does not stand up to any scrutiny. For how can a 'reasonable apprehension' be known and hence guarded against by any owner if has no idea his dog is going to be poked in the eye by a child with a stick? That would require the owner to be blessed with a chiromancy and clairvoyance denied to most except an end-of-the-pier fortune-teller. Moreover what if instead of a stick it is a knife or a vicious kick by a passing drunken thug? If the principle is right then he should act before it happens because he somehow knows it will happen. Or that reasoning is wrong.

The court then refrained from considering the position where the intervention, or the possible intervention, of third parties who would let the dogs out. The situation and the cited South African and New Zealand cases were not relevant on the facts of this case. However both the courts and legal advisers have obviously accepted that strict liability still lies as many people plead on that precise basis. Indeed even where a defendant did plead not guilty the jury convicted him. In *R. v. Haynes* [2004] 2 Cr. App. R. (S) 9 in the Court of Appeal HHJ Roberts said, 'However, the offence under section 3 is an offence of strict liability and the jury had little alternative but to convict him.' [See **G32**]

G54 Will

After *Bezzina* the High Court had another opportunity to properly interpret section 10(3) in *Rafiq v DPP* [1997] 161 JP R 412. Karen Rafiq was the owner of a dog, a German Shepherd, called with a less than felicitous name, Venom. On 23 December 1995 Jane Rusen visited Fariq's garage in Souldrop in Bedford. Rusen parked her car and went into the garage to buy a Christmas tree. Venom was loose on the forecourt. Then 'with the oral permission of the owner's daughter she let Venom into the shop.' Rusen bought some items and was handing back over the counter a knife she had borrowed. As she was passing the knife over Venom jumped up and bit her on the thigh. The Crown Court found that prior to jumping up and biting Rusen, Venom had 'given no indication at all of his intention to do so.'

Fariq was convicted at the magistrates' court. Her appeal was dismissed by the Crown Court as they relied on *Bezzina*. This was a case stated application which presented the Court with the chance to grasp the gauntlet and distinguish *Bezzina*. For it was obvious that the judges knew the *ratio* of that case could not be followed relying on logic. The view of Kennedy LJ and the reason he gave was not reasonable in fact or law.

So given that choice, Popplewell J referred to *Bezzina* and said, 'It seems to me that in order to impose some logic in this case the proper way to approach these cases is to take the view that if there is a bite without a reasonable apprehension immediately before that, the use of the word 'any occasion' is sufficient to impose a liability because there are grounds thereafter for reasonable apprehension that it will injure some other person.'

Then Auld LJ referred to *Bezzina* and said, 'Depending on the circumstances, the time for apprehension, even by the notional reasonable bystander, may be so minimal as for practical purposes to be non-existent. The notion of reasonable apprehension of injury before it occurs in such circumstances, is artificial and the court should strain against adding that unhappy element to an already difficult statutory formulation. It seems to me that Kennedy LJ in that passage was unnecessarily focusing on the injury as if it were a necessary culmination and demonstration of anterior reasonable apprehension of injury. In my view there is no need for such an approach. The act of a dog causing injury, a bite or otherwise, is itself capable of being conduct giving grounds for reasonable apprehension of injury.'

Both judges fudged the real issue namely that the sections in question, 3(3) and 10(3), are each concerned with something happening which 'will' confirm the reasonable apprehension of the owner. Thus it is concerned with a present situation which causes the owner to be aware that his dog 'will' injure a person. That is an immediate warning of an impending risk. Certainly it is not dealing with a present position that is a contingency in the future. The problem for the court was that the attempts to uphold *Bezzina* meant they had to bend words out of shape to give the section a meaning that was not specified or intended. For where an injury in fact occurs there may have been, immediately before, a reasonable apprehension that it would occur. That may be true in given circumstances, but it is not the case it 'must' be true in all cases. It is not relating to 'some other person' at all. It indicates a present position that causes the owner to know an injury will immediately fructify.

G55 Ruling

The Court of Appeal had the opportunity to consider the position yet again in *R. v. Edita Gedminintaite* [2008] EWCA Crim 814. It was an application for leave to appeal against a ruling by HHJ Gibson as to how he would address a jury in a case of an offence under section 3(1). Following that ruling Edita Gedminintaite pleaded guilty and was sentenced. She challenged that ruling by seeking leave to appeal against it.

In the Court of Appeal HHJ Hall outlined the background and the legal issue: 'The facts are simple. The second applicant is the owner of two Rottweiler dogs. The first applicant and her friend took them for a walk. While passing a young lad on the pavement, one of the Rottweilers, Rocky, went for him, bit him and tore his scrotum. A Good Samaritan came to his rescue. He went to hospital. Seemingly there are no long-term effects but it was extraordinarily painful for him at the time.

In presenting the legal argument, it was acknowledged that neither of the Rottweiler dogs had ever shown a propensity to attack. It was accepted that at the time both were on a lead. It was also accepted that it was in a public place and that injury was caused to the victim. Therefore the question for the court was: 'was that behaviour of the dog such that the applicants were guilty of the offences under section 3…?'

The court considered the two decided cases on the topic, *Rafiq v. DPP*. [1997] 161 JP 412 and *R. v. Bezzina* [1994] 99 Cr. App. R. 356. In giving the judgment of the Divisional Court, Popplewell J. referred to *R. v. Bezzina* where Kennedy L.J. said:

"Of course, if injury does result then, on the face of it, there must have been immediately before the injury resulted, grounds for reasonable apprehension that injury would occur."

HHJ Hall then relied upon the view of each judge in *Rafiq*. He said that 'Popplewell J slightly dissented from that approach. He said:

"The use of the word 'any occasion' is sufficient to impose a liability because there are grounds thereafter for reasonable apprehension that it will injure some other person."

'Auld LJ commented:

"The act of a dog causing injury, a bite or otherwise, is itself capable of being conduct giving grounds for reasonable apprehension of injury."

Counsel for both applicants submitted the Court should consider the type of occasion when a dog reacts to provocative behaviour. HHJ Hall said, 'He submits that it is possible to conceive a factual situation where it would be unjust to impose actual liability in such circumstances. The teasing schoolboy – a stick with the horse's head handle – comes to mind. But that is not this case. This was an ordinary pedestrian walking past a woman in charge of a Rottweiler dog which swung round and bit him.'

HHJ Hall then referred the ruling of Judge Gibson at the Crown Court when he ruled:

"My conclusion is that the directions to the jury should include a direction that in law the occasion on which the boy was bitten was an occasion on which there arose grounds for reasonable apprehension that the dog would injure a person, and that in consequence the dog was to be regarded, immediately it administered the bite, as being dangerously out of control."

HHJ Hall then posed and answered the question raised by the application namely, 'We ask ourselves: was this dog under control? The answer is patent: No. What is the evidence of that? It bit someone else who was innocently walking past it on the pavement and who exhibited no provocative behaviour. Was it dangerous? Yes, because the dog bit the boy.

On either the interpretation propounded in *Rafiq* or that of Kennedy LJ in *Bezzina,* this dog was dangerously out of control. We are inclined to go further. In any event the definitions section, section 10, is not exclusive. It does not read as a matter of construction, "For the purposes of this Act, a dog shall only be regarded as dangerously out of control…" and then proceed to the definition. Therefore we feel ourselves entitled to go back to the straightforward words of section 3: "If a dog is dangerously out of control in a public place…" In our judgment, this dog was dangerously out of control in a public place. That was amply evidenced by the way it behaved and the fact that it was not controlled by its handler.' So the application was refused.

In Blackstone's Criminal Practice 2012 it is suggested that, 'Even where it seems likely that a dog may injure someone, the words "dangerously out of control" must be given their natural meaning. If, for example, X teases Y's Doberman in a cruel and stupid way, it may be apparent to any onlooker that X is likely to be bitten unless he desists, but it does not follow that the dog is out of control.' That may be true jurisprudentially but alas it is subsumed by the *ratio* of *Bezzina* as Kennedy LJ puts the onus plainly on the owner to keep the dog away from the child wielding the stick. If he fails to do so he is guilty.

This is a case and this area itself that requires a careful analysis as it is rare for a dog with no propensity at all to bite to do so without provocation or reason. This decision was an attempt to introduce a sense of reason to an area that now defies law and logic. The result is four different judges effectively giving four different interpretations of the same section in an attempt to use words to fit a situation which is not covered by either section. Their collective conclusions are a hotchpotch that is at odds with the plain words of each respective section. On their conclusions in this run of cases, especially *Gedminintaite,* they impute knowledge to an owner that is neither real nor reasonable: an apprehension cannot exist if you are unaware of it. The strict position is under section 3(3)(b) the reasonable apprehension the owner must possess is that his dog 'will' do so, namely act in that way. That element of 'will' is also in section 10(3) and qualifies the same condition. The vain attempt to justify it is an exercise in semantics that smacks of Alice: 'When *I* use a word it means just what I choose it to mean – neither more nor less.'

When the four different views of the four judges are analysed you have a situation where on 'any occasion' that a dog who is poked in the eye with a stick by a child then bites the child there is on the part of the owner an immediate 'reasonable apprehension' that it will bite 'some other person'. The owner is blessed and cursed with such knowledge as he 'will' know that will happen and as the dog is dangerously out of control, he is guilty.

Two recent unrelated examples magnify the problem the courts have created plus the confusion for a responsible owner. On 9 August 2012 while Anne-Marie was walking in Yeovil with her 4 year old daughter, Lucy-Ann, the child tried to stroke a Staffordshire bull terrier which lunged at her and grabbed her arm. The owner of the dog was arrested. On a separate point the RSPCA said in *The Times* on 10 August 2012: 'Children tend to treat pet dogs as their peers. They hug them, try to cuddle them and scold them. Children express their affection through very close facial contact, often kissing. Much of this is exactly opposite to dog social behaviour and your dog may find it threatening.'

G56 Draft Bill

In 2012 the Coalition Programme for Government included a promise 'to ensure that enforcement agencies target irresponsible owners of dogs'. The result was on 9 April 2013 a draft Dangerous Dogs (Amendment) Bill was published. Interested parties were expected to submit written evidence to the Committee by 22 April. The EFRA Committee was requested to do the same by 29 April.

According to Lord de Mauley the reason for the requested swift response is: 'Given the pressure in Parliament for these changes to be brought forward quickly, the Government's intention is to legislate for these changes at the earliest opportunity'.

The draft Bill has two Clauses namely 1 entitled 'Keeping dogs under proper control' and 2 'Whether a dog is a danger to public safety'. [See Appendix 6]

Clause 1 extends criminal responsibility to all places whether public or private. Given the understandable concern of the public that that could be harsh where their dog attacks an intruder, there is an exemption for householders in the event of a 'trespasser'. That is an essential exemption as there is little point in having a guard dog that does not sink its teeth deep into a burglar's buttocks. That is an occupational risk for any burglar and so one he should be legally deemed to accept before any intended entry. However the definition of who is a trespasser could be laden with doubt and perhaps blurred by an unwelcome hawker or a nosy neighbour. [See **G49**]

The proposed extension of the law to include attacks on 'assistance' dogs becoming an aggravated offence is already overdue. It applies to the vulnerable person in charge of the dog too. The reason according to Lord de Mauley is 'This is in line with the Government's policy on encouraging responsible ownership by ensuring dog owners are fully aware of the consequences of their actions or inaction...' It is beyond time that they should realise the root of all those problems stems from irresponsible owners. Those who are vulnerable, both people and dogs, have long deserved protection from that breed of owner.

It clarifies the position by extending the problematic 'reasonable apprehension' provision to assistance dogs as it is an offence if the grounds for fear of an attack exist even if there is no injury.

If there is an actual injury to the dog then it would become an aggravated offence. [See **G18**; **G53**]

Clause 2 is proposed 'to address the consequences of an adverse judgement in the High Court (*The Queen on the Application of Sandhu v. Isleworth Crown Court and Defra* [2012] EWHC 1658 (Admin)). Somewhat ironically that is one of the soundest decisions under such a badly-drafted Act. So the Government's view it is 'adverse' seems perverse. [See **G34**; **G37**]

The proposed amendment will require a court to consider the (a) character of the owner or keeper and (b) the temperament of the dog and its past behaviour and (c) any other relevant circumstances.

Given that the 'character' of a person is now such a wide-ranging provision within criminal law, this is a welcome change. It could and certainly should mean that a person who is not deemed to be 'a fit and proper person' to be in 'charge' of a dog is denied ownership at all. That would result in a direct improvement to the present position where 'character' is barely considered in or out of court in respect of animals. [See **G33**]

These changes, if enacted, will affect sections 3, 4, 4A and 4 B of the DDA. In relation to section 4B it is proposed that a destruction order can be made even where there is no conviction. That proposal is a myopic provision and seeks to revive the negative position that previously prevailed. Indeed that is the precise reason that section 4B amended the DDA. Moreover the amendment by section 4B was necessary because the Government introduced the DDA too swiftly and thought too loosely, if at all, about the consequences of that Act. That was a 'knee-jerk' reaction by the Government following police and public concern about too many dogs being branded as out of control and then too many being killed without good reason. As

Lord de Mauley again referred to the 'pressure of Parliament' as the reason for the changes, it would be rash to seek to revive the corpse of bad legislation that was also condemned by numerous judges. [See **G1**; **G38**; **G40**]

Peter Jones, the President of the British Veterinary Association, in response to these proposals said on 9/4/13: 'The law will still be focused on dealing with incidents after they have occurred rather than attempting to prevent them. The BVA strongly supports the introduction of more preventative measures, such as Dog Control Notices, to identify problem behaviour before it become s serious.' He is right. The answer is harsher measures aimed at irresponsible owners, not simply death for their dogs. If it is otherwise the same self-engendered problem caused by the previous Government who acted on impulse will be revisited. [See **G1**]

G57 Conclusion

It is usually only when a microphone remains on unknown to the speaker or a secret e-mail is discovered that we get a modicum of truth about the real thoughts of a politician. In Matthew Parris' column in *The Times* in January 2012 he recalls how in 1978 a photograph was taken of him with a politician. Parris was receiving an award from the RSPCA for rescuing a dog. The politician was presenting it to him. Just prior to the presentation, Parris says, 'off-camera she had said to me, "A dog? Did you really rescue a dog? What a stupid thing to do?" '

A year later that politician became the Prime Minister. When Margaret Thatcher left in 1991 her role was taken on by her protégé John Major. He then introduced the DDA.

Conversely with the uncanny insight of a woman who has every reason to know, Melanie Reid assesses the truth with typical accuracy in her column in *The Times* of August 2012 when observing her rescued dog, Princess Tippytoes, a Stafffordshire bull terrier: 'Her breed, unfairly, casts a long shadow. Some delivery van drivers refuse to get out of their vehicles when they see her. Strangers recoil when she approaches. She's a beautiful specimen, lightweight, brindled black, but she's stigmatised as socially ugly, purely because of human uglies who have given her type a bad name.'

It is truistic that dangerous dogs are a problem within many modern societies. Yet the approach of our politicians has been to introduce legislation as a sop to Cerberus in the hope it will gain them a few more votes. That is so in Australia no less than England. Dr Stephen Collier asked the loaded question, 'Breed-specific legislation and the pit bull terrier: Are the laws justified?' in the *Journal of Veterinary Behaviour* [2006]. He answers it in a clear-cut manner saying, 'Dog attacks are a significant public safety issue in Australia, as elsewhere. However, a tiny minority of the 4 million dogs in our communities bite people in any given year...It is questionable whether laws to extirpate a breed can be justified when, by the worst case data, 90% of its individuals are not recorded to attack a person or animal over their life span...there are many other breeds' individuals of which irresponsible owners could render dangerous.'

The RSPCA in its analytical report, *Response to Defra consultation on dangerous dogs*, in 2010 considers the precise problem the politicians are intent on ignoring: 'Q4. Do you think that breed-specific legislation, in its current form, is effective in protecting the public from dangerous dogs? Why? The short answer is no. The RSPCA's long-standing position is that breed-specific legislation is unfair and unjustifiable and that Government should adopt an approach that recognises that any individual dog, irrespective of breed or type, can display aggression towards people, and that responsibility for this lies with the owners.'

For while it is understandable that the courts wish to uphold such legislation on public policy and social safety grounds, the reality is that there are far too many examples of bad cases reflecting a bad law. To that extent they are intent on using legal pliers to bend the law out of shape to fit their views on the distorted concerns of society. The DDA should be replaced by an Act that focuses on fairness for the victims and the dogs while punishing the human deviants. For demon dogs are created by demon humans.

8

Sentence

H1 Effect

The DDA has been in force for over two decades. In origin it attempted to put an onus on the owner of dogs who were either dangerous by type or specially so by behaviour to keep them under control. The price for the dog of the owner's non-compliance was death. While that is still available as a sentence, it can now be suspended. Given that the DDA was introduced as deterrent legislation, how far it has failed or succeeded is finally reflected in the policy and the punishment.

Under section 3(4) the penalties for the simple offence of the dog being dangerously out of control on summary conviction is 6 months' imprisonment or a level 5 fine or both. The penalties for the aggravated offence are on (a) summary conviction is 6 months' imprisonment or a fine up to the statutory maximum or both and (b) on indictment imprisonment for two years or a fine or both.

The present position reflects the seriousness of the aggravated offence which could be committed to the Crown Court by the magistrates of their own volition. It could also be sent there on the application of the prosecution or by the election of the defendant.

Normally it is rare for the court to impose a prison sentence in cases under the DDA. However in *R. v. Cox* [2004] 2 Cr. App. R. (S) 54 the Court of Appeal confirmed it was right in principle to do so. Jacqueline Cox pleaded guilty at Burnley Crown Court to an aggravated offence of keeping a dog which was dangerously out of control contrary to section 3. A man exercising his dogs in a park saw 7 dogs run into the park. They came to a halt as a pack and attacked a seven-year-old boy. Cox pleaded guilty on the basis that she failed to ensure that the dogs were kept indoors. She claimed she was upstairs having a bath when the dogs escaped. She was sentenced to 9 months' imprisonment. All the dogs were destroyed.

After reciting the facts Leveson J. said, 'No prior example of a sentence in a case such as this is apparent from a study of the authorities. We approach it from first principles... Thus Parliament demonstrated the clearest intention that the courts should in no small measure look at the consequences of the offence when determining the ultimate penalty. An analogy can be seen by comparing the offence of dangerous driving, which has a maximum of two years' imprisonment, and causing death by dangerous driving, which has a maximum of 10 years' imprisonment.

We have come to the conclusion that it was entirely appropriate for the recorder to pass a custodial sentence to mark the nature and extent of the obligation which owners of dogs owe to all who might be affected if they roam free. Nevertheless, we do not consider it necessary for the appellant to be deprived of her liberty for as long as nine months. She was, after all, a lady of good character whose plea was on the basis that she should have ensured that the dogs stayed at her home, not on the basis that she had frequently allowed the dogs to terrorise others... In the circumstances we reduce the term of nine months' imprisonment to one of three months' imprisonment. The 10 years' disqualification order in relation to dogs remains.'

The sentences thereafter have varied in degrees of leniency. In *R. v. Donnelly* [2007] EWCA Crim 2548 the defendant was subject to an Anti-Social Behaviour Order [ASBO] in relation to an injury by the same dog. He pleaded to another offence in 2006 involving the same dog. This was the third appearance with the same dog. He was sentenced to consecutive sentences with a total of 12 months' which was suspended. The Court of Appeal followed *Cox* and reduced his sentence to 35 weeks. The dog was destroyed.

In *R. v. Richards* [2009] 1 Cr. App. R. (S) 48 there was a serious sustained attack on a postman by two dogs owned by Jamal Richards. There was a hole in the fence through which they had escaped. Richards knew about that and that his dogs had 'broken out before.' A concurrent sentence of 9 months was imposed on two charges. The Court of Appeal followed *Cox* and reduced the sentence to 4 months. The dog was destroyed.

However the courts in subsequent cases have been anxious to avoid any view that *Cox* served as any kind of guideline.

The Court of Appeal was concerned about that position which was addressed in *R. v. Lee* [2010] 1 Cr. App. R. (S) 94. Lee pleaded guilty to two counts of allowing his dog to enter a public place and injure a person. Lee had two pit bull terriers which lived in his rear garden. One of them escaped and went into his neighbour's garden and killed one of her cats. As a result she stayed out of her garden. On Boxing Day, about 2.30 a.m., she heard noises from her garden and saw one of Lee's dogs with her cat in his mouth. She went into the garden with a broom. The dogs attacked and bit her and dragged her to the ground. She said she thought that she would be killed. Eventually the dog backed off. The police heard her screams and found her 'bleeding heavily.' She needed a skin graft to her arm. The judge said, 'She had been almost a prisoner in her house because of his dogs; there was a gross failure to ensure the dogs were restrained.' He imposed a sentence of 10 months' imprisonment concurrently on each count. The Court of Appeal allowed the appeal by reducing the term to six months.

That was a rather strange decision as the court had stated specifically that *Cox* was not a guideline. While the sentence at the Crown Court was not severe, the one imposed by the Court of Appeal in reducing it bordered on undue leniency. It is unlikely most of those authorities will survive the new guidelines introduced on 20 August 2012.

Yet in *R. v. Baballa* [2011] 1 Cr. App. R. (S) 50 four dogs belonging to Moses Baballa attacked and injured Jalal Dawad in Melfort Park in Thorton Heath. Baballa pleaded guilty to an aggravated offence in respect of one dog, a mongrel, and three counts of a simple offence relating to the other three pit bull terriers. A suspended sentenced of 8 months' in total was imposed at Croydon Crown Court. The mongrel was destroyed.

H2 Aim

The Sentencing Council [SC] was created by the Coroners and Justice Act 2009 to combine the functions of the two previous bodies, the Sentencing Guidelines Council and Sentencing Advisory Panel, which were disbanded. Leveson LJ who was the judge in *R. v. Cox* [2004] 2 Cr. App. R. (S) 54 is the Head of the SC. The SC is a more streamlined body with a greater remit to make progressive sentencing policy through the introduction of guidelines. In doing so its development is based on evidence and by engaging more with the public. The aim is to avoid inconsistency as well as improving the public's general understanding of and about the sentencing process.

Up until 20 August 2012 there were no guidelines of any nature issued by the Sentencing Council in relation to the DDA. As a consequence of various factors including an increase in the number of attacks by dogs, the seriousness of the injuries, the disparity of sentences around the country and the natural public concern, a consultation paper was produced. That took account of the views of those parties who contributed to the consultation and the conclusions which in turn led to the new SC introducing the first guideline on the DDA. The guidelines are detailed and positive in aim and approach. They are the result of an in-depth consultation where numerous people and bodies were consulted for their views. As a result there are '8 Steps' which have to be taken by the court in relation to an offence under sections 1 and 3. The guideline deals with all aspects of the offences particularly the character of the owner. Allied to that position it has to take into account the character of the dog. Both points are a welcome aspect of the sentencing process because prior to it the courts sometimes seemed intent on disregarding any references for the owner and equally for the dog.

The guideline has been published following a consultation which received more than 500 responses from members of the public, judges and magistrates, the police, animal welfare organisations and many others with expertise or interest in this issue. Those responses have helped shape the final guideline in a number of ways:

(a) The guideline has widened the definition of vulnerable victims so that it applies not only to children, but to others such as the elderly, disabled and blind or visually impaired people.

(b) The guideline has also been extended to include injuries to other animals as an aggravating factor in the offence of allowing a dog to be out of control and causing injury. There was very strong support for this in a large number of responses including the CPS and the Association of Chief Police Officers.

(c) The problem of dog fighting has been taken into account in the offence of possession of a prohibited dog, training a dog to fight or possessing paraphernalia for dog fighting is now included as a factor increasing the seriousness of this offence. This follows concerns from the Police Federation about this issue.

H3 ABC

The SC for England and Wales has issued a definitive guideline, applying to all offenders aged 18 or over who are sentenced on or after 20 August 2012, regardless of the date of the offence. The definitive guideline has been published both in a Crown Court version and as an update to the Magistrates' Court Sentencing Guidelines. The offences it relates to are:

A   1.   Owning or being in charge of a dog that injures a person whilst dangerously out of control in a public place: section 3(1);

     2.   Allowing a dog to enter a private place where it is not permitted to be where it then injures any person: section 3(3)(a);

B   3.   Owning or being in charge of a dog dangerously out of control in a public place: section 3(1);

     4.   Allowing a dog to enter a private place where the dog is not permitted to be and while it is there, there are grounds for reasonable apprehension that it will injure any person: section 3(3)(b);

C   5.   Possession of a prohibited dog: section 1(3);

     6.   Breeding, selling, exchanging or advertising a prohibited dog: section 1(2).

The categories of **A** relate to offences 1 to 2, **B** relate to offences 3 to 4 and **C** relate to offences 5 to 6, respectively. The maximum sentence for those within A is 2 years' imprisonment so it is a hybrid offence. The maximum sentence for those within B and C is 6 months' imprisonment so they are only summary offences.

The categories A and B and C reflect the various degrees of seriousness in which the offence fits. Step 1 requires the court to determine which of the three categories, A or B or C, applies. When determining the offender's culpability and the harm caused or intended, the court has to refer only to the factors indicating that harm and culpability outlined in the specific section relating to A to C. Those factors in turn comprise the main factual elements of the offence.

The guideline sets out *8 Steps* which apply and have to be followed in order by the court. After deciding on the starting point the court then has to proceed to Step 2 by using the determined relevant category of A or B or C to consider a sentence within the respective category range. The starting point applies to all offenders regardless of the plea or their antecedents. The court then has to further consider adjusting the position according a list of aggravating or mitigating features set out in each of the specific sections A to C. At that point the court can take into account an offender's previous convictions.

Each one contains a list, which is not exclusive, of additional factual elements relating directly to both the offence and the offender. When the court has considered all of those and any other relevant factors, it might decide it is appropriate to move from the identified category range.

The SC emphasises, consistent with previous guidelines, that where it is appropriate the court should consider whether the community or custodial threshold have been passed. Then if the custodial threshold is passed, the court has to consider whether it is avoidable to impose such a sentence. If not and a custodial sentence must be imposed the court then has to consider whether it can be suspended.

There are bands for the level of fines which again reflect the level of seriousness. Allied to that specifically in Step 5 it sets out the factors the court has to consider in relation to compensation and ancillary orders. An Annex to the guideline lists the requirements, which are not exclusive, the court might consider appropriate for either a low or a medium or a high level community order. They reflect the seriousness of the offence and cover from 40 to 300 hours of community work.

The key aim of the guideline is to provide clear guidance to the various sentencers so there is a consistent approach to sentencing and appropriate sentences are given to owners of dangerous dogs. It will help courts make best use of their powers so that irresponsible owners who put the public at risk can be imprisoned and banned from keeping dogs

According to a press release published on 15 May 2012 by the SC the sentencing ranges mark an increase in sentencing levels from current practice. The top of the sentencing range for owners allowing their dog to be dangerously out of control injuring someone has been set at 18 months' custody in order to encourage the courts to use more severe sentences when it would be appropriate to do so. The top of the sentencing range for possession of a prohibited dog has been set at the legal maximum of six months' custody to encourage courts to use the full range of their sentencing powers for the most serious offences. As a result the new guideline will mean that more offenders will face jail sentences, more will get community orders and fewer will receive discharges.

The guideline covers the most commonly sentenced offences in the DDA, such as allowing a dog to be dangerously out of control causing injury and possession of a prohibited dog. In situations where someone deliberately sets a dog on another person intending to injure them, the offender is likely be charged with assault, rather than one of these offences.

Anne Arnold, a District Judge and member of the SC said:

'As a result, this new sentencing guideline encourages courts to use their full powers when dealing with offenders so that they are jailed where appropriate. It also gives guidance to courts on making the best use of their powers so that people can be banned from keeping dogs, genuinely dangerous dogs can be put down and compensation can be paid to victims.'

On the very day the guideline was introduced a man recalled the trauma of seeing his 6-year-old daughter and wife savaged by a dog owned by an irresponsible owner. When the father remonstrated with the owner his response was to blame and claim the child was at fault as, 'She shouldn't have run away.' [BBC Radio 4 *PM* 20/8/12] The father gave evidence to the SC. He was informed his evidence assisted in drafting the final guideline. [See Appendix 5]

The guideline is aimed at both of those people. For the father is a victim if he has witnessed an attack on his family and thereafter has to share in the sheer trauma caused by that out of control dog. Then there is the real culprit namely the feckless owner who is reckless with regard to the lives of other people as well as the fate of his dog. At present the DDA has failed the man and his family by being too lenient with those typical owners. To merely keep killing the dogs as happens at present does not begin to address the problem at all. For all you end up with is a pile of dead dogs matched by irresponsible owners who will in due course just get another dog. To be effective this guideline needs a delivery to match its promise. It has to show the public that its legal teeth will bite the criminal owner. At present the victim is barely and rarely compensated and the dog is routinely destroyed. This guideline should target the one who is responsible as a matter of fact and law yet so often escapes from the fate he deserves, while the victim and the dog continue to reap the whirlwind of the actions of every irresponsible owner.

The maximum sentence should be increased to at least 5 years. For the public need protection from those who treat their dogs in such a way as to transmute their character. The dogs do too. Ultimately dangerous dogs are not born that way but created by dangerous owners. It is that type of owner rather than the type of dog that should be restrained by the law.

9

The Legal Role and Status of Animals

I1 Profit

The relationship between animals and law is a cycle of cruelty caused and controlled by and for man. Where man's benefit is balanced against a beast's burden, the human animal usually wins. Even such limited legal rights as animals have are subject to human interests.

Most legal abuse of animals is committed in the name of commerce or science and related, directly or indirectly, to profit. When that position was originally considered in *Ford v Wiley* it was held to be irrelevant. In *Lewis v. Fermor* [1887] 18 QBD 532 a vet spayed a number of sows, an 'unnecessary and useless' operation which was very painful. He performed it because farmers and buyers believed it improved the quality of the meat. That belief was wholly wrong as the operation did nothing but cause the animal pain. Fermor was acquitted of causing cruelty as the operation was 'carried out for the bona fide purpose of benefiting the owner by increasing the value of the animal.' That decision was expressly disapproved in *Ford v Wiley*. Further Hawkins J said, 'Many instances might be put in which, at the cost of extreme suffering to the animal, it might be rendered more serviceable for the use of man, by means of an operation which it is impossible to suppose that any Legislature would sanction. What would be said of a man who sewed up the eyelids of his sheep, or cut the hoofs of his cattle to the quick to keep them from moving about as nature dictated, in order that they should more quickly fatten in his field for his profit?' The judge considered acts such as sewing eyelids of sheep were not reasonably necessary. Hawkins J chose those examples to indicate extreme measures which were not legal on pure economic grounds. That was in 1889. Now experiments and farming practices are legal which make them seem by no means extreme.

Most human beings now have 'rights' because they are human beings. In essence these allow a person to act freely providing he does not infringe another's rights. These have arisen because of man's special status as a rational, sentient being. However in formulating and granting these rights, they have not been limited to humans who are rational. Rights extend to all within the category of *homo sapiens*. But that is the limit. Man has chosen deliberately to deny those rights to animals. Therefore the same practice may be legal or illegal according to the victim and the profit to us.

12 Speciesism

It has been long known and accepted that animals feel pain, mentally and physically as well as psychologically. If an animal is a sentient being and in some ways a kindred spirit of man, why then is it so often treated purely as property, a thing to be owned, used or consumed? The answer lies in what Richard Ryder has termed 'speciesism' in *The Ethics of Animal Abuse* [1979]: human life being treated as having a special priority over animal life simply because it is human. That is at the root of man's assumed control and power over animals. This convenient conclusion is based on two assumptions, both borne of self-interest: man has a moral claim because of his superiority and animals are not deserving of moral rights.

Speciesism is similar to other forms of discrimination such as racism and sexism. Most of the arguments based on race and sex including biological differences, inferiority and intelligence are equally applicable to animals. Much of Western thought, in terms of philosophy and religion which was later filtered and expressed in law, was influenced by Aristotle. He believed that slaves, women and animals were inferior to freemen. Strangely though significantly it is no surprise to learn he was in the favoured superior category. Aristotle considered that 'since nature makes nothing purposeless or in vain, it is undeniably true that she has made all animals for the sake of man.' It is a self-mined streak of hubris and vainglory for one of the foremost philosophers of all time to assume a state and rely on it as a presumption without evidence and then just declare it to be true. You may as well say only humans have souls and then rely on the premise as the proof. Where is the proof for such a perverse theological notion any more than Aristotle's own?

13 Masters

Yet the idea of superiority is the base of man's legal rights over and duty towards animals. They are his property to be used, worked and killed at will. It was acceptance of this property-concept that led to Martin's Act. [See **A1**] For it protected the property rights of the owner in the animal rather than the animal itself. The same idea has permeated and is perpetuated throughout English law. The Theft Act 1968 defines 'property' as including 'money and all other property, real or personal...Wild creatures, tamed or untamed, shall be regarded as property...' Thus the animal is not deemed to count in its own right. It status is dependent on its use to man. However the idea is not limited to English law, but affects and forms judicial thinking in its own right. Our relationship with animals was considered in *R. v. Menard* [1978] 43 CCC (2d) 458l by the Quebec Court of Appeal where Lamer JA said: 'Within the hierarchy of our planet the animal occupies a place which, if it does not give rights to the animal, at least prompts us, being animals who claim to be rational beings, to impose on ourselves behaviour which will reflect in our relations with them those virtues we seek to promote in our relationships among humans. On the other hand, the animal is inferior to man, and takes its place within a hierarchy which is the hierarchy of animals, and above all is part of nature with all its "racial and natural" selections. The animal is subordinate to nature and to man. It will often be in the interests of man to kill and mutilate wild or domestic animals, to subjugate them and, to this end, to tame them with all the painful consequence this may entail for them and, if they are too old, or too numerous, or abandoned, to kill them.'

This explanation denies rights to animals and denotes our duties towards them when it is considered necessary to control human behaviour. So in the legal sense the animal as a defendant is tried by a human prosecutor and a human judge and jury. It has neither a defence counsel nor a defence. Nor can it have a defence. For the crime it has committed is solely being born and the figurative trial is a denial of natural justice.

Lamer JA candidly claimed that any rules made are purely in the 'interests of man'. Consistent with that concept he continued to explain our self-importance: 'It does not mean that man, when a thing is susceptible of causing pain to an animal, must abstain unless it is necessary but means that man in the pursuit of his purposes as a superior being, in the pursuit of his well-being, is obliged not to inflict on animals pain, suffering or injury which is not inevitable taking into account the purpose sought and the circumstances of the particular case. In effect, even if it is not necessary for man to eat meat if he could abstain from doing so, as many in fact do, it is the privilege of man to eat it.'

The words used by Lamer JA namely 'interests' and 'superior' and 'privilege' all underline the reasons why animals are exploited. So there was no possible doubt about it he explained in detail that animals are in 'our world' and so any protection given to them is a result of 'The responsibilities that we impose on ourselves as their masters.' His judgment was no less than legal speciesism based on the warped morals of Aristotle.

14 Single

However there is nothing surprising about His Lordship's view. For the tone and bias only echoes English law. In 1895 a society formed to promote the abolition of vivisection was held to be charity. The judge said, 'Cruelty is degrading to man and its suppression advances morals and education among men'. That view did not persuade the judges in England's then highest court. The House of Lords reversed that decision in *National Anti-vivisection Society v. IRC* [1948] AC 31 holding that the abolition was outweighed by the advantages of its continuance: 'It would destroy a source of enormous blessings to mankind. That is a positive and calamitous detriment of appalling magnitude'. Lord Wright made his position clear: 'The scientists who inflicts pain in the course of vivisection is fulfilling a moral duty to mankind which is higher in degree than the moralist or sentimentalist who thinks only of the animals. Nor do I agree that animals ought not be sacrificed to man when necessary. A strictly regulated amount of pain to some hundreds of animals may save and avert incalculable suffering to innumerable millions of mankind. I cannot doubt what the moral choice should be. There is only one single issue.'

This Aristotelian spirit places each and every animal below anyone within the category of *homo sapiens*. But is there really 'only one single issue'? Is it not pure prejudice to consider without question that that which you have control of and over is bound to be morally and legally inferior?

In truth there are two stark polar positions at play in respect of vivisection namely (a) animals are unlike us and so any experiment is likely to produce an unreliable result and hence morally should not be undertaken at all or (b) animals are so like us they will be subject to such pain it is morally unacceptable to cause them to undergo any experiment. Whichever way it is spliced the result is the same in that we do it because might is right. Like every robber baron in history we do it because we can get away with it.

15 Voice

Animals and bias and cruelty are connected as they suffer both at the hands of humans. That is reasonable as it is the natural order where prejudice and power intersect. The nature of prejudice is to first deem another group as inferior and then treat them that way. It is easy to form a prejudice against a group that is 'different' to your own. It is even easier to find a victim that you can rule by virtue of reason. At the bottom of the pile that leaves one group. After blacks, Jews, women and children, we have animals. They are ideal as a man-made victim because they are different, identifiable and vulnerable: animals are the underdog's underdog.

Animals are treated as they are in law because they have neither a voice nor a vote. Jeremy Bentham claimed, in comparing their plight to slavery, that their 'Rights have been withheld from them by the hand of tyranny.' This is because they are weak. Anywhere that a person has others in his control so that they are mentally and/or physically weak, the opportunity presents itself.

Aristotle made much of the value of the intellect and the fact that 'Man is the only animal endowed with speech.' Without these qualities he believed the person would be a man in name only. Yet what of people, be they slaves or otherwise, who do not possess these faculties? Is a person who is paralysed or insane or in a coma not a real person?

Many of Aristotle's views were found to be without substance or unjust or immoral and so rejected. Similarly his opinions regarding animals were irrational. Animals show altruism, have learned to communicate, have defined intellects, can exhibit grief, can die of heartache and show a greater perception than most advanced scientific instruments in detecting earthquakes. Yet though the argument has disappeared the fallacy persists. Aristotle wisely said, 'It is the mark of an educated mind to be able to entertain a thought without accepting it.' So given his sapience we should respect and reject his thoughts on natural-born superiority.

16 *Jus animalium*

Anthony Storr, in his classic book *Human Aggression*, concluded that of all the animals on the face of the Earth man is the cruellest. If this is so then the law should curb this characteristic. For if it is right that man can assume a superior role over animals and then treat or ill-treat them accordingly, then morality has no meaning.

In 1796 Lawrence wrote in *Philosophical Treatise on the Moral duties of Man towards the Brute Creation*, 'The grand source of the unmerited and superfluous misery of beasts exists in a defect in the constitution of all communities. No human government, I believe, has ever recognised the *jus animalium*, which ought surely to form a part of the jurisprudence of every system founded on the principles of justice and humanity.' The basis of *jus animalium* [justice for animals] lies in the actual existence of animals. By virtue of being alive and sentient they are entitled to have rights.

A right is not a concession grudgingly given to an animal by a superior species. At the lowest animals have a right to live. Rights run with life itself. They have a right not to suffer because they have the ability to suffer. By comparison humans owe duties to other humans which are generally endorsed by corresponding rights: if A has a duty not to kill people, B has a right not be killed by A. This is generally true as some humans have rights but owe no duties. A newborn baby or mentally ill person has a right to life but does not owe a duty not to kill people. This springs from their lack of sense and conscience, not sentience. Hence as *homo sapiens* they share the legal rights accorded to everyone in that group, but morally they are not held legally liable for their actions.

Yet the position with animals is exactly the same. Possessing a higher degree of intelligence does not justify one human denying rights to another. The greatest genius is on par morally with the most illiterate, insane person. How then can humans justify exploiting animals regardless of feelings, intelligence and perception? The real answer is morally we cannot do so. Human life has no 'intrinsic value' *per se*. To adopt that view which is constantly used by philosophers as a shallow justification is but speciesism written in water. Why should say a human vegetable kept artificially alive on a life-machine have some intrinsic value denied to a dolphin? While we know that many animals possess qualities similar to normal human characteristics and sensibilities, man has persuaded himself that he has absolute and arbitrary rights over them. That notion is persuasive by the consent of other men and the benefit we all derive from that belief.

It is all too easy to accept that animals are only to be used for man's gain. But that is as logical as saying black people were born to be slaves and women were to be used by men. All living creatures have a right to live and die with dignity. Animals must take their place within the community or outside it, in either case their worth being recognised by law. Henry Salt wrote in *Animals' Rights Considered in Relation to Social Progress* [1894]: 'To live one's life – to realise one's true self – is the highest moral purpose of man and animal alike...[then] if we have to kill, whether it be man or animal, let us kill and have done with it; if we must inflict pain, let us do what is inevitable, without hypocrisy, or evasion, or cant. But (here is the cardinal point) let us first be assured it is necessary, let us not wantonly trade on the needless miseries of other beings, and then attempt to lull our consciences by a series of shuffling excuses which cannot endure a moment's candid investigation.'

The acceptance of animal rights and human duties undoubtedly causes problems for humans. Experiments on animals would be illegal, but then so are they on humans unless they consent. Moreover it is not an exchange but a gift. Therein lies the problem. If man extends legal protection to other species on ethical grounds he has no tangible gain. Conversely his loss is readily apparent as it was to the slave-trader and the wife-seller. So as it raises more questions than answers, it is ignored in a conspiracy of our complacency.

It is immoral to assume rights for members of your own kind only. Indeed in general the reverse occurs. The law attempts to protect the weak: including minors, the blind, the mentally ill and those liable to discrimination on the grounds of age or race or sex. With greater intelligence comes compassion and responsibility. Thus in civil and criminal law there are special exemptions and privileges extended to those who might otherwise be disadvantaged. In logic and morality such protection should equally apply to animals.

JS Mill wrote in *The Principles of Political Economy* [1929] 'The reasons for legal intervention in favour of children apply not less strongly to the case of those unfortunate slaves and victims of the most brutal part of mankind – the lower animals. It is by the grossest misunderstanding of the principle of liberty that the infliction of exemplary punishment on ruffianism practised towards these defenceless creatures has been treated as a meddling by Government in things beyond its province; an interference with domestic life. The domestic life of domestic tyrants is one of the things which it is the most imperative on the law to interfere with...What it would be the duty of a human being, possessed of the requisite physical strength, to prevent by force, if attempted in his presence, it cannot be less incumbent on society generally to repress.'

That is true. While there are numerous flaws in our laws in relation to animals, there are three major matters that should be addressed now in order that a degree of justice is introduced so that they have some legal protection from their ultimate predator:

1. An Animals' Ombudswoman should be appointed to promote and protect the rights and interests of animals in and out of court. She should liase with the Law Commission to introduce a new Act.

2. Vivisection and experiments on animals should become illegal.

3. A new Animal Rights Act should replace all the existing legislation. The paramount principle of the Act should be to protect the life and well-being of any animal, wild and domesticated.

Although at first glance these reforms look revolutionary, in truth they are not. The only unusual aspect is that they relate to animals. These reforms are essential if animals are to have a legal *personality.* Without such a personality there can be no progress towards justice for animals. Philosophical discussions about rights will fade into verbal smoke-rings unless and until animals possess a defined legal status.

I7 Mirror

The legal comparison between people and things and animals is instructive and illuminating. In the 13th Century Henry de Bracton, the English jurist, confirmed that 'A Jew cannot have anything of his own, because whatever he acquires he acquires not for himself but for the King...' The reason relied upon for their legal standing was Jews were 'Men *ferae naturae*, protected by a quasi forest law. Like the roe and the deer, they form an order apart.' The same principle of prejudice was used by American judges when a statute provided, 'No Black or Mulatto person, or Indian shall be allowed to give evidence in favor of, or against a white man...' The statute was silent as to the position of a Chinese man who wanted to testify. So the highest court in California held he had no right to do so because he was one of 'A race of people whom nature has marked as inferior, and who are incapable of progress or intellectual development beyond a certain point...between whom and ourselves nature has placed an impassable difference.' Women were similarly legally marked as inferior from birth and merely the property of men. When the first woman wanted to practise law in Wisconsin she was laughed out of court: 'The law of nature destines and qualifies the female sex for the bearing and nurture of the children of our race and for the custody of the homes of the world...Nature has tempered woman as little for the judicial conflicts of the court room, as for the physical conflicts of the battle field...' [See M. Bateson; Medieval England 139 [1904]; *People v Hall* [1854] 4 Cal. 399; *In re Goddell* [1875] 39 Wisc. 232]

The same mind-set was inherent in the Founding Fathers who drafted the American Declaration of Independence in 1776. Those who drafted it limited the protection to men and even then only white men. Moreover most of them owned slaves and used and abused their 'property'. At first glance all these examples appear to be pure hypocrisy riddled with myopia. The truth is different. For in each example the Jew and the Chinese man and the woman and the slave were not seen by them to be human at all. By each of those in authority they were seen to be *things*. That is the reason they were denied legal rights. It is why animals are seen in the same way as legally mere things, just property, rather than fellow creatures.

Pythagoras was so far ahead of his time that according to Jones, *Legal Theory of the Greeks* [1956], he believed that killing an animal was murder. Though that seems extreme the very thought was echoed in 2007 by a judge. St Clair Shores deliberately left his dog to starve to death by abandoning him when he left the house where they were living together. The judge in sentencing Shores to prison said, 'This was murder. An animal, in this court's opinion, is no different than a child.' [*Detroit Free Press* 19/7/07]

In the American *Sido Case*, [*In Re Murphy* [1980] Cal. Super. Ct 17/6/80], the California court held that an animal has a 'right to life'. Mary Murphy, the owner of a dog made a Will specifying he should be killed after her death. She was concerned that Sido might 'Fall into the hands of an uncaring animal shelter or some worse fate.' She died and arrangements were being made to comply with the condition in the Will. Richard Avazino, the President of the San Francisco Society for the Prevention of Cruelty to Animals, (SPCA) had custody of Sido. He refused to deliver Sido to the executrix for euthanasia. So the executrix took action against the Society. Meanwhile, a few hours before the court hearing, a new Californian law was introduced to prevent the 'malicious and unnecessary destruction of animals'. It was drafted with Sido in mind. The court overruled the clause in the Will. Jay Pfotenhaven J interpreting the new law said, 'The Will seeks to have carried out an act I find to be illegal and a violation of public policy... Now, stray dogs, abandoned dogs, have rights under our statute which must be carefully followed. Our Sido cannot be deemed an abandoned dog or a stray dog, her plight resulted due to the death of her mistress. Her Sido is entitled to nothing less than [that] which we afford to stray dogs. To permit the direction of the decedent here to be carried out would, again, violate existing statute and be contrary to public policy.'

This portentous decision should serve as a model for other jurisdictions. It recognises and respects an animal's basic right to life. Why should English law sanction the killing of an animal according to the wishes of its owner? Why should English law accept the notion even if it is based on some idle fancy or whim however capricious, or ill-founded or selfish or wrong? Mary Murphy's Will stated that as Sido would not be able to find a happy home after she was gone, he must be put to death. She committed suicide. That was her choice. The dog had no choice. Sido, a ten-year-old mongrel, was to die because she chose to die. If that situation happened in England today, Sido would not be saved. That death sentence is a continuing failure of our jurisprudence.

There is a small glimmer of a change in judicial thinking that can be gleaned from a decision in the High Court of Israel. The court was ruling on whether force-feeding of geese was cruel. During the judgment in *NOAH (Israeli Federation of Animal Protection Organizations) v. Attorney-General* [2003] 57(6) Piskei Din 212 Rivlin J said, 'As for myself, there is no doubt in my heart that wild creatures, like pets, have emotions. They were endowed with a soul that experiences the emotions of joy and sorrow, happiness and grief, affection and fear. Some of them nurture special feelings towards their friend-enemy: man. Not all think so; but no one denies that these creatures also feel the pain inflicted upon them through physical harm or a violent intrusion into their bodies. Indeed, whoever wishes may find, in the circumstances of this appeal, prima facie evidence for the acts of artificial force-feeding, justification whose essence is the need to retain the farmer's source of livelihood and enhance the gastronomic delight of others...But this has a price – and the price is reducing the dignity of Man himself.'

Rivlin J ruled it was cruel. It was abolished in 2005.

When the gain to man is measured by the pain inflicted on an innocent unwilling victim, it is inhumane and unethical for the practice to continue. Where it does the law thereby sanctions tyranny. To do so detracts not only from the man but the law itself. For part of the role of law is to quell the base desires of man. Another part is to promote the noble side of man's nature. Jurisprudentially the law is not concerned only with ideas but ideals: it is the aspiration more than the attainment. Law is the universal language of natural justice. Granting animal rights will in turn strengthen human rights. Ultimately the fate of man and animal is inextricably linked. In the mystery of living their destinies are interdependent and interrelated and interwoven. Much like the slave needed to be freed from his owner, animals need a legal status which recognises their sentience. For that status alone guarantees the quintessence of natural justice that rights run with life itself. Law as man's mirror of morality should reflect the self-evident truth that we are all animals-in-law.

Appendices

Animal Welfare Act 2006

Animal Welfare Act 2006

CHAPTER 45

Animal Welfare Act 2006

CHAPTER 45

CONTENTS

Animal Welfare Act 2006

2006 CHAPTER 45

An Act to make provision about animal welfare; and for connected purposes.

[8th November 2006]

B E IT ENACTED by the Queen's most Excellent Majesty, by and with the advice and consent of the Lords Spiritual and Temporal, and Commons, in this present Parliament assembled, and by the authority of the same, as follows: —

Introductory

1 Animals to which the Act applies

(1) In this Act, except subsections (4) and (5), "animal" means a vertebrate other than man.

(2) Nothing in this Act applies to an animal while it is in its foetal or embryonic form.

(3) The appropriate national authority may by regulations for all or any of the purposes of this Act—

    (a) extend the definition of "animal" so as to include invertebrates of any description;

    (b) make provision in lieu of subsection (2) as respects any invertebrates included in the definition of "animal";

    (c) amend subsection (2) to extend the application of this Act to an animal from such earlier stage of its development as may be specified in the regulations.

(4) The power under subsection (3)(a) or (c) may only be exercised if the appropriate national authority is satisfied, on the basis of scientific evidence, that animals of the kind concerned are capable of experiencing pain or suffering.

(5) In this section, "vertebrate" means any animal of the Sub-phylum Vertebrata of the Phylum Chordata and "invertebrate" means any animal not of that Sub-phylum.

2 "Protected animal"

An animal is a "protected animal" for the purposes of this Act if —

(a) it is of a kind which is commonly domesticated in the British Islands,

(b) it is under the control of man whether on a permanent or temporary basis, or

(c) it is not living in a wild state.

3 Responsibility for animals

(1) In this Act, references to a person responsible for an animal are to a person responsible for an animal whether on a permanent or temporary basis.

(2) In this Act, references to being responsible for an animal include being in charge of it.

(3) For the purposes of this Act, a person who owns an animal shall always be regarded as being a person who is responsible for it.

(4) For the purposes of this Act, a person shall be treated as responsible for any animal for which a person under the age of 16 years of whom he has actual care and control is responsible.

Prevention of harm

4 Unnecessary suffering

(1) A person commits an offence if —

(a) an act of his, or a failure of his to act, causes an animal to suffer,

(b) he knew, or ought reasonably to have known, that the act, or failure to act, would have that effect or be likely to do so,

(c) the animal is a protected animal, and

(d) the suffering is unnecessary.

(2) A person commits an offence if —

(a) he is responsible for an animal,

(b) an act, or failure to act, of another person causes the animal to suffer,

(c) he permitted that to happen or failed to take such steps (whether by way of supervising the other person or otherwise) as were reasonable in all the circumstances to prevent that happening, and

(d) the suffering is unnecessary.

(3) The considerations to which it is relevant to have regard when determining for the purposes of this section whether suffering is unnecessary include —

(a) whether the suffering could reasonably have been avoided or reduced;

(b) whether the conduct which caused the suffering was in compliance with any relevant enactment or any relevant provisions of a licence or code of practice issued under an enactment;

(c) whether the conduct which caused the suffering was for a legitimate purpose, such as —
   (i) the purpose of benefiting the animal, or
   (ii) the purpose of protecting a person, property or another animal;

(d) whether the suffering was proportionate to the purpose of the conduct concerned;

(e) whether the conduct concerned was in all the circumstances that of a reasonably competent and humane person.

(4) Nothing in this section applies to the destruction of an animal in an appropriate and humane manner.

5 Mutilation

(1) A person commits an offence if —
   (a) he carries out a prohibited procedure on a protected animal;
   (b) he causes such a procedure to be carried out on such an animal.

(2) A person commits an offence if —
   (a) he is responsible for an animal,
   (b) another person carries out a prohibited procedure on the animal, and
   (c) he permitted that to happen or failed to take such steps (whether by way of supervising the other person or otherwise) as were reasonable in all the circumstances to prevent that happening.

(3) References in this section to the carrying out of a prohibited procedure on an animal are to the carrying out of a procedure which involves interference with the sensitive tissues or bone structure of the animal, otherwise than for the purpose of its medical treatment.

(4) Subsections (1) and (2) do not apply in such circumstances as the appropriate national authority may specify by regulations.

(5) Before making regulations under subsection (4), the appropriate national authority shall consult such persons appearing to the authority to represent any interests concerned as the authority considers appropriate.

(6) Nothing in this section applies to the removal of the whole or any part of a dog's tail.

6 Docking of dogs' tails

(1) A person commits an offence if —
   (a) he removes the whole or any part of a dog's tail, otherwise than for the purpose of its medical treatment;
   (b) he causes the whole or any part of a dog's tail to be removed by another person, otherwise than for the purpose of its medical treatment.

(2) A person commits an offence if —
   (a) he is responsible for a dog,
   (b) another person removes the whole or any part of the dog's tail, otherwise than for the purpose of its medical treatment, and
   (c) he permitted that to happen or failed to take such steps (whether by way of supervising the other person or otherwise) as were reasonable in all the circumstances to prevent that happening.

(3)   Subsections (1) and (2) do not apply if the dog is a certified working dog that is not more than 5 days old.

(4)   For the purposes of subsection (3), a dog is a certified working dog if a veterinary surgeon has certified, in accordance with regulations made by the appropriate national authority, that the first and second conditions mentioned below are met.

(5)   The first condition referred to in subsection (4) is that there has been produced to the veterinary surgeon such evidence as the appropriate national authority may by regulations require for the purpose of showing that the dog is likely to be used for work in connection with —

     (a)   law enforcement,

     (b)   activities of Her Majesty's armed forces,

     (c)   emergency rescue,

     (d)   lawful pest control, or

     (e)   the lawful shooting of animals.

(6)   The second condition referred to in subsection (4) is that the dog is of a type specified for the purposes of this subsection by regulations made by the appropriate national authority.

(7)   It is a defence for a person accused of an offence under subsection (1) or (2) to show that he reasonably believed that the dog was one in relation to which subsection (3) applies.

(8)   A person commits an offence if —

     (a)   he owns a subsection (3) dog, and

     (b)   fails to take reasonable steps to secure that, before the dog is 3 months old, it is identified as a subsection (3) dog in accordance with regulations made by the appropriate national authority.

(9)   A person commits an offence if —

     (a)   he shows a dog at an event to which members of the public are admitted on payment of a fee,

     (b)   the dog's tail has been wholly or partly removed (in England and Wales or elsewhere), and

     (c)   removal took place on or after the commencement day.

(10)   Where a dog is shown only for the purpose of demonstrating its working ability, subsection (9) does not apply if the dog is a subsection (3) dog.

(11)   It is a defence for a person accused of an offence under subsection (9) to show that he reasonably believed —

     (a)   that the event was not one to which members of the public were admitted on payment of an entrance fee,

     (b)   that the removal took place before the commencement day, or

     (c)   that the dog was one in relation to which subsection (10) applies.

(12)   A person commits an offence if he knowingly gives false information to a veterinary surgeon in connection with the giving of a certificate for the purposes of this section.

(13)   The appropriate national authority may by regulations make provision about the functions of inspectors in relation to —

     (a)   certificates for the purposes of this section, and

(b)   the identification of dogs as subsection (3) dogs.

(14)   Power to make regulations under this section includes power –

(a)   to make different provision for different cases, and

(b)   to make incidental, supplementary, consequential or transitional provision or savings.

(15)   Before making regulations under this section, the appropriate national authority shall consult such persons appearing to the authority to represent any interests concerned as the authority considers appropriate.

(16)   In this section –

"commencement day" means the day on which this section comes into force;

"subsection (3) dog" means a dog whose tail has, on or after the commencement day, been wholly or partly removed without contravening subsection (1), because of the application of subsection (3).

7   Administration of poisons etc.

(1)   A person commits an offence if, without lawful authority or reasonable excuse, he –

(a)   administers any poisonous or injurious drug or substance to a protected animal, knowing it to be poisonous or injurious, or

(b)   causes any poisonous or injurious drug or substance to be taken by a protected animal, knowing it to be poisonous or injurious.

(2)   A person commits an offence if –

(a)   he is responsible for an animal,

(b)   without lawful authority or reasonable excuse, another person administers a poisonous or injurious drug or substance to the animal or causes the animal to take such a drug or substance, and

(c)   he permitted that to happen or, knowing the drug or substance to be poisonous or injurious, he failed to take such steps (whether by way of supervising the other person or otherwise) as were reasonable in all the circumstances to prevent that happening.

(3)   In this section, references to a poisonous or injurious drug or substance include a drug or substance which, by virtue of the quantity or manner in which it is administered or taken, has the effect of a poisonous or injurious drug or substance.

8   Fighting etc.

(1)   A person commits an offence if he –

(a)   causes an animal fight to take place, or attempts to do so;

(b)   knowingly receives money for admission to an animal fight;

(c)   knowingly publicises a proposed animal fight;

(d)   provides information about an animal fight to another with the intention of enabling or encouraging attendance at the fight;

(e)   makes or accepts a bet on the outcome of an animal fight or on the likelihood of anything occurring or not occurring in the course of an animal fight;

(f)   takes part in an animal fight;

(g)   has in his possession anything designed or adapted for use in connection with an animal fight with the intention of its being so used;

(h)   keeps or trains an animal for use for in connection with an animal fight;

(i)   keeps any premises for use for an animal fight.

(2)   A person commits an offence if, without lawful authority or reasonable excuse, he is present at an animal fight.

(3)   A person commits an offence if, without lawful authority or reasonable excuse, he —

(a)   knowingly supplies a video recording of an animal fight,

(b)   knowingly publishes a video recording of an animal fight,

(c)   knowingly shows a video recording of an animal fight to another, or

(d)   possesses a video recording of an animal fight, knowing it to be such a recording, with the intention of supplying it.

(4)   Subsection (3) does not apply if the video recording is of an animal fight that took place —

(a)   outside Great Britain, or

(b)   before the commencement date.

(5)   Subsection (3) does not apply —

(a)   in the case of paragraph (a), to the supply of a video recording for inclusion in a programme service;

(b)   in the case of paragraph (b) or (c), to the publication or showing of a video recording by means of its inclusion in a programme service;

(c)   in the case of paragraph (d), by virtue of intention to supply for inclusion in a programme service.

(6)   Provision extending the application of an offence under subsection (3), so far as relating to the provision of information society services, may be made under section 2(2) of the European Communities Act 1972 (c. 68) (powers to implement Community obligations by regulations) notwithstanding the limits imposed by paragraph 1(1)(d) of Schedule 2 to that Act on the penalties with which an offence may be punishable on summary conviction.

(7)   In this section —

"animal fight" means an occasion on which a protected animal is placed with an animal, or with a human, for the purpose of fighting, wrestling or baiting;

"commencement date" means the date on which subsection (3) comes into force;

"information society services" has the meaning given in Article 2(a) of Directive 2000/31/EC of the European Parliament and of the Council of 8 June 2000 on certain legal aspects of information society services, in particular electronic commerce in the Internal Market (Directive on electronic commerce);

"programme service" has the same meaning as in the Communications Act 2003 (c. 21);

"video recording" means a recording, in any form, from which a moving image may by any means be reproduced and includes data stored on a computer disc or by other electronic means which is capable of conversion into a moving image.

(8)   In this section —

    (a)   references to supplying or publishing a video recording are to supplying or publishing a video recording in any manner, including, in relation to a video recording in the form of data stored electronically, by means of transmitting such data;

    (b)   references to showing a video recording are to showing a moving image reproduced from a video recording by any means.

Promotion of welfare

9   Duty of person responsible for animal to ensure welfare

(1)   A person commits an offence if he does not take such steps as are reasonable in all the circumstances to ensure that the needs of an animal for which he is responsible are met to the extent required by good practice.

(2)   For the purposes of this Act, an animal's needs shall be taken to include —

    (a)   its need for a suitable environment,

    (b)   its need for a suitable diet,

    (c)   its need to be able to exhibit normal behaviour patterns,

    (d)   any need it has to be housed with, or apart from, other animals, and

    (e)   its need to be protected from pain, suffering, injury and disease.

(3)   The circumstances to which it is relevant to have regard when applying subsection (1) include, in particular —

    (a)   any lawful purpose for which the animal is kept, and

    (b)   any lawful activity undertaken in relation to the animal.

(4)   Nothing in this section applies to the destruction of an animal in an appropriate and humane manner.

10   Improvement notices

(1)   If an inspector is of the opinion that a person is failing to comply with section 9(1), he may serve on the person a notice which —

    (a)   states that he is of that opinion,

    (b)   specifies the respects in which he considers the person is failing to comply with that provision,

    (c)   specifies the steps he considers need to be taken in order to comply with the provision,

    (d)   specifies a period for the taking of those steps, and

    (e)   explains the effect of subsections (2) and (3).

(2)   Where a notice under subsection (1) ("an improvement notice") is served, no proceedings for an offence under section 9(1) may be instituted before the end of the period specified for the purposes of subsection (1)(d) ("the compliance period") in respect of —

    (a)   the non-compliance which gave rise to the notice, or

    (b)   any continuation of that non-compliance.

(3)   If the steps specified in an improvement notice are taken at any time before the end of the compliance period, no proceedings for an offence under section 9(1) may be instituted in respect of —

(a) the non-compliance which gave rise to the notice, or

(b) any continuation of that non-compliance prior to the taking of the steps specified in the notice.

(4) An inspector may extend, or further extend, the compliance period specified in an improvement notice.

11 Transfer of animals by way of sale or prize to persons under 16

(1) A person commits an offence if he sells an animal to a person whom he has reasonable cause to believe to be under the age of 16 years.

(2) For the purposes of subsection (1), selling an animal includes transferring, or agreeing to transfer, ownership of the animal in consideration of entry by the transferee into another transaction.

(3) Subject to subsections (4) to (6), a person commits an offence if —

(a) he enters into an arrangement with a person whom he has reasonable cause to believe to be under the age of 16 years, and

(b) the arrangement is one under which that person has the chance to win an animal as a prize.

(4) A person does not commit an offence under subsection (3) if —

(a) he enters into the arrangement in the presence of the person with whom the arrangement is made, and

(b) he has reasonable cause to believe that the person with whom the arrangement is made is accompanied by a person who is not under the age of 16 years.

(5) A person does not commit an offence under subsection (3) if —

(a) he enters into the arrangement otherwise than in the presence of the person with whom the arrangement is made, and

(b) he has reasonable cause to believe that a person who has actual care and control of the person with whom the arrangement is made has consented to the arrangement.

(6) A person does not commit an offence under subsection (3) if he enters into the arrangement in a family context.

12 Regulations to promote welfare

(1) The appropriate national authority may by regulations make such provision as the authority thinks fit for the purpose of promoting the welfare of animals for which a person is responsible, or the progeny of such animals.

(2) Without prejudice to the generality of the power under subsection (1), regulations under that subsection may, in particular —

(a) make provision imposing specific requirements for the purpose of securing that the needs of animals are met;

(b) make provision to facilitate or improve co-ordination in relation to the carrying out by different persons of functions relating to the welfare of animals;

(c) make provision for the establishment of one or more bodies with functions relating to advice about the welfare of animals.

(3) Power to make regulations under subsection (1) includes power —

     (a)   to provide that breach of a provision of the regulations is an offence;

     (b)   to apply a relevant post-conviction power in relation to conviction for an offence under the regulations;

     (c)   to make provision for fees or other charges in relation to the carrying out of functions under the regulations;

     (d)   to make different provision for different cases or areas;

     (e)   to provide for exemptions from a provision of the regulations, either subject to specified conditions or without conditions;

     (f)   to make incidental, supplementary, consequential or transitional provision or savings.

(4)   Power to make regulations under subsection (1) does not include power to create an offence triable on indictment or punishable with —

     (a)   imprisonment for a term exceeding 51 weeks, or

     (b)   a fine exceeding level 5 on the standard scale.

(5)   Regulations under subsection (1) may provide that a specified offence under the regulations is to be treated as a relevant offence for the purposes of section 23.

(6)   Before making regulations under subsection (1), the appropriate national authority shall consult such persons appearing to the authority to represent any interests concerned as the authority considers appropriate.

(7)   In this section, "specified" means specified in regulations under subsection (1).

Licensing and registration

13   **Licensing or registration of activities involving animals**

(1)   No person shall carry on an activity to which this subsection applies except under the authority of a licence for the purposes of this section.

(2)   Subsection (1) applies to an activity which —

     (a)   involves animals for which a person is responsible, and

     (b)   is specified for the purposes of the subsection by regulations made by the appropriate national authority.

(3)   No person shall carry on an activity to which this subsection applies unless registered for the purposes of this section.

(4)   Subsection (3) applies to an activity which —

     (a)   involves animals for which a person is responsible, and

     (b)   is specified for the purposes of the subsection by regulations made by the appropriate national authority.

(5)   Regulations under subsection (2) or (4) may only be made for the purpose of promoting the welfare of animals for which a person is responsible, or the progeny of such animals.

(6)   A person commits an offence if he contravenes subsection (1) or (3).

(7)   The appropriate national authority may by regulations make provision about licences or registration for the purposes of this section.

(8) The appropriate national authority may by regulations repeal any of the following enactments (which impose licence or registration requirements in relation to activities involving animals) —

  (a) section 1(1) of the Performing Animals (Regulation) Act 1925 (c. 38);

  (b) section 1(1) of the Pet Animals Act 1951 (c. 35);

  (c) section 1(1) of the Animal Boarding Establishments Act 1963 (c. 43);

  (d) section 1(1) of the Riding Establishments Act 1964 (c. 70);

  (e) section 1(1) of the Breeding of Dogs Act 1973 (c. 60).

(9) Before making regulations under this section, the appropriate national authority shall consult such persons appearing to the authority to represent any interests concerned as the authority considers appropriate.

(10) Schedule 1 (which makes provision about regulations under this section) has effect.

Codes of practice

14   Codes of practice

(1) The appropriate national authority may issue, and may from time to time revise, codes of practice for the purpose of providing practical guidance in respect of any provision made by or under this Act.

(2) The authority responsible for issuing a code of practice under subsection (1) shall publish the code, and any revision of it, in such manner as it considers appropriate.

(3) A person's failure to comply with a provision of a code of practice issued under this section shall not of itself render him liable to proceedings of any kind.

(4) In any proceedings against a person for an offence under this Act or an offence under regulations under section 12 or 13 —

  (a) failure to comply with a relevant provision of a code of practice issued under this section may be relied upon as tending to establish liability, and

  (b) compliance with a relevant provision of such a code of practice may be relied upon as tending to negative liability.

15   Making and approval of codes of practice: England

(1) Where the Secretary of State proposes to issue (or revise) a code of practice under section 14, he shall —

  (a) prepare a draft of the code (or revised code),

  (b) consult about the draft such persons appearing to him to represent any interests concerned as he considers appropriate, and

  (c) consider any representations made by them.

(2) If following consultation under subsection (1) the Secretary of State decides to proceed with a draft (either in its original form or with such modifications as he thinks fit), he shall lay a copy of it before Parliament.

(3) If, within the 40-day period, either House of Parliament resolves not to approve a draft laid under subsection (2), the Secretary of State shall take no further steps in relation to it.

(4) If, within the 40-day period, neither House resolves not to approve a draft laid under subsection (2), the Secretary of State shall issue (or revise) the code in the form of the draft.

(5) A code (or revised code) shall come into force on such day as the Secretary of State may by order appoint.

(6) Subsection (3) does not prevent a new draft of a code (or revised code) from being laid before Parliament.

(7) An order under subsection (5) may include transitional provision or savings.

(8) In this section, "the 40-day period", in relation to a draft laid under subsection (2), means —

    (a) if the draft is laid before the Houses on different days, the period of 40 days beginning with the later of the two days, and

    (b) in any other case, the period of 40 days beginning with the day on which the draft is laid before each House,

no account being taken of any period during which Parliament is dissolved or prorogued or during which both Houses are adjourned for more than four days.

16 Making of codes of practice: Wales

(1) Where the National Assembly for Wales proposes to issue (or revise) a code of practice under section 14, it shall —

    (a) prepare a draft of the code (or revised code),

    (b) consult about the draft such persons appearing to it to represent any interests concerned as it considers appropriate, and

    (c) consider any representations made by them.

(2) The Assembly may issue (or revise) a code either in the form of the draft prepared under subsection (1)(a) or with such modification as it thinks fit.

(3) A code (or revised code) shall come into force in accordance with its provisions.

(4) A code (or revised code) may include transitional provision or savings.

17 Revocation of codes of practice

(1) The appropriate national authority may by order revoke a code of practice issued by it under section 14.

(2) An order under subsection (1) may include transitional provision or savings.

(3) Before making an order under subsection (1), the appropriate national authority shall consult such persons appearing to the authority to represent any interests concerned as the authority considers appropriate.

(4) Subsection (3) does not apply in relation to an order revoking a code of practice in connection with its replacement by a new one.

Animals in distress

18   Powers in relation to animals in distress

(1)   If an inspector or a constable reasonably believes that a protected animal is suffering, he may take, or arrange for the taking of, such steps as appear to him to be immediately necessary to alleviate the animal's suffering.

(2)   Subsection (1) does not authorise destruction of an animal.

(3)   If a veterinary surgeon certifies that the condition of a protected animal is such that it should in its own interests be destroyed, an inspector or a constable may —

     (a)   destroy the animal where it is or take it to another place and destroy it there, or

     (b)   arrange for the doing of any of the things mentioned in paragraph (a).

(4)   An inspector or a constable may act under subsection (3) without the certificate of a veterinary surgeon if it appears to him —

     (a)   that the condition of the animal is such that there is no reasonable alternative to destroying it, and

     (b)   that the need for action is such that it is not reasonably practicable to wait for a veterinary surgeon.

(5)   An inspector or a constable may take a protected animal into possession if a veterinary surgeon certifies —

     (a)   that it is suffering, or

     (b)   that it is likely to suffer if its circumstances do not change.

(6)   An inspector or a constable may act under subsection (5) without the certificate of a veterinary surgeon if it appears to him —

     (a)   that the animal is suffering or that it is likely to do so if its circumstances do not change, and

     (b)   that the need for action is such that it is not reasonably practicable to wait for a veterinary surgeon.

(7)   The power conferred by subsection (5) includes power to take into possession dependent offspring of an animal taken into possession under that subsection.

(8)   Where an animal is taken into possession under subsection (5), an inspector or a constable may —

     (a)   remove it, or arrange for it to be removed, to a place of safety;

     (b)   care for it, or arrange for it to be cared for —

          (i)   on the premises where it was being kept when it was taken into possession, or

          (ii)   at such other place as he thinks fit;

     (c)   mark it, or arrange for it to be marked, for identification purposes.

(9)   A person acting under subsection (8)(b)(i), or under an arrangement under that provision, may make use of any equipment on the premises.

(10)   A veterinary surgeon may examine and take samples from an animal for the purpose of determining whether to issue a certificate under subsection (3) or (5) with respect to the animal.

(11) If a person exercises a power under this section otherwise than with the knowledge of a person who is responsible for the animal concerned, he must, as soon as reasonably practicable after exercising the power, take such steps as are reasonable in the circumstances to bring the exercise of the power to the notice of such a person.

(12) A person commits an offence if he intentionally obstructs a person in the exercise of power conferred by this section.

(13) A magistrates' court may, on application by a person who incurs expenses in acting under this section, order that he be reimbursed by such person as it thinks fit.

(14) A person affected by a decision under subsection (13) may appeal against the decision to the Crown Court.

19 Power of entry for section 18 purposes

(1) An inspector or a constable may enter premises for the purpose of searching for a protected animal and of exercising any power under section 18 in relation to it if he reasonably believes —
   (a) that there is a protected animal on the premises, and
   (b) that the animal is suffering or, if the circumstances of the animal do not change, it is likely to suffer.

(2) Subsection (1) does not authorise entry to any part of premises which is used as a private dwelling.

(3) An inspector or a constable may (if necessary) use reasonable force in exercising the power conferred by subsection (1), but only if it appears to him that entry is required before a warrant under subsection (4) can be obtained and executed.

(4) Subject to subsection (5), a justice of the peace may, on the application of an inspector or constable, issue a warrant authorising an inspector or a constable to enter premises for the purpose mentioned in subsection (1), if necessary using reasonable force.

(5) The power to issue a warrant under subsection (4) is exercisable only if the justice of the peace is satisfied —
   (a) that there are reasonable grounds for believing that there is a protected animal on the premises and that the animal is suffering or is likely to suffer if its circumstances do not change, and
   (b) that section 52 is satisfied in relation to the premises.

20 Orders in relation to animals taken under section 18(5)

(1) A magistrates' court may order any of the following in relation to an animal taken into possession under section 18(5) —
   (a) that specified treatment be administered to the animal;
   (b) that possession of the animal be given up to a specified person;
   (c) that the animal be sold;
   (d) that the animal be disposed of otherwise than by way of sale;
   (e) that the animal be destroyed.

(2) If an animal is taken into possession under section 18(5) when it is pregnant, the power conferred by subsection (1) shall also be exercisable in relation to any offspring that results from the pregnancy.

(3) The power conferred by subsection (1) shall be exercisable on application by—
  (a) the owner of the animal, or
  (b) any other person appearing to the court to have a sufficient interest in the animal.

(4) A court may not make an order under subsection (1) unless—
  (a) it has given the owner of the animal an opportunity to be heard, or
  (b) it is satisfied that it is not reasonably practicable to communicate with the owner.

(5) Where a court makes an order under subsection (1), it may—
  (a) appoint a person to carry out, or arrange for the carrying out, of the order;
  (b) give directions with respect to the carrying out of the order;
  (c) confer additional powers (including power to enter premises where the animal is being kept) for the purpose of, or in connection with, the carrying out of the order;
  (d) order a person to reimburse the expenses of carrying out the order.

(6) In determining how to exercise its powers under this section, the court shall have regard, amongst other things, to the desirability of protecting the animal's value and avoiding increasing any expenses which a person may be ordered to reimburse.

(7) A person commits an offence if he intentionally obstructs a person in the exercise of any power conferred by virtue of this section.

(8) If the owner of the animal is subject to a liability by virtue of section 18(13) or subsection (5)(d) above, any amount to which he is entitled as a result of sale of the animal may be reduced by an amount equal to that liability.

21 Orders under section 20: appeals

(1) Where a court makes an order under section 20(1), the owner of the animal to which the order relates may appeal against the order to the Crown Court.

(2) Nothing may be done under an order under section 20(1) unless—
  (a) the period for giving notice of appeal against the order has expired, and
  (b) if the order is the subject of an appeal, the appeal has been determined or withdrawn.

(3) Where the effect of an order is suspended under subsection (2)—
  (a) no directions given in connection with the order shall have effect, but
  (b) the court may give directions about how any animal to which the order applies is to be dealt with during the suspension.

(4) Directions under subsection (3)(b) may, in particular—
  (a) appoint a person to carry out, or arrange for the carrying out, of the directions;
  (b) require any person who has possession of the animal to deliver it up for the purposes of the directions;

(c)   confer additional powers (including power to enter premises where the animal is being kept) for the purpose of, or in connection with, the carrying out of the directions;

(d)   provide for the recovery of any expenses which are reasonably incurred in carrying out the directions.

(5)   Where a court decides on an application under section 20(3)(a) not to exercise the power conferred by subsection (1) of that section, the applicant may appeal against the decision to the Crown Court.

(6)   Where a court makes an order under section 20(5)(d), the person against whom the order is made may appeal against the order to the Crown Court.

Enforcement powers

22   Seizure of animals involved in fighting offences

(1)   A constable may seize an animal if it appears to him that it is one in relation to which an offence under section 8(1) or (2) has been committed.

(2)   A constable may enter and search premises for the purpose of exercising the power under subsection (1) if he reasonably believes —
    (a)   that there is an animal on the premises, and
    (b)   that the animal is one in relation to which the power under subsection (1) is exercisable.

(3)   Subsection (2) does not authorise entry to any part of premises which is used as a private dwelling.

(4)   Subject to subsection (5), a justice of the peace may, on the application of a constable, issue a warrant authorising a constable to enter and search premises, if necessary using reasonable force, for the purpose of exercising the power under subsection (1).

(5)   The power to issue a warrant under subsection (4) is exercisable only if the justice of the peace is satisfied —
    (a)   that there are reasonable grounds for believing that there is on the premises an animal in relation to which an offence under section 8(1) or (2) has been committed, and
    (b)   that section 52 is satisfied in relation to the premises.

(6)   In this section, references to an animal in relation to which an offence under section 8(1) or (2) has been committed include an animal which took part in an animal fight in relation to which such an offence was committed.

23   Entry and search under warrant in connection with offences

(1)   Subject to subsection (2), a justice of the peace may, on the application of an inspector or constable, issue a warrant authorising an inspector or a constable to enter premises, if necessary using reasonable force, in order to search for evidence of the commission of a relevant offence.

(2)   The power to issue a warrant under subsection (1) is exercisable only if the justice of the peace is satisfied —
    (a)   that there are reasonable grounds for believing —
        (i)   that a relevant offence has been committed on the premises, or

        (ii)   that evidence of the commission of a relevant offence is to be found on the premises, and

    (b)   that section 52 is satisfied in relation to the premises.

(3)   In this section, "relevant offence" means an offence under any of sections 4 to 9, 13(6) and 34(9).

24   Entry for purposes of arrest

In section 17(1)(c) of the Police and Criminal Evidence Act 1984 (c. 60) (power of constable to enter and search premises for purpose of arresting a person for offence under specified enactments), at end insert —

        "(v)   any of sections 4, 5, 6(1) and (2), 7 and 8(1) and (2) of the Animal Welfare Act 2006 (offences relating to the prevention of harm to animals);".

25   Inspection of records required to be kept by holder of licence

(1)   An inspector may require the holder of a licence to produce for inspection any records which he is required to keep by a condition of the licence.

(2)   Where records which a person is so required to keep are stored in electronic form, the power under subsection (1) includes power to require the records to be made available for inspection —

    (a)   in a visible and legible form, or

    (b)   in a form from which they can readily be produced in a visible and legible form.

(3)   An inspector may inspect and take copies of any records produced for inspection in pursuance of a requirement under this section.

26   Inspection in connection with licences

(1)   An inspector may carry out an inspection in order to check compliance with —

    (a)   the conditions subject to which a licence is granted;

    (b)   provision made by or under this Act which is relevant to the carrying on of an activity to which a licence relates.

(2)   An inspector may, for the purpose of carrying out an inspection under subsection (1), enter —

    (a)   premises specified in a licence as premises on which the carrying on of an activity is authorised;

    (b)   premises on which he reasonably believes an activity to which a licence relates is being carried on.

(3)   Subsection (2) does not authorise entry to any part of premises which is used as a private dwelling unless 24 hours' notice of the intended entry is given to the occupier.

27   Inspection in connection with registration

(1)   An inspector may carry out an inspection in order to check compliance with provision made by or under this Act which is relevant to the carrying on of an activity to which a registration for the purposes of section 13 relates.

(2) An inspector may, for the purpose of carrying out an inspection under subsection (1), enter premises on which he reasonably believes a person registered for the purposes of section 13 is carrying on an activity to which the registration relates.

(3) Subsection (2) does not authorise entry to any part of premises which is used as a private dwelling unless 24 hours' notice of the intended entry is given to the occupier.

28 Inspection of farm premises

(1) An inspector may carry out an inspection in order to —
   (a) check compliance with regulations under section 12 which relate to animals bred or kept for farming purposes;
   (b) ascertain whether any offence under or by virtue of this Act has been or is being committed in relation to such animals.

(2) An inspector may enter premises which he reasonably believes to be premises on which animals are bred or kept for farming purposes in order to carry out an inspection under subsection (1).

(3) Subsection (2) does not authorise entry to any part of premises which is used as a private dwelling.

(4) Subject to subsection (5), a justice of the peace may, on the application of an inspector, issue a warrant authorising an inspector to enter premises, if necessary using reasonable force, in order to carry out an inspection under subsection (1).

(5) The power to issue a warrant under subsection (4) is exercisable only if the justice of the peace is satisfied —
   (a) that it is reasonable to carry out an inspection on the premises, and
   (b) that section 52 is satisfied in relation to the premises.

29 Inspection relating to Community obligations

(1) An inspector may carry out an inspection in order to check compliance with regulations under section 12 which implement a Community obligation.

(2) An inspector may enter any premises in order to carry out an inspection under subsection (1).

(3) Subsection (2) does not authorise entry to any part of premises which is used as a private dwelling.

Prosecutions

30 Power of local authority to prosecute offences

A local authority in England or Wales may prosecute proceedings for any offence under this Act.

445

31   Time limits for prosecutions

(1)   Notwithstanding anything in section 127(1) of the Magistrates' Courts Act 1980
       (c. 43), a magistrates' court may try an information relating to an offence under
       this Act if the information is laid —
       (a)   before the end of the period of three years beginning with the date of
              the commission of the offence, and
       (b)   before the end of the period of six months beginning with the date on
              which evidence which the prosecutor thinks is sufficient to justify the
              proceedings comes to his knowledge.

(2)   For the purposes of subsection (1)(b) —
       (a)   a certificate signed by or on behalf of the prosecutor and stating the
              date on which such evidence came to his knowledge shall be conclusive
              evidence of that fact, and
       (b)   a certificate stating that matter and purporting to be so signed shall be
              treated as so signed unless the contrary is proved.

Post-conviction powers

32   Imprisonment or fine

(1)   A person guilty of an offence under any of sections 4, 5, 6(1) and (2), 7 and 8
       shall be liable on summary conviction to —
       (a)   imprisonment for a term not exceeding 51 weeks, or
       (b)   a fine not exceeding £20,000,
       or to both.

(2)   A person guilty of an offence under section 9, 13(6) or 34(9) shall be liable on
       summary conviction to —
       (a)   imprisonment for a term not exceeding 51 weeks, or
       (b)   a fine not exceeding level 5 on the standard scale,
       or to both.

(3)   A person guilty of an offence under regulations under section 12 or 13 shall be
       liable on summary conviction to such penalty by way of imprisonment or fine
       as may be provided by regulations under that section.

(4)   A person guilty of any other offence under this Act shall be liable on summary
       conviction to —
       (a)   imprisonment for a term not exceeding 51 weeks, or
       (b)   a fine not exceeding level 4 on the standard scale,
       or to both.

(5)   In relation to an offence committed before the commencement of section 281(5)
       of the Criminal Justice Act 2003 (c. 44), the reference in each of subsections
       (1)(a), (2)(a) and (4)(a) to 51 weeks is to be read as a reference to 6 months.

33   Deprivation

(1)   If the person convicted of an offence under any of sections 4, 5, 6(1) and (2), 7,
       8 and 9 is the owner of an animal in relation to which the offence was
       committed, the court by or before which he is convicted may, instead of or in

addition to dealing with him in any other way, make an order depriving him of ownership of the animal and for its disposal.

(2) Where the owner of an animal is convicted of an offence under section 34(9) because ownership of the animal is in breach of a disqualification under section 34(2), the court by or before which he is convicted may, instead of or in addition to dealing with him in any other way, make an order depriving him of ownership of the animal and for its disposal.

(3) Where the animal in respect of which an order under subsection (1) or (2) is made has any dependent offspring, the order may include provision depriving the person to whom it relates of ownership of the offspring and for its disposal.

(4) Where a court makes an order under subsection (1) or (2), it may —

   (a) appoint a person to carry out, or arrange for the carrying out of, the order;

   (b) require any person who has possession of an animal to which the order applies to deliver it up to enable the order to be carried out;

   (c) give directions with respect to the carrying out of the order;

   (d) confer additional powers (including power to enter premises where an animal to which the order applies is being kept) for the purpose of, or in connection with, the carrying out of the order;

   (e) order the offender to reimburse the expenses of carrying out the order.

(5) Directions under subsection (4)(c) may —

   (a) specify the manner in which an animal is to be disposed of, or

   (b) delegate the decision about the manner in which an animal is to be disposed of to a person appointed under subsection (4)(a).

(6) Where a court decides not to make an order under subsection (1) or (2) in relation to an offender, it shall —

   (a) give its reasons for the decision in open court, and

   (b) if it is a magistrates' court, cause them to be entered in the register of its proceedings.

(7) Subsection (6) does not apply where the court makes an order under section 34(1) in relation to the offender.

(8) In subsection (1), the reference to an animal in relation to which an offence was committed includes, in the case of an offence under section 8, an animal which took part in an animal fight in relation to which the offence was committed.

(9) In this section, references to disposing of an animal include destroying it.

34 Disqualification

(1) If a person is convicted of an offence to which this section applies, the court by or before which he is convicted may, instead of or in addition to dealing with him in any other way, make an order disqualifying him under any one or more of subsections (2) to (4) for such period as it thinks fit.

(2) Disqualification under this subsection disqualifies a person —

   (a) from owning animals,

   (b) from keeping animals,

   (c) from participating in the keeping of animals, and

(d)   from being party to an arrangement under which he is entitled to control or influence the way in which animals are kept.

(3)   Disqualification under this subsection disqualifies a person from dealing in animals.

(4)   Disqualification under this subsection disqualifies a person —
    (a)   from transporting animals, and
    (b)   from arranging for the transport of animals.

(5)   Disqualification under subsection (2), (3) or (4) may be imposed in relation to animals generally, or in relation to animals of one or more kinds.

(6)   The court by which an order under subsection (1) is made may specify a period during which the offender may not make an application under section 43(1) for termination of the order.

(7)   The court by which an order under subsection (1) is made may —
    (a)   suspend the operation of the order pending an appeal, or
    (b)   where it appears to the court that the offender owns or keeps an animal to which the order applies, suspend the operation of the order, and of any order made under section 35 in connection with the disqualification, for such period as it thinks necessary for enabling alternative arrangements to be made in respect of the animal.

(8)   Where a court decides not to make an order under subsection (1) in relation to an offender, it shall —
    (a)   give its reasons for the decision in open court, and
    (b)   if it is a magistrates' court, cause them to be entered in the register of its proceedings.

(9)   A person who breaches a disqualification imposed by an order under subsection (1) commits an offence.

(10)   This section applies to an offence under any of sections 4, 5, 6(1) and (2), 7, 8, 9 and 13(6) and subsection (9).

35   Seizure of animals in connection with disqualification

(1)   Where —
    (a)   a court makes an order under section 34(1), and
    (b)   it appears to the court that the person to whom the order applies owns or keeps any animal contrary to the disqualification imposed by the order,
it may order that all animals he owns or keeps contrary to the disqualification be taken into possession.

(2)   Where a person is convicted of an offence under section 34(9) because of owning or keeping an animal in breach of disqualification under section 34(2), the court by or before which he is convicted may order that all animals he owns or keeps in breach of the disqualification be taken into possession.

(3)   An order under subsection (1) or (2), so far as relating to any animal owned by the person subject to disqualification, shall have effect as an order for the disposal of the animal.

(4)   Any animal taken into possession in pursuance of an order under subsection (1) or (2) that is not owned by the person subject to disqualification shall be dealt with in such manner as the appropriate court may order.

(5)   A court may not make an order for disposal under subsection (4) unless —
    (a)   it has given the owner of the animal an opportunity to be heard, or
    (b)   it is satisfied that it is not reasonably practicable to communicate with the owner.

(6)   Where a court makes an order under subsection (4) for the disposal of an animal, the owner may —
    (a)   in the case of an order made by a magistrates' court, appeal against the order to the Crown Court;
    (b)   in the case of an order made by the Crown Court, appeal against the order to the Court of Appeal.

(7)   In subsection (4), the reference to the appropriate court is to —
    (a)   the court which made the order under subsection (1) or (2), or
    (b)   in the case of an order made by a magistrates' court, to a magistrates' court for the same local justice area as that court.

(8)   In this section, references to disposing of an animal include destroying it.

36   Section 35: supplementary

(1)   The court by which an order under section 35 is made may —
    (a)   appoint a person to carry out, or arrange for the carrying out of, the order;
    (b)   require any person who has possession of an animal to which the order applies to deliver it up to enable the order to be carried out;
    (c)   give directions with respect to the carrying out of the order;
    (d)   confer additional powers (including power to enter premises where an animal to which the order applies is being kept) for the purpose of, or in connection with, the carrying out of the order;
    (e)   order the person subject to disqualification, or another person, to reimburse the expenses of carrying out the order.

(2)   Directions under subsection (1)(c) may —
    (a)   specify the manner in which an animal is to be disposed of, or
    (b)   delegate the decision about the manner in which an animal is to be disposed of to a person appointed under subsection (1)(a).

(3)   In determining how to exercise its powers under section 35 and this section, the court shall have regard, amongst other things, to —
    (a)   the desirability of protecting the value of any animal to which the order applies, and
    (b)   the desirability of avoiding increasing any expenses which a person may be ordered to reimburse.

(4)   In determining how to exercise a power delegated under subsection (2)(b), a person shall have regard, amongst other things, to the things mentioned in subsection (3)(a) and (b).

(5)   If the owner of an animal ordered to be disposed of under section 35 is subject to a liability by virtue of subsection (1)(e), any amount to which he is entitled

as a result of sale of the animal may be reduced by an amount equal to that liability.

37 Destruction in the interests of the animal

(1) The court by or before which a person is convicted of an offence under any of sections 4, 5, 6(1) and (2), 7, 8(1) and (2) and 9 may order the destruction of an animal in relation to which the offence was committed if it is satisfied, on the basis of evidence given by a veterinary surgeon, that it is appropriate to do so in the interests of the animal.

(2) A court may not make an order under subsection (1) unless —
    (a) it has given the owner of the animal an opportunity to be heard, or
    (b) it is satisfied that it is not reasonably practicable to communicate with the owner.

(3) Where a court makes an order under subsection (1), it may —
    (a) appoint a person to carry out, or arrange for the carrying out of, the order;
    (b) require a person who has possession of the animal to deliver it up to enable the order to be carried out;
    (c) give directions with respect to the carrying out of the order (including directions about how the animal is to be dealt with until it is destroyed);
    (d) confer additional powers (including power to enter premises where the animal is being kept) for the purpose of, or in connection with, the carrying out of the order;
    (e) order the offender or another person to reimburse the expenses of carrying out the order.

(4) Where a court makes an order under subsection (1), each of the offender and, if different, the owner of the animal may —
    (a) in the case of an order made by a magistrates' court, appeal against the order to the Crown Court;
    (b) in the case of an order made by the Crown Court, appeal against the order to the Court of Appeal.

(5) Subsection (4) does not apply if the court by which the order is made directs that it is appropriate in the interests of the animal that the carrying out of the order should not be delayed.

(6) In subsection (1), the reference to an animal in relation to which an offence was committed includes, in the case of an offence under section 8(1) or (2), an animal which took part in an animal fight in relation to which the offence was committed.

38 Destruction of animals involved in fighting offences

(1) The court by or before which a person is convicted of an offence under section 8(1) or (2) may order the destruction of an animal in relation to which the offence was committed on grounds other than the interests of the animal.

(2) A court may not make an order under subsection (1) unless —
    (a) it has given the owner of the animal an opportunity to be heard, or
    (b) it is satisfied that it is not reasonably practicable to communicate with the owner.

(3) Where a court makes an order under subsection (1), it may —

    (a) appoint a person to carry out, or arrange for the carrying out of, the order;

    (b) require a person who has possession of the animal to deliver it up to enable the order to be carried out;

    (c) give directions with respect to the carrying out of the order (including directions about how the animal is to be dealt with until it is destroyed);

    (d) confer additional powers (including power to enter premises where the animal is being kept) for the purpose of, or in connection with, the carrying out of the order;

    (e) order the offender or another person to reimburse the expenses of carrying out the order.

(4) Where a court makes an order under subsection (1) in relation to an animal which is owned by a person other than the offender, that person may —

    (a) in the case of an order made by a magistrates' court, appeal against the order to the Crown Court;

    (b) in the case of an order made by the Crown Court, appeal against the order to the Court of Appeal.

(5) In subsection (1), the reference to an animal in relation to which the offence was committed includes an animal which took part in an animal fight in relation to which the offence was committed.

39 Reimbursement of expenses relating to animals involved in fighting offences

(1) The court by or before which a person is convicted of an offence under section 8(1) or (2) may order the offender or another person to reimburse any expenses incurred by the police in connection with the keeping of an animal in relation to which the offence was committed.

(2) In subsection (1), the reference to an animal in relation to which the offence was committed includes an animal which took part in a fight in relation to which the offence was committed.

40 Forfeiture of equipment used in offences

(1) Where a person is convicted of an offence under any of sections 4, 5, 6(1) and (2), 7 and 8, the court by or before which he is convicted may order any qualifying item which is shown to the satisfaction of the court to relate to the offence to be —

    (a) forfeited, and

    (b) destroyed or dealt with in such manner as may be specified in the order.

(2) The reference in subsection (1) to any qualifying item is —

    (a) in the case of a conviction for an offence under section 4, to anything designed or adapted for causing suffering to an animal;

    (b) in the case of a conviction for an offence under section 5, to anything designed or adapted for carrying out a prohibited procedure on an animal;

    (c) in the case of a conviction for an offence under section 6(1) or (2), to anything designed or adapted for removing the whole or any part of a dog's tail;

(d) in the case of a conviction for an offence under section 7, to anything designed or adapted for administering any drug or substance to an animal;

(e) in the case of a conviction for an offence under section 8(1) or (2), to anything designed or adapted for use in connection with an animal fight;

(f) in the case of a conviction for an offence under section 8(3), to a video recording of an animal fight, including anything on or in which the recording is kept.

(3) The court shall not order anything to be forfeited under subsection (1) if a person claiming to be the owner of it or otherwise interested in it applies to be heard by the court, unless he has been given an opportunity to show cause why the order should not be made.

(4) An expression used in any of paragraphs (a) to (f) of subsection (2) has the same meaning as in the provision referred to in that paragraph.

41 Orders under section 33, 35, 37, 38 or 40: pending appeals

(1) Nothing may be done under an order under section 33, 35, 37 or 38 with respect to an animal or an order under section 40 unless —

(a) the period for giving notice of appeal against the order has expired,

(b) the period for giving notice of appeal against the conviction on which the order was made has expired, and

(c) if the order or conviction is the subject of an appeal, the appeal has been determined or withdrawn.

(2) Subsection (1) does not apply to an order under section 37(1) if the order is the subject of a direction under subsection (5) of that section.

(3) Where the effect of an order is suspended under subsection (1) —

(a) no requirement imposed or directions given in connection with the order shall have effect, but

(b) the court may give directions about how any animal to which the order applies is to be dealt with during the suspension.

(4) Directions under subsection (3)(b) may, in particular —

(a) authorise the animal to be taken into possession;

(b) authorise the removal of the animal to a place of safety;

(c) authorise the animal to be cared for either on the premises where it was being kept when it was taken into possession or at some other place;

(d) appoint a person to carry out, or arrange for the carrying out, of the directions;

(e) require any person who has possession of the animal to deliver it up for the purposes of the directions;

(f) confer additional powers (including power to enter premises where the animal is being kept) for the purpose of, or in connection with, the carrying out of the directions;

(g) provide for the recovery of any expenses in relation to removal or care of the animal which are incurred in carrying out the directions.

(5) Any expenses a person is directed to pay under subsection (4)(g) shall be recoverable summarily as a civil debt.

(6) Where the effect of an order under section 33 is suspended under subsection (1) the person to whom the order relates may not sell or part with any animal to which the order applies.

(7) Failure to comply with subsection (6) is an offence.

42 Orders with respect to licences

(1) If a person is convicted of an offence under any of sections 4, 5, 6(1) and (2), 7 to 9, 11 and 13(6), the court by or before which he is convicted may, instead of or in addition to dealing with him in any other way —

    (a) make an order cancelling any licence held by him;

    (b) make an order disqualifying him, for such period as it thinks fit, from holding a licence.

(2) Disqualification under subsection (1)(b) may be imposed in relation to licences generally or in relation to licences of one or more kinds.

(3) The court by which an order under subsection (1)(b) is made may specify a period during which the offender may not make an application under section 43(1) for termination of the order.

(4) The court by which an order under subsection (1) is made may suspend the operation of the order pending an appeal.

43 Termination of disqualification under section 34 or 42

(1) A person who is disqualified by virtue of an order under section 34 or 42 may apply to the appropriate court for the termination of the order.

(2) No application under subsection (1) may be made —

    (a) before the end of the period of one year beginning with the date on which the order is made,

    (b) where a previous application under that subsection has been made in relation to the same order, before the end of the period of one year beginning with the date on which the previous application was determined, or

    (c) before the end of any period specified under section 34(6), 42(3) or subsection (5) below in relation to the order.

(3) On an application under subsection (1), the court may —

    (a) terminate the disqualification,

    (b) vary the disqualification so as to make it less onerous, or

    (c) refuse the application.

(4) When determining an application under subsection (1), the court shall have regard to the character of the applicant, his conduct since the imposition of the disqualification and any other circumstances of the case.

(5) Where the court refuses an application under subsection (1), it may specify a period during which the applicant may not make a further application under that subsection in relation to the order concerned.

(6) The court may order an applicant under subsection (1) to pay all or part of the costs of the application.

(7) In subsection (1), the reference to the appropriate court is to —

(a) the court which made the order under section 34 or 42, or

(b) in the case of an order made by a magistrates' court, to a magistrates' court acting for the same local justice area as that court.

44 Orders made on conviction for reimbursement of expenses

Where an order is made under section 33(4)(e), 36(1)(e), 37(3)(e), 38(3)(e) or 39(1), the expenses that are required by the order to be reimbursed shall not be regarded for the purposes of the Magistrates' Courts Act 1980 (c. 43) as a sum adjudged to be paid by a summary conviction, but shall be recoverable summarily as a civil debt.

45 Orders for reimbursement of expenses: right of appeal for non-offenders

(1) Where a court makes an order to which this section applies, the person against whom the order is made may —

(a) in the case of an order made by a magistrates' court, appeal against the order to the Crown Court;

(b) in the case of an order made by the Crown Court, appeal against the order to the Court of Appeal.

(2) This section applies to —

(a) an order under section 36(1)(e) against a person other than the person subject to disqualification, and

(b) an order under section 37(3)(e), 38(3)(e) or 39(1) against a person other than the offender.

Scotland

46 Effect in Scotland of disqualification under section 34

(1) Disqualification by virtue of an order under section 34(1) has effect in relation to Scotland.

(2) A person who breaches a disqualification under section 34 commits an offence.

(3) A person guilty of an offence under subsection (2) is liable on summary conviction to —

(a) imprisonment for a term not exceeding 6 months, or

(b) a fine not exceeding level 5 on the standard scale,

or to both.

47 Deprivation orders in connection with offence under section 46(2)

(1) Where a person is convicted of an offence under section 46(2) because of owning or keeping an animal in breach of disqualification under section 34(2), the convicting court may make an order (in this section and sections 49 and 50 referred to as a "deprivation order") in respect of any animal in relation to which the offence was committed.

(2) A deprivation order is an order —

(a) depriving a person of possession or ownership (or both) of an animal, and

(b) for —

      (i)   the destruction,

      (ii)   the sale, or

      (iii) another disposal,

of the animal.

(3) Where the court decides not to make a deprivation order, it must state its reasons.

(4) A deprivation order may be made in addition to, or instead of, any other penalty or order which may be imposed in relation to the offence.

(5) A deprivation order may make provision in respect of any dependent offspring of an animal to which it applies.

(6) A deprivation order may include —

    (a)   provision —

        (i)   appointing a person who is to secure that the order is carried out,

        (ii)   requiring any person possessing an animal to which the order applies to give it up to a person appointed under sub-paragraph (i),

    (b)   provision authorising —

        (i)   a person appointed under paragraph (a)(i), and

        (ii)   any person acting on that person's behalf,

    to enter, for the purposes of securing that the order is carried out, any premises where an animal to which the order applies is kept,

    (c)   such other provisions as the court considers appropriate in connection with the order.

(7) Provision under subsection (6)(c) may, in particular —

    (a)   require reimbursement of any expenses reasonably incurred in carrying out the order,

    (b)   relate to the retention of any proceeds of the disposal.

(8) The court may not make a deprivation order which involves the destruction of an animal unless it is satisfied, on evidence provided (orally or in writing) by a veterinary surgeon, that destruction would be in the interests of the animal.

(9) Before making a deprivation order, the court must give the owner of the animal concerned an opportunity to make representations unless it is not practicable for it to do so.

48   Seizure orders where disqualification breached: Scotland

(1) Where the court is satisfied that a person who is subject to disqualification under section 34 owns or keeps an animal in breach of the disqualification, the court may make an order (in this section and sections 49 and 50 referred to as a "seizure order") in respect of all animals which the person owns or keeps in breach of the disqualification.

(2) A seizure order may be made —

    (a)   on summary application by an inspector,

    (b)   even if proceedings have not been, or are not likely to be, taken against the person for an offence under section 46(2).

(3)   A seizure order is an order —
- (a)   depriving a person of possession or ownership (or both) of an animal, and
- (b)   for —
    - (i)   the destruction,
    - (ii)   the sale, or
    - (iii) another disposal,
    of the animal.

(4)   A seizure order may include —
- (a)   provision —
    - (i)   appointing a person who is to secure that the order is carried out,
    - (ii)   requiring any person possessing an animal to which the order applies to give it up to a person appointed under sub-paragraph (i),
- (b)   provision authorising —
    - (i)   a person appointed under paragraph (a)(i), and
    - (ii)   any person acting on that person's behalf,
    to enter, for the purposes of securing that the order is carried out, any premises where an animal to which the order applies is kept,
- (c)   such other provision as the court considers appropriate in connection with the order.

(5)   Provision under subsection (4)(c) may, in particular —
- (a)   require reimbursement of any expenses reasonably incurred in carrying out the order,
- (b)   relate to the retention of any proceeds of the disposal.

(6)   The court may not make a seizure order which involves the destruction of an animal unless it is satisfied, on evidence provided (orally or in writing) by a veterinary surgeon, that destruction would be in the interests of the animal.

(7)   Before making a seizure order, the court must give the owner of the animals concerned an opportunity to make representations unless it is not practicable for it to do so.

(8)   In determining whether or how to make a seizure order, the court must have regard to the desirability of —
- (a)   protecting the value of any animal to which the order applies, and
- (b)   avoiding increasing any expenses which a person may be required to reimburse.

(9)   When an application is made under subsection (2)(a), the court may make an order under this subsection (an "interim order") containing such provision as the court considers appropriate in relation to the keeping of an animal until the application is finally determined.

(10) Subsections (4), (5)(a) and (8) apply in relation to an interim order as they apply in relation to a seizure order.

(11) In subsection (2)(a), an "inspector" is a person —
- (a)   appointed as inspector by the Scottish Ministers, or authorised by them, for the purposes of this section, or

(b)   appointed as inspector by a local authority for the purposes of this section.

(12)   In subsection (11)(b), a "local authority" means a council constituted under section 2 of the Local Government etc. (Scotland) Act 1994 (c. 39).

49   Appeals against deprivation orders and seizure orders

(1)   Any deprivation order is, for the purposes of any appeal under the Criminal Procedure (Scotland) Act 1995 (c. 46), to be treated as a sentence.

(2)   Where a deprivation order is made, any person (apart from a person who may appeal against the order by virtue of subsection (1)) who has an interest in any animal to which the order applies may appeal to the High Court of Justiciary against the order by the same procedure as applies under subsection (1) in relation to a deprivation order.

(3)   The disqualified person by reference to whom a seizure order is made, or any person (apart from that disqualified person) who entered the process prior to the making of the order, may appeal to the sheriff principal against the order.

(4)   The operation of any deprivation order or seizure order is suspended until —
       (a)   any period for an appeal against the order has expired,
       (b)   the period for an appeal against the conviction on which the order depends has expired, and
       (c)   any appeal against the order or that conviction has been withdrawn or finally determined.

(5)   Where the operation of a deprivation order or seizure order is suspended under subsection (4), or such an order is not executable because decree has not been extracted, the court which made the order may make an order under this subsection (an "interim order") containing such provisions as the court considers appropriate in relation to the keeping of an animal for so long as the first-mentioned order remains suspended or inexecutable.

(6)   An interim order may, in particular —
       (a)   make provision —
              (i)   appointing a person who is to secure that the order is carried out,
              (ii)   requiring any person possessing an animal to which the order applies to give it up to a person appointed under sub-paragraph (i),
       (b)   make provision authorising —
              (i)   a person appointed under paragraph (a)(i), and
              (ii)   any person acting on that person's behalf,
              to enter, for the purposes of securing that the order is carried out, any premises where an animal to which the order applies is kept,
       (c)   for reimbursement of any expenses reasonably incurred in carrying out the order.

(7)   In determining whether or how to make an interim order, the court must have regard to the desirability of —
       (a)   protecting the value of any animal to which the order applies, and
       (b)   avoiding increasing any expenses which a person may be required to reimburse.

50 Deprivation orders, seizure orders and interim orders: offences

(1) Where the operation of a deprivation order is suspended under section 49(4), a person commits an offence if the person sells or otherwise parts with an animal to which the order applies.

(2) A person commits an offence if the person intentionally obstructs a person in the carrying out of —

(a) a deprivation order,

(b) a seizure order,

(c) an interim order under section 48(9) or 49(5).

(3) A person guilty of an offence under subsection (1) or (2) is liable on summary conviction to —

(a) imprisonment for a term not exceeding 6 months, or

(b) a fine not exceeding level 5 on the standard scale,

or to both.

General

51 Inspectors

(1) In this Act, "inspector", in the context of any provision, means a person appointed to be an inspector for the purposes of that provision by —

(a) the appropriate national authority, or

(b) a local authority.

(2) In appointing a person to be an inspector for purposes of this Act, a local authority shall have regard to guidance issued by the appropriate national authority.

(3) The appropriate national authority may, in connection with guidance under subsection (2), draw up a list of persons whom the authority considers suitable for appointment by a local authority to be an inspector for purposes of this Act.

(4) A person may be included in a list under subsection (3) as suitable for appointment as an inspector for all the purposes of this Act or only for such one or more of those purposes as may be specified in the list.

(5) An inspector shall not be liable in any civil or criminal proceedings for anything done in the purported performance of his functions under this Act if the court is satisfied that the act was done in good faith and that there were reasonable grounds for doing it.

(6) Relief from liability of an inspector under subsection (5) shall not affect any liability of any other person in respect of the inspector's act.

52 Conditions for grant of warrant

(1) This section is satisfied in relation to premises if any of the following four conditions is met.

(2) The first condition is that the whole of the premises is used as a private dwelling and the occupier has been informed of the decision to apply for a warrant.

(3) The second condition is that any part of the premises is not used as a private dwelling and that each of the following applies to the occupier of the premises —

    (a) he has been informed of the decision to seek entry to the premises and of the reasons for that decision;

    (b) he has failed to allow entry to the premises on being requested to do so by an inspector or a constable;

    (c) he has been informed of the decision to apply for a warrant.

(4) The third condition is that —

    (a) the premises are unoccupied or the occupier is absent, and

    (b) notice of intention to apply for a warrant has been left in a conspicuous place on the premises.

(5) The fourth condition is that it is inappropriate to inform the occupier of the decision to apply for a warrant because —

    (a) it would defeat the object of entering the premises, or

    (b) entry is required as a matter of urgency.

53 Powers of entry, inspection and search: supplementary

Schedule 2 (which makes supplementary provision in relation to powers of entry, inspection and search) has effect.

54 Power to stop and detain vehicles

(1) A constable in uniform or, if accompanied by such a constable, an inspector may stop and detain a vehicle for the purpose of entering and searching it in the exercise of a power conferred —

    (a) by section 19(1), or

    (b) by a warrant under section 19(4) or 23(1).

(2) A constable in uniform may stop and detain a vehicle for the purpose of entering and searching it in the exercise of a power conferred —

    (a) by section 22(2), or

    (b) by a warrant under section 22(4).

(3) If accompanied by a constable in uniform, an inspector may stop and detain a vehicle for the purpose of entering it and carrying out an inspection in the exercise of a power conferred —

    (a) by section 26(2), 27(2), 28(2) or 29(2), or

    (b) by a warrant under section 28(4).

(4) A vehicle may be detained for as long as is reasonably required to permit a search or inspection to be carried out (including the exercise of any related power under this Act) either at the place where the vehicle was first detained or nearby.

55 Power to detain vessels, aircraft and hovercraft

(1) Where an inspector appointed by the appropriate national authority certifies in writing that he is satisfied that an offence under or by virtue of this Act is being or has been committed on board a vessel in port, the vessel may be detained.

(2) A certificate under subsection (1) shall —

    (a) specify each offence to which it relates, and

    (b) set out the inspector's reasons for being satisfied that each offence to which it relates is being or has been committed.

(3) Section 284 of the Merchant Shipping Act 1995 (c. 21) (which provides for enforcement of the detention of a ship under that Act by specified officers) shall apply as if the power of detention under subsection (1) were conferred by that Act.

(4) An officer who detains a vessel in reliance on a certificate under subsection (1) shall as soon as is reasonably practicable give a copy of it to the master or person in charge of the vessel.

(5) A vessel may be detained under subsection (1) until the appropriate national authority otherwise directs.

(6) The appropriate national authority may by regulations —

    (a) apply this section to aircraft or hovercraft, with such modifications as the authority thinks fit, or

    (b) make such other provision for the detention of aircraft or hovercraft in relation to offences under or by virtue of this Act as the authority thinks fit.

56   Obtaining of documents in connection with carrying out orders etc.

(1) Where —

    (a) an order under section 20(1), 33(1) or (2), 35(1) or (2) or 37(1) has effect, and

    (b) the owner of an animal to which the order relates has in his possession, or under his control, documents which are relevant to the carrying out of the order or any directions given in connection with it,

the owner shall, if so required by a person authorised to carry out the order, deliver the documents to that person as soon as practicable and in any event before the end of the period of 10 days beginning with the date on which he is notified of the requirement.

(2) Where —

    (a) directions under section 41(3)(b) have effect, and

    (b) the owner of an animal to which the directions relate has in his possession, or under his control, documents which are relevant to the carrying out of the directions,

the owner shall, if so required by a person authorised to carry out the directions, deliver the documents to that person as soon as practicable and in any event before the end of the period of 10 days beginning with the date on which he is notified of the requirement.

(3) A person who fails without reasonable excuse to comply with subsection (1) or (2) commits an offence.

57   Offences by bodies corporate

(1) Where an offence under this Act is committed by a body corporate and is proved to have been committed with the consent or connivance of or to be attributable to any neglect on the part of —

(a) any director, manager, secretary or other similar officer of the body corporate, or

(b) any person who was purporting to act in any such capacity,

he (as well as the body corporate) commits the offence and shall be liable to be proceeded against and punished accordingly.

(2) Where the affairs of a body corporate are managed by its members, subsection (1) applies in relation to the acts and defaults of a member in connection with his functions of management as if he were a director of the body corporate.

58 Scientific research

(1) Nothing in this Act applies to anything lawfully done under the Animals (Scientific Procedures) Act 1986 (c. 14).

(2) No power of entry, inspection or search conferred by or under this Act, except for any such power conferred by section 28, may be exercised in relation to a place which is—

(a) designated under section 6 of the Animals (Scientific Procedures) Act 1986 as a scientific procedure establishment, or

(b) designated under section 7 of that Act as a breeding establishment or as a supplying establishment.

(3) Section 9 does not apply in relation to an animal which—

(a) is being kept, at a place designated under section 6 of the Animals (Scientific Procedures) Act 1986 as a scientific procedure establishment, for use in regulated procedures,

(b) is being kept, at a place designated under section 7 of that Act as a breeding establishment, for use for breeding animals for use in regulated procedures,

(c) is being kept at such a place, having been bred there for use in regulated procedures, or

(d) is being kept, at a place designated under section 7 of that Act as a supplying establishment, for the purpose of being supplied for use elsewhere in regulated procedures.

(4) In subsection (3), "regulated procedure" has the same meaning as in the Animals (Scientific Procedures) Act 1986.

59 Fishing

Nothing in this Act applies in relation to anything which occurs in the normal course of fishing.

60 Crown application

(1) Subject to the provisions of this section, this Act and regulations and orders made under it shall bind the Crown.

(2) No contravention by the Crown of any provision made by or under this Act shall make the Crown criminally liable; but the High Court may declare unlawful any act or omission of the Crown which constitutes such a contravention.

(3)   Notwithstanding subsection (2), the provisions of this Act and of regulations and orders made under it shall apply to persons in the service of the Crown as they apply to other persons.

(4)   If the Secretary of State certifies that it appears to him appropriate in the interests of national security that powers of entry conferred by or under this Act should not be exercisable in relation to Crown premises specified in the certificate, those powers shall not be exercisable in relation to those premises.

(5)   In subsection (4), "Crown premises" means premises held, or used, by or on behalf of the Crown.

(6)   No power of entry conferred by or under this Act may be exercised in relation to land belonging to Her Majesty in right of Her private estates.

(7)   In subsection (6), the reference to Her Majesty's private estates shall be construed in accordance with section 1 of the Crown Private Estates Act 1862 (c. 37).

61   Orders and regulations

(1)   Any power of the Secretary of State, the National Assembly for Wales or the Scottish Ministers to make orders or regulations under this Act, except the power under section 17(1) of the National Assembly for Wales, is exercisable by statutory instrument.

(2)   No regulations under section 1(3), 5(4), 6, 12 or 13 shall be made by the Secretary of State unless a draft of the instrument containing the regulations has been laid before, and approved by a resolution of, each House of Parliament.

(3)   No order under section 17(1) shall be made by the Secretary of State unless a draft of the instrument containing the order has been laid before Parliament.

(4)   Subsection (3) does not apply in relation to an order revoking a code of practice in connection with its replacement by a new one.

(5)   A statutory instrument containing regulations under section 55(6) made by the Secretary of State shall be subject to annulment in pursuance of a resolution of either House of Parliament.

62   General interpretation

(1)   In this Act—
    "animal" has the meaning given by section 1(1);
    "appropriate national authority" means—
        (a)   in relation to England, the Secretary of State;
        (b)   in relation to Wales, the National Assembly for Wales;
    "enactment" includes an enactment contained in subordinate legislation (within the meaning of the Interpretation Act 1978 (c. 30));
    "licence" means a licence for the purposes of section 13;
    "local authority" means—
        (a)   in relation to England, a county council, a district council, a London borough council, the Common Council of the City of London or the Council of the Isles of Scilly;

462

    (b) in relation to Wales, a county council or a county borough council;

"premises" includes any place and, in particular, includes —

    (a) any vehicle, vessel, aircraft or hovercraft;

    (b) any tent or movable structure;

"protected animal" has the meaning given by section 2;

"'suffering" means physical or mental suffering and related expressions shall be construed accordingly;

"veterinary surgeon" means a person registered in the register of veterinary surgeons, or the supplementary veterinary register, kept under the Veterinary Surgeons Act 1966 (c. 36).

(2) In this Act, references to the occupier of premises, in relation to any vehicle, vessel, aircraft or hovercraft, are to the person who appears to be in charge of the vehicle, vessel, aircraft or hovercraft, and "unoccupied" shall be construed accordingly.

(3) In this Act, references to a part of premises which is used as a private dwelling include any yard, garden, garage or outhouse which is used for purposes in connection with it.

(4) In this Act, references to responsibility, in relation to an animal, are to be read in accordance with section 3.

(5) In this Act, references to the needs of an animal are to be read in accordance with section 9(2).

(6) In this Act, references to a "relevant post-conviction power" are to a power conferred by —

    (a) section 33, 34, 37 or 42 of this Act,

    (b) section 4(2) of the Performing Animals (Regulation) Act 1925 (c. 38) (power to remove name from register under Act and disqualify from registration),

    (c) section 5(3) of the Pet Animals Act 1951 (c. 35) (power to cancel licence under Act and disqualify from carrying on licensable activity),

    (d) section 3(3) of the Animal Boarding Establishments Act 1963 (c. 43) (provision corresponding to that mentioned in paragraph (c) above),

    (e) section 4(3) of the Riding Establishments Act 1964 (c. 70) (further corresponding provision),

    (f) section 3(4) of the Guard Dogs Act 1975 (c. 50) (power to cancel licence under Act),

    (g) section 6(2) of the Dangerous Wild Animals Act 1976 (c. 38) (power to cancel licence under Act and disqualify from carrying on licensable activity), or

    (h) section 4(4) of the Zoo Licensing Act 1981 (c. 37) (power to refuse licence under Act for conviction for an offence).

63 Financial provisions

(1) There shall be paid out of money provided by Parliament —

    (a) any expenditure under this Act of the Secretary of State, and

    (b) any increase attributable to this Act in the sums payable out of money so provided under any other enactment.

(2)   There shall be paid into the Consolidated Fund any increase attributable to this Act in the sums payable into that Fund under any other enactment.

64   Minor and consequential amendments

Schedule 3 (minor and consequential amendments) has effect.

65   Repeals

The enactments specified in Schedule 4 are hereby repealed to the extent specified.

66   Transition

(1)   Each of the Secretary of State, the National Assembly for Wales and the Scottish Ministers may by order make such transitional provision or savings as are considered necessary or expedient in connection with the coming into force of any provision of this Act.

(2)   Power under subsection (1) includes power to make different provision for different cases.

(3)   Section 34(9) shall apply in relation to a disqualification imposed by an order under section 1 of the Protection of Animals (Amendment) Act 1954 (c. 40) (power to disqualify persons convicted of cruelty to animals) as it applies in relation to a disqualification imposed by an order under section 34(1).

(4)   In relation to a person convicted of an offence under section 34(9) by virtue of breaching a disqualification imposed by an order under section 1 of the Protection of Animals (Amendment) Act 1954, section 35(2) shall have effect with the substitution for the words from "owning" to "keeps" of "having custody of an animal in breach of disqualification under section 1 of the Protection of Animals (Amendment) Act 1954, the court by or before which he is convicted may order that all animals of which he has custody".

(5)   Section 43 shall apply in relation to a person who is disqualified by virtue of an order under section 1 of the Protection of Animals (Amendment) Act 1954 as it applies in relation to a person who is disqualified by virtue of an order under section 34 or 42.

(6)   In its application by virtue of subsection (5), section 43(2)(c) shall have effect with the omission of the words "section 34(6), 42(3) or".

67   Extent

(1)   Subject to the following provisions, this Act extends to England and Wales only.

(2)   Sections 46 to 50 and 68(2) extend to Scotland only.

(3)   The following provisions also extend to Scotland —
   (a)   sections 57 and 60(1) and (4) to (7), so far as relating to sections 46 to 50,
   (b)   section 61(1), so far as relating to sections 66 and 68,
   (c)   section 66(1) and (2), this section and sections 68(1), (3) and (4) and 69,
   (d)   paragraphs 2, 12 and 14 of Schedule 3, and section 64 so far as relating to them, and

(e)   such of the repeals in Schedule 4 as are mentioned in subsection (4), and section 65 so far as relating to them.

(4)   The repeals referred to are—

    (a)   in section 1(3) of the Protection of Animals Act 1934 (c. 21), the provision about the meaning of "horse" and "bull";

    (b)   in the Protection of Animals (Amendment) Act 1954 (c. 40) —

        (i)   in section 1(1), the words "the Protection of Animals Act 1911 or", and

        (ii)   in section 4(1)(a), the words from ", in relation to England" to "in relation to Scotland,";

    (c)   in the Protection of Animals (Anaesthetics) Act 1954 (c. 46), section 2(2) and Part 1 of Schedule 2;

    (d)   in the Abandonment of Animals Act 1960 (c. 43) —

        (i)   section 2(a), and

        (ii)   in section 3(2), the words "the Protection of Animals Acts 1911 to 1960, or" and the words ", as the case may be";

    (e)   in section 4(2) of the Animals (Cruel Poisons) Act 1962 (c. 26), the words from "and the Protection of Animals Acts 1911" to "and this Act";

    (f)   in the Protection of Animals (Anaesthetics) Act 1964 (c. 39), section 2(1)(a);

    (g)   in the Agriculture (Miscellaneous Provisions) Act 1968 (c. 34) —

        (i)   section 7(3), and

        (ii)   in section 8(5), the words "the Protection of Animals Acts 1911 to 1964 or".

(5)   The following provisions also extend to Northern Ireland—

    (a)   section 61(1), so far as relating to sections 66 and 68,

    (b)   section 66(1) and (2), this section and sections 68(1), (3) and (4) and 69, and

    (c)   paragraphs 12 and 14 of Schedule 3, and section 64 so far as relating to them.

68   Commencement

(1)   This section and sections 61, 67 and 69 shall come into force on the day on which this Act is passed.

(2)   Sections 46 to 50 shall come into force on such day as the Scottish Ministers may by order appoint.

(3)   The remaining provisions of this Act—

    (a)   so far as relating to England, Scotland or Northern Ireland, shall come into force on such day as the Secretary of State may by order appoint, and

    (b)   so far as relating to Wales, shall come into force on such day as the National Assembly for Wales may by order appoint.

(4)   Power under subsection (3) includes power to appoint different days for different purposes.

69 Short title

This Act may be cited as the Animal Welfare Act 2006.

SCHEDULES

SCHEDULE 1

REGULATIONS UNDER SECTION 13

PART 1

LICENCES FOR THE PURPOSES OF THE SECTION

Introductory

1   This Part has effect in relation to regulations under section 13(7) about licences for the purposes of section 13.

Licensing authority

2   Regulations shall provide for the licensing authority to be —
     (a)   a local authority, or
     (b)   the appropriate national authority.

3   Where the licensing authority is a local authority, regulations may require the licensing authority to have regard in carrying out its functions under the regulations to such guidance as may be issued by the appropriate national authority.

Period of licence

4   Regulations may, in particular —
     (a)   make provision about the period for which licences are to be granted;
     (b)   make provision, in connection with the death of the holder of a licence, for the continuation in force of the licence for such period and subject to such conditions as the regulations may provide.

5   Regulations may not provide for licences to be granted for a period of more than 3 years.

Exercise of licensing functions

6   Regulations may, in particular —
     (a)   require a licensing authority not to grant a licence unless satisfied as to a matter specified in the regulations;
     (b)   require a licensing authority to have regard, in deciding whether to grant a licence, to a matter specified in the regulations.

40

Animal Welfare Act 2006 (c. 45)
Schedule 1 — Regulations under section 13
Part 1 — Licences for the purposes of the section

7   Regulations shall make provision requiring a licensing authority not to grant a licence authorising the carrying on of an activity on specific premises unless the premises have been inspected as the regulations may provide.

Grant of licence subject to conditions

8   (1) Regulations may, in particular, make provision for the grant of a licence subject to conditions.

     (2) Provision of the kind mentioned in sub-paragraph (1) may —
         (a) enable a licensing authority to attach conditions to a licence;
         (b) require a licensing authority to attach to a licence conditions specified in the regulations.

Breach of licence condition

9   (1) Regulations may provide for breach of a condition of a licence to be an offence.

     (2) Regulations may not provide for an offence of breach of condition of a licence to be triable on indictment or punishable with —
         (a) imprisonment for a term exceeding 51 weeks, or
         (b) a fine exceeding level 5 on the standard scale.

     (3) Regulations may provide that an offence of breach of condition of a licence is to be treated as a relevant offence for the purposes of section 23.

     (4) Regulations may apply a relevant post-conviction power in relation to conviction for an offence of breach of condition of a licence.

Appeals

10   Regulations may, in particular, make provision for appeals in relation to decisions of a licensing authority under the regulations.

Fees

11   Regulations may include provision for fees or other charges in relation to the carrying out of functions of the licensing authority under the regulations.

PART 2

REGISTRATION FOR THE PURPOSES OF THE SECTION

Introductory

12   This Part has effect in relation to regulations under section 13(7) about registration for the purposes of section 13.

Registering authority

13   Regulations shall provide for the registering authority to be —
         (a) a local authority, or
         (b) the appropriate national authority.

Animal Welfare Act 2006 (c. 45)
Schedule 1 — Regulations under section 13
Part 2 — Registration for the purposes of the section

41

14 Where the registering authority is a local authority, regulations may require the registering authority to have regard in carrying out its functions under the regulations to such guidance as may be issued by the appropriate national authority.

Exercise of registration functions

15 Regulations may, in particular —

(a) require a registering authority not to register an applicant for registration unless satisfied as to a matter specified in the regulations;

(b) require a registering authority to have regard, in deciding whether to register an applicant for registration, to a matter specified in the regulations.

Appeals

16 Regulations may, in particular, make provision for appeals in relation to decisions of a registering authority under the regulations.

Fees

17 Regulations may include provision for fees or other charges in relation to the carrying out of functions of the registering authority under the regulations.

PART 3

SUPPLEMENTARY

18 Power to make regulations under section 13(7) includes power —

(a) to make provision for purposes other than the purpose of promoting the welfare of animals for which a person is responsible;

(b) to make different provision for different cases or areas;

(c) to provide for exemptions from a provision of the regulations, either subject to specified conditions or without conditions.

19 (1) Power to make regulations under section 13 includes power to make incidental, supplementary, consequential or transitional provision or savings.

(2) In the case of provision consequential on the repeal of an enactment specified in section 13(8), the power under sub-paragraph (1) includes power —

(a) to amend or repeal an enactment;

(b) to make provision for the purpose of continuing the effect of an enactment repealed under paragraph (a).

(3) The power under sub-paragraph (2)(b) includes power to provide that breach of a provision of the regulations is an offence, but does not include power to create an offence triable on indictment or punishable with —

(a) imprisonment for a term exceeding 51 weeks, or

(b) a fine exceeding level 5 on the standard scale.

SCHEDULE 2

Section 53

POWERS OF ENTRY, INSPECTION AND SEARCH: SUPPLEMENTARY

Safeguards etc. in connection with powers of entry conferred by warrant

1   (1) Sections 15 and 16 of the Police and Criminal Evidence Act 1984 (c. 60) shall have effect in relation to the issue of a warrant under section 19(4) or 23(1) to an inspector as they have effect in relation to the issue of a warrant under that provision to a constable.

  (2) In their application in relation to the issue of a warrant under section 19(4) or 23(1), sections 15 and 16 of that Act shall have effect with the following modifications.

  (3) In section 15 —
      (a)   in subsection (2), omit the words from the end of paragraph (a)(ii) to the end of paragraph (b);
      (b)   omit subsections (2A) and (5A);
      (c)   in subsection (5), omit the words from "unless" to the end;
      (d)   in subsection (6)(a), omit the words from the end of sub-paragraph (iii) to the end of sub-paragraph (iv);
      (e)   in subsection (7), omit the words from "(see" to the end.

  (4) In section 16 —
      (a)   omit subsections (3A) and (3B);
      (b)   in subsection (9), omit the words after paragraph (b).

2   (1) This paragraph and paragraph 3 have effect in relation to the issue to inspectors of warrants under section 28(4); and an entry on premises under such a warrant is unlawful unless it complies with this paragraph and paragraph 3.

  (2) Where an inspector applies for a warrant, he shall —
      (a)   state the ground on which he makes the application,
      (b)   state the enactment under which the warrant would be issued, and
      (c)   specify the premises which it is desired to enter.

  (3) An application for a warrant shall be made without notice and supported by an information in writing.

  (4) The inspector shall answer on oath any question that the justice of the peace hearing the application asks him.

  (5) A warrant shall authorise an entry on one occasion only.

  (6) A warrant shall specify —
      (a)   the name of the person who applies for it,
      (b)   the date on which it is issued, and
      (c)   the enactment under which it is issued.

  (7) Two copies shall be made of a warrant.

  (8) The copies shall be clearly certified as copies.

3   (1) A warrant may be executed by any inspector.

470

(2) A warrant may authorise persons to accompany any inspector who is executing it.

(3) A person authorised under sub-paragraph (2) has the same powers as the inspector whom he accompanies in respect of the execution of the warrant, but may exercise those powers only in the company, and under the supervision, of an inspector.

(4) Execution of a warrant must be within three months from the date of its issue.

(5) Execution of a warrant must be at a reasonable hour unless it appears to the inspector executing it that the purpose of entry may be frustrated on an entry at a reasonable hour.

(6) Where the occupier of premises which are to be entered under a warrant is present at the time when an inspector seeks to execute it, the inspector shall—

    (a) identify himself to the occupier and shall produce to him documentary evidence that he is an inspector,

    (b) produce the warrant to him, and

    (c) supply him with a copy of it.

(7) Where—

    (a) the occupier of premises which are to be entered under a warrant is not present when an inspector seeks to execute it, but

    (b) some other person who appears to the inspector to be in charge of the premises is present,

sub-paragraph (6) shall have effect as if any reference to the occupier were a reference to that other person.

(8) If there is no person present who appears to the inspector to be in charge of the premises, he shall leave a copy of the warrant in a prominent place on the premises.

(9) A warrant which—

    (a) has been executed, or

    (b) has not been executed within the time authorised for its execution,

shall be returned to the designated officer for the local justice area in which the justice of the peace who issued the warrant was acting when he issued it.

(10) A warrant which is returned under sub-paragraph (9) shall be retained by the officer to whom it is returned for 12 months from its return.

(11) If during the period for which a warrant is to be retained the occupier of the premises to which it relates asks to inspect it, he shall be allowed to do so.

Duty to produce evidence of identity

4   (1) This paragraph applies to a power of entry conferred by section 19(1), 22(2), 26(2), 27(2), 28(2) or 29(2).

    (2) A person may only exercise a power of entry to which this paragraph applies if on request—

        (a) he produces evidence of his identity and of his entitlement to exercise the power;

        (b) he outlines the purpose for which the power is exercised.

Power to take persons onto premises

5   In exercising a power to which paragraph 4 applies, a person may take with him onto the premises such persons as he thinks appropriate.

Duty to exercise power of entry at reasonable time

6   Entry under a power to which paragraph 4 applies shall be at a reasonable time, unless it appears to the person exercising the power that the purpose for which he is exercising the power would be frustrated on entry at a reasonable time.

Power to require assistance

7   (1) This paragraph applies to a power of entry conferred by —
         (a)   section 19(1), 22(2), 26(2), 27(2), 28(2) or 29(2), or
         (b)   a warrant under section 19(4), 22(4), 23(1) or 28(4).

     (2) Where a person enters premises in the exercise of a power of entry to which this paragraph applies, he may require any qualifying person on the premises to give him such assistance as he may reasonably require for the purpose for which entry is made.

     (3) The reference in sub-paragraph (2) to a qualifying person is to —
         (a)   the occupier of the premises;
         (b)   any person who appears to the person exercising the power to be responsible for animals on the premises;
         (c)   any person who appears to the person exercising the power to be under the direction or control of a person mentioned in paragraph (a) or (b).

     (4) In the case of a power under section 26(2), the reference in sub-paragraph (2) to a qualifying person also includes the holder of a licence —
         (a)   specifying the premises as premises on which the carrying on of an activity is authorised, or
         (b)   relating to an activity which is being carried on on the premises.

Power to take equipment onto premises

8   In exercising a power to which paragraph 7 applies, a person may take with him such equipment and materials as he thinks appropriate.

Duty to leave premises secured

9   If, in the exercise of a power of entry to which paragraph 7 applies, a person enters premises which are unoccupied, he shall leave them as effectively secured against entry as he found them.

Functions in connection with inspection and search

10   (1) This paragraph applies to —
         (a)   a power of inspection conferred by section 26(1), 27(1), 28(1) or 29(1), and
         (b)   a power of search conferred by a warrant under section 23(1).

(2) A person exercising a power to which this paragraph applies may —

    (a) inspect an animal found on the premises;

    (b) inspect any other thing found on the premises, including a document or record (in whatever form it is held);

    (c) carry out a measurement or test (including a measurement or test of an animal found on the premises);

    (d) take a sample (including a sample from an animal found on the premises or from any substance on the premises which appears to be intended for use as food for such an animal);

    (e) mark an animal found on the premises for identification purposes;

    (f) remove a carcass found on the premises for the purpose of carrying out a post-mortem examination on it;

    (g) take copies of a document or record found on the premises (in whatever form it is held);

    (h) require information stored in an electronic form and accessible from the premises to be produced in a form in which it can be taken away and in which it is visible and legible or from which it can readily be produced in a visible and legible form;

    (i) take a photograph of anything on the premises;

    (j) seize and detain or remove anything which the person exercising the power reasonably believes to be evidence of any non-compliance, or of the commission of any offence, relevant to the purpose for which the inspection or search is made.

(3) A person taken onto premises under paragraph 5 may exercise any power conferred by sub-paragraph (2) if he is in the company, and under the supervision, of a person exercising a power to which this paragraph applies.

11   A person who takes a sample from an animal pursuant to paragraph 10(2)(d) shall give a part of the sample, or a similar sample, to any person appearing to be responsible for the animal, if, before the sample is taken, he is requested to do so by that person.

12 (1) Paragraph 10(2)(j) does not include power to seize an item which the person exercising the power has reasonable grounds for believing to be subject to legal privilege (within the meaning of section 10 of the Police and Criminal Evidence Act 1984 (c. 60)).

(2) A person who seizes anything in exercise of the power under paragraph 10(2)(j) shall on request provide a record of the thing seized to a person showing himself —

    (a) to be the occupier of premises on which it was seized, or

    (b) to have had possession or control of it immediately before its seizure.

(3) Subject to sub-paragraph (4), anything which has been seized in the exercise of a power under paragraph 10(2)(j) may be retained so long as is necessary in all the circumstances and in particular —

    (a) for use as evidence at a trial for a relevant offence, or

    (b) for forensic examination or for investigation in connection with a relevant offence.

(4) Nothing may be retained for either of the purposes mentioned in sub-paragraph (3) if a photograph or a copy would be sufficient for that purpose.

13   As soon as reasonably practicable after having exercised a power to which paragraph 10 applies, the person who exercised the power shall —
    (a)   prepare a written report of the inspection or search, and
    (b)   if requested to do so by the occupier of the premises, give him a copy of the report.

14   (1)   A person exercising a power of search conferred by a warrant under section 23(1) may (if necessary) use reasonable force in the exercise of powers under paragraph 10 in connection with the execution of the warrant.

    (2)   A person carrying out an inspection under section 28(1) on premises which he is authorised to enter by a warrant under section 28(4) may (if necessary) use reasonable force in the exercise of powers under paragraph 10 in connection with the inspection.

Functions in connection with entry under section 19

15   (1)   Where a person enters premises in exercise of a power of entry conferred by section 19(1), or by a warrant under section 19(4), he may —
    (a)   inspect an animal found on the premises;
    (b)   remove a carcass found on the premises for the purposes of carrying out a post-mortem examination on it;
    (c)   remove for those purposes the carcass of an animal destroyed on the premises in exercise of power conferred by section 18(3) or (4);
    (d)   take a photograph of anything on the premises.

    (2)   Where a person exercising a power of entry under section 19(1) takes another person with him under paragraph 5, the other person may exercise any power conferred by sub-paragraph (1) if he is in the company, and under the supervision, of the person exercising the power of entry.

Offences

16   A person commits an offence if he —
    (a)   intentionally obstructs a person in the lawful exercise of a power to which paragraph 7 or 10 applies;
    (b)   intentionally obstructs a person in the lawful exercise of a power conferred by this Schedule;
    (c)   fails without reasonable excuse to give any assistance which he is required to give under paragraph 7.

SCHEDULE 3   Section 64

MINOR AND CONSEQUENTIAL AMENDMENTS

Performing Animals (Regulation) Act 1925 (c. 38)

1   In section 4 of the Performing Animals (Regulation) Act 1925 (offences and legal proceedings), in subsection (2), after "enactment," insert "or of an offence under any of sections 4, 5, 6(1) and (2), 7 to 9 and 11 of the Animal Welfare Act 2006".

Cinematograph Films (Animals) Act 1937 (c. 59)

2   In section 1 of the Cinematograph Films (Animals) Act 1937 (prohibition of films involving cruelty to animals), in subsection (4), for paragraph (b) substitute—

          "(b)   in relation to England and Wales, the expression "animal" means a "protected animal" within the meaning of the Animal Welfare Act 2006."

Pet Animals Act 1951 (c. 35)

3   (1) Section 2 of the Pet Animals Act 1951 (pets not to be sold in streets etc.) ceases to have effect.

        (2) In section 5 of that Act (offences and disqualifications), in subsection (3), after "1912," insert "or of any offence under any of sections 4, 5, 6(1) and (2), 7 to 9 and 11 of the Animal Welfare Act 2006,".

Protection of Animals (Amendment) Act 1954 (c. 40)

4   (1) In the Protection of Animals (Amendment) Act 1954, after section 2 insert—

      "2A   Breach of disqualification order

          (1)   If a person has custody of any animal in contravention of an order made under this Act by a court in Scotland, he shall be liable on summary conviction to—

               (a)   imprisonment for a term not exceeding 51 weeks, or

               (b)   a fine not exceeding level 3 on the standard scale.

          or to both.

          (2)   This section applies to orders made before, as well as to orders made after, the coming into force of this section."

        (2) In relation to an offence under the inserted section 2A committed before the commencement of section 281(5) of the Criminal Justice Act 2003 (c. 44), the reference in subsection (1)(a) of the section to 51 weeks is to be read as a reference to 6 months.

Animal Boarding Establishments Act 1963 (c. 43)

5   (1) In section 1 of the Animal Boarding Establishments Act 1963 (licensing of boarding establishments for animals), in subsection (2), at the end of paragraph (e) insert "or—

          (f)   under section 34(2), (3) or (4) of the Animal Welfare Act 2006,".

        (2) In section 3 of that Act (offences and disqualification), in subsection (3), after "1951," insert "or of any offence under any of sections 4, 5, 6(1) and (2), 7 to 9 and 11 of the Animal Welfare Act 2006,".

Riding Establishments Act 1964 (c. 70)

6   (1) In section 1 of the Riding Establishments Act 1964 (licensing of riding

establishments), in subsection (2), at the end of paragraph (f) insert "or —

> (g) under section 34(2), (3) or (4) of the Animal Welfare Act 2006".

(2) In section 4 of that Act (penalties and disqualification), in subsection (3), after "1963," insert "or of any offence under any of sections 4, 5, 6(1) and (2), 7 to 9 and 11 of the Animal Welfare Act 2006,".

Breeding of Dogs Act 1973 (c. 60)

7   In section 1 of the Breeding of Dogs Act 1973 (licensing of breeding establishments for dogs), in subsection (2), at the end of paragraph (f) insert "or —

> (g) under section 34(2), (3) or (4) of the Animal Welfare Act 2006,".

Guard Dogs Act 1975 (c. 50)

8   In section 3 of the Guard Dogs Act 1975 (guard dog kennel licences), in subsection (4), after "1973," insert "or of an offence under any of sections 4, 5, 6(1) and (2), 7 to 9 and 11 of the Animal Welfare Act 2006,".

Dangerous Wild Animals Act 1976 (c. 38)

9   In section 6 of the Dangerous Wild Animals Act 1976 (penalties), in subsection (2) —

> (a) for "Protection of Animals Acts 1911 to 1964," substitute "Protection of Animals Act 1911,",
>
> (b) after "1912 to 1964," insert "the Performing Animals (Regulation) Act 1925,",
>
> (c) after "1951," insert "the Animals (Cruel Poisons) Act 1962,", and
>
> (d) after "1973," insert "or of an offence under any of sections 4, 5, 6(1) and (2), 7 to 9 and 11 of the Animal Welfare Act 2006,".

Magistrates' Courts Act 1980 (c. 43)

10   In section 108 of the Magistrates' Courts Act 1980 (right of appeal to the Crown Court), in subsection (3)(c), for "section 2 of the Protection of Animals Act 1911" substitute "section 37(1) of the Animal Welfare Act 2006".

Zoo Licensing Act 1981 (c. 37)

11   In section 4 of the Zoo Licensing Act 1981 (grant or refusal of licence), in subsection (5) —

> (a) for "the Protection of Animals Acts 1911 to 1964" substitute "the Protection of Animals Act 1911",
>
> (b) after the entry for the Protection of Animals (Scotland) Acts 1912 to 1964, insert —
>
> > "the Performing Animals (Regulation) Act 1925;",
>
> (c) after the entry for the Pet Animals 1951, insert —
>
> > "the Animals (Cruel Poisons) Act 1962;", and

(d)   at the end, insert —

> "sections 4, 5, 6(1) and (2), 7 to 9 and 11 of the Animal
> Welfare Act 2006."

Animals (Scientific Procedures) Act 1986 (c. 14)

12   (1)   In section 22(5) of the Animals (Scientific Procedures) Act 1986 (penalties for
contraventions) —

(a)   for "section 1 of the Protection of Animals Act 1911" substitute "any
of sections 4, 5, 6(1) and (2), 7 and 8 of the Animal Welfare Act 2006",
and

(b)   at the end insert "(rather than any penalty by way of imprisonment
or fine provided for in those Acts)".

(2)   In section 26 of that Act (prosecutions), in subsection (1)(b), for "section 1 of
the Protection of Animals Act 1911" substitute "any of sections 4, 5, 6(1) and
(2) and 7 to 9 of the Animal Welfare Act 2006".

(3)   In section 29 of that Act (application to Northern Ireland), for subsection (5)
substitute —

> "(5)   In section 22(5) above for the reference to sections 4, 5, 6(1) and (2), 7
> and 8 of the Animal Welfare Act 2006 there shall be substituted a
> reference to sections 13 and 14 of the Welfare of Animals Act
> (Northern Ireland) 1972.
>
> (5A)   In section 26(1)(b) above for the reference to sections 4, 5, 6(1) and (2)
> and 7 to 9 of the Animal Welfare Act 2006 there shall be substituted
> a reference to sections 13 and 14 of the Welfare of Animals Act
> (Northern Ireland) 1972."

Wild Mammals (Protection) Act 1996 (c. 3)

13   For section 3 of the Wild Mammals (Protection) Act 1996 (interpretation)
substitute —

"3   Interpretation

> In this Act "wild mammal" means any mammal which is not a
> "protected animal" within the meaning of the Animal Welfare Act
> 2006."

Criminal Justice and Police Act 2001 (c. 16)

14   (1)   In section 57 of the Criminal Justice and Police Act 2001 (retention of seized
items), in subsection (1), at the end insert —

> "(r)   paragraph 12(3) of Schedule 2 to the Animal Welfare Act
> 2006."

(2)   In section 66 of that Act (general interpretation of Part 2), in subsection (4),
at the end insert —

> "(p)   sections 26(1), 27(1), 28(1) and 29(1) of the Animal Welfare
> Act 2006 (inspection in connection with licences, inspection
> in connection with registration, inspection of farm premises
> and inspection relating to Community obligations)."

(3)   In Part 1 of Schedule 1 to that Act (powers of seizure to which section 50

applies), at the end insert—

"*Animal Welfare Act 2006*

731   The power of seizure conferred by paragraph 10(2)(j) of Schedule 2 to the Animal Welfare Act 2006."

SCHEDULE 4   Section 65

REPEALS

Short title and chapter	Extent of repeal
Metropolitan Police Act 1839 (c. 47)	Section 47.
Town Police Clauses Act 1847 (c. 89)	Section 36.
Protection of Animals Act 1911 (c. 27)	Sections 1 to 3, 5 to 5B, 7, 9 and 11 to 14. In section 15, paragraphs (a), (c), (e) and (f).
Protection of Animals (1911) Amendment Act 1921 (c. 14)	The whole Act.
Protection of Animals Act 1934 (c. 21)	The whole Act.
Docking and Nicking of Horses Act 1949 (c. 70)	Section 1. In section 3, the definition of "nicking".
Pet Animals Act 1951 (c. 35)	Sections 2 and 3.
Cockfighting Act 1952 (c. 59)	The whole Act.
Protection of Animals (Amendment) Act 1954 (c. 40)	Sections 1, 2 and 4(1).
Protection of Animals (Anaesthetics) Act 1954 (c. 46)	The whole Act.
Abandonment of Animals Act 1960 (c. 43)	The whole Act.
Animals (Cruel Poisons) Act 1962 (c. 26)	In section 4(2), the words from "and the Protection of Animals Acts 1911" to "and this Act".
Protection of Animals (Anaesthetics) Act 1964 (c. 39)	The whole Act.
Agriculture (Miscellaneous Provisions) Act 1968 (c. 34)	Part 1.
Animal Health Act 1981 (c. 22)	Sections 37 to 39. In Schedule 5, paragraph 8.
Animals (Scientific Procedures) Act 1986 (c. 14)	In Schedule 3, paragraphs 1 and 7.

Short title and chapter	Extent of repeal
Protection of Animals (Penalties) Act 1987 (c. 35)	The whole Act.
Protection of Animals (Amendment) Act 1988 (c. 29)	Section 1. In section 2 — (a) in subsection (1), the words "section 47 of the Metropolitan Police Act 1839," and the words "and section 36 of the Town Police Clauses Act 1847", and (b) subsection (2).
Protection against Cruel Tethering Act 1988 (c. 31)	The whole Act.
Protection of Animals (Amendment) Act 2000 (c. 40)	The whole Act.

Printed in the UK by The Stationery Office Limited
under the authority and superintendence of Carol Tullo, Controller of
Her Majesty's Stationery Office and Queen's Printer of Acts of Parliament

11/2006   352429   19585

The Welfare of Farmed Animals (England) Regulations 2007

2007 No. 2078

ANIMALS, ENGLAND

ANIMAL WELFARE

The Welfare of Farmed Animals (England) Regulations 2007

Made - - - -		*19th July 2007*
Coming into force - -		*1st October 2007*

The Secretary of State is, in relation to England, the appropriate national authority for the purposes of exercising the powers conferred by section 12(1), (2) and (3) of the Animal Welfare Act 2006(**a**), and makes the following Regulations in exercise of those powers.

In accordance with section 12(6) of that Act, the Secretary of State has consulted such persons appearing to him to represent interests with which these Regulations are concerned as he considered appropriate.

In accordance with section 61(2) of that Act, a draft of these Regulations has been laid before Parliament and approved by a resolution of each House of Parliament.

Citation, commencement and application

1. These Regulations—

(a) may be cited as the Welfare of Farmed Animals (England) Regulations 2007;

(b) come into force on 1st October 2007; and

(c) apply in England only.

Definitions and interpretation

2.—(1) In these Regulations—

"calf" means a bovine animal up to six months old;

"laying hen" means a hen of the species *Gallus gallus* which has reached laying maturity and is kept for the production of eggs not intended for hatching;

"litter" means, in relation to laying hens, any friable material enabling the hens to satisfy their ethological needs;

"nest" means a separate space for egg laying, the floor component of which may not include wire mesh that can come into contact with the birds, for an individual hen or for a group of hens;

(**a**) 2006 c.45.

"person responsible" for an animal has the same meaning as in section 3 of the Animal Welfare Act 2006;

"pig" means an animal of the porcine species of any age, kept for breeding or fattening;

"usable area" means an area, other than that taken up by a nest, used by laying hens which is at least 30cm wide with a floor slope not exceeding 14% and with headroom of at least 45cm.

(2) Expressions used in these Regulations that are not defined in these Regulations and are used in the following Directives, have the meaning they bear in those Directives—

    (a) in relation to pigs, Directive 91/630/EEC(**a**), 2001/88/EC(**b**) and 2001/93/EC(**c**);

    (b) in relation to laying hens, Directive 99/74/EC(**d**); and

    (c) in relation to calves, Directive 91/629/EEC(**e**), 97/2/EC(**f**) and 97/182/EC(**g**).

(3) An expression used in regulation 4 or Schedule 1, which is not defined in these Regulations and which appears in Directive 98/58/EC(**h**), has the same meaning as it has for the purposes of that Directive.

Animals to which these Regulations apply

3.—(1) These Regulations apply to farmed animals only.

(2) In these Regulations, a "farmed animal" means an animal bred or kept for the production of food, wool or skin or other farming purposes, but not including—

    (a) a fish, reptile or amphibian;

    (b) an animal whilst at, or solely intended for use in, a competition, show or cultural or sporting event or activity;

    (c) an experimental or laboratory animal; or

    (d) an animal living in the wild.

Duties on persons responsible for farmed animals

4.—(1) A person responsible for a farmed animal must take all reasonable steps to ensure that the conditions under which it is bred or kept comply with Schedule 1.

(2) In complying with the duty in paragraph (1), a person responsible for a farmed animal must have regard to its—

    (a) species;

    (b) degree of development;

    (c) adaptation and domestication; and

    (d) physiological and ethological needs in accordance with good practice and scientific knowledge.

Additional duties on persons responsible for poultry, laying hens, calves, cattle, pigs or rabbits

5.—(1) A person responsible for—

(**a**) OJ No L340, 11.12.91, p 33
(**b**) OJ No L316, 1.12.2001, p 1
(**c**) OJ No L316, 1.12.2001, p 36
(**d**) OJ No L203, 3.8.99, p 53
(**e**) OJ No L340, 11.12.91, p 28
(**f**) OJ No L25, 28.1.97, p 24
(**g**) OJ No L76, 18.3.97, p 30
(**h**) OJ No L221, 8.8.98, p 23

(a) poultry (other than those kept in the systems referred to in Schedules 2 to 4) kept in a building must ensure they are kept on, or have access at all times to, well-maintained litter or a well-drained area for resting;

(b) laying hens kept in establishments with 350 or more laying hens must comply with Schedules 2, 3, 4 and 5, as applicable;

(c) calves confined for rearing and fattening must comply with Schedule 6;

(d) cattle must comply with Schedule 7;

(e) pigs must, subject to paragraph (2), comply with Part 2 of Schedule 8 and, where applicable, the requirements of Parts 3, 4, 5 and 6 of Schedule 8; or

(f) rabbits must comply with Schedule 9.

(2) Paragraphs 12, 28, 29 and 30 of Schedule 8 apply to all holdings newly built, rebuilt or brought into use for the first time on or after 1st January 2003, but in the case of all other holdings, those paragraphs do not apply until 1st January 2013.

(3) Part 1 of Schedule 8 has effect.

Codes of Practice

6.—(1) A person responsible for a farmed animal—

(a) must not attend to the animal unless he is acquainted with any relevant code of practice and has access to the code while attending to the animal; and

(b) must take all reasonable steps to ensure that a person employed or engaged by him does not attend to the animal unless that other person—

(i) is acquainted with any relevant code of practice;

(ii) has access to the code while attending to the animal; and

(iii) has received instruction and guidance on the code.

(2) In this section, a "relevant code of practice" means a code of practice issued under section 14 of the Animal Welfare Act 2006 or a statutory welfare code issued under section 3 of the Agriculture (Miscellaneous Provisions) Act 1968(**a**) relating to the particular species of farmed animal to which a person is attending.

Offences

7. A person commits an offence if, without lawful authority or excuse, he—

(a) contravenes, or does not comply with a duty in, regulation 4, 5 or 6;

(b) makes an entry in a record, or gives any information for the purposes of these Regulations which he knows to be false in any material particular or, for those purposes, recklessly makes a statement or gives any information which is false in any material particular; or

(c) causes or permits any of the above.

Prosecutions

8.—(1) A local authority may prosecute proceedings for an offence under these Regulations.

(2) The Secretary of State may direct that he, and not the local authority, prosecutes proceedings for an offence under these Regulations in relation to cases of a particular description or any particular case.

Penalties

9.—(1) A person guilty of an offence under regulation 7 is liable on summary conviction to—

(**a**) 1968 c. 34.

(a) imprisonment for a term not exceeding 51 weeks;

(b) a fine not exceeding level 4 on the standard scale; or

(c) both the term of imprisonment referred to sub-paragraph (a) and the fine referred to in sub-paragraph (b).

(2) In relation to an offence committed before the commencement of section 281(5) of the Criminal Justice Act 2003(**a**), the reference in paragraph (1)(a) to 51 weeks must be taken as a reference to 6 months.

Jeff Rooker
Minister of State

19th July 2007   Department for Environment, Food and Rural Affairs

SCHEDULE 1

Regulation 4

General conditions under which farmed animals must be kept

Staffing

1. Animals must be cared for by a sufficient number of staff who possess the appropriate ability, knowledge and professional competence.

Inspection

2.—(1) Subject to sub-paragraph (3), animals kept in husbandry systems in which their welfare depends on frequent human attention must be thoroughly inspected at least once a day to check that they are in a state of well-being.

(2) Subject to sub-paragraph (3), animals kept in husbandry systems in which their welfare does not depend on frequent human attention must be inspected at intervals sufficient to avoid any suffering.

(3) In the following cases it is sufficient for the purposes of this paragraph to comply with the following provisions—

(a) in the case of laying hens, paragraph 1 of Schedule 5;

(b) in the case of calves, paragraph 2 or 3 of Schedule 6; and

(c) in the case of pigs, paragraph 2 of Schedule 8.

3. Where animals are kept in a building, adequate lighting (whether fixed or portable) must be available to enable them to be thoroughly inspected at any time.

4. Where any animals (other than poultry) are kept in a building they must be kept on, or have access at all times to, a lying area which either has well-maintained dry bedding or is well-drained.

5. Any animals which appear to be ill or injured must be cared for appropriately and without delay; where they do not respond to such care, veterinary advice must be obtained as soon as possible.

6. Where necessary, sick or injured animals must be isolated in suitable accommodation with, where appropriate, dry comfortable bedding.

(a) 2003 c. 44.

Record keeping

7. A record must be maintained of—

(a) any medicinal treatment given to animals; and

(b) the number of mortalities found on each inspection of animals carried out in accordance with any of the following provisions—

    (i) in the case of laying hens, paragraph 1 of Schedule 5;

    (ii) in the case of calves, paragraph 2 or 3 of Schedule 6; or

    (iii) in the case of pigs, paragraph 2 of Schedule 8; or

    (iv) in any other case, paragraph 2(1) or (2) of this Schedule.

8. The record referred to in paragraph 7 must be retained for a period of at least three years from the date on which the medicinal treatment was given, or the date of the inspection, and must be made available to an inspector on request.

Freedom of movement

9. The freedom of movement of animals, having regard to their species and in accordance with good practice and scientific knowledge, must not be restricted in such a way as to cause them unnecessary suffering or injury.

10. Where animals are continuously or regularly tethered or confined, they must be given the space appropriate to their physiological and ethological needs in accordance with good practice and scientific knowledge.

Buildings and accommodation

11. Materials used for the construction of accommodation, and in particular for the construction of pens, cages, stalls and equipment with which the animals may come into contact, must not be harmful to them and must be capable of being thoroughly cleaned and disinfected.

12. Accommodation and fittings for securing animals must be constructed and maintained so that there are no sharp edges or protrusions likely to cause injury to them.

13. Air circulation, dust levels, temperature, relative air humidity and gas concentrations must be kept within limits which are not harmful to the animals.

14. Animals kept in buildings must not be kept in permanent darkness.

15. Where the natural light available in a building is insufficient to meet the physiological or ethological needs of any animals being kept in it, appropriate artificial lighting must be provided.

16. Animals kept in buildings must not be kept without an appropriate period of rest from artificial lighting.

Animals not kept in buildings

17. Animals not kept in buildings must, where necessary and possible, be given protection from adverse weather conditions, predators and risks to their health and must, at all times, have access to a well-drained lying area.

Automatic or mechanical equipment

18. All automated or mechanical equipment essential for the health and well-being of the animals must be inspected at least once a day to check that there is no defect in it.

19. Where defects in automated or mechanical equipment of the type referred to in paragraph 18 are discovered, these must be rectified immediately or, if this is impossible, appropriate steps must be taken to safeguard the health and well-being of the animals pending the rectification of those defects including the use of alternative methods of feeding and watering and methods of providing and maintaining a satisfactory environment.

20. Where the health and well-being of the animals is dependent on an artificial ventilation system—

(a) provision must be made for an appropriate back-up system to guarantee sufficient air renewal to preserve the health and well-being of the animals in the event of failure of the system; and

(b) an alarm system (which will operate even if the principal electricity supply to it has failed) must be provided to give warning of any failure of the system.

21. The back-up system referred to in paragraph 20(a) must be thoroughly inspected and the alarm system referred to in paragraph 20(b) tested at least once every seven days in order to check that there is no defect, and, if any defect is found at any time, it must be rectified immediately.

Feed, water and other substances

22. Animals must be fed a wholesome diet which is appropriate to their age and species and which is fed to them in sufficient quantity to maintain them in good health, to satisfy their nutritional needs and to promote a positive state of well-being.

23. Animals must not be provided with food or liquid that contains any substance that may cause them unnecessary suffering or injury and must be provided with food and liquid in a manner that does not cause them unnecessary suffering or injury.

24. All animals must have access to feed at intervals appropriate to their physiological needs (and, in any case, at least once a day), except where a veterinary surgeon acting in the exercise of his profession otherwise directs.

25. All animals must either have access to a suitable water supply and be provided with an adequate supply of fresh drinking water each day, or be able to satisfy their fluid intake needs by other means.

26. Feeding and watering equipment must be designed, constructed, placed and maintained so that contamination of food or water and the harmful effects of competition between animals are minimised.

27.—(1) — No other substance, with the exception of those given for therapeutic or prophylactic purposes or for the purpose of zootechnical treatment, may be administered to animals unless it has been demonstrated by scientific studies of animal welfare or established practice that the effect of that substance is not detrimental to the health or welfare of the animals.

(2) In sub-paragraph (1), "zootechnical treatment" has the meaning given in Article 1(2)(c) of Directive 96/22/EEC(**a**) concerning the prohibition on the use in stockfarming of certain substances having a hormonal or thyrostatic action and of beta-agonists.

Breeding procedures

28.—(1) — Natural or artificial breeding or breeding procedures which cause, or are likely to cause, suffering or injury to any of the animals concerned, must not be practised.

(2) Sub-paragraph (1) does not preclude the use of natural or artificial breeding procedures that are likely to cause minimal or momentary suffering or injury or that might necessitate interventions which would not cause lasting injury.

(**a**) OJ No L125, 23.5.96, p 3

29. Animals may only be kept for farming purposes if it can reasonably be expected, on the basis of their genotype or phenotype, that they can be kept without any detrimental effect on their health or welfare.

Electrical immobilisation

30. An electrical current must not be applied to an animal for the purpose of immobilisation.

SCHEDULE 2

Regulation 5

Additional conditions that apply to the keeping of laying hens in non-cage systems

1. All non-cage systems of production for keeping laying hens must comply with the requirements of this Schedule.

2. All systems must be equipped in such a way that all laying hens have—

(a) linear feeders providing at least 10cm per bird or circular feeders providing at least 4cm per bird;

(b) continuous drinking troughs providing at least 2.5 cm per hen or circular drinking troughs providing at least 1 cm per hen;

(c) at least one nest for every seven hens and, if group nests are used, there must be at least 1 m² of nest space for a maximum of 120 hens;

(d) perches without sharp edges and providing at least 15 cm per hen, which must not be mounted above the litter, and the horizontal distance between perches must be at least 30 cm and the horizontal distance between the perch and the wall must be at least 20 cm; and

(e) at least 250 cm² of littered area per hen, the litter occupying at least one third of the ground surface.

3. Where a system is equipped with nipple drinkers or cups, there must be at least one nipple drinker or cup for every 10 hens.

4. Where a system has drinking points plumbed in, at least two cups or two nipple drinkers must be within reach of each hen.

5. The floors of installations must be constructed so as to support each of the forward-facing claws of each bird's foot.

6. If systems are used where the laying hens can move freely between different levels—

(a) there must be no more than four levels;

(b) the headroom between the levels must be at least 45 cm;

(c) the drinking and feeding facilities must be distributed in such a way as to provide equal access for all hens; and

(d) the levels must be so arranged as to prevent droppings falling on the levels below.

7. If laying hens have access to open runs —

(a) there must be several popholes giving direct access to the outer area, at least 35 cm high and 40 cm wide, and extending along the entire length of the building; and in any case, a total opening of 2 m must be available per group of 1,000 hens; and

(b) the open runs must be—

(i) of an area appropriate to the stocking density and to the nature of the ground, in order to prevent any contamination; and

(ii) equipped with shelter from adverse weather conditions and predators and, if necessary, drinking troughs.

8. Subject to paragraph (9), the stocking density must not exceed nine laying hens per m² of usable area.

9. Where on 3rd August 1999 the establishment applied a system where the usable area corresponded to the available ground surface, and the establishment was still applying this system on 25th June 2002, a stocking density of not more than 12 hens per m² is authorised until 31st December 2011.

SCHEDULE 3

Regulation 5

Additional conditions that apply to the keeping of laying hens in conventional cages

1. All conventional (unenriched) cage systems must comply with the requirements of this Schedule.

2. Cage systems must have at least 550 cm² per hen of cage area, measured in a horizontal plane, which may be used without restriction, in particular not including non-waste deflection plates liable to restrict the area available unless they are placed so as not to restrict the area available for the hens to use.

3. A feed trough must be provided which may be used without restriction, the length of which must be at least 10 cm multiplied by the number of hens in the cage.

4.—(1) Unless nipple drinkers or drinking cups are provided, each cage must have a continuous drinking channel of the same length as the feed trough mentioned in paragraph 3.

(2) Where drinking points are plumbed in, at least two nipple drinkers or two cups must be within reach from each cage.

5. Cages must be at least 40 cm high over at least 65% of the cage area and not less than 35 cm at any point, the area being obtained by multiplying 550 cm² by the number of birds kept in the cage.

6.—(1) Floors of cages must be constructed so as to support each of the forward-facing claws of each foot of each bird.

(2) The floor slope must not exceed 14% or 8 degrees when made of rectangular wire mesh and must not exceed 21.3% or 12 degrees for other types of floor.

7. Cages must be fitted with suitable claw-shortening devices.

8. No person may build or bring into service for the first time any cage system referred to in this Schedule for the keeping of laying hens.

9. On and after 1st January 2012, no person may keep laying hens in any cage system referred to in this Schedule.

SCHEDULE 4

Regulation 5

Additional conditions that apply to the keeping of laying hens in enriched cages

1. All laying hens not kept in a cage system referred to in Schedule 3 must be kept in an enriched cage system which complies with the requirements of this Schedule.

2. Laying hens must have—

(a) at least 750 cm² of cage area per hen, 600 cm² of which must be usable; the height of the cage other than that above the usable area must be at least 20 cm at every point and the minimum total area for any cage must be 2000 cm²;

(b) access to a nest;

(c) litter such that pecking and scratching are possible; and

(d) appropriate perches allowing at least 15 cm per hen.

3. A feed trough which can be used without restriction must be provided, the length of which must be at least 12 cm multiplied by the number of hens in the cage.

4. Each cage must have a drinking system appropriate to the size of the group; where nipple drinkers are provided, at least two nipple drinkers or two cups must be within reach of each hen.

5. To facilitate inspection, installation and depopulation of hens there must be a minimum aisle width of 90 cm between tiers of cages and a space of at least 35 cm must be allowed between the floor of the building and the bottom tier of cages.

6. Cages must be fitted with suitable claw-shortening devices.

SCHEDULE 5

Regulation 5

Additional conditions applicable to all systems in which laying hens are kept

1. All hens must be inspected by the owner or other person responsible for the hens at least once a day.

2. In all systems in which laying hens are kept—

(a) the sound level must be minimised;

(b) constant or sudden noise must be avoided; and

(c) ventilation fans, feeding machinery and other equipment must be constructed, placed, operated and maintained in such a way that they cause the least possible noise.

3.—(1) All buildings must have light levels sufficient to allow hens to see other hens and be seen clearly, to investigate their surroundings visually and to show normal levels of activity.

(2) Where there is natural light, light apertures must be arranged in such a way that light is distributed evenly within the accommodation.

(3) After the first days of conditioning, the lighting regime must be such as to prevent health and behavioural problems and accordingly it must follow a 24-hour rhythm and include an adequate uninterrupted period of darkness lasting, by way of indication, about one third of the day.

(4) A period of twilight of sufficient duration should if possible be provided when the light is dimmed so that the hens may settle down without disturbance or injury.

4.—(1) Those parts of buildings, equipment or utensils which are in contact with the hens must be thoroughly cleaned and disinfected regularly and, in any case, every time depopulation is carried out and before a new batch of hens is brought in.

(2) While the cages are occupied—

(a) the surfaces and all equipment must be kept satisfactorily clean;

(b) droppings must be removed; and

(c) dead hens must be removed every day.

5. Cages must be suitably equipped to prevent hens escaping.

6. Accommodation comprising two or more tiers of cages must have devices, or appropriate measures must be taken, to allow inspection of all tiers without difficulty and to facilitate the removal of hens.

7. The design and dimensions of the cage door must be such that an adult hen can be removed without undergoing unnecessary suffering or sustaining injury.

SCHEDULE 6

Regulation 5

Additional conditions that apply to the keeping of calves confined for rearing and fattening

Accommodation

1.—(1) No calf may be confined in an individual stall or pen after the age of eight weeks unless a veterinary surgeon certifies that its health or behaviour requires it to be isolated in order to receive treatment.

(2) The width of any individual stall or pen for a calf must be at least equal to the height of the calf at the withers, measured in the standing position, and the length must be at least equal to the body length of the calf, measured from the tip of the nose to the caudal edge of the *tuber ishii* (pin bones), multiplied by 1.1.

(3) Individual stalls or pens for calves (except for those isolating sick animals) must have perforated walls which allow calves to have direct visual and tactile contact.

(4) For calves kept in groups, the unobstructed space allowance available to each calf must be—

    (a) at least 1.5 m² for each calf with a live weight of less than 150 kg;

    (b) at least 2 m² for each calf with a live weight of 150 kg or more but less than 200 kg; and

    (c) at least 3 m² for each calf with a live weight of 200 kg or more.

(5) Each calf must be able to stand up, lie down, turn around, rest and groom itself without hindrance.

(6) Each calf that is kept on a holding on which two or more calves are kept, must be able to see at least one other calf.

(7) Sub-paragraph (6) does not apply to any calf that is kept in isolation on a holding on veterinary advice or in accordance with sub-paragraph (1).

(8) For the purpose of calculating the number of calves kept on a holding in order to determine whether sub-paragraph (6) applies, no account may be taken of any calf that is being kept in isolation on veterinary advice or in accordance with sub-paragraph (1).

Inspection

2. All housed calves must be inspected by the owner or other person responsible for the calves at least twice a day to check that they are in a state of well-being.

3. Calves which are kept outside must be inspected by the owner or other person responsible for the calves at least once a day to check that they are in a state of well-being.

Tethering

4.—(1) No person responsible for a calf may tether it or cause it to be tethered, with the exception of group-housed calves which may be tethered for a period of not more than one hour when being fed milk or milk substitute.

492

(2) Where tethers are used in accordance with sub-paragraph (1), the tether must not cause pain or injury to the calves and must be inspected regularly and adjusted as necessary to ensure a comfortable fit.

(3) Each tether must be designed to avoid the risk of strangulation, pain or injury and allow the calf to stand up, lie down, rest and groom itself without hindrance.

Artificially lit buildings

5. Where calves are kept in an artificially lit building then, subject to paragraph 16 of Schedule 1, artificial lighting must be provided for a period at least equivalent to the period of natural light normally available between 9.00 am and 5.00 pm.

Cleaning and disinfection

6.—(1) Housing, stalls, pens, equipment and utensils used for calves must be properly cleaned and disinfected as often as necessary to prevent cross-infection and the build-up of disease-carrying organisms.

(2) Faeces, urine and uneaten or spilt food must be removed as often as necessary to minimise smell and to avoid attracting flies or rodents.

Floors

7. Where calves are kept in a building, floors must—

(a) be smooth but not slippery;

(b) be designed, constructed and maintained so as not to cause injury or suffering to calves standing or lying on them;

(c) be suitable for the size and weight of the calves; and

(d) form a rigid, even and stable surface.

Bedding and lying area

8.—(1) All calves must be provided with appropriate bedding.

(2) All calves must be kept on, or at all times have access to, a lying area which is clean, comfortable and adequately drained and which does not adversely affect the calves.

(3) All housed calves and calves kept in hutches or temporary structures must be kept on, or at all times have access to, a lying area which is well-maintained with dry bedding.

Bovine colostrum

9. Each calf must receive bovine colostrum as soon as possible after it is born and, in any event, within the first six hours of life.

Additional dietary requirements

10.—(1) All calves must be provided with food which contains sufficient iron to ensure a blood haemoglobin level of at least 4.5 mmol/litre.

(2) A minimum daily ration of fibrous food must be provided for each calf over 2 weeks old, the quantity being raised in line with the growth of the calf from a minimum of 100g at 2 weeks old, to a minimum of 250g at 20 weeks old.

Muzzling

11. Calves must not be muzzled.

Feeding

12.—(1) All calves must be fed at least twice a day.

(2) Where calves are housed in a group and do not have continuous access to food, or are not fed by an automatic feeding system, each calf must have access to food at the same time as the others in the feeding group.

Drinking water

13.—(1) All calves must be provided with a sufficient quantity of fresh drinking water each day.

(2) Calves must be provided with fresh drinking water at all times—

    (a) in hot weather conditions; or

    (b) when they are ill.

SCHEDULE 7 Regulation 5

Additional conditions that apply to the keeping of cattle

1. Where lactating dairy cows or calving cows are kept in a building, they must have access at all times to a well-drained and bedded lying area.

2. A pen or yard in a building used for calving cows must be of such a size as to permit a person to attend the cows.

3. Calving cows which are kept in a building must be kept separate from livestock other than calving cows.

SCHEDULE 8 Regulation 5

Additional conditions that apply to the keeping of pigs

PART 1

Interpretation

1. In this Schedule—

  "boar" means a male pig after puberty, intended for breeding;

  "gilt" means a female pig intended for breeding after puberty and before farrowing;

  "piglet" means a pig from birth to weaning;

  "rearing pig" means a pig from the age of ten weeks to slaughter or service;

  "sow" means a female pig after the first farrowing;

  "weaner" means a pig from weaning to the age of ten weeks.

PART 2

General additional conditions

Inspection

2. All pigs must be inspected by the owner or other person responsible for the pigs at least once a day to check that they are in a state of well-being.

Tethering

3. No person responsible for a pig may tether it or cause it to be tethered, except while it is undergoing any examination, test, treatment or operation carried out for any veterinary purpose.

4.—(1) Where tethers are used in accordance with paragraph 3, they must not cause injury to the pigs and must be inspected regularly and adjusted as necessary to ensure a comfortable fit.

(2) Each tether must be of sufficient length to allow the pigs to move as stipulated in paragraph 5(2)(a) and (e) and the design must be such as to avoid, as far as possible, any risk of strangulation, pain or injury.

Accommodation

5.—(1) A pig must be free to turn around without difficulty at all times.

(2) The accommodation used for pigs must be constructed in such a way as to allow each pig to—

    (a) stand up, lie down and rest without difficulty;

    (b) have a clean, comfortable and adequately drained place in which it can rest;

    (c) see other pigs, except—

        (i) where the pig is isolated for veterinary reasons; or

        (ii) in the week before the expected farrowing time and during farrowing, when sows and gilts may be kept out of sight of other pigs;

    (d) maintain a comfortable temperature; and

    (e) have enough space to allow all the animals to lie down at the same time.

6.—(1) The dimensions of any stall or pen used for holding individual pigs must be such that the internal area is not less than the square of the length of the pig, and no internal side is less than 75% of the length of the pig, the length of the pig in each case being measured from the tip of its snout to the base of its tail while it is standing with its back straight.

(2) Sub-paragraph (1) does not apply to a female pig for the period beginning with seven days before the predicted day of her farrowing and ending when the weaning of her piglets (including any piglets fostered by her) is complete.

(3) Sub-paragraph (1) does not apply to a pig held in a stall or pen—

    (a) while it is undergoing any examination, test, treatment or operation carried out for veterinary purposes;

    (b) for the purposes of service, artificial insemination or collection of semen;

    (c) while it is fed on any particular occasion;

    (d) for the purposes of marking, washing or weighing it;

    (e) while its accommodation is being cleaned; or

    (f) while it is awaiting loading for transportation,

provided that the period during which it is so kept is not longer than necessary for that purpose.

(4) Sub-paragraph (1) does not apply to a pig held in a stall or pen which the pig can enter or leave at will, provided that the stall or pen is entered from a stall or pen in which the pig is kept without contravention of this paragraph.

Artificially lit buildings

7. Where pigs are kept in an artificially lit building, lighting with an intensity of at least 40 lux must be provided for a minimum period of 8 hours per day subject to paragraph 16 of Schedule 1.

Prevention of fighting

8.—(1) If pigs are kept together, measures must be taken to prevent fighting which goes beyond normal behaviour.

(2) Pigs which show persistent aggression towards others or are victims of such aggression must be separated from the group.

Cleaning and disinfection

9.—(1) Housing, pens, equipment and utensils used for pigs must be properly cleaned and disinfected as often as necessary to prevent cross-infection and build-up of disease-carrying organisms.

(2) Faeces, urine and uneaten or spilt food must be removed as often as necessary to minimise smell and to avoid attracting flies or rodents.

Bedding

10. Where bedding is provided, it must be clean, dry and not harmful to the pigs.

Floors

11. Where pigs are kept in a building, floors must—

    (a) be smooth but not slippery;

    (b) be designed, constructed and maintained so as not to cause injury or suffering to pigs standing or lying on them;

    (c) be suitable for the size and weight of the pigs; and

    (d) where no litter is provided, form a rigid, even and stable surface.

12.—(1) Where concrete slatted floors are used for pigs kept in groups, the maximum width of the openings must be—

    (a) 11 mm for piglets;

    (b) 14 mm for weaners;

    (c) 18 mm for rearing pigs; and

    (d) 20 mm for gilts after service and sows.

(2) The minimum slat width must be—

    (a) 50 mm for piglets and weaners; and

    (b) 80 mm for rearing pigs, gilts after service and sows.

Feeding

13.—(1) All pigs must be fed at least once a day.

(2) Where pigs are housed in a group and do not have continuous access to feed, or are not fed by an automatic feeding system feeding the animals individually, each pig must have access to the food at the same time as the others in the feeding group.

Drinking water

14. All pigs over two weeks of age must have continuous access to a sufficient quantity of fresh drinking water.

Environmental enrichment

15. To enable proper investigation and manipulation activities, all pigs must have permanent access to a sufficient quantity of material such as straw, hay, wood, sawdust, mushroom compost, peat or a mixture of such which does not adversely affect the health of the animals.

Prohibition on the use of the sweat-box system

16. Pigs must not be kept in an environment which involves maintaining high temperatures and high humidity (known as the "sweat-box system").

Noise levels

17. Pigs must not be exposed to constant or sudden noise.

18. Noise levels above 85 dBA must be avoided in that part of any building where pigs are kept.

PART 3

Boars

19. Boar pens must be sited and constructed so as to allow the boar to turn around and to hear, see and smell other pigs, and must contain clean resting areas.

20. The lying area must be dry and comfortable.

21.—(1) Subject to sub-paragraph (2), the minimum unobstructed floor area for a boar must be 6 m².

(2) When boar pens are also used for natural service, the floor area must be at least 10 m² and must be free of any obstacles.

PART 4

Sows and Gilts

22. Pregnant sows and gilts must, where necessary, be treated against external and internal parasites.

Farrowing

23. Pregnant sows and gilts must be thoroughly cleaned before being placed in farrowing crates.

24. In the week before the expected farrowing time, sows and gilts must be given suitable nesting material in sufficient quantity unless it is not technically feasible for the slurry system used.

25. During farrowing, an unobstructed area behind the sow or gilt must be available for the ease of natural or assisted farrowing.

26. Farrowing pens where sows or gilts are kept loose must have some means of protecting the piglets, such as farrowing rails.

Group housing

27. Sows and gilts must be kept in groups except during the period between seven days before the predicted day of farrowing and the day on which the weaning of piglets (including any piglets fostered) is complete.

28. The pen where the group is kept must have sides greater than 2.8 m in length, except when there are six or fewer individuals in the group, when the sides of the pen must be no less than 2.4 m in length.

29. The unobstructed floor area available to each gilt after service and to each sow when gilts and/or sows are kept in groups must be at least 1.64 m² and 2.25 m² respectively. When these animals are kept in groups of six or fewer individuals, the unobstructed floor area must be increased by 10%. When these animals are kept in groups of 40 or more individuals, the unobstructed floor area may be decreased by 10%.

30. For gilts after service and pregnant sows, a part of the area required in paragraph 29 equal to at least 0.95 m² per gilt and at least 1.3 m² per sow must be of continuous solid floor of which a maximum of 15% is reserved for drainage openings.

31. Sows and gilts kept on holdings of 10 or fewer sows may be kept individually provided that their accommodation complies with the requirements of paragraphs 5 and 6 of this Schedule.

32. In addition to the requirements of paragraph 13 of this Schedule, sows and gilts must be fed using a system which ensures that each individual can obtain sufficient food even when competitors for the food are present.

33. All dry pregnant sows and gilts must be given a sufficient quantity of bulky or high-fibre food as well as high-energy food to satisfy their hunger and need to chew.

PART 5

Piglets

34. Where a farrowing crate system is used, piglets must be provided with a source of heat and a solid, dry and comfortable lying area away from the sow where all of them can rest at the same time.

35. A part of the floor area where the piglets are kept, and which is large enough to allow the animals to rest together at the same time, must be solid or covered with a mat, or be littered with straw or other suitable material.

36. Where a farrowing crate system is used, the piglets must have sufficient space so they can be suckled without difficulty.

37. Subject to paragraph 38, piglets must not be weaned from the sow at an age less than 28 days, unless the health or welfare of the sow or piglets would otherwise be adversely affected.

38. Piglets may be weaned up to seven days earlier than the age referred to in paragraph 37 if they are moved into specialised housing which is—

    (a) emptied and thoroughly cleaned and disinfected before the introduction of a new group; and

    (b) separate from housing where other sows are kept.

PART 6

Weaners and rearing pigs

39. As soon as possible after weaning, weaners and rearing pigs must be kept in stable groups, with as little mixing as possible.

40. If weaners and rearing pigs unfamiliar with one another have to be mixed—

(a) this must if possible be done before weaning or up to one week after weaning, or otherwise when the pigs are as young as possible; and

(b) they must be provided with adequate opportunities to escape and hide from other pigs.

41. The use of tranquilising medication in order to facilitate mixing must be limited to exceptional conditions and only after consultation with a veterinary surgeon.

42. If there are signs of severe fighting, the causes must be immediately investigated and appropriate measures taken.

43. The unobstructed floor area available to each weaner or rearing pig reared in a group must be at least—

(a) 0.15 m² for each pig where the average weight of the pigs in the group is 10 kg or less;

(b) 0.20 m² for each pig where the average weight of the pigs in the group is more than 10 kg, but less than or equal to 20 kg;

(c) 0.30 m² for each pig where the average weight of the pigs in the group is more than 20 kg but less than or equal to 30 kg;

(d) 0.40 m² for each pig where the average weight of the pigs in the group is more than 30 kg but less than or equal to 50 kg;

(e) 0.55 m² for each pig where the average weight of the pigs in the group is more than 50 kg but less than or equal to 85 kg;

(f) 0.65 m² for each pig where the average weight of the pigs in the group is more than 85 kg but less than or equal to 110 kg; and

(g) 1.00 m² for each pig where the average weight of the pigs in the group is more than 110 kg.

SCHEDULE 9

Regulation 5

Additional conditions that apply to the keeping of rabbits

1. Hutches or cages in which rabbits are kept must be—

(a) of sufficient size to allow the rabbits to move around and to feed and drink without difficulty and to allow them all to lie on their sides at the same time; and

(b) of sufficient height to allow the rabbits to sit upright on all four feet without their ears touching the top of the hutch or cage.

2. Where rabbits are kept in accommodation which is exposed to the weather, suitable steps must be taken so as to ensure that the rabbits have access to shelter from the weather, including direct sunlight.

EXPLANATORY NOTE

(This note is not part of the Regulations)

These Regulations, which apply to England only, substantially replace (with amendments):

The Welfare of Farmed Animals (England) Regulations 2000 (SI 2002/1870);

The Welfare of Farmed Animals (England) (Amendment) Regulations 2002 (SI 2002/1646);

The Welfare of Farmed Animals (England) (Amendment) Regulations 2003 (SI 2003/299); and

Section 7 of the Agriculture (Miscellaneous Provisions) Act 1968(**a**).

The above legislation will be repealed at the same time as these Regulations come into force.

These Regulations implement Community legislation which had previously been implemented in the three Regulations mentioned above (SI 2000/1870; 2002/1646 and 2003/299). The Community legislation which these Regulations continue to implement is—

Council Directive 98/58/EC concerning the protection of animals kept for farming purposes (**b**);

Council Directive 99/74/EC laying down minimum standards for the protection of laying hens (**c**);

Council Directive 91/629/EEC laying down minimum standards for the protection of calves (**d**), as amended by Council Directive 97/2/EC (**e**) and Commission decision 97/182/EC (**f**); and

Council Directive 91/630/EEC laying down minimum standards for the protection of pigs (**g**), as amended by Council Directive 2001/88/EC (**h**) and Council Directive 2001/93/EC (**i**).

These Regulations (and the Community legislation which they implement) reflect the obligations contained in the European Convention for the Protection of Animals kept for Farming Purposes of 10th March 1976 (European Treaty series No 98), as read with the Protocol of Amendment to the European Convention for the Protection of Animals kept for Farming Purposes of 6th February 1992 (European Treaty Series No 145).

The Regulations are made under section 12(1), (2) and (3) of the Animal Welfare Act 2006(**j**) and apply to all animals kept for farming purposes, subject to certain limited exceptions set out in regulation 3(2).

Regulation 4(1) lays down the general principle that persons responsible for farmed animals must take reasonable steps to ensure that the animals are kept in conditions complying with Schedule 1. This principle applies to all vertebrate animals (other than man) which are bred or kept for the production of food, wool or skin or other farming purposes, but does not include a fish, reptile or amphibian.

A "person responsible" for an animal takes its meaning from section 3 of the Animal Welfare Act 2006, which includes a person responsible for an animal on a permanent or temporary basis, a person who is in charge of an animal, an owner of an animal and a person responsible for a child under the age of 16 years who has actual care and control of an animal.

(**a**) 1968 c. 34.
(**b**) OJ No L221, 8.8.98, p23
(**c**) OJ No. L203, 3.8.99, p53
(**d**) OJ No. L340. 11.12.91, p28
(**e**) OJ No. L25, 28.1.97, p24
(**f**) OJ No. L76, 24.2.97, p30
(**g**) OJ No. L340, 11.12.91, p33
(**h**) OJ No. L316, 1.12.2001
(**i**) OJ No. L316, 1.12.2001, p36
(**j**) 2006 c. 45.

The Regulations provide for the conditions under which all farmed animals must be kept (regulation 4(1) and Schedule 1) and for specific additional conditions applying to the following farmed animals—

laying hens in establishments with 350 or more laying hens, kept in—

- non-cage systems (regulation 5(1) (b) and Schedule 2);
- conventional (battery) cages (regulation 5(1) (b) and Schedule 3);
- enriched cages (regulation 5(1) (b) and Schedule 4);
- all cage and non-cage systems (regulation 5(1) (b) and Schedule 5);

laying hens, whether or not in establishments with 350 or more hens (regulation 5(1)(a));

calves (regulation 5(1) (c) and Schedule 6);

cattle (regulation 5(1) (d) and Schedule 7);

pigs (regulation 5(1) (e) and Schedule 8); and

rabbits (regulation 5(1) (f) and Schedule 9).

Conventional or battery cage systems cannot be built or used for the first time (paragraph 8 of Schedule 3) and are prohibited on and after 1st January 2012 (paragraph 9 of Schedule 3).

Regulation 6 imposes obligations on persons responsible for farmed animals to be acquainted with and have access to codes of practice while attending to animals and ensure that employees have the same knowledge and access.

Regulation 7(a) makes it an offence for a person responsible for a farmed animal, without lawful authority or excuse, not to comply with either the general duty to comply with Schedule 1 or any of the additional duties to comply with Schedules 2 to 9, as applicable. It also creates an offence if any of the duties in respect of codes of practice in Regulation 6 are not met.

An offence is committed under Regulation 7(b) where a false record is made or false information is given.

The maximum penalty for an offence under regulation 7(a) or (b) is 6 months imprisonment and/or a fine at level 4 on the standard scale (currently £2,500). When section 281(5) of the Criminal Justice Act 2003(a) comes into force, the maximum imprisonment will increase to 51 weeks.

A Regulatory Impact Assessment has been prepared and placed in the library of each House of Parliament. Copies may be obtained from the Department for Environment, Food and Rural Affairs (On-farm Animal Welfare Team), 5th Floor, 1A Page Street, London SW1P 4PQ.

(a) 2003 c. 44.

Appendix 3

Dangerous Dogs Act 1991

Dangerous Dogs Act 1991

CHAPTER 65

ARRANGEMENT OF SECTIONS

Dangerous Dogs Act 1991

1991 CHAPTER 65

An Act to prohibit persons from having in their possession or custody dogs belonging to types bred for fighting; to impose restrictions in respect of such dogs pending the coming into force of the prohibition; to enable restrictions to be imposed in relation to other types of dog which present a serious danger to the public; to make further provision for securing that dogs are kept under proper control; and for connected purposes.

[25th July 1991]

B E IT ENACTED by the Queen's most Excellent Majesty, by and with the advice and consent of the Lords Spiritual and Temporal, and Commons, in this present Parliament assembled, and by the authority of the same, as follows:—

1.—(1) This section applies to—

    (a) any dog of the type known as the pit bull terrier;

    (b) any dog of the type known as the Japanese tosa; and

    (c) any dog of any type designated for the purposes of this section by an order of the Secretary of State, being a type appearing to him to be bred for fighting or to have the characteristics of a type bred for that purpose.

    (2) No person shall—

    (a) breed, or breed from, a dog to which this section applies;

    (b) sell or exchange such a dog or offer, advertise or expose such a dog for sale or exchange;

    (c) make or offer to make a gift of such a dog or advertise or expose such a dog as a gift;

    (d) allow such a dog of which he is the owner or of which he is for the time being in charge to be in a public place without being muzzled and kept on a lead; or

Dogs bred for fighting.

504

(e) abandon such a dog of which he is the owner or, being the owner or for the time being in charge of such a dog, allow it to stray.

(3) After such day as the Secretary of State may by order appoint for the purposes of this subsection no person shall have any dog to which this section applies in his possession or custody except—

    (a) in pursuance of the power of seizure conferred by the subsequent provisions of this Act; or

    (b) in accordance with an order for its destruction made under those provisions;

but the Secretary of State shall by order make a scheme for the payment to the owners of such dogs who arrange for them to be destroyed before that day of sums specified in or determined under the scheme in respect of those dogs and the cost of their destruction.

(4) Subsection (2)(b) and (c) above shall not make unlawful anything done with a view to the dog in question being removed from the United Kingdom before the day appointed under subsection (3) above.

(5) The Secretary of State may by order provide that the prohibition in subsection (3) above shall not apply in such cases and subject to compliance with such conditions as are specified in the order and any such provision may take the form of a scheme of exemption containing such arrangements (including provision for the payment of charges or fees) as he thinks appropriate.

(6) A scheme under subsection (3) or (5) above may provide for specified functions under the scheme to be discharged by such persons or bodies as the Secretary of State thinks appropriate.

(7) Any person who contravenes this section is guilty of an offence and liable on summary conviction to imprisonment for a term not exceeding six months or a fine not exceeding level 5 on the standard scale or both except that a person who publishes an advertisement in contravention of subsection (2)(b) or (c)—

    (a) shall not on being convicted be liable to imprisonment if he shows that he published the advertisement to the order of someone else and did not himself devise it; and

    (b) shall not be convicted if, in addition, he shows that he did not know and had no reasonable cause to suspect that it related to a dog to which this section applies.

(8) An order under subsection (1)(c) above adding dogs of any type to those to which this section applies may provide that subsections (3) and (4) above shall apply in relation to those dogs with the substitution for the day appointed under subsection (3) of a later day specified in the order.

(9) The power to make orders under this section shall be exercisable by statutory instrument which, in the case of an order under subsection (1) or (5) or an order containing a scheme under subsection (3), shall be subject to annulment in pursuance of a resolution of either House of Parliament.

2.—(1) If it appears to the Secretary of State that dogs of any type to which section 1 above does not apply present a serious danger to the public he may by order impose in relation to dogs of that type restrictions corresponding, with such modifications, if any, as he thinks appropriate, to all or any of those in subsection (2)(d) and (e) of that section.

(2) An order under this section may provide for exceptions from any restriction imposed by the order in such cases and subject to compliance with such conditions as are specified in the order.

(3) An order under this section may contain such supplementary or transitional provisions as the Secretary of State thinks necessary or expedient and may create offences punishable on summary conviction with imprisonment for a term not exceeding six months or a fine not exceeding level 5 on the standard scale or both.

(4) In determining whether to make an order under this section in relation to dogs of any type and, if so, what the provisions of the order should be, the Secretary of State shall consult with such persons or bodies as appear to him to have relevant knowledge or experience, including a body concerned with animal welfare, a body concerned with veterinary science and practice and a body concerned with breeds of dogs.

(5) The power to make an order under this section shall be exercisable by statutory instrument and no such order shall be made unless a draft of it has been laid before and approved by a resolution of each House of Parliament.

3.—(1) If a dog is dangerously out of control in a public place—

(a) the owner; and

(b) if different, the person for the time being in charge of the dog,

is guilty of an offence, or, if the dog while so out of control injures any person, an aggravated offence, under this subsection.

(2) In proceedings for an offence under subsection (1) above against a person who is the owner of a dog but was not at the material time in charge of it, it shall be a defence for the accused to prove that the dog was at the material time in the charge of a person whom he reasonably believed to be a fit and proper person to be in charge of it.

(3) If the owner or, if different, the person for the time being in charge of a dog allows it to enter a place which is not a public place but where it is not permitted to be and while it is there—

(a) it injures any person; or

(b) there are grounds for reasonable apprehension that it will do so,

he is guilty of an offence, or, if the dog injures any person, an aggravated offence, under this subsection.

(4) A person guilty of an offence under subsection (1) or (3) above other than an aggravated offence is liable on summary conviction to imprisonment for a term not exceeding six months or a fine not exceeding level 5 on the standard scale or both; and a person guilty of an aggravated offence under either of those subsections is liable—

(a) on summary conviction, to imprisonment for a term not exceeding six months or a fine not exceeding the statutory maximum or both;

(b) on conviction on indictment, to imprisonment for a term not exceeding two years or a fine or both.

1871 c.56.

(5) It is hereby declared for the avoidance of doubt that an order under section 2 of the Dogs Act 1871 (order on complaint that dog is dangerous and not kept under proper control)—

(a) may be made whether or not the dog is shown to have injured any person; and

(b) may specify the measures to be taken for keeping the dog under proper control, whether by muzzling, keeping on a lead, excluding it from specified places or otherwise.

(6) If it appears to a court on a complaint under section 2 of the said Act of 1871 that the dog to which the complaint relates is a male and would be less dangerous if neutered the court may under that section make an order requiring it to be neutered.

1989 c. 30.

(7) The reference in section 1(3) of the Dangerous Dogs Act 1989 (penalties) to failing to comply with an order under section 2 of the said Act of 1871 to keep a dog under proper control shall include a reference to failing to comply with any other order made under that section; but no order shall be made under that section by virtue of subsection (6) above where the matters complained of arose before the coming into force of that subsection.

Destruction and disqualification orders.

4.—(1) Where a person is convicted of an offence under section 1 or 3(1) or (3) above or of an offence under an order made under section 2 above the court—

(a) may order the destruction of any dog in respect of which the offence was committed and shall do so in the case of an offence under section 1 or an aggravated offence under section 3(1) or (3) above; and

(b) may order the offender to be disqualified, for such period as the court thinks fit, for having custody of a dog.

(2) Where a court makes an order under subsection (1)(a) above for the destruction of a dog owned by a person other than the offender, then, unless the order is one that the court is required to make, the owner may appeal to the Crown Court against the order.

(3) A dog shall not be destroyed pursuant to an order under subsection (1)(a) above—

(a) until the end of the period for giving notice of appeal against the conviction or, where the order was not one which the court was required to make, against the order; and

(b) if notice of appeal is given within that period, until the appeal is determined or withdrawn,

unless the offender and, in a case to which subsection (2) above applies, the owner of the dog give notice to the court that made the order that there is to be no appeal.

(4) Where a court makes an order under subsection (1)(a) above it may—

(a) appoint a person to undertake the destruction of the dog and require any person having custody of it to deliver it up for that purpose; and

(b) order the offender to pay such sum as the court may determine to be the reasonable expenses of destroying the dog and of keeping it pending its destruction.

(5) Any sum ordered to be paid under subsection (4)(b) above shall be treated for the purposes of enforcement as if it were a fine imposed on conviction.

(6) Any person who is disqualified for having custody of a dog by virtue of an order under subsection (1)(b) above may, at any time after the end of the period of one year beginning with the date of the order, apply to the court that made it (or a magistrates' court acting for the same petty sessions area as that court) for a direction terminating the disqualification.

(7) On an application under subsection (6) above the court may—

(a) having regard to the applicant's character, his conduct since the disqualification was imposed and any other circumstances of the case, grant or refuse the application; and

(b) order the applicant to pay all or any part of the costs of the application;

and where an application in respect of an order is refused no further application in respect of that order shall be entertained if made before the end of the period of one year beginning with the date of the refusal.

(8) Any person who—

(a) has custody of a dog in contravention of an order under subsection (1)(b) above; or

(b) fails to comply with a requirement imposed on him under subsection (4)(a) above,

is guilty of an offence and liable on summary conviction to a fine not exceeding level 5 on the standard scale.

(9) In the application of this section to Scotland—

(a) in subsection (2) for the words "Crown Court against the order" there shall be substituted the words "High Court of Justiciary against the order within the period of seven days beginning with the date of the order";

(b) for subsection (3)(a) there shall be substituted—

"(a) until the end of the period of seven days beginning with the date of the order";

(c) for subsection (5) there shall be substituted—

"(5) Section 411 of the Criminal Procedure (Scotland) Act 1975 shall apply in relation to the recovery of sums ordered to be paid under subsection (4)(b) above as it applies to fines ordered to be recovered by civil diligence in pursuance of Part II of that Act."; and 1975 c. 21.

(d) in subsection (6) the words "(or a magistrates' court acting for the same petty sessions area as that court)" shall be omitted.

5.—(1) A constable or an officer of a local authority authorised by it to exercise the powers conferred by this subsection may seize— Seizure, entry of premises and evidence.

(a) any dog which appears to him to be a dog to which section 1 above applies and which is in a public place—

(i) after the time when possession or custody of it has become unlawful by virtue of that section; or

(ii) before that time, without being muzzled and kept on a lead;

(b) any dog in a public place which appears to him to be a dog to which an order under section 2 above applies and in respect of which an offence against the order has been or is being committed; and

(c) any dog in a public place (whether or not one to which that section or such an order applies) which appears to him to be dangerously out of control.

(2) If a justice of the peace is satisfied by information on oath, or in Scotland a justice of the peace or sheriff is satisfied by evidence on oath, that there are reasonable grounds for believing—

(a) that an offence under any provision of this Act or of an order under section 2 above is being or has been committed; or

(b) that evidence of the commission of any such offence is to be found,

on any premises he may issue a warrant authorising a constable to enter those premises (using such force as is reasonably necessary) and to search them and seize any dog or other thing found there which is evidence of the commission of such an offence.

(3) A warrant issued under this section in Scotland shall be authority for opening lockfast places and may authorise persons named in the warrant to accompany a constable who is executing it.

(4) Where a dog is seized under subsection (1) or (2) above and it appears to a justice of the peace, or in Scotland a justice of the peace or sheriff, that no person has been or is to be prosecuted for an offence under this Act or an order under section 2 above in respect of that dog (whether because the owner cannot be found or for any other reason) he may order the destruction of the dog and shall do so if it is one to which section 1 above applies.

(5) If in any proceedings it is alleged by the prosecution that a dog is one to which section 1 or an order under section 2 above applies it shall be presumed that it is such a dog unless the contrary is shown by the accused by such evidence as the court considers sufficient; and the accused shall not be permitted to adduce such evidence unless he has given the prosecution notice of his intention to do so not later than the fourteenth day before that on which the evidence is to be adduced.

Dogs owned by young persons.

6. Where a dog is owned by a person who is less than sixteen years old any reference to its owner in section 1(2)(d) or (e) or 3 above shall include a reference to the head of the household, if any, of which that person is a member or, in Scotland, to the person who has his actual care and control.

Muzzling and leads.

7.—(1) In this Act—

(a) references to a dog being muzzled are to its being securely fitted with a muzzle sufficient to prevent it biting any person; and

(b) references to its being kept on a lead are to its being securely held on a lead by a person who is not less than sixteen years old.

509

(2) If the Secretary of State thinks it desirable to do so he may by order prescribe the kind of muzzle or lead to be used for the purpose of complying, in the case of a dog of any type, with section 1 or an order under section 2 above; and if a muzzle or lead of a particular kind is for the time being prescribed in relation to any type of dog the references in subsection (1) above to a muzzle or lead shall, in relation to any dog of that type, be construed as references to a muzzle or lead of that kind.

(3) The power to make an order under subsection (2) above shall be exercisable by statutory instrument subject to annulment in pursuance of a resolution of either House of Parliament.

8. An Order in Council under paragraph 1(1)(b) of Schedule 1 to the Northern Ireland Act 1974 (legislation for Northern Ireland in the interim period) which states that it is made only for purposes corresponding to the purposes of this Act— Power to make corresponding provision for Northern Ireland. 1974 c. 28.

   (a) shall not be subject to paragraph 1(4) and (5) of that Schedule (affirmative resolution of both Houses of Parliament); but

   (b) shall be subject to annulment in pursuance of a resolution of either House.

9. Any expenses incurred by the Secretary of State in consequence of this Act shall be paid out of money provided by Parliament. Expenses.

10.—(1) This Act may be cited as the Dangerous Dogs Act 1991. Short title, interpretation, commencement and extent.

(2) In this Act—

   "advertisement" includes any means of bringing a matter to the attention of the public and "advertise" shall be construed accordingly;

   "public place" means any street, road or other place (whether or not enclosed) to which the public have or are permitted to have access whether for payment or otherwise and includes the common parts of a building containing two or more separate dwellings.

(3) For the purposes of this Act a dog shall be regarded as dangerously out of control on any occasion on which there are grounds for reasonable apprehension that it will injure any person, whether or not it actually does so, but references to a dog injuring a person or there being grounds for reasonable apprehension that it will do so do not include references to any case in which the dog is being used for a lawful purpose by a constable or a person in the service of the Crown.

(4) Except for section 8, this Act shall not come into force until such day as the Secretary of State may appoint by an order made by statutory instrument and different days may be appointed for different provisions or different purposes.

(5) Except for section 8, this Act does not extend to Northern Ireland.

Dangerous Dogs (Amendment) Act 1997

Dangerous Dogs (Amendment) Act 1997

1997 CHAPTER 53

An Act to amend the Dangerous Dogs Act 1991; and for connected purposes. [21st March 1997]

Be it enacted by the Queen's most Excellent Majesty, by and with the advice and consent of the Lords Spiritual and Temporal, and Commons, in this present Parliament assembled, and by the authority of the same, as follows:—

1   Destruction orders

(1) In paragraph (a) of subsection (1) of section 4 (destruction and disqualification orders) of the Dangerous Dogs Act 1991 ("the 1991 Act"), after the words "committed and" there shall be inserted the words ", subject to subsection (1A) below,".

(2) After that subsection there shall be inserted the following subsection—

"(1A) Nothing in subsection (1)(a) above shall require the court to order the destruction of a dog if the court is satisfied—

(a) that the dog would not constitute a danger to public safety; and

(b) where the dog was born before 30th November 1991 and is subject to the prohibition in section 1(3) above, that there is a good reason why the dog has not been exempted from that prohibition."

(3) In subsection (2) of that section, the words "then, unless the order is one that the court is required to make" shall cease to have effect.

(4) In subsection (3)(a) of that section, the words ", where the order was not one that the court was required to make" shall cease to have effect.

2   Contingent destruction orders

After section 4 of the 1991 Act there shall be inserted the following section—

"4A   Contingent destruction orders

(1) Where—

(a)   a person is convicted of an offence under section 1 above or an aggravated offence under section 3(1) or (3) above;

(b)   the court does not order the destruction of the dog under section 4(1) (a) above; and

(c)   in the case of an offence under section 1 above, the dog is subject to the prohibition in section 1(3) above,

the court shall order that, unless the dog is exempted from that prohibition within the requisite period, the dog shall be destroyed.

(2) Where an order is made under subsection (1) above in respect of a dog, and the dog is not exempted from the prohibition in section 1(3) above within the requisite period, the court may extend that period.

(3) Subject to subsection (2) above, the requisite period for the purposes of such an order is the period of two months beginning with the date of the order.

(4) Where a person is convicted of an offence under section 3(1) or (3) above, the court may order that, unless the owner of the dog keeps it under proper control, the dog shall be destroyed.

(5) An order under subsection (4) above—

(a)   may specify the measures to be taken for keeping the dog under proper control, whether by muzzling, keeping on a lead, excluding it from specified places or otherwise; and

(b)   if it appears to the court that the dog is a male and would be less dangerous if neutered, may require it to be neutered.

(6) Subsections (2) to (4) of section 4 above shall apply in relation to an order under subsection (1) or (4) above as they apply in relation to an order under subsection (1)(a) of that section."

3   Destruction orders otherwise than on a conviction

(1) After section 4A of the 1991 Act there shall be inserted the following section—

"4B   Destruction orders otherwise than on a conviction

(1) Where a dog is seized under section 5(1) or (2) below and it appears to a justice of the peace, or in Scotland a justice of the peace or sheriff—

(a)   that no person has been or is to be prosecuted for an offence under this Act or an order under section 2 above in respect of that dog (whether because the owner cannot be found or for any other reason); or

(b)   that the dog cannot be released into the custody or possession of its owner without the owner contravening the prohibition in section 1(3) above,

he may order the destruction of the dog and, subject to subsection (2) below, shall do so if it is one to which section 1 above applies.

(2) Nothing in subsection (1)(b) above shall require the justice or sheriff to order the destruction of a dog if he is satisfied—

    (a)   that the dog would not constitute a danger to public safety; and

    (b)   where the dog was born before 30th November 1991 and is subject to the prohibition in section 1(3) above, that there is a good reason why the dog has not been exempted from that prohibition.

(3) Where in a case falling within subsection (1)(b) above the justice or sheriff does not order the destruction of the dog, he shall order that, unless the dog is exempted from the prohibition in section 1(3) above within the requisite period, the dog shall be destroyed.

(4) Subsections (2) to (4) of section 4 above shall apply in relation to an order under subsection (1)(b) or (3) above as they apply in relation to an order under subsection (1)(a) of that section.

(5) Subsections (2) and (3) of section 4A above shall apply in relation to an order under subsection (3) above as they apply in relation to an order under subsection (1) of that section, except that the reference to the court in subsection (2) of that section shall be construed as a reference to the justice or sheriff."

(2) In section 5 of the 1991 Act (seizure, entry of premises and evidence), subsection (4) (which is superseded by this section) shall cease to have effect.

4   Extended application of 1991 Order

(1) Where an order is made under section 4A(1) or 4B(3) of the 1991 Act, Part III of the Dangerous Dogs Compensation and Exemption Schemes Order 1991 (exemption scheme) shall have effect as if—

    (a)   any reference to the appointed day were a reference to the end of the requisite period within the meaning of section 4A or, as the case may be, section 4B of the 1991 Act;

    (b)   paragraph (a) of Article 4 and Article 6 were omitted; and

    (c)   the fee payable to the Agency under Article 9 were a fee of such amount as the Secretary of State may by order prescribe.

(2) The power to make an order under this section shall be exercisable by statutory instrument which shall be subject to annulment in pursuance of a resolution of either House of Parliament.

5   Transitional provisions

(1) This Act shall apply in relation to cases where proceedings have been instituted before, as well as after, the commencement of this Act.

(2) In a case where, before the commencement of this Act—

    (a)   the court has ordered the destruction of a dog in respect of which an offence under section 1, or an aggravated offence under section 3(1) or (3), of the 1991 Act has been committed, but

    (b)   the dog has not been destroyed,

that destruction order shall cease to have effect and the case shall be remitted to the court for reconsideration.

(3) Where a case is so remitted, the court may make any order in respect of the dog which it would have power to make if the person in question had been convicted of the offence after the commencement of this Act.

6   Short title, commencement and extent

(1) This Act may be cited as the Dangerous Dogs (Amendment) Act 1997.

(2) This Act does not extend to Northern Ireland.

(3) This Act shall come into force on such day as the Secretary of State may by order made by statutory instrument appoint.

Sentencing Council Dangerous Dog Offences Difinitive Guideline

Sentencing
Council

Dangerous Dog Offences
Definitive Guideline

Contents

Effective from 20 August 2012

Applicability of guideline

I n accordance with section 120 of the Coroners and Justice Act 2009, the Sentencing Council issues this definitive guideline. It applies to all offenders aged 18 and older, who are sentenced on or after 20 August 2012, regardless of the date of the offence.

Section 125(1) of the Coroners and Justice Act 2009 provides that when sentencing offences committed after 6 April 2010:

"Every court –

(a) must, in sentencing an offender, follow any sentencing guideline which is relevant to the offender's case, and

(b) must, in exercising any other function relating to the sentencing of offenders, follow any sentencing guidelines which are relevant to the exercise of the function,

unless the court is satisfied that it would be contrary to the interests of justice to do so."

This guideline applies only to offenders aged 18 and older. General principles to be considered in the sentencing of youths are in the Sentencing Guidelines Council's definitive guideline, *Overarching Principles – Sentencing Youths*.

Structure, ranges and starting points
For the purposes of section 125(3)–(4) of the Coroners and Justice Act 2009, the guideline specifies *offence ranges* – the range of sentences appropriate for each type of offence. Within each offence, the Council has specified three *categories* which reflect varying degrees of seriousness. The offence range is split into *category ranges* – sentences appropriate for each level of seriousness. The Council has also identified a starting point within each category.

Starting points define the position within a category range from which to start calculating the provisional sentence. **Starting points apply to all offences within the corresponding category and are applicable to all offenders, in all cases.** Once the starting point is established, the court should consider further aggravating and mitigating factors and previous convictions so as to adjust the sentence within the range. Starting points and ranges apply to all offenders, whether they have pleaded guilty or been convicted after trial. Credit for a guilty plea is taken into consideration only at step four in the decision making process, after the appropriate sentence has been identified.

Information on community orders and fine bands is set out in the annex at page 20.

Effective from 20 August 2012

Owner or person in charge of a dog dangerously out of control in a public place, injuring any person

Dangerous Dogs Act 1991 (section 3(1))

Owner or person in charge allowing a dog to be in a private place where the dog is not permitted to be, injuring any person

Dangerous Dogs Act 1991 (section 3(3)(a))

OUT OF CONTROL (CAUSING INJURY)

Triable either way
Maximum: 2 years' custody

Offence range: Discharge – 18 months' custody

Effective from 20 August 2012

518

OUT OF CONTROL (CAUSING INJURY)

Determining the offence category

The court should determine the offence category using the table below.

Category 1	Greater harm **and** higher culpability
Category 2	Greater harm **and** lower culpability; **or** lesser harm **and** higher culpability
Category 3	Lesser harm **and** lower culpability

The court should determine culpability and harm caused or intended, by reference **only** to the factors below, which comprise the principal factual elements of the offence. Where an offence does not fall squarely into a category, individual factors may require a degree of weighting before making an overall assessment and determining the appropriate offence category.

Factors indicating greater harm

Serious injury (which includes disease transmission and/or psychological harm)

Sustained or repeated attack

Victim is a child or otherwise vulnerable because of personal circumstances

Factor indicating lesser harm

Minor injury

Factors indicating higher culpability

Statutory aggravating factors:

Offence racially or religiously aggravated

Offence motivated by, or demonstrating, hostility to the victim based on his or her sexual orientation (or presumed sexual orientation)

Offence motivated by, or demonstrating, hostility to the victim based on the victim's disability (or presumed disability)

Factors indicating higher culpability *(continued)*

Other aggravating factors:

Failure to respond to warnings or concerns expressed by others about the dog's behaviour

Goading, or allowing goading, of dog

Dog used as weapon or to intimidate victim

Offence motivated by, or demonstrating, hostility based on the victim's age, sex, gender identity (or presumed gender identity)

Factors indicating lower culpability

Attempts made to regain control of dog and/or intervene

Provocation of dog without fault of the offender

Evidence of safety or control measures having been taken

Mental disorder or learning disability, where linked to the commission of the offence

Starting point and category range

Having determined the category, the court should use the corresponding starting points to reach a sentence within the category range below. The starting point applies to all offenders irrespective of plea or previous convictions. A case of particular gravity, reflected by multiple features of culpability or harm in step 1, could merit upward adjustment from the starting point before further adjustment for aggravating or mitigating features, set out on the next page.

Offence Category	Starting Point *(Applicable to all offenders)*	Category Range *(Applicable to all offenders)*
Category 1	6 months' custody	Medium level community order – 18 months' custody
Category 2	Medium level community order	Band B fine – 6 months' custody
Category 3	Band B fine	Discharge – Band C fine

Effective from 20 August 2012

The table below contains a **non-exhaustive** list of additional factual elements providing the context of the offence and factors relating to the offender. Identify whether any combination of these, or other relevant factors, should result in an upward or downward adjustment from the starting point. In some cases, having considered these factors, it may be appropriate to move outside the identified category range.

When sentencing **category 1 or 2** offences, the court should also consider the custody threshold as follows:
- has the custody threshold been passed?
- if so, is it unavoidable that a custodial sentence be imposed?
- if so, can that sentence be suspended?

When sentencing **category 2** offences, the court should also consider the community order threshold as follows:
- has the community order threshold been passed?

Factors increasing seriousness	Factors reducing seriousness or reflecting personal mitigation
Statutory aggravating factors:	No previous convictions **or** no relevant/recent convictions
Previous convictions, having regard to a) the nature of the offence to which the conviction relates and its relevance to the current offence; and b) the time that has elapsed since the conviction	Isolated incident
	No previous complaints against, or incidents involving, the dog
Offence committed whilst on bail	Remorse
Other aggravating factors include:	Good character and/or exemplary conduct
Injury to another animal(s)	Evidence of responsible ownership
Location of the offence	Determination and/or demonstration of steps taken to address addiction or offending behaviour
Ongoing effect upon the victim and/or others	
Failure to take adequate precautions to prevent dog escaping	Serious medical conditions requiring urgent, intensive or long-term treatment
Allowing person insufficiently experienced or trained, to be in charge of dog	Age and/or lack of maturity where it affects the responsibility of the offender
Ill treatment or failure to ensure welfare needs of dog, where not charged separately	Mental disorder or learning disability, where not linked to the commission of the offence
Dog known to be prohibited	Sole or primary carer for dependent relatives
Lack or loss of control of dog due to influence of alcohol or drugs	
Offence committed against those working in the public sector or providing a service to the public	
Established evidence of community impact	
Failure to comply with current court orders	
Offence committed whilst on licence	

OUT OF CONTROL (CAUSING INJURY)

OUT OF CONTROL (CAUSING INJURY)

STEP THREE
Consider any factors which indicate a reduction, such as assistance to the prosecution
The court should take into account sections 73 and 74 of the Serious Organised Crime and Police Act 2005 (assistance by defendants: reduction or review of sentence) and any other rule of law by virtue of which an offender may receive a discounted sentence in consequence of assistance given (or offered) to the prosecutor or investigator.

STEP FOUR
Reduction for guilty pleas
The court should take account of any potential reduction for a guilty plea in accordance with section 144 of the Criminal Justice Act 2003 and the *Guilty Plea* guideline.

STEP FIVE
Compensation and ancillary orders
In all cases, the court should consider whether to make a compensation order and/or other ancillary orders.

Compensation order
The court should consider compensation orders in all cases where personal injury, loss or damage has resulted from the offence.[1] The court must give reasons if it decides not to award compensation in such cases.

Other ancillary orders available include:

Disqualification from having custody of a dog
The court **may** disqualify the offender from having custody of a dog.[2] The test the court should consider is whether the offender is a fit and proper person to have custody of a dog.

Destruction order/contingent destruction order
In any case where the offender is not the owner of the dog, the owner must be given an opportunity to be present and make representations to the court.

The court **shall** make a destruction order unless the court is satisfied that the dog would not constitute a danger to public safety.[3]

In reaching a decision, the court should consider the relevant circumstances which include:
• the incident – what degree of harm was caused by the dog's behaviour?
• past behaviour of the dog – is this an isolated incident or have there been previous warnings or incidents? and
• owner's character – is the owner a fit and proper person to own this particular dog?

(step 5 continues on next page)

---

1   s.130 Powers of Criminal Courts (Sentencing) Act 2000
2   s.4(1)(b) Dangerous Dogs Act 1991
3   s.4(1)(a) ibid

STEP FIVE (continued)

If the court is satisfied that the dog would not constitute a danger to public safety, it **shall** make a contingent destruction order imposing certain available conditions.[4] A contingent destruction order should specify the measures to be taken by the owner for keeping the dog under proper control, which include:

- muzzling;
- keeping on a lead;
- neutering in appropriate cases; and
- excluding it from a specified place.[5]

Where the court makes a destruction order, it **may** order the offender to pay what it determines to be the reasonable expenses of destroying the dog and of keeping it pending its destruction.[6]

STEP SIX

Totality principle

If sentencing an offender for more than one offence, or where the offender is already serving a sentence, consider whether the total sentence is just and proportionate to the offending behaviour.

STEP SEVEN

Reasons

Section 174 of the Criminal Justice Act 2003 imposes a duty to give reasons for, and explain the effect of, the sentence.

STEP EIGHT

Consideration for remand time

Sentencers should take into consideration any remand time served in relation to the final sentence at this final step. The court should consider whether to give credit for time spent on remand in custody or on bail in accordance with sections 240 and 240A of the Criminal Justice Act 2003.

OUT OF CONTROL (CAUSING INJURY)

4   s.4A(4) Dangerous Dogs Act 1991
5   s.4A(5) ibid
6   s.4(4)(b) ibid

Owner or person in charge of a dog dangerously out of control in a public place

Dangerous Dogs Act 1991 (section 3(1))

Owner or person in charge allowing a dog to be in a private place where the dog is not permitted to be, which makes a person fear injury

Dangerous Dogs Act 1991 (section 3(3)(b))

OUT OF CONTROL

Triable summarily only
Maximum: 6 months' custody

Offence range: Discharge – 6 months' custody

STEP ONE
Determining the offence category

The court should determine the offence category using the table below.

Category 1	Greater harm **and** higher culpability
Category 2	Greater harm **and** lower culpability; **or** lesser harm **and** higher culpability
Category 3	Lesser harm **and** lower culpability

The court should determine culpability and harm caused or intended, by reference **only** to the factors below, which comprise the principal factual elements of the offence. Where an offence does not fall squarely into a category, individual factors may require a degree of weighting before making an overall assessment and determining the appropriate offence category.

Factors indicating greater harm	**Factors indicating higher culpability** *(continued)*
Presence of children or others who are vulnerable because of personal circumstances	*Other aggravating factors:*
Injury to another animal(s)	Failure to respond to warnings or concerns expressed by others about the dog's behaviour
Factors indicating lesser harm	Goading, or allowing goading, of dog
Low risk to the public	Dog used as weapon or to intimidate victim
Factors indicating higher culpability	Offence motivated by, or demonstrating, hostility based on the victim's age, sex, gender identity (or presumed gender identity)
Statutory aggravating factors:	
Offence racially or religiously aggravated	**Factors indicating lower culpability**
Offence motivated by, or demonstrating, hostility to the victim based on his or her sexual orientation (or presumed sexual orientation)	Attempts made to regain control of dog and/or intervene
	Provocation of dog without fault of the offender
Offence motivated by, or demonstrating, hostility to the victim based on the victim's disability (or presumed disability)	Evidence of safety or control measures having been taken
	Mental disorder or learning disability, where linked to the commission of the offence

STEP TWO
Starting point and category range

Having determined the category, the court should use the corresponding starting points to reach a sentence within the category range below. The starting point applies to all offenders irrespective of plea or previous convictions. A case of particular gravity, reflected by multiple features of culpability or harm in step 1, could merit upward adjustment from the starting point before further adjustment for aggravating or mitigating features, set out on the next page.

Offence Category	**Starting Point** *(Applicable to all offenders)*	**Category Range** *(Applicable to all offenders)*
Category 1	Medium level community order	Band C fine – 6 months' custody
Category 2	Band B fine	Band A fine – Low level community order
Category 3	Band A fine	Discharge – Band B fine

OUT OF CONTROL

The table below contains a **non-exhaustive** list of additional factual elements providing the context of the offence and factors relating to the offender. Identify whether any combination of these, or other relevant factors, should result in an upward or downward adjustment from the starting point. In some cases, having considered these factors, it may be appropriate to move outside the identified category range.

When sentencing **category 1** offences, the court should also consider the custody threshold as follows:
- has the custody threshold been passed?
- if so, is it unavoidable that a custodial sentence be imposed?
- if so, can that sentence be suspended?

When sentencing **category 1 or 2** offences, the court should also consider the community order threshold as follows:
- has the community order threshold been passed?

Factors increasing seriousness	Factors reducing seriousness or reflecting personal mitigation
Statutory aggravating factors:	No previous convictions **or** no relevant/recent convictions
Previous convictions, having regard to a) the nature of the offence to which the conviction relates and its relevance to the current offence; and b) the time that has elapsed since the conviction	Isolated incident
	No previous complaints against, or incidents involving, the dog
Offence committed whilst on bail	Remorse
Other aggravating factors include:	Good character and/or exemplary conduct
Location of the offence	Evidence of responsible ownership
Ongoing effect upon the victim and/or others	Determination and/or demonstration of steps taken to address addiction or offending behaviour
Failure to take adequate precautions to prevent dog escaping	Serious medical conditions requiring urgent, intensive or long-term treatment
Allowing person insufficiently experienced or trained, to be in charge of dog	Age and/or lack of maturity where it affects the responsibility of the offender
Ill treatment or failure to ensure welfare needs of dog, where not charged separately	Mental disorder or learning disability, where not linked to the commission of the offence
Dog known to be prohibited	Sole or primary carer for dependent relatives
Lack or loss of control of dog due to the influence of alcohol or drugs	
Offence committed against those working in the public sector or providing a service to the public	
Established evidence of community impact	
Failure to comply with current court orders	
Offence committed whilst on licence	

OUT OF CONTROL

STEP THREE
Consider any factors which indicate a reduction, such as assistance to the prosecution
The court should take into account sections 73 and 74 of the Serious Organised Crime and Police Act 2005 (assistance by defendants: reduction or review of sentence) and any other rule of law by virtue of which an offender may receive a discounted sentence in consequence of assistance given (or offered) to the prosecutor or investigator.

STEP FOUR
Reduction for guilty pleas
The court should take account of any potential reduction for a guilty plea in accordance with section 144 of the Criminal Justice Act 2003 and the *Guilty Plea* guideline.

STEP FIVE
Compensation and ancillary orders
In all cases, the court should consider whether to make a compensation order and/or other ancillary orders.

Compensation order
The court should consider compensation orders in all cases where personal injury, loss or damage has resulted from the offence.[7] The court must give reasons if it decides not to award compensation in such cases.

Other ancillary orders available include:

Disqualification from having custody of a dog
The court **may** disqualify the offender from having custody of a dog.[8] The test the court should consider is whether the offender is a fit and proper person to have custody of a dog.

Destruction order/contingent destruction order
In any case where the offender is not the owner of the dog, the owner must be given an opportunity to be present and make representations to the court.

The court **may** make a destruction order.[9] Alternatively, it **may** make a contingent destruction order imposing certain available conditions.[10] A contingent destruction order should specify the measures to be taken by the owner for keeping the dog under proper control, which include:
• muzzling;
• keeping on a lead;
• neutering in appropriate cases; and
• excluding it from a specified place.[11]

In reaching a decision, the court should consider the relevant circumstances which include:
• the incident – what degree of harm was caused by the dog's behaviour?
• past behaviour of the dog – is this an isolated incident or have there been previous warnings or incidents? and
• owner's character – is the owner a fit and proper person to own this particular dog?

Where the court makes a destruction order, it **may** order the offender to pay what it determines to be the reasonable expenses of destroying the dog and of keeping it pending its destruction.[12]

---

7 s.130 Powers of Criminal Courts (Sentencing) Act 2000
8 s.4(1)(b) Dangerous Dogs Act 1991
9 s.4(1)(a) ibid
10 s.4A(4) ibid
11 s.4A(5) ibid
12 s.4(4)(b) ibid

STEP SIX
Totality principle
If sentencing an offender for more than one offence, or where the offender is already serving a sentence, consider whether the total sentence is just and proportionate to the offending behaviour.

STEP SEVEN
Reasons
Section 174 of the Criminal Justice Act 2003 imposes a duty to give reasons for, and explain the effect of, the sentence.

STEP EIGHT
Consideration for remand time
Sentencers should take into consideration any remand time served in relation to the final sentence at this final step. The court should consider whether to give credit for time spent on remand in custody or on bail in accordance with sections 240 and 240A of the Criminal Justice Act 2003.

OUT OF CONTROL

Possession of a prohibited dog

Dangerous Dogs Act 1991 (section 1(3))

Breeding, selling, exchanging or advertising a prohibited dog

Dangerous Dogs Act 1991 (section 1(2))

Triable only summarily
Maximum: 6 months' custody

Offence range: Discharge – 6 months' custody

POSSESSION

Determining the offence category

The court should determine the offence category using the table below.

Category 1	Greater harm **and** higher culpability
Category 2	Greater harm **or** higher culpability
Category 3	**Neither** greater harm **nor** higher culpability

The court should determine culpability and harm caused or intended, by reference **only** to the factors below, which comprise the principal factual elements of the offence. Where an offence does not fall squarely into a category, individual factors may require a degree of weighting before making an overall assessment and determining the appropriate offence category.

Factors indicating greater harm	Factors indicating higher culpability
Injury to person	Possessing a dog known to be prohibited
Injury to another animal(s)	Breeding from a dog known to be prohibited
	Selling, exchanging or advertising a dog known to be prohibited
	Offence committed for gain
	Dog used to threaten or intimidate
	Permitting fighting
	Training and/or possession of paraphernalia for dog fighting

Starting point and category range

Having determined the category, the court should use the corresponding starting points to reach a sentence within the category range below. The starting point applies to all offenders irrespective of plea or previous convictions. A case of particular gravity, reflected by multiple features of culpability or harm in step 1, could merit upward adjustment from the starting point before further adjustment for aggravating or mitigating features, set out on the next page.

Offence Category	Starting Point *(Applicable to all offenders)*	Category Range *(Applicable to all offenders)*
Category 1	Medium level community order	Band C fine – 6 months' custody*
Category 2	Band C fine	Band A fine – Medium level community order
Category 3	Band A fine	Discharge – Band B fine

POSSESSION

* Imprisonment is not available if the provisions of s.1(7) Dangerous Dogs Act 1991 apply

Effective from 20 August 2012

The table below contains a **non-exhaustive** list of additional factual elements providing the context of the offence and factors relating to the offender. Identify whether any combination of these, or other relevant factors, should result in an upward or downward adjustment from the starting point. In some cases, having considered these factors, it may be appropriate to move outside the identified category range.

When sentencing **category 1** offences, the court should also consider the custody threshold as follows:
• has the custody threshold been passed?
• if so, is it unavoidable that a custodial sentence be imposed?
• if so, can that sentence be suspended?

When sentencing **category 1 or 2** offences, the court should also consider the community order threshold as follows:
• has the community order threshold been passed?

Factors increasing seriousness	Factors reducing seriousness or reflecting personal mitigation
Statutory aggravating factors:	
	No previous convictions **or** no relevant/recent convictions
Previous convictions, having regard to a) the nature of the offence to which the conviction relates and its relevance to the current offence; and b) the time that has elapsed since the conviction	Unaware that dog was prohibited type despite reasonable efforts to identify type
Offence committed whilst on bail	Evidence of safety or control measures having been taken by owner
Other aggravating factors include:	Prosecution results from owner notification
Presence of children or others who are vulnerable because of personal circumstances	Remorse
Ill treatment or failure to ensure welfare needs of dog, where not charged separately	Good character and/or exemplary conduct
	Evidence of responsible ownership
Established evidence of community impact	Determination and/or demonstration of steps taken to address addiction or offending behaviour
Failure to comply with current court orders	
Offence committed whilst on licence	Serious medical conditions requiring urgent, intensive or long-term treatment
	Age and/or lack of maturity where it affects the responsibility of the offender
	Lapse of time since the offence where this is not the fault of the offender
	Mental disorder or learning disability
	Sole or primary carer for dependent relatives

POSSESSION

STEP THREE
Consider any factors which indicate a reduction, such as assistance to the prosecution
The court should take into account sections 73 and 74 of the Serious Organised Crime and Police Act 2005 (assistance by defendants: reduction or review of sentence) and any other rule of law by virtue of which an offender may receive a discounted sentence in consequence of assistance given (or offered) to the prosecutor or investigator.

STEP FOUR
Reduction for guilty pleas
The court should take account of any potential reduction for a guilty plea in accordance with section 144 of the Criminal Justice Act 2003 and the *Guilty Plea* guideline.

STEP FIVE
Ancillary orders
In all cases, the court should consider whether to make any ancillary orders.

Ancillary orders available include:

Disqualification from having custody of a dog
The court **may** disqualify the offender from having custody of a dog.[13] The test the court should consider is whether the offender is a fit and proper person to have custody of a dog.

Destruction order/contingent destruction order
The court **shall** make a destruction order unless the court is satisfied that the dog would not constitute a danger to public safety.[14]

In reaching a decision, the court should consider the relevant circumstances which include:
• danger to the public – what is the potential risk of harm posed by the dog?
• behaviour of the dog – have there been any warnings or incidents involving the dog? and
• owner's character – is the owner a fit and proper person to own this particular dog?

If the court does not make a destruction order, the court **shall** make a contingent destruction order providing that unless the dog is exempted from the prohibition within two months it shall be destroyed.[15] Statutory procedures and conditions automatically apply to exempted dogs and no other conditions can be imposed.[16] Where the offender is the owner of the dog, it would not normally be appropriate to make a contingent destruction order in conjunction with a disqualification order.

Furthermore, the court **must not** transfer ownership of the dog to another.[17]

Where the court makes a destruction order, it **may** order the offender to pay what it determines to be the reasonable expenses of destroying the dog and of keeping it pending its destruction.[18]

STEP SIX
Totality principle
If sentencing an offender for more than one offence, or where the offender is already serving a sentence, consider whether the total sentence is just and proportionate to the offending behaviour.

---

13 s.4(1)(b) Dangerous Dogs Act 1991
14 s.4(1)(a) ibid
15 s.4A(1) ibid
16 The Dangerous Dogs Compensation and Exemption Schemes Order 1991 SI No. 1744 (as amended by The Dangerous Dogs Compensation and Exemption Schemes (Amendment) Order 1991 SI No. 2297)
17 s.1(2)(b) Dangerous Dogs Act 1991
18 s.4(4)(b) ibid

STEP SEVEN

Reasons

Section 174 of the Criminal Justice Act 2003 imposes a duty to give reasons for, and explain the effect of, the sentence.

STEP EIGHT

Consideration for remand time

Sentencers should take into consideration any remand time served in relation to the final sentence at this final step. The court should consider whether to give credit for time spent on remand in custody or on bail in accordance with sections 240 and 240A of the Criminal Justice Act 2003.

Effective from 20 August 2012

POSSESSION

Annex:
Fine bands and community orders

FINE BANDS

In this guideline, fines are expressed as one of three fine bands (A, B or C).

Fine Band	**Starting Point** *(Applicable to all offenders)*	**Category Range** *(Applicable to all offenders)*
Band A	50% of relevant weekly income	25–75% of relevant weekly income
Band B	100% of relevant weekly income	75–125% of relevant weekly income
Band C	150% of relevant weekly income	125–175% of relevant weekly income

COMMUNITY ORDERS

In this guideline, community orders are expressed as one of three levels (low, medium and high).

An illustrative description of examples of requirements that might be appropriate for each level is provided below. Where two or more requirements are ordered, they must be compatible with each other.

LOW	MEDIUM	HIGH
In general, only one requirement will be appropriate and the length may be curtailed if additional requirements are necessary		More intensive sentences which combine two or more requirements may be appropriate
Suitable requirements might include: • 40–80 hours unpaid work; • curfew requirement within the lowest range (for example, up to 12 hours per day for a few weeks); • exclusion requirement, without electronic monitoring, for a few months; • prohibited activity requirement; • attendance centre requirement (where available).	Suitable requirements might include: • greater number of hours of unpaid work (for example, 80–150 hours); • an activity requirement in the middle range (20–30 days); • curfew requirement within the middle range (for example, up to 12 hours for 2–3 months); • exclusion requirement, lasting in the region of 6 months; • prohibited activity requirement.	Suitable requirements might include: • 150–300 hours unpaid work; • activity requirement up to the maximum of 60 days; • curfew requirement up to 12 hours per day for 4–6 months; • exclusion order lasting in the region of 12 months.

The tables above are also set out in the *Magistrates' Court Sentencing Guidelines* which includes further guidance on fines and community orders.

Effective from 20 August 2012

Dangerous Dogs (Amendment) Bill 2013

DRAFT

OF A

B I L L

TO

Make provision

B E IT ENACTED by the Queen's most Excellent Majesty, by and with the advice and consent of the Lords Spiritual and Temporal, and Commons, in this present Parliament assembled, and by the authority of the same, as follows: —

1   Keeping dogs under proper control

(1)   The Dangerous Dogs Act 1991 is amended as follows.

(2)   In section 3 (keeping dogs under proper control) —
    (a)   in subsection (1) —
        (i)   for "a public place" substitute "any place in England or Wales   5
            (whether or not a public place)", and
        (ii)   after "injures any person" insert "or assistance dog";
    (b)   after subsection (1) insert —

        "(1A)   A person ("D") is not guilty of an offence under subsection (1)
            in a case which is a householder case.   10

        (1B)   For the purposes of subsection (1A) "a householder case" is a
            case where —
            (a)   the dog is dangerously out of control while D is in or
                partly in a building, or part of a building, that is a
                dwelling or is forces accommodation (or is both),   15
            (b)   D is not a trespasser at the time the dog is dangerously
                out of control, and
            (c)   at that time —
                (i)   the person in relation to whom the dog is
                    dangerously out of control ("V") is in, or is   20
                    entering, the building or part as a trespasser, or
                (ii)   D believed V to be in, or entering, the building or
                    part as a trespasser.

54/1

Section 76(8B) to (8F) of the Criminal Justice and Immigration Act 2008 (use of force at place of residence) apply for the purposes of this subsection as they apply for the purposes of subsection (8A) of that section (and for those purposes the reference in section 76(8D) to subsection (8A)(d) is to be read as   5
if it were a reference to paragraph (c)(ii) of this subsection).";

    (c)   omit subsection (3);

    (d)   in subsection (4) —

         (i)   omit "or (3)", and

        (ii)   for "either of those subsections" substitute "that subsection".   10

(3)   In section 4 (destruction and disqualification orders), in both places where it occurs in subsection (1) omit "or (3)".

(4)   In section 4A (contingent destruction orders) —

    (a)   in subsection (1)(a) omit "or (3)", and

    (b)   in subsection (4) omit "or (3)".   15

(5)   In section 5 (seizure, entry of premises and evidence) —

    (a)   in subsection (1)(c) for "one" substitute "a dog";

    (b)   after subsection (1) insert —

     "(1A)   A constable or an officer of a local authority authorised by it to exercise the powers conferred by this subsection may seize any   20
dog in a place in England or Wales which is not a public place, if the dog appears to the constable or officer to be dangerously out of control.".

(6)   In section 10 (interpretation) —

    (a)   in subsection (2) after the definition of "advertisement" insert —   25
          ""assistance dog" has the meaning given by section 173(1) of the Equality Act 2010;";

    (b)   in subsection (3) —

         (i)   after "injure any person" insert "or assistance dog", and

        (ii)   after "injuring a person" insert "or assistance dog".   30

2   Whether a dog is a danger to public safety

(1)   The Dangerous Dogs Act 1991 is amended as follows.

(2)   In section 1 (dogs bred for fighting) after subsection (6) insert —

    "(6A)   A scheme under subsection (3) or (5) may in particular include provision requiring a court to consider whether a person is a fit and   35
proper person to be in charge of a dog."

(3)   In section 4 (destruction and disqualification orders) after subsection (1A) insert —

    "(1B)   For the purposes of subsection (1A)(a), when deciding whether a dog would constitute a danger to public safety, the court —   40

        (a)   must consider —

            (i)   the temperament of the dog and its past behaviour, and

             (ii)   whether the owner of the dog, or the person for the time being in charge of it, is a fit and proper person to be in charge of the dog, and

      (b)   may consider any other relevant circumstances.

(4)   Section 4B (destruction orders otherwise than on a conviction) is amended as follows — 5

      (a)   in subsection (1) after "section 5(1) or (2) below" insert "or in exercise of a power of seizure conferred by any other enactment";

      (b)   after subsection (2) insert —

        "(2A)   For the purposes of subsection (2)(a), when deciding whether a dog would constitute a danger to public safety, the justice or sheriff — 10

             (a)   must consider —

                  (i)   the temperament of the dog and its past behaviour, and 15

                  (ii)   whether the owner of the dog, or the person for the time being in charge of it, is a fit and proper person to be in charge of the dog, and

             (b)   may consider any other relevant circumstances."

Index

index

Biograph: Noël Sweeney

Noël Sweeney is a practising barrister who specialises in criminal law and human rights and animal law. He had lectured widely on all those subjects at Conferences and in Universities. He has also written on all aspects of the legal status of animals and particularly the connexion between racism and sexism and speciesism. He is a member of the Association of Lawyers for Animal Welfare and the Animal Welfare Science Ethics and Law Veterinary Association.